DERACINATION

SUNY Series in Psychoanalysis and Culture
Henry Sussman, editor

DERACINATION

Historicity, Hiroshima, and the
Tragic Imperative

Walter A. Davis

State University of New York Press

Cover illustration: detail of *Hiroshima*, mixed media, 1999, by Breck J. Hapner, courtesy of Breck J. Hapner, Imagescape Design, Columbus, Ohio

Published by
State University of New York Press, Albany

© 2001 State University of New York

For information, address State University of New York Press
90 State Street, Suite 700, Albany, New York 12207

Production by Dana Foote
Marketing by Patrick Durocher

Library of Congress Cataloging-in-Publication Data

Davis, Walter A., 1942–
Deracination : historicity, Hiroshima, and the tragic imperative / Walter A. Davis.
p. cm. — (SUNY series in psychoanalysis and culture)
Includes bibliographical references and index.
ISBN 0–7914–4833–9 (alk. paper) — ISBN 0–7914–4834–7 (pbk. : alk. paper)
1. Social sciences and psychoanalysis. 2. Political psychology.
3. History—Philosophy. I. Title. II. Series.

BF175.4 S65 D38 2001
901—dc21
00–049238

10 9 8 7 6 5 4 4 3 2 1

TO
Sensei Bill Evans
(1947–1998)
who led me to the inner readiness
AND
Stephen Lacey
(1943–2000)
who taught me how to write

CONTENTS

ACKNOWLEDGMENTS

Doing final revisions is like going to your own wake and trying to convince the bereaved that the corpse looks good. During that labor I was sustained by memories of the friends and colleagues who contributed to this book: Lee Abbott, Alex Blazer, Paul Boyer, Paul Eisenstein, Rino della Flora, William Gaddis, William Gass, Garth Gillan, Gary Heim, Nick Kaldis, Gretchen Luidens, Todd McGowan, Laura Pauley, James Peltz, David Riede, Marjorie Rowe, Bennett Simon, Henry Sussman, Melanie Rae Thon, Lois Tyson, Sensei Lu Yarbrough, and Slavoj Žižek.

A special word of thanks to my brother John Davis, as well as to David Gross, James Hemmer, and Nathan Moore.

PREFACE

In my first book, I was still transfiguring things—I'll never do
that again.

—Paul Celan

This work will develop four related theses that go "against the grain" of the
methods of thinking that define the parameters of current discourse. Briefly
stated:

1. My goal is to develop a new theory of the tragic and to show how a
tragic understanding offers the most accurate comprehension of what is
termed "the postmodern condition." I hasten to add that the tragic, so
understood, is not a "master discourse" rooted in nostalgia for the dis-
credited metaphysical assumptions of traditional humanism. It is, rather, an
attempt to go beyond postmodern irony—that playful, ironic, self-demysti-
fying discourse dedicated to the endless deferral of meaning—without returning to the essentialistic assumptions that inform the logic of the *ratio*.[1]
The ruling assumption in current intellectual debate is that one must
choose between these two positions. The basic flaw in this reasoning is the
belief that this opposition offers a choice between two genuine alternatives,
when the actual truth of our historical condition is that both constitute
flights from a tragic comprehension.[2]
2. The theory of the tragic I will construct strives to recapture the
demands of the *existential*. Not, I would add, in order to return to Sartre or
Heidegger, but to reconstitute a way of thinking about history and lived
experience that is freed of the contradictions that limited their efforts. The
book thus advances a new understanding, and practice, of what it means to
think and live existentially.
3. That understanding is itself grounded in a psychoanalytic inquiry
into the dynamics of the psyche, one that establishes an order of affective
inwardness in which existential awareness and action emerge as direct functions of an in-depth inquiry into deeply repressed conflicts. Since this is
perhaps the most radical dimension of the book, let me add that the psychoanalytic theory I will develop here is sharply opposed to currently available
alternatives. Briefly, I will argue that ego psychology (including its recent

incorporation of object-relations psychology) is best understood as a massive defense against psychological reality, while Lacanian psychoanalysis constitutes an exceedingly formalistic and neo-Kantian displacement of tragic anxiety into a series of ironic impasses. To go beyond both, another way of thinking about the psyche is required. The one I will offer grows out of a reflection on two of Freud's richest insights. (A) Psychoanalysis, as a discipline and profession, is marked by an effort to repress and contain its most disruptive insights. (B) When Freud acknowledged that the "poets knew it [the unconscious] first" he failed to see something even more significant: they know it better. As I have shown in *Get the Guests: Psychoanalysis, Modern American Drama, and the Audience* (Madison: University of Wisconsin Press, 1995) great literature offers us insights into the dynamics of the psyche that exceed the concepts and frameworks that have informed psychoanalysis thus far. A literary work, accordingly, should not be used as the example that illustrates fixed psychoanalytic concepts, which are simply imposed on it, as is generally the case; literature must become, instead, the basis for original advances in psychoanalysis, the source of new concepts and from them, eventually, a new theory.

4. History, I will argue, contains the same power, the power to lead us to a new theory of the psyche. The primary goal of the present work is to unlock and articulate that power. Such an effort needs an "example," one that will reveal the past as something that we often do not want to know and yet are compelled to know, because it weighs like a "nightmare" on the brains of the living, revealing the dilemmas, impasses, and anxieties that contemporary intellectual alternatives strive to exorcize by proclaiming the dogmas whereby we rush blindly into the future. History eludes us not primarily because language differs, defers, delays, and spins itself out in endless arrays of fabulation and signification without closure, but because we lack a theory of history grounded in a tragic and existential understanding of the psyche.

For an American reflecting on these issues, one event presents itself ineluctably as a matter of infinite historical concern. I refer, of course, to Hiroshima. A recent book by Robert Jay Lifton and Greg Mitchell, *Hiroshima in America,* is subtitled *A Half Century of Denial.* I will show later that this book itself contributes to the situation it would correct.[3] My purpose in citing it here is to foreground an issue that will always remain both controversial and self-evident: something is lacking, something is "out of joint," in the discourse American historians have developed to deal with Hiroshima. And as we will see, that something highlights and challenges the *system of guarantees* that informs history as a discipline. Such a demonstration entails for the discipline what Heidegger regards as the most creative situation any discipline can attain—that of a crisis in which "the very relationship between positively investigative inquiry and those things themselves that are under interrogation comes to a point where it begins to totter."[4] As I will show, that crisis derives from the contradiction between the system of guarantees that inform the discipline of history and the tragic realities that are thereby consigned to silence.

For several reasons, Hiroshima presents an ideal forum for developing these issues. Auschwitz and Hiroshima are often joined both in the popular and the poetic imagination. Their treatment by historians, however, is marked by a striking dissonance. Historians of the Holocaust foreground ethical, theological, and ontological questions about human nature and the nature of evil. Empirically and ontologically those questions constitute the terms under which research is conducted in the field, as witnessed most recently by the controversies surrounding Daniel Jonah Goldhagen's *Hitler's Willing Executioners*. Considerations of Hiroshima, in contrast, turn on a single issue. Was the United States justified in using the Bomb? Was that decision taken "to end the war, saving perhaps a million lives," or do the "facts" suggest another story? The current consensus among historians, with one noteworthy exception, is that the official justification for using the Bomb is a carefully constructed myth that cannot withstand historical scrutiny.[5] Be that as it may, after fifty years of debate another function of the fixation of historians on this issue becomes apparent. As long as this issue remains primary, other questions are deferred and effectively rendered moot. There is even a tacit assumption shared (with few exceptions) by both sides in the debate that once the issue of "justification" has been settled— and the last incorrigible fact finally in place—the concern of historians with Hiroshima will have attained its proper end.

We thereby see one of the meanings of Walter Benjamin's idea that "the dead remain in danger."[6] For what if the most important questions about Hiroshima as a historical Event transcend the terms of the debate and the underlying framework it serves? That is, what if the true function of the dominant system of rules and protocols of inquiry that structure history as a discipline is to prevent other, deeper inquiries until their traces, like fine radioactive particles, have been diffused in the general atmosphere of academic discourse and mastery?[7] From this perspective, the long march to the current consensus about why America dropped the Bomb reveals itself as an act of deliberate, if unconscious, repression. We ask certain questions so that we don't have to ask others. A single issue and a single way of conducting research on that issue attain dominance in academic discourse so that other ways of thinking will not be able to constitute themselves. We need fear no Auschwitz of the American psyche, no psychoanalytic inquiry into the Bomb as an event that marks a turning point in the history of our humanity. The possibility that studying history may turn on such issues, with certain events having the power to enforce major revisions in our understanding of "human nature," has been contained. Unless, that is, an end to the debate about America's reasons for dropping the Bomb means the beginning of another kind of discourse about Hiroshima: one that poses the kind of moral, psychological, and ontological questions we find necessary when talking about Auschwitz. But with a significant difference. For as we'll see, Auschwitz was the "end" of modernism, Hiroshima the inaugural post-modern act.

This book attempts to construct that long overdue discourse about Hiroshima in order to develop a new theory of history. To engage the reader in that inquiry existentially and psychologically, as well as intellectually, I begin with an assertion that for many Americans remains a matter of heated resistance. After fifty years spent dispelling lies and carefully constructed myths, the truth can now be said: Hiroshima was a crime against humanity, an act of atrocity without justification and, in its way, without precedent.[8] Moreover, something deeply rooted in "the American character" and im-plicit in the logos of Western thought informed that act and was changed— in depth and perhaps irreversibly—as a result. The effects of that change continue to proliferate, defining the present and revealing the "postmod-ern sensibility" in terms of its true referent: what I will call the nuclear Unconscious.[9] Hiroshima as event is that moment, that Heideggerian "*ec-stases* of temporality,"[10] which is uniquely revelatory of all that we do not know—and do not want to know—about our culture. As such, it will func-tion in this book as the traumatic kernel[11] that flares up at each crucial step in the inquiry to point the way toward the next necessary stage of its dialecti-cal progression.

Virginia Woolf said that "in or about December 1910 human nature changed." She would have recorded a similar shock in August of 1945. The change Woolf witnessed has now, of course, been safely domesticated and has a local habitation and a name: modernism. The second change also has a name—postmodernism—but the ideologies most closely associated with its development remain mired in the first moment of an arrested dialectic.[12] Irony and aporia dominate the "postmodern sensibility" because its con-siderable energies are devoted to a displacement of the Event that remains at the center of our collective historical Unconscious—the referent that serves as the motive behind the denial of reference. Reference must be continually deferred, then rendered impossible, because anxiety and flight from that anxiety define our actual response to the one referent that will continue to weigh on our consciousness until we restore the proper dialecti-cal direction and move from the delights of skeptical play to a recovery of the demands of unhappy consciousness.

Einstein said "the Bomb changed everything—except the ways we think." As such, it is the inwardness of our inwardness, never more so perhaps than when we use deconstructive irony as the master trope that delivers us from the burden of a historically situated subjectivity or, at that opposite extreme that amounts to the same thing, when we reassert an essentialist humanism as the fixed and universal system of understanding and explanation that washes us clean of history and its contingencies. What if we broke with both strategies—and rather than deconstructing the Bomb or containing it we tried to **internalize** it and then trace the ways it explodes and implodes within the psyche?

Such an effort would take as its goal a reconstitution of the tragic as the dialectical category that provides the only adequate idea for comprehending—and existing—in the present. Such a humanism, however, confronts as its prior and primary task a deracination of the **system of guarantees** on which previous "humanisms" have depended. For the function of that system, with respect to history, has been to establish, as canons of research and explanation, a set of essentialistic concepts of meaning, logic, and human nature that function to insulate historians and their audiences so that horror can never be more than the temporary aberration from which we always, of necessity, recover. The narration of History thereby becomes yet another occasion for deploying—and thereby reinforcing—the central beliefs and values of the humanistic tradition. That tradition thus provides the ego, or identity-principle, that "we" (the community of humanistic interpreters) move *from* and *to* in dealing with events that challenge our certainties.[13] We love to read and write histories because such stories tell us who we already know we are, while conveniently exorcizing the threat of those accounts that would hold up a different mirror to our nature. History is, indeed, a "fiction," the corpse over which we warm ourselves[14] so that we may rise cleansed, catharted, the system of needs, beliefs, and guarantees restored—with existence the self-reference perpetually deferred.[15]

What if, instead, we approached history as a reality—and a discipline—in which we must risk ourselves utterly? One in which to know is to suffer irreversible change in one's beliefs, values, and even in one's "identity," with nothing in the logos of thought able to protect us from that possibility? The reign of the *a priori* would thereby come to an end, the principle of hope a category we'd risk, not one we'd need to renew at whatever cost. Could such an engagement constitute the true "force and signification" of Hiroshima[16] and thereby evidence that events in history are the true "Absolute" that abide with us—the gift of the past to the future as that call of conscience requiring of us no less than a fundamentally new understanding of the human psyche and the human condition?[17]

Whether such will be the result of our inquiry remains to be seen. A final consideration, however, reinforces the claim of Hiroshima on our attention. It's ours. If horror comes into history here in a new way, the horror also comes from us and not from somewhere else. As such, it offers us a chance, as Americans, to learn that "the knowledge most worth having" is the opportunity to learn that about ourselves which we do not want to know.

When the subject under investigation impinges on the inquirer in this way, the process of understanding is one with the depth of one's engagement.[18] Thus, I end this overture with that term—**existential engagement**—to underscore again my primary heresy: the effort to reclaim the existential as the category that has not been rendered passé by the postmodern sensibility but, rather, the one that haunts it as its conscience. It does so because it teaches us, as I will show, that authentic "deconstruction" is *deracination:* that dialectical and psychological process in which "spirit is the life that cuts back into life" because thought is the process of actively reversing one's psyche from within by eradicating every belief, value, and need that stands in the way of taking up one's responsibility to history, a responsibility that derives from the discovery that our being as subjects is utterly delivered over to history. As those who live it know, such an effort begins not in the head but in the pores. Asked why she is there, the woman in Duras' *Hiroshima Mon Amour* says, "I came to Hiroshima because I feel that perception must be learned."[19] Such will be our task. (It is important to note here, however, that this task requires two works: the present one, which develops a concept of artistic cognition as the way of knowing required for the comprehension of traumatic Events; and a companion piece, *The Holocaust Memorial: A Play About Hiroshima,* (Bloomington, IN: First Books, 2000), in which I attempt to realize artistically what *Deracination* theorizes. The two works dialectically depend upon and complete one another.[19]

Let me add in closing a brief note on a book dealing with one of the historical figures I will discuss that I had an opportunity to read only when my own work was nearing publication. After a fifty-five-year search Paul Tibbets finally found his Vergil in Bob Greene, whose recently published book *Duty* (New York: Morrow, 2000) repeats all the myths about why we bombed Hiroshima, about Tibbets (represented by Greene as a "reluctant hero" and as the author of a book that Tibbets did not, in fact, write), and, sadly, about how the sons of World War II veterans should mourn their fathers—by perpetuating the lies those fathers were told.

One

The Way to Hiroshima

Humanus sum, nihil humanum me alienum puto.
—Terence

No, this is not a disentanglement from, but a progressive *knotting into.*
—Thomas Pynchon, *Gravity's Rainbow*

Half of history is revenge, the other half is its provocation.
—William Gass, *The Tunnel*

I. Only Connect: Trauma in/and History

In August 1945 Elias Canetti writes the following in his journal: "A tormenting thought; as of a certain point, history was no longer *real*. Without noticing it, all mankind suddenly left reality; everything happening since then was supposedly not true; but we supposedly didn't notice. Our task would now be to find that point, and as long as we didn't have it, we would be forced to abide in our present destruction."[1] What Canetti can't see is that the point he refers to is the one he inhabits. He can't see it because it is too close and blinds him (as it would soon the inhabitants of two cities) with a light not of this world.

The proliferation of new theories of history in recent decades is itself a response to a historical situation—that defined by the Bomb. That connection is also what these theories cannot know about themselves and ceaselessly displace in teaching us all the new ways we can know and write about the past. What they *do* know is that the assumptions and guarantees on which historians have traditionally relied in constituting their subject and the needs that histories fulfill in offering us an account of events structured by these guarantees are no longer adequate to a contemporary awareness of history and historicity.[2]

To cite the major developments (though in no necessary order of importance):[3]

1. Foucault's concept of geneological history and the archeology of knowledge and its creative extension in the new historicist methodologies developed by Stephen Greenblatt and his circle.

1

2. The hermeneutic theories of history and historical explanation developed by Gadamer, Habermas, and Ricoeur, with special note given to Ricoeur's development of a complex theory of time and narrative.
3. Derrida's recent work on Marx and Benjamin and his continuing effort to expose the Hegelian assumptions about history, progress, and the logos which structure the way history is narrated by historians who know little or nothing of Hegel.
4. Althusser, Sartre, Gramsci, and the many often sharply opposed approaches to history developed in recent years by Marxists as different as Frederic Jameson, G. A. Cohen, Perry Anderson, and Stuart Hall.
5. The recovery of Kant's speculations on history and its recent extension in Lyotard's theory of the differend.
6. The attempts by Slavoj Žižek, Joan Copjec, and Teresa Brennan to articulate the theory of history implicit in Lacan.
7. The massive significance of Walter Benjamin's speculations, the continued vitality of Adorno and the Frankfurt school, and the renewed interest in the thought of Kenneth Burke.
8. The work of Louis O. Mink, Hayden White, Dominick LaCapra, Roy Schafer, and others on the narrative and tropological principles that shape the writing of history.

To this list one can add Collingwood and McKeon's earlier theorizing about history, the work of Braudel, Baudrillard, deCerteau, Calinescu, and Bourdieu and the new modes of historical writing and historical investigation developed by anthropologists such as Clifford Geertz, James Clifford, and Natalie Zemon Davis. The list is by no means complete because one must add to it two developments that may be of greater significance and that complicate the issue of the historical.

I refer, first, to the number of alternative histories that have emerged in recent years thanks to feminist, multicultural, postcolonial, subaltern, and queer studies. Such works have contributed more than new knowledge to our understanding of the past. They have broken with the logic, the procedures, and the ruling assumptions of traditional historical methodologies by showing how that logic has as its primary function the exclusion (or marginalization) of "voices" that challenge its hegemony and the motives that inform its explanations. Such studies are not merely of local interest. They entail a theoretical *crisis:* the recognition that the principles of historical explanation that we regard as true, rational, objective, and universal are cultural, conventional, ideological, and deeply implicated in power and the repressions required for its maintenance. Ways of thinking derived from other cultures or voices silenced by the dominant culture may provide precisely the critical handle required to understand what is really at work in the privileging of certain canons of reasoning and explanation as scientific and "objective" and the rejection of other experiences and ways of thinking as illegitimate and unfounded. The true bite of the multicultural—seldom honored because it cuts in every direction—is the idea that none of us are locked into privileging our own culture and "subject position(s)." We can gain distance from our frameworks by immersing ourselves in other ways of thinking. We can then use that experience to become aware of things that our culture and its dominant interest groups do not want to know about themselves. The implication of such an orientation for history is considerable, since historical explanation is perhaps the primary way in which a community establishes the structures of belief, mind, and feeling on which it depends in giving an "identity" to its members.[4] Thanks to the explosion of the multicultural, we now have a way to internally distance ourselves from such beliefs and practices, even perhaps, following Nietzsche, to touch all that "goes without saying" with the hammer as with a tuning fork.

The second development goes even further in revealing history to us in new ways. I refer to the work of those thinkers I term the true empiricists—writers such as Faulkner and Morrison, Gaddis and Pynchon, Garcia-Marquez and David Grossman—whose explorations of new narrative strategies for the understanding of history deepen and redefine the crisis implicit in recent work in historiography. For what such writers explore is the *cognitive* power of new *narrative* methods for the very apprehension of history. In evolving new ways to write and represent history such writers thereby constitute the past as precisely what has eluded dominant modes of conceptualization and explanation. Their works thus become the primary texts we must grapple with in order to grasp the "complexity" of history as well as the ways we must learn to write in order to sustain that comprehension. It may turn out, in fact, that the concepts of history developed by the theorists listed above are but dim reflections of the concrete models of knowing offered by such writers—the implication being that we shouldn't use Derrida (say) to read Pynchon or Ricoeur to understand Faulkner, but must take up the proper dialectical relationship and grant the literary work the power to challenge and even overturn the theoretical frameworks we impose on it.[5] My purpose in this book is to develop that possibility: (1) to show that Literature is an independent way of knowing, prior to logic and the order of the concept, and (2) to demonstrate that its cognitive power comes to fruition in the apprehension of the historical.

Here is one way to think about this possiblity. If conceptualization, especially as practiced within the ratio, alters and falsifies what artists such as Faulkner and Pynchon enable us to grasp, the problem is not to resolve this difference, but to sustain it as a way of thinking about history. After spending a week in El Salvador, Joan Didion said "I now regard Garcia-Marquez as a social realist." The implication of Didion's remark is that "magical realism" is not fiction but revelation—that way of writing which first cognizes and represents the truth of Latin American history. My purpose is to sustain the disruptive implications of this idea and nurture it into theory for a discipline that still by and large wants to set strict limits to the ways in which it will understand itself as narrative, to say nothing of using the modes of writing contemporary novelists place at its disposal.

The idea that history, like literature and philosophy, is a way of writing, and that this circumstance is not incidental but constitutive in determining the "facts," has been in the air for quite some time now. It derives from what we can list as a fourth major development behind the current rethinking of history. I refer to the explosion of theories of narrative and to what Clifford Geertz calls the "blurred genres" and new ways of writing history that have emerged in the work of historical scholars in a number of disciplines in recent years.[6]

What are we to make of these developments? Is it possible that Aristotle was wrong when he said that "poetry is more philosophic than history" since, qua narrative, it is impossible to fix the difference? The kinds of stories we are able to tell determine what counts as fact and inference. A narrative paradigm functions from the beginning of any historical inquiry. For example: assume agents with rational intentions that they formulated through careful deliberation before taking action and that is what one finds in "evidence" when one interprets the documents they left behind; documents that one then uses to construct a narrative that will offer a structured, orderly, reasoned account of why those agents were justified in raining nuclear fire on two cities.[7]

Narrative assumptions about human nature and the motives determining the intentions and actions of the agents who make history inform the act of historical interpretation. The very constitution of data is inextricably tied to the narrative framework in which one will "later" cast and represent the data. Such is the hermeneutic circle in which every historian moves. If here too "there are no facts, only interpretations" (Nietzsche), narrative is the reason because it provides the a priori framework that shapes the materials of historical inquiry from the beginning. What Flaubert teaches us about Emma Bovary, and Joyce about virtually every language our culture employs to make sense of experience, is true also for the historian. The limits of a person's narrative framework—of the kinds of stories one can tell—establish the limits of what that person can know and experience. That is why narrative has become the neo-Kantian preoccupation of the day.[8] As Frederic Jameson argues, the need to tell stories is the superordinate a priori, the deepest desire and structuring principle whereby "the human mind" makes sense of personal and cultural experience.[9]

Approach and avoidance, however, has characterized the response of those historiographers who have worked hardest to bring this condition to our attention. While historiographers such as White, LaCapra, and Ricoeur foreground the ways in which narrative genres, tropes, and conventions shape historical writing, their fascination with narrative halts at precisely the point where I will argue one should begin—with writers such as Joyce, Pynchon, Faulkner, Woolf, Gaddis, and Morrison as opposed to the models of omniscient and reliable narration provided by the nineteenth century novel. For when one begins with "modern" and "post-modern" writers, fascinating complications arise concerning the cognitive inseparability of historical knowledge and narrative "method"; complications which exceed the framework a metahistorian such as Hayden White uses to contain the Kantian turn in historical inquiry by establishing, through the use of Northrop Frye, an essentialistic and curiously ahistorical theory of the four literary forms or modes (romance, comedy, tragedy, irony) that for White inform and exhaust the possibilities of historical narration.[10]

In his recent work, White has opened himself to new possibilities, but the way he frames them involves assumptions that in effect cancel everything radical in those possibilities. Consider the following statement: "Such a conception of historical inquiry . . . would permit historians to conceive of the possibility of using impressionistic, expressionistic, surrealistic, and (perhaps) even actionist modes of representation for dramatizing the significance of data which they have uncovered but which, all too frequently, they are prohibited from seriously contemplating as evidence."[11] Implicit here is the assumption that there is still some way to separate the "data" and its comprehension from what is finally "rhetoric"—a way of presenting, even dramatizing things but not a mode of cognition whereby the data is had and known in the first place. What White holds back from is this: *representation is cognition.* For once take that step and there is no way to limit the narrative experiments historians may have to undertake in order to know their subject.

Re-enter Faulkner and Pynchon, Morrison and Gaddis with the recognition that the extant modes of narration—Frye's essentialistic cycle, whether suitably ironized by White and Roy Schafer or grounded in Wayne Booth's humanistic rhetoric of reliable narration—are not adequate to the "facts" of contemporary history or to the relationship authors must form to readers if those facts are to be comprehended.[12] The task of the historian is not to recycle the old forms, as if they constitute and exhaust all narrative possibilities a priori, but to evolve new and unprecedented ways of narrating experiences that cannot be cognized until modes of representation adequate to them have been invented. Narrative, so understood, is not tied to an a priori structure of explanatory paradigms (comedy, tragedy, romance, irony), nor is it tied to the need for a reliable authorial voice of reason wedded to the essential beliefs of the humanistic tradition. It is a project made new and dangerous by the historical contingencies that are the historian's subject or become so whenever the paradise of the a priori is rent by the force of traumatic events.[13]

The leads offered by great writers of fiction will be of little use to us, however, as long as the discipline of history remains tied to epistemologies that rest on concepts of perception and explanation that render such narratological experiments irrelevant and finally intrusive to the pursuit of an objective, scientific knowledge that one restores to history once experimental writing has been cast aside for factual "narratives" that dare not know themselves as such, lest in doing so they "deconstruct" the line that somehow separates them from "fiction." This non-existent line, however, is only sustained by keeping the narrative dimension of historical writing to a minimum or by establishing, through the consensus of all "responsible" historians, [14] a set of conventions regarding those ways of telling that are inherently proper to history and that save the historian from having to attempt the kind of narrative "inventions" and strategies one finds in Faulkner or Pynchon.

The appeal of such arguments derives, of course, from a recognition of what would happen if historians actually tried to constitute the radical possibility. What, for example, would result if an "academic" historian attempted to represent the Middle Passage in a voice similar to the one Toni Morrison finds necessary to its evocation in *Beloved?* Or if Shelby Foote attempted to rewrite a history of the South after internalizing *Absalom, Absalom!?* Or, imagine a consciousness of the Bomb as deep and tortured as that possessed by the narrator of *Gravity's Rainbow* made the basis for an actual historical narrative about Hiroshima that would of necessity become as expressive, as fantastic, and as appalling as anything one finds in Pynchon's fiction. Imagine: Oppenheimer in the dessert chewing on the *Gita;* Tibbets naming the plane Enola Gay, after his mother; a rapt and cheering crowd of 100,000 gathered in the L.A. Coliseum two months after the war to celebrate a simulated re-enactment of Hiroshima complete with "mushroom cloud"—and, in juxtaposition, the experience of the *hibakusha,* agents who never existed before in history.

As these examples indicate, the force of narrative is both epistemological and ontological. For the richest implication of this line of thought is that the way artists know is not only different; it liberates a knowledge of the Real that official historical methods are designed to conceal. One way to think of the artist is as a consciousness that internalizes and then sustains the traumatic impact of events by refusing to sacrifice the revelatory power of image and affect to the order of the concept and the rule of the ratio. The artist's task, as Rilke put it, "is to wait for that which has become concept to become again image." Such is the process from which the search for new artistic forms, new narrative ways to grasp and articulate experience begins; in the image, say, of Morrison's Sethe dashing her child's brains out to prevent that child's return to slavery. For the artist, the image in its traumatic impact is the first historical fact and the last one: that primary datum that gives us the world in its power to enter us with the severity of a judgment that eradicates defenses and conceptual shields. A historian who takes up this possibility knows two things in their dialectical connection: (1) that conceptualization and the structures of explanation it offers prove inadequate to the affective reality of experience and (2) that it is possible, by refusing their pull, to recover what official accounts consign to silence.

Such a route, however, leads inevitably to a *crisis* for the discipline: one in which virtually everything on which historians have traditionally depended is subjected to a skeptical interrogation; a crisis that can't be resolved by reasserting pragmatic or academic consensual limits since the ground and motives from which such solutions derive are part and parcel of the very circle of understanding that has become problematic. History as a discipline is not an archive of monumental empirical labors. **It is a practice grounded in a system of guarantees.** That system and the reassurances it gives us are the primary things we read—and internalize—when we read histories. And, as we will see, that system has as its deepest motive and appeal the assurance that certain things will not be known.

II. The Concept of Crisis and a Hermeneutics of Engagement

Early in *Being and Time,* Heidegger makes one of his major and insufficiently appreciated contributions to methodology: "a discipline is mature only insofar as it is capable of 'undergoing' a crisis in all of its basic concepts and procedures."[15] Rather than something to be avoided, this condition for Heidegger is something to be sought, something reflection must endeavor to produce. Moreover, when it happens, the first sign is this: the relationship between the objects under investigation and the frameworks of knowing "begins to totter." We start to see the ways in which our frameworks set up positive barriers to knowledge. The objects of inquiry then announce themselves in a new way: in terms of how they exceed, resist, challenge, and even mock the frameworks. The normal post-Kantian epistemological operation—concepts superimposed upon data—becomes problematic. A discipline in crisis is one where the very nature of knowledge—of what it is we want to know and why—is at issue. Because that is so, crisis in any discipline is valuable because it renews our contact with something else that Heidegger formulates in an equally memorable way when he defines a "metaphysical" question as one that "puts the very being of the questioner into question."[16] Such a situation, like crisis, is of course for most people unintelligible, impossible, and intolerable. For some, however, it is the only time one feels truly alive in the act of thinking.

A *hermeneutics of engagement* is the term I have coined for the method of interpretation that develops and sustains the experience that gives birth to "metaphysical" questioning. I first coined this term in a memorable conversation I had with Paul Ricoeur in 1971. My effort was to distinguish my idea of interpretation from Ricoeur's "hermeneutics of recovery."[17] A hermeneutics of recovery strives to find those "meanings" and values that are constant and repeatable across time, and that can be found in diverse cultural products once we develop the correct method of humanist, essentialistic interpretation. Engagement begins when all such assurances are in doubt. Contingency, existence, and anxiety then bite deep into the human subject, constituting a situation we can sustain only by resisting the ways in which we are predisposed to flee or resolve it. Crisis thereby generates its true complement: the questioner as a being in crisis, existentially at issue in the act of thinking and forced by it to descend to the most hidden places of the psyche.[18]

For one who sustains this condition as a methodological principle, the goal of thinking becomes to constitute a criticism that is radical and radically self-critical in principle, one where reflection strives to sustain the disruptiveness of experience, not resolve it.[19] Most thinkers of course reject this possibility—or find it pragmatically unnecessary and undesirable—since it breaks with the Cartesian and rationalist assumptions that have traditionally informed the concept and the practice of reflection. Engaged reflection, in contrast, is a process that is itself existentialized from within through a principled sustenance and deepening of anxiety. Thereby, what others see as infinite regress, or the inability to "begin," becomes an authentic constitution of a third major insight we can derive from Heidegger.

He terms it the hermeneutic circle and derives striking implications from a recognition of its inescapability.[20] Briefly, Heidegger argues that (1) circularity cannot be avoided because thinking is always situated; (2) the authentic response being not to bewail this situation or try to escape it but to enter it fully in the recognition that it contains a positive possibility. *Engagement* is the act that preserves this situation as the agon through which thinking existentializes the thinker.[21] One result is an existentializing of epistemology. Discovering a framework's limitations is no longer the basis of its "affirmation" through the Kantian acquiescence in necessary a priori limits. It has become, rather, the beginning of a search for underlying motives and the need for their critique. The rationality of pure mind now reveals the psyche beneath. The sufferance of painful insights into oneself becomes the circumstance that defines the possibility of self-knowledge.

Nietzsche's ideal of "self-contempt" thereby becomes the basis for a thought in which reflection on one's motives transforms the way in which one subsequently knows the world.[22] With psychological self-consciousness comes an awareness of how deeply our thoughts, attitudes, beliefs, and feelings have been chosen for us, implanted in us by others; and of how altering this condition requires taking issue with oneself at a register of inwardness to which few subjects ever "descend" given the intense anxiety that attends it. Suffering is here not only the result of reflection, it is the way to it. And it begets as the basis for "self-overcoming" the need to cast the cold eye of a withering contempt not simply on the values we hold, but on the deeper ties that bind us to them. Tearing out of one's heart certain desires and the complex internal relations that bind us to them has become the prime agent of human perception. Self-contempt of this order is neither a pathological state nor a psychological impossibility. It is a discipline of courage in suffering and self-mediation through suffering: the act whereby the quest for knowledge takes on the status of an ethical and psychological imperative. Knowledge (and the "self") can no longer be consigned to the purely intellectual space of a world we construct solely in the head to assure the presence of the human mind to itself in endless pure tautology, a ratio secure in its transcendence of anything that doesn't make "sense." Engaged reflection lives, in contrast, the readiness to make uncompromising self-examination one's innermost imperative. This is the engagement one carries as hermeneutic into every situation, every inquiry, which is why *deracination* is the best word for this method since the process is one in which taking action within oneself depends upon a repeated reversal that uproots the motives upon which the "self" depends for its identity. This process, by way of transition, is what this book attempts for both the author—and the audience.

III. Only Connect: Why Hiroshima?

A prospectus outlining this inquiry called forth the following comments from two National Endowment for the Humanities reviewers. I quote both reviews in their entirety.

1. The first, scrawled across the page: "Pure nonsense. What is his discipline? There are perfectly good justifications for Hiroshima. Not 'Humanities' at all but vapid, subjective philosophizing."
2. The second, typed, serenely transcendent: "Why the insistence that Hiroshima is 'concealed and forgotten'? Why the emphasis on a city's *instantaneous* obliteration as a Sign more *horrific* than the cumulative engineered deaths of millions in World War II, millions in the holocaust, tens of millions in the Gulag, Cambodia, Rwanda, back to tens of thousands killed and blinded by Basil II Bulgaroktonos, and back into time immemorial?"

Clearly, it's not a good idea to get downwind of the post-Cheney NEH. That noted, we can profitably derive from these comments a preliminary understanding of five issues that inevitably arise in any discussion of historical method.

A. Fact-Document

Joe Friday is always with us, but in doing history the unmediated vision is no more than a self-deluding myth. Consider the following headline in an American Newspaper, August 7, 1945:

"ATOM" CITY IN ASHES
HOLOCAUST IN HIROSHIMA
JAP PITTSBURGH HIT

Just the facts, or a first textualization. Understandable, as a sign of war weariness and thus easily purged through a more disinterested, "objective" account? Or would that account, by its very "objectivity," elide what is set forth with uncommon clarity in the headline—the inseparability of an Event from its contextualization. The sentiments laid forth baldly in the newspaper headline may have been, in fact, the primary "cause" or motive in the decisions that led to the act; and to the subsequent effort of historians (and apologists) to conceal those motives and justify the bombing of Hiroshima on the basis of the "objective" evidence that can be obtained by consulting the official records left behind by the architects of that decision. But that does not free one from the circle. For to establish their veracity one must read and interpret those texts: some of which are similar to the newspaper headline, others quite different; some fashioned on the spot and apparently free of motives; others darkly ambiguous and intended primarily for public consumption; some created co-temporal with the event, or shortly thereafter, as a record of official *intentions;* others long after, late in the winter of one's reflections.[23] In all cases, one thing is common—text. In consulting the historical "record" one never comes at long last on pure factual data, but always on yet another text open to interpretation. Moreover, in interpreting such documents, the search for "reasons" and the privileging of certain statements and explanations (albeit from the mouths of politicians) because they take that form is a perfect instance of the kind of circularity that many thinkers find so appealing: that is, the privileging of reason and intention as a way to limit what can happen in history so that we will achieve explanations that make "sense" and are reassuring to reason.

History, as event and as discipline, is inherently textual. with no way out of the circle.[24] The correct response is not to persist in the effort to remove such impurities in order to attain that mythical beast dear to the positivist's heart—the brute, unmediated fact that puts an end to debate—but, following Heidegger, to enter the circle fully by recognizing that history is a hermeneutic discipline and not an empirical one. The primary data of history are the documents that historians can only read through the frameworks of interpretation they employ to wrestle with that "data" in all its elusive, ambiguous complexity and frequent duplicity. When Truman, Byrnes, and Stimson speak and write the concealing of their intention may in fact be their primary intention.[25] Evidence for this hypothesis was inadvertently provided by the cry against "rewriting history," sounded most recently by the VFW in its successful campaign against the Smithsonian.[26] For the cry belies the basic fact. History is always being rewritten because it is only through that process that historians ever come to know it.

B. Explanation

Out of that process, in some cases, a general consensus about "reasons" eventually emerges. Such is the case with the Bomb where, fifty years after, the "perfectly good justifications for Hiroshima" have finally been established. Since this book is *not* about that issue, but about a deeper history underlying it, I take this opportunity to list those justifications here. Thus: on August 6, 1945 and then again on August 9, 1945, the United States dropped atomic bombs on Japan for four reasons: (1) to avenge Pearl Harbor; (2) to justify to the American people the amount of money invested in the development of the Bomb; (3) to create a laboratory wherein scientists and military personnel could study its effects; and (4) to "impress" the Russians with this opening salvo of the Cold War. Furthermore: (5) the action was taken in full knowledge that the Japanese, at Hirohito's direction, were pursuing terms of surrender through several diplomatic channels. (6) It was also taken in the knowledge that the planned "invasion of Japan"—which would cost a "million [sic] American lives"—had become, thanks to the success of Curtis LeMay's fire-bombing campaign[27] unnecessary; except, that is, as a ruse perpetrated on our own servicemen and as a rhetorical prop in postwar propaganda. The first act of revisionism, of rewriting history was the myth fabricated after the war by Stimson and others to hide what America had done: namely, the myth that we dropped the Bomb "to end the war and save lives."[28]

Two observations follow the above that are crucial to the definition and understanding of my purpose. The production of the "case closed" account of any historical debate predictably generates the next new account, which depends, for its possibility, on the production or unearthing of the next new "fact."[29] This is not simply the way dissertations get written or bar-room battles sustained. It is, with far more troubling results, the process whereby certain issues come to regulate the discussion of a historical event to the exclusion or repression of other concerns. If we can keep in place the assumption that there are two sides to every question, with the two camps fixated forever on debating whether dropping the Bomb was "justified," we can avoid dealing with the reality that is thereby displaced—the brute fact of August 6, 1945 and the historical meaning of that event as a human action. That is the subject of this book. And to the consternation of my NEH reviewers it necessarily entails matters that are all too conveniently labelled "subjective."

C. Subjectivity and History

As Hegel shows in *The Phenomenology of Spirit*, objectivity and the stance of observational reason is neither the primary nor the proper stance toward the real; it is, rather, one of the most abstract and self-contradictory attitudes we can adopt toward both the object of knowledge (especially in the "human sciences") and the relationship of the knower to that object. Subjectivity, moreover, is not a lawless flight into self-indulgent projections breeding nothing but emotional and cognitive confusion, but a principle of self-reference and of knowing that is rigorous and supremely lawful because it develops through its own immanent critique. As such, subjectivity is precisely that self-mediation that enables us to get beyond the dualism of objectivity and subjectivity and the reified concepts of both terms required to sustain that dualism. For the right subject that is: one for whom subjectivity is the most rigorous and determinate relationship one can take up toward the objects of one's inquiry; with knowledge a dialectic in which reference is always secured because the imperatives imposed by events in their traumatic impact on subjects generate the self-transformations one must undertake in order to become adequate to the task of knowing. To know the Bomb is to live a relationship to it that is subjective in the most exacting determination of that term. Those who seek the pure facticity of the fact, who regard "objectivity" in positivistic terms and "subjectivity" a woeful lapse from that stance, fail to see two conditions that blind them to the very subject matter of history: (1) objectivity is an attempt by a subject to limit the terms and conditions of its engagement; (2) it produces, as its necessary corollary, a drastic limitation of what can be known. The ideology of objectivity is not a purgation of subjective considerations but an attempt to reduce them to their most dogmatic and self-reifying form, to impose rigid controls on history so that its knowing will not "trouble us / With thoughts beyond the reaches of our souls."

D. Disciplinarity

Deracination is an interdisciplinary work, based on a self-conscious awareness of the methodology that makes interdisciplinary knowledge possible. That method is *dialectic* as that way of thinking that establishes necessary connections that cut across the separations that isolate questions and disciplines. To get a quick idea of what is distinctive about this way of thinking—and why the current practice of attaining the interdisciplinary by simply piling the results of distinct disciplines atop one another is its inadvertent parody—imagine Aristotle's exasperation when he looked on the Platonic corpus and saw issues that must be separated into distinct disciplines jumbled together under hypostatized categories with no locus in "experience" save pure speculation. "What's his discipline?" was the question Aristotle asked of Plato before correcting the situation by creating an organon for inquiry based on what Aristotle made his primary methodological task: the separation of distinct questions into distinct disciplines so that particular "sciences" could be constructed, each with their own univocal definitions and distinct, fixed procedures.[30] We who live habituated to that way of doing things forget what Aristotle knew (as did Kant and Dewey): separating questions and disciplines is just as difficult as joining them. Both operations are philosophic acts and depend on distinct philosophic principles.[31]

For some thinkers the task of thought is to find and establish necessary connections. The question "what's his discipline?" is inappropriate to such a discourse. The proper question concerns architectonic principles: what is the nature of the categories that cut across and bind "disciplines" and in what ontological principle are they grounded?[32] That ground principle may derive from a single discipline—logic in Plato and Hegel, history in Marx, psychology in Nietzsche and Freud. But that only happens if the grounding discipline is comprehensive and provides the dialectical thinker with a way to join together, in an inseparable unity, questions and phenomena that disciplinary thought is intent on keeping separate. To cite a simple example, this is the logic that allows Plato in *The Republic* to bring together education, poetry, justice, and the soul in an inquiry into the nature of Knowledge that is capped by an understanding that, qua Being, the good, the true, and the beautiful are and must be one. For the dialectical thinker, disciplinary thought rends the unity of experience, resulting in splits and bifurcations that destroy those connections that are lived before they are cognized and that require for their articulation modes of engagement and reflection that make preserving "the unity of lived-experience" more than just a pleasant phrase.[33]

The effort to evolve such categories is here taken up in a new way because the architectonic principles I use are derived from art, and specifically from literature, and not from a conceptual or logical framework of comprehensive mediation such as characterizes the dialectical tradition from Plato through Hegel. The basic argument I will mount is that the image gives us an awareness of history that transcends the order of the concept and of what can be known within the conceptual medium. In so doing image brings to perception concrete connections that are sundered, even in the best interdisciplinary work, insofar as that work remains based on the conceptual because the connections made by the image are radically different from the logical connections made possible by rational, conceptual mediation. Sustaining the ontological status of such connections, however, requires establishing art—and specifically literature—as an original, primary way of thinking and knowing that is capable of preserving its uniquely revelatory power over and against the effort of other ways of thinking to reduce that awareness to rational canons of discourse and intelligibility. Brought before the bar of historical investigation and forced to speak, Itzhak Zuckerman, soldier in the Warsaw ghetto and survivor of Auschwitz, responded to the insistent demand of Claude Lanzmann to contribute to the historical record with a deathless poem: "If you could lick my heart it would poison you."[34] After such knowledge, the historian's task is to sustain what Heidegger calls "the poetizing of discourse." For when history is one's concern, artistic knowing is perhaps the only mode of cognition and representation that proves adequate to the subject. Which brings us to a final observation.

E. Inhumanity Has No/A History: Basil II Bulgaroktonos Vivant

Boundless compassion is a wonderful thing. But Hiroshima has something to recommend it to our souls that other historical atrocities lack. It's ours. As such it gives us a chance to learn something about history that is easy to miss. I refer to the resistance we put up against knowing certain things; the ways in which the writing of history often serves to confirm what we want to believe, not what we ought to know. As we will see, a system of *guarantees* structures the activity of most historians, providing the *glue* that holds together the assumptions about fact, inference, and explanation that unify historical inquiry. One of the primary motives behind the writing of history is to show the power of these guarantees to subsume historical contingency in ways that enable us to live in a world that has been given the shape of that intelligibility. The inestimable value of Hiroshima, in contrast, is its ability to foreground these guarantees as principles of resistence to knowing, and not as the one true a priori logic of explanation. The power of Hiroshima is that of a vast alienation or *Entfremdungseffekt:* that is, the opportunity to detect and thereby make a fresh decision about categories of mind and feeling that have become habitual.

It may even entail the knowledge that there is something new under the sun; that August 6, 1945 was unprecedented and remains so as an object for understanding. It is comforting to proclaim that inhumanity is one and the same from time immemorial, rather than a historical process where great and irreversible changes can occur. One is thereby delivered from the specter that haunts history—that "human nature" is historical to the core, with no guarantee present to deliver us from the power of an event to complete processes of change that are irreversible and that produce results in which, as Virginia Woolf said, "human nature" itself changes utterly. Such a process, ripened through the use of poison gas and the erosion during the Great War of the protection accorded non-combatants matured to monstrous proportions in the years between 1937 and 1945. A new inhumanity was then ratified when an entire city—of no military significance, its population an undifferentiated mass—became the proper object of military strategy and military action.[35] A rough beast, its hour come round at last, was then born, ushering in a "new world order." That order contained as its innermost, nuclear secret the recognition that the psyche—individual and collective—is historical and continues to evolve forms appropriate to itself long after the traumatic events that bring its disorders to apotheosis have been explained, justified, and thereby rendered Unconscious.[36]

IV. On Psychoanalytic Method: No "Return to Freud"

This book attempts a psychoanalytic reading of Hiroshima—and of the American psyche. That reading is not based, however, on Freud, Lacan, Kohut, or any other current psychoanalytic orthodoxy. Such practices abridge the primary canon of engagement, depriving us of the most valuable lesson we can learn from Freud. The vitality of "psychoanalysis" resides in the effort to sustain a radically new way of thinking, not in a set of dogmas that are imposed a priori on phenomena without allowing the latter any power to challenge, extend, or revise the framework of interpretation. Genuine psychoanalytic thinking necessarily outstrips that practice because the logic that animates it is the effort to strip away defenses and resistances, to advance knowledge by seeking out what we do not want to know—about ourselves. That hermeneutic implies a complex epistemological relationship both to Freud's texts and to their use as conceptual tools in studying phenomena that exceed their explanatory powers and thus contain the power to produce new theoretical developments within psychoanalysis itself. Sustaining that possibility is why no "return to Freud" is attempted here. Such returns invariably take one of two forms, both inherently limiting. The first involves the repeated attempt—most recently by Grunbaum and Dennett[37] to see if psychoanalysis is a "science," and the recurrent discovery that its central concepts fail that test. To perform this operation one selects certain supposedly canonical statements in Freud's texts— statements that are established as such through a literal and distinctly unproblematic reading of those "texts"—then tests those statements by seeing if they stand up to what we now know scientifically, given the latest developments in cognitive psychology and the neurosciences. Not surprisingly, some of Freud's most provocative ideas—about the image, the nature of

depth memory, psyche as agon—are cast aside a priori since there is no way
they can even be constituted as hypotheses within the empiricizing methods
demanded by the "hard sciences."

The second return follows an opposite route, to a radically different
end. Through an exceedingly complicated, and somewhat hermetic, reading of Freud's canonical texts, the original and undiluted "truth" of the
master is recaptured, purged of revisionary errors. Lacan is, of course, the
most eloquent, elusive, and at times profound example of this hermeneutic
and its power to preserve the deep, and often previously undisclosed, meaning of Freud's discoveries against the simplifications to which subsequent
"developments," such as ego psychology, have reduced them in adapting
psychoanalysis to the social designs of the American "health-industry."

Neither approach will be used here, for good psychoanalytic and hermeneutic reasons. Freud is a giant but also only a beginning. Return, even
when purest, begets reification. And, of greater importance, a twofold resistance to history. First, to the genuine discoveries and advances that have
been made since Freud by psychoanalysts as diverse as Melanie Klein and
William Faulkner, Bion, Pynchon, Winnicott, Gaddis, Fairbairn, and Morrison. Second, to the ways in which these developments address the situation Freud only dimly foresaw when World War I convinced him that he had
underestimated the force of Thanatos in the psyche. My effort is to develop
the theory of psyche required to constitute Freud's most radical insights and
to extend them by tracing their development in those subsequent historical
events that confirm everything Freud feared. In thus situating psychoanalysis before that Event which has the power to put all its confidences and
concepts into crisis, my goal is to wrest from concealment and constitute a
theory of the psyche that other psychoanalytic theories have worked overtime to contain.

V. Engaging the Audience: Agonistic Intersubjectivity

Such a project entails an exacting rhetorical contract that I hope to form
with the reader. One of the interesting things about rhetoric is that when we
"agree" with an author we scarcely notice it. Or we find an author's rhetoric
"sensible, restrained, and rational" when it confirms our assumptions and
beliefs, when we are a member of the intellectual community whose needs
and interests it serves. It's when language breaks with any of this that we
object to tone and emotional tenor, to the author's voice and persona, the
questionable nature of the examples used, and so on. All this invariably
happens when a discourse tries to get to places in the psyche that we do not
care to visit. Reassuring one's audience while taking care not to give "of-
fense" is the magna carta of successful rhetoric, which turns on the implicit

assurance that anything traumatic that comes up will be resolved in a way that contributes to the maintenance of the "identity" and the guarantees upon which one's audience depends to sustain its beliefs in the basic order of experience. But that is also the inherent limitation of the circle in which such rhetoric moves. When we proceed *from* and *to* a coherent identity or fixed framework of interpretation, the topic under discussion becomes the medium through which we confirm—via repetition—what we already know, the fruit of inquiry being the reinforcement through that process of what has thereby proven its ability to master yet another experience.

An agonistic relationship to the reader is something quite different. It necessarily risks dismissal, especially when an author's purpose is to unearth and then challenge some of our culture's deeply cherished assumptions and guarantees. There is, however, an irony in the situation. For perhaps an agonistic relationship is the only one that truly respects the reader and shows the proper regard for the reader's possibilities. It does so by asking readers to open themselves to the possibility that we are strongly opposed to self-knowledge; that we have constructed elaborate systems of defense to protect us from things we do not want to know; and that we are quick to react with hostility to anyone who presumes to speak in ways that suggest that in "doing history" we must place our lives, as well as our concepts, into question. Such an agon is possible only if author and audience bind one another to a drama in which painful, strongly resisted discoveries drive a discourse that is thus about the psyche confronting itself at that register where true change first becomes possible: change in depth through a reversal in which the subject is existentialized from within through a process in which the anxiety that was previously displaced through the construction of defenses and conceptual guarantees has become that "wakeful anguish of the soul," which purges defenses in order to take up the burdens of one's historical and psychological being.

As the previous sentence shows, such a process employs terms that are currently dismissed as signs of the worst kind of nostalgia, terms that invoke what has been thoroughly, utterly deconstructed: the subject. What I hope to show is that the only commonality between the principle I'm talking about and those theories of subject now happily refuted is the term. Rhetorically, however, the problem remains, since one of the primary barriers to communication in professional discourse is that the popular meaning that readers attach to one's terms predetermines whether one's discourse is warranted by current commonplaces and thus worthy of attention. Four cardinal terms I use are especially noteworthy in this regard. To forestall misunderstanding, and to give a further sense of what the agon I'm after involves, I here offer brief comments on each.

First and foremost is the *subject,* a term that enters any discourse today trailing clouds of reflected pre- and mis-conceptions. For the "postmodern" audience, administering the *quietus* to the subject—that is, the Cartesian, humanistic, substantialist subject, begetter of the Kantian mind and the Hegelian logos—has been the primary achievement of recent thought. Any use today of terms or concepts tied to it (human nature, essences, universals) condemns one to ahistorical phallogocentrism, or, to appropriation, since the only legitimate meaning left to the term is that given it by Foucault (discursive subject-positions), Althusser (the effects of interpellation) or Lacan (schema L).[38] For the traditional humanistic audience, the equally easy assumption is that any use of the term subject implies agreement with a host of humanistic assumptions about "identity," ethical development, and the social process that tie one to ego psychology, a rationalistic theory of the ideal communicative speech act, and a reassertion of the timeless, universal values of the *Aufklarung*.[39] My effort is to chart a course that cuts between these views in order to recover a specifically *existential* meaning for the term subject, one that fully situates subject in the world as that possibility which arises through a *self-reference* that is radically different from the essentialistic assumptions in which the concepts of subject mentioned above are grounded.

My use of the term *humanism* entails a different problem. One of my primary efforts is to show the ways in which humanism's various representatives are attached to the "system of guarantees" that I strive to deracinate. In doing so, however, I argue for a way of being that is itself clearly and deeply "humanistic." In fact, my project could be described as an attempt to reclaim humanism from essentialistic, ahistorical misprisionings by bringing it to the crisis that its current representatives continue to resist and deny by refusing to undertake an immanent critique that rethinks and revalues the "human" in terms of the *tragic*.

This brings us to the third term in need of clarification, since tragedy is one of the most essentialized and ahistorical concepts in our cultural lexicon, as thinkers from Aristotle through Frye show. Tragedy is readily essentialized, whereas the tragic is something different: what our inquiry will strive to produce, as what we proceed toward, not from. It is the comprehensive concept (*Begriff*) the entire discourse moves toward, but only insofar as the process constitutes an effort to sustain and concretize what Nietzsche was after when he defined *geist* thus: "Spirit is the life that cuts back into life; with its suffering it increases its knowledge." Such a process is dedicated to the effort to purge thought of all efforts to transcend experience so that we may know and inhabit the world in its contingency, cleansed of guarantees. When this happens, it then becomes possible to see tragic drama (unlike comedy, romance, and irony, and in opposition to previous theories of tragedy) as that literary form which is historical in its being, and has the ontological status of an *existential a priori:* that is, a way of thinking that is *at issue with itself* and that submits its ways of structuring experience to immanent critique and transformation by referring them to those historical realities that exceed the power of comprehension implicit in its previous forms. To the Kantian tradition, most a priori principles are categorical and subsume experience under concepts that remain fixed and universal.[40] Tragic mediation is a radically different process. As a *form*, the tragic is engaged in the immanent critique of itself, with history the force that generates this necessity. The resulting epistemological relationship is unique and decidedly non-Kantian. The *self-reference* of tragedy is the effort to detect and purge the *form* of its inadequacies, especially those connected to emotions (such as pity and fear) that are tied to the desire for transcendence and guarantees.[41] The tragic sensibility readies itself to know what history calls on us to know by deracinating the internal limitations that save us from that knowledge. While other literary forms remain enduringly popular precisely because they offer us ways of fleeing history, the goal of the tragic is to evolve artistic forms that will enable us to know our situation in a way that is existential—and that radically existentializes us.

Which brings us to the last term and perhaps my most difficult task—the effort to reclaim and reconstitute existentialism as a meaningful position in contemporary thought. If existentialism functions here as what Kenneth Burke would call my "god-term," it also conjures up for most readers an intellectual movement that one scarcely hears mentioned anymore except as passé and with disdain. Reclaiming it involves not only rescuing the existential from what R. D. Cumming called its "vagabondage," that is, the set of absurdist commonplaces and adolescent postures it assumed during its fifteen minutes of fame in American pop culture and the academy.[42] The real task is to think one's way through to it again. To begin again from within the experiences that gave it birth so that one might bring it to life again from the ground up and in the integrity of passion appropriate to it. That, rather than a return to certain texts of Sartre or Kierkegaard or Heidegger, is the starting point I will try to reclaim. It is, of course, what I've been practicing throughout these pages in an effort to engage the reader in a preliminary experience of what happens when questioning and anxiety come together in a thinking that strives to maximize the ways in which a subject's being can become at issue to it in and through the study of history. When that happens, thought and the thinker are existentialized utterly and from within because inquiry turns on a probing of the deepest hiding places of the psyche. The term existential thus refers to an engagement in which dialectic is drama: thought develops out of an agon in which every structure on which the psyche depends is put at issue because the subject has once again become a being at issue to itself.

VI. Only Connect: Immanence—The Existentializing Process

The arguments of Hegel and Derrida against "Prefaces" are at base arguments for the radical immanence of thought, for the process of thinking as the emergence of concepts and of connections that can only be grasped through radical immersion in a drama where self-criticism is the moving and radically destabilizing principle that structures thought.[43] For most thinkers such a situation is intolerable and betrays a prior confusion: a lack of first principles, clear and distinct ideas, valid methodological procedures based on fixed canons of evidence and explanation, sound hypotheses capable of development and leading to conclusions and a body of doctrines that will be communicable to a coherent intellectual community.[44] This difference is worth noting here to indicate that what Hegel and Derrida say is true only of those philosophic systems that are *dialectical* and that make radical self-interrogation their through-line and moving dynamic. There are different modes of immanence, however, depending upon the nature of the *principle* in which a dialectical system is grounded and the relationship of that principle to experience. The immanence of the *Forms* in Plato, of *logos* in Hegel, of linguistic *différance* in Derrida and of *existential engagement* as practiced here are quite different things.[45] All affirm the primacy of the adverbial, of thinking and writing as agon. Here, however, the immanent "origin" and "end" resides in what I call the existentializing process, which is something quite different in its "results" from what happens in the other dialectical philosophies mentioned above. For those who engage their existence existentially, the process of thinking generates a content—what I term the deracination of guarantees—that is one with the sequence of irreversible acts whereby a subject, in internalizing that content, is changed utterly—and in depth—by it. That is why existential anxiety is not an abstract and self-reifying mood (as most popular accounts would have it) but a principle of action that, in Hegelian terms, is "its own notion immediately" or immanently because anxiety when authentic is a Keatsian "wakeful anguish of the soul." It does not flee or bewail its state but seeks to sustain and maximize its power to reveal to the subject the concrete ways in which its being is at issue in a situation for which it can become responsible only by existentializing its being: that is, by purging oneself, at the deepest register of the psyche, of the protections and guarantees that would resolve the situation by denying everything that makes it vital—and one's own. For the subject who sustains it, anxiety thus generates a complete transformation of anxiety itself; a complete change in how anxiety is lived and the attitude one must take up, in a spirit of gladness, whenever one finds oneself delivered over to the gift of its revelatory power to expose our inauthenticities. The circle of existential engagement ends only with a complete transformation of the condition with which it began. As subjects, we are that process—or the self-reifications whereby we refuse it.

As existentializing process, engagement evolves as a way of thinking that necessarily gives discourse the structure of an *Aufhebung*[46] in which each stage "cancels, preserves, and uplifts" what went before by discovering connections and complications requiring a new inquiry, which often involves the shift to a field or topic that could not have been anticipated but that now emerges as necessary. Such a necessity is not a product of abstract Hegelian mediation. It arises instead as an outgrowth of the concrete circumstance in which the inquiry is grounded: as a process of internalization in which the deepening of the subject's relationship to itself produces an *Aufhebung* that has the following structure. Each stage of the inquiry *cancels* an entire way of living: an "identity," a psychological economy, a relationship that the subject can adopt toward its being. The inquiry then preserves the product of that labor as an anguish that becomes determinate through its projection into the larger complex of problems that have emerged as the true fruit of the prior inquiry. To use "uplift" or words of similar connotation for the third movement of the process would be doubly inappropriate since a movement which existentializes reverses the very direction of Hegelian thought. For us, *fur uns,* progress always points downward, to a deeper descent into the buried disorders and discontents of the psyche and the deracination that must be affected there if we are to overcome the guarantees that blind us to history and a knowledge of the actual forces that shape it.[47] (As we'll see, this paragraph describes the logic behind the sequence of chapters that follow.)

The best way to introduce the result of that labor comes from a question that a friend asked recently after reading the entire manuscript:

"If the psyche—in its crypt—is as you say it is, why would anyone want to know it? That is, know themselves in these ways—and with these results? In eradicating all defenses, deracinating all guarantees, you seem to ask the reader to suffer to no purpose, with no resolution, and no direction other than endless tunneling into "the heart of darkness.""[48]

Though I'd quarrel with this description, the reaction is genuine and deserves an honest reply. For some human beings suffering is an innermost imperative because resentment begins precisely when we set limits to what we can let ourselves know and suffer about the world. Sustaining sufferance thus provides the beginnings of an ethic based on an existential and not a categorical imperative, an ethic that is concretely historical and opposed, in principle, to the system of guarantees that the ratio superimposes upon history in order to deliver us from it. The value of suffering is its power to historicize us in our pores. As such, it is not a passive state or a masochistic disorder but, as Nietzsche knew, an active principle of willing determining

the "degree" to which we have attained "spirit" in the existentializing meaning of that term.

Because our time is a tragic one we refuse to see it as such. One of the
ways we do so is by defining tragedy in essentialistic terms and then classify-
ing it as one of the modes writers have devised to give a narrative order to
experience. Suitably aestheticized, it is then troped by deconstructive *irony;*
for when we classify modes and forms of writing in this way the ironic
sensibility always carries the day since it provides both the principle of
knowing and the rhetorical trope that generates and comprehends the
entire system of classification. For the "postmodern sensibility" irony is the
rhetoric of rhetoric: through its application the tragic becomes just another
mystification, consigned to the nostalgic fringes of the modern, which the
postmodern "subject" looks down on from that serene and superior position that irony confers on those who have internalized it and are now blind
to the danger Rilke foresaw as its lure.[49]

As long as the tragic is contained in such ways there is no way to
retrieve it as a vital voice in the postmodern world; even perhaps as the
dialectical category that comprehends our time in a way irony cannot and that
breaks the hold irony has over us by revealing it as a *moment* within the
reconstitution of a thinking that sees fragmentation, dissolution, and cultural breakdown not as an occasion for *aporia,* free play, and the double-
binding of the ironized psyche to the abstract circle in which a self-dissolving thought moves, but as one of the many "signs" that suffering this condition is the act that restores the true dialectical relationship, which Hegel
described as the movement from stoicism (structuralism) to skepticism
(deconstruction) to "unhappy consciousness." Most theories of the postmodern condition reverse the relationship of the last two terms: irony
thereby cancels and delivers us from existence. The correct way to regain
what is "living" in Hegel is to "negate the negation" and restore the tragic as
the category that concretizes and existentializes the "unhappy consciousness," as that engagement which underlies and measures all the attitudes
and philosophies we adopt toward the world.

Developing such a dialectic informs the "suspensive" structure of the
inquiry that follows and underlies the necessary connections it establishes
among issues and disciplines that are usually held at considerable distance
from one another. It may be helpful here to list that sequence as a further
instance of the kind of dialectical thinking that will be attempted here. (1)
The development of a theory of internalization that exposes the ruling
assumptions of American ego psychology. (2) An interpretation of the Kantian sublime as the historical category required to understand the desire
that finds fulfillment in the Bomb. (3) An examination of the inner world of
"the psyche that dropped the bomb" and the evolution thereby of a new

theory of Thanatos as a force in history. (4) The possibility for a reversal of
that condition through a reflection on Hamlet and the concept of existential reflection that Shakespeare develops in that character. (5) A new theory
of the tragic is thereby advanced, leading to (6) a theory of the dialectical
image and of artistic cognition as a way of knowing that has the reality of
history as its referent. As we will see, this sequence, strange as it may initially
appear, is the structure of thought required to connect two issues that are
themselves necessarily connected: the bombing of Hiroshima and the need,
after that event, to take up Einstein's challenge and internalize the Bomb by
changing the way we think about and write history.

When Plato defined dialectic as that way of thinking that discovers the
necessary connections that bind together separate phenomena and disciplines, the sequence outlined above is *not* the kind of structure he had in
mind. Nor could he have imagined a historical situation in which the greatest dialectical thinker of our time would redefine that task thus: "paranoia is
the ability to make connections."[50] Only connect: If, with Plato or Hegel,
rational mediation is the route to one's dialectical totality one will build vast
structures of mind, clouds of contemplation, winged with dusk: a world in
the head, better far than that which one has sacrificed to the need for
transcendental guarantees—and the need to be free at last from the burdens of existence. If, following the way of the artist, connections flare up as
lighting products of that imaginative perception which comes when the
world assaults the astonished heart with images that cannot be subsumed by
the ratio, one will build structures of a radically different order, ones that
deliver us from nothing.

The bombing of Hiroshima is the traumatic through-line that binds
together the various inquiries undertaken here as the Event requiring such
a dialectic of one who would constitute its historical meaning. As such, the
Bomb is not discussed here in a continuous manner but flares up throughout the book, similar to the way a traumatic kernel forms the deepest nodal
point of a dream—the nightmare from which the rest of the dream forms,
in a sense, the effort to awake.[51] The connections that the Bomb enables us
to make are of a similar order: depth-psychological rather than rational or
empirical. Thereby the dead of Hiroshima never become what would be
truly horrible—an example used to illustrate a thesis. Their status, rather, is
that of a cause—that which drives the discourse and constitutes the heart of
its inwardness. If, as Benjamin argues, "the dead are in danger," the only
adequate response is to give them a voice that fully unleashes their power to
vex the minds of the living.[52]

To which I would add a final, heretical idea as the true stake of the
following inquiry. If the connections we establish lead us to rethink thought
in a way that supplants the logic of rationalistic mediation, our inquiry will

constitute, for history, a recovery of what Shelley had in mind when he claimed that "the poets are the unacknowledged legislators of the world."[53]

But to see how that might be so we must begin with Shelley's burning coal at that moment when it is lit, when experience first breaks through the shields and forces the astounded and terrified subject to engage the dynamics of *internalization*.

Two
Cutting Back into Life

> If the personality is once emptied of its subjectivity and comes to what men call an "objective" condition, nothing can have any more effect on it.
> —Nietzsche, "The Use and Abuse of History for Life"

> The unexamined life is not worth living.

I. History as Hermeneutic of Engagement

What does it mean to internalize an historical event? Is history the discipline in which this process takes place or the system of discursive and psychological defenses constructed to assure that it won't? These questions involve others, which are central to a hermeneutics of engagement. What does it mean to risk oneself in the act of interpretation and to do so in a way that is rigorous and systematic and not merely a nostalgic yearning, late in the winter of our deconstruction, for a return to pop-existentialism American-style? My goal is to constitute a reply to these questions that will enable history to impinge on us in a way that calls into question the system of guarantees that structure the ratio.

What happened on August 6, 1945? Has a history adequate to of that *event* been written? By a historian willing to approach it with this question: what would it mean to *internalize* the *Bomb*? Is such an act within the historian's purview or does the discipline depend on suppressing such concerns? Most histories come down on the issue somewhere in the middle. Few historians work from a developed concept of internalization, yet almost all recognize it as an ineluctable part of what they do. The issue is inescapable, however, because our interest in history is defined by the following variables: the impact of contingencies we want to master on guarantees we wish to reaffirm through the study of events so that certain ideas, beliefs, and explanatory principles will gain ratification through the narratives we construct in order to explain the past. Of course, a good historian is ready to call the concepts and values implicit in this formulation into question, whenever "the facts" warrant. That readiness is, indeed, the article of faith on which the discipline rests.

Internalization is what happens when we take a troubling experience into ourselves—or find, to our dismay, that it has already taken up residence there. In thinking on disruptive events we try deal with the insurrection within us by practicing what Freud calls *Durcharbeit* or working through.

That task comes to all of us often in the course of experience; often, for example, when, casting our eye across what Hegel called our morning prayer, a new horror and a new duty blazes itself into our consciousness. Something happened on August 6, 1945 and for fifty years all of us have been trying to find "the words to say it," to write, if only on the tablet of a memory deep within, an account that will comprehend what happened that day. In that sense we all come to Hiroshima with the female protagonist in Duras' *Hiroshima Mon Amour* in the knowledge "that perception must be learned." As we will see, pursuing that task entails a new way of thinking about certain problems central to historical method: the fact-opinion split, the opposition between objectivity and subjective considerations; the method of multiple working hypotheses and its use in determining historical explanations; and the possibility of bringing certain historical debates to closure.

When the young Nietzsche wrote "On the Use and Abuse of History for Life," he was troubled by far more than the fixations of the scholarly, objectifying attitude toward the past. His larger goal was to assess the value of history for the life of spirit—a concept he later defined in this exacting formula: "spirit is the life that cuts back into life; with its agony it increases its knowledge." What would history become if one brought such a principle to its study? If, that is, the object of study were given the power to probe the deepest registers of the knower's psyche? In such a hermeneutic one knows insofar as one discovers things about oneself one does not want to know. Getting inside a historical event and probing one's own conflicts are of a piece and their keynote is *ontological risk,* the courage to pursue a knowledge that brackets the appeal of ontological and conceptual guarantees.[1]

This possibility offers a sharp contrast to the typical way epistemological considerations are foregrounded and deployed to safeguard the act of interpretation. A good example is the way the Kantian turn is generally used in the humanities today to short-circuit interpretive difficulties and assure self-confirming resolutions. We are all "Kantians" now and this is what we know. Percepts depend on concepts. Knowledge is a product of one's framework. That which makes knowledge possible also establishes its limits as the condition in which every inquiry must acquiesce. Internal coherence is all. Your framework is all ye know on earth, and all ye need to know. In fact, any framework, in knowing, finally knows primarily itself, a limit reinforced by the metatheoretical support provided by the umbrella of pluralism. The fore-ordained result is this impasse: each framework can know only itself, with whatever internal rigor and conceptual transparency it can muster. "Pluralism" then grants legitimacy to all frameworks and their eclectic usefulness to one another in the loose, ad hoc "relationships" we can establish by ignoring the older issue of the "conflict of interpretations" and heaping approaches atop one another in a conglomerate masquerading as a dialectical synthesis.[2]

Two problems are thereby avoided: (1) the possibility that the phenomena exceed my framework(s), and (2) the consequent recognition that I must subject any framework to another kind of critique, one that necessarily breaks with the friendly confines of Kantian reflection. With these recognitions the innermost possibility that is present whenever interpretation occurs is found: we can be put at issue existentially by the objects we study. As a result the elaborate defenses that have been constructed to avoid that possibility begin to emerge. Engagement changes the act of interpretation radically. Engaging oneself as a subject is not one epistemological stance among others. It is the act that activates what the others need to deny: that knowing involves motives that determine the object of knowledge in ways that have little to do with disinterested objectivity. Epistemological frameworks and philosophic methodologies are a realization of complex psychological desires and harbor the contradictions of their origins. This is the kind of connection Hegel was getting at in the *Phenomenology* before rationalist mediation intervened to save the day by making every experience part of the confident march to—and by—reason. The dialectical connection between *methodology* and *existence* points in another direction, one that implies a crisis for our continued neo-Kantian fixation on the epistemological bases of frameworks and a new way to deepen that kind of inquiry.

Engagement, however, is rendered impossible by the methods currently dominant in "the human sciences." Interpretation is deprived of danger whenever it becomes an issue of how a fixed subject, with a fixed identity, knows an object outside itself by imposing fixed concepts and interpretive frameworks upon it. The virtue of the procedure is that the subject using it works free of anxiety, knowing that inquiry will not bring the existential registers of one's being into question. Once internalization gets on the agenda, however, that issue is reopened. Or closed down once and for all, since an application of Kantian methods to motivational and psychological questions offer the possibility of confining reigning epistemological practices by providing the "human sciences" with a solid and essentializing understanding of the fixed psychological bases of "moral development and ego-identity."[3] Historians seeking reassurances about interiority have not far to seek. The theory of internalization that is currently dominant in American ego psychology is a monument to such needs. Which is why recovering a different and "darker" understanding of internalization begins of necessity with its interrogation. To highlight the contrast, the two sections that follow describe each view of internalization in its essentials.

II. Internalization and Bad Faith: The Disorder Called the Ego

According to the dominant theory, the purpose of internalization is to build up and then reinforce the ego by eliminating anything that threatens the system of beliefs, motives, and reasons it needs in order to maintain a coherent identity fully plugged into the social, consensual order of things and what it determines as reality and the reality principle. Internalization serves this system in two ways: (1) we incorporate good experiences, ones that increase our self-esteem, and (2) we take in bad things so that we can discharge their force by placing them within a larger context of meaning. Through internalization we incorporate and then identify with the storehouse of commonplaces and operations that our culture has developed in order to make adaptation, consensual validation, and shared meanings the primary processes that shape the inwardness of most human beings. Internalization, so understood, has two grand products: the ego and the ratio. Because the entire system functions to solidify the socialized self, the guarantees thereby circulated through it assure that internalization will not go beyond a certain point. Or to put it another way, so that nothing will prevent internalization from being a magical operation: a system of self-regulation composed of the measures we take to protect ourselves from disruptive experiences and regain control whenever such experiences strike a dissonant chord within.

Aside from its popularity, there are many things wrong with this position. The most important one derives from the simple observation made by the psychoanalyst who has done more than any other to understand internalization in a way that preserves its disruptive *origin*. I refer to W. R. D. Fairbairn, who advances the striking idea that internalization begins with the bad object, there being no motive for internalization other than the necessity to rework that which has had a traumatic impact on us.[4] Inwardness here has its birth in a violent necessity. Contra ego psychology, it is not the case that we develop as psyches by taking in good, positive experiences, one after another, as we slowly and harmoniously build upon the "bonds of love," the egosyntonic structures that will enable us to achieve normalcy and a stable identity. Internalization for Fairbairn is a true "labor of the negative." There is, as he sees it, only one kind of "object" or experience we take into ourselves—one that terrifies us. And only one reason we do so—the desperate hope that somehow the inner world thereby created will be less horrifying than the traumatic events from which it derives. Such an inner world in its "contents" and modes of operation is a product of the most primitive psychical processes: a world of Aeschylean agons that have not yet been bleached out into concepts. When we first take events into ourselves, we have not yet constructed a world in the head, but suffer terrors that strike at the very heart of the psyche. The kind of conceptual and rhetorical guarantees and defenses that coincide with the ego as a psychic structure do not yet exist. The world here is suffered in a way that offers no smooth transition from psyche to ego. Instead, we find the grounds for a permanent rift between ego and psyche. That rift may in fact be the primary motive for repression, since the world of our most primitive conflicts, longings, and ways of mediating experience is precisely what we forget once we attain the ego. We forget them because we have attained a structure and a way of dealing with things that is vigorously opposed to the inner world of the psyche and to anything in the external world that recalls and reawakens its traumatic impact. That is why the ego busies itself with internalizing everything it can to fortify its burrow; to reassure itself by exorcizing in one and the same act the two realities that threaten it: the deep traumatic pull of the core conflicts that make up our inner world and the power of experience to strike through defenses and impinge directly on that realm, reawakening the "life" buried there. The reason why most people internalize "positive" experiences all the time, some even becoming experts in it (ego psychologists, professors of humanities, etc.) comes into view. The more we build up a reassuring world, the more we are protected from the real one. We construct massive worlds in the head to assure ourselves that they, rather than something else, constitute what's real. The ego is "the knowledge most worth having," our civic duty and a massive cultural production because it assures the final dissolution of inner drama, and the transformation of everything into mind through the conceptual thematizing of experience. That is why a traumatic event comes as such a staggering blow to most subjects. It shatters the only way they can internalize things and asks them to return to another and more "primitive" way of "functioning," a way in which the psyche, through agonistic engagement—as opposed to logical and conceptual—mediates itself directly within the alembic of those primary affects, which overpower the defenses we habitually use to make the life of feeling no more than yet another discharge mechanism. When an Event finds us, we are profoundly wounded because experience has brought us before something with a character similar to that of the original world of our primitive, founding internalizations. Only now, thanks to the ego, we have no way to deal with them because experience has been the process whereby we live ever more estranged from the deeper offices of our being. And so to save ourselves we again shuffle off this mortal coil by consigning the traumatic event to silence and the flames.

There is thus only one thing wrong with the dominant view of internalization. It neglects to consider the motive that informs—and invalidates it. And because it presents internalization as a quasinaturalistic process that is wholly "positive" in its genesis and principles of operation—that is, we slowly build up solid structures by incorporating positive experiences and evolving from them the consensual, reality testing frameworks that make us good, healthy, functioning social agents—it is unable to address the contradiction that informs its most revealing definition. As Winnicott put it, "The ego is that which is vigorously opposed to reality."[5] It is essentially a system of defenses whereby we contain and deny what we cannot deal with, what we do not want to know about ourselves and our world.

Out of this need we eventually evolve the ratio: the system of concepts, definitions, and principles of explanation that solidify the ego by creating a coincidence between reality and the sensible, the reasonable. The functions of reasoning are many. The most profound is what I call the *system of guarantees:* the principles of explanation that enable us to account for events in such a way that we always, somehow, attain a ratification of what we want to believe and an exorcism of anything that disrupts our defense-barriers. Such is the achievement and the prime function of the ego in its refusal to let certain realities inside our heads.

Comprehending history is one of the necessary occasions for the operation of this system. History may also be the primary force behind the development of guarantees, since in history contingency often rises up with a force that gives the need for explanation, reassurance, and resolution a special urgency. Perhaps Aristotle, that canny Platonist, had it backwards: maybe history is more philosophic than either philosophy or poetry; and in order to displace its ontological force we build towers in the head—while Ilium burns. History is not just what hurts, and then conveniently proves unknowable to the conceptual, "symbolic" order.[6] It is what shatters and wounds us with traumatic force. As long as the ego-ratio remains its author, however, history as a discipline will have as its grandest function what amounts to an exorcism, the ushering from the stage of whatever threatens the system of guarantees.

As I will show, the writing of history remains for the most part confined in a circle it is unable to break since each explanation of events provides a ratification of the guarantees contributing to that circle's reification. Doing so may, in fact, be the ground motive underlying the discipline. Through meticulous, scholarly research yet another spectre of contingency—of an unintelligibility in events full of distressing implications—will be conquered: for reason and a world suited to the needs of the ego, a mighty fortress we can inhabit in equanimity as long as we banish the thought that Svidrigailov's bathhouse is the actual space we inhabit when we construct the dream of a history shaped by the explanatory power of reason.

III. Authentic Internalization: The Birth of Psyche

Challenging the reign of the ego turns on the possibility that traumatic experience is determinative in the first instance and the last because internalization has its origin when a sudden blow from some experience puts one at risk by shattering the structure of one's self-reference. Humpty Dumpty usually gets put back together again. But that is not our concern. That happens after. Our concern is to constitute the "before," without giving ontological preference to its sequel. What's too painful to remember we may choose to forget, the primary lesson about human beings being that defenses work—with intellectualization providing the perfect capstone to the edifice. But we can also try to reverse that process. Because there is another register of human inwardness; that in which the subject is a *who* not a *what* and where the question *why* arises with the urgency and anxiety that necessarily attends it whenever we find ourselves in situations where to risk oneself has become an imperative.

What I want to do here is open up this dimension of experience by setting forth a series of definitions of what I term authentic internalization, with each definition taking us a step deeper into the complexities of the process. The sequence can be seen as an effort to move in a dialectical progression toward a concept of internalization that will be adequate to the agon that any traumatic event unleashes in the psyche. It can also be read as a drama, a series of actions that attempt to engage the reader at a register that remains heavily defended in most subjects. My goal here is to advance an order of concepts that will produce an affective change in the reader and, thereby, the possibility of change at that register of the psyche where our self-reference awaits us, even though we are usually quick to expel the depth-charge that sounds whenever experience touches the life buried deep within us. (As a dialectical structure, creating such an agon is the overriding purpose of the book as a whole and the process it enacts at each step in its development.)

1. Internalization is the agon that begins whenever experience shatters the economy of ideas and beliefs on which the identity of the ego depends. Sustained, it is the act in which we take that experience inside ourselves and *brood*[7] its implications as a challenge to the guarantees on which we have based our previous understanding of experience. Even though it composes the assumptions and principles of explanation that wed the egosyntonic parts of the personality to the consensual agreements and practices that structure one's *socius* world, the system of guarantees is for the most part habitual and unconscious. Shock puts this system, however momentarily, at issue. Where discharge of tension usually reigns, something else now happens. Cognitive dissonance produces affective discord: ideas, shattered, regress to the motives and desires on which they are based. Internalization reopens the subject's relationship to its inner world.

"The shock of recognition" drives us inward. In response, most subjects seek an adjustment that will restore their prior psychological economy. Adaptation, reductionism, identity-maintenance and control, discharge of tension at whatever cost to the "phenomena," re-assert themselves. In some subjects, however, these operations give way to a more fundamental and exacting process. Its originary form: a subject awakened from dormancy, burdened with itself, brought in anxiety before the importance of experiences that exceed our concepts and our control while opening up within us all we've sought to escape through our allegiance to the concept. Experience here announces *reversal* as the existential possibility whereby we *mediate* ourselves. To constitute that possibility, however, we must accept and engage that abrupt, and always potentially catastrophic, turning around in which one's entire life presents itself as a flight from situations that one now realizes are most one's own and bear the burden of the deepest self-knowledge. Subject as psyche, and not as mind, here experiences identity and subjectivity not as presence but as agon. Indeed, as that engaged agon reveals, most "agons" are unworthy of the name. The basic difference between people reveals itself : it derives from the imperative of that choice whereby we humanize ourselves from within or fail in the duty we bear to ourselves as subjects.

2. In internalization, *experience* assumes the status given it by C. S. Peirce: "experience is what occurs when our conceptual frameworks break down."[8] We then face this choice: we can mend the breach or we can sustain the insurrection. In either case reality and reference have here revealed themselves, however momentarily, in terms of something that is independent of epistemological games, an experience that measures us and our knowing by a canon of seriousness that cannot finally be abrogated. Reference here bears the weight of a world that gives birth to thought and inhabits it even when thought strives thereafter to perfect the epistemological circles needed to contain and then deny that fact. Because then experience laughs last in the power of events to shatter the epistemological economy that protects the psyche sequestered in the framework. Reference to that exacting psychological reality is the constant, the heresy of situated thought. Frameworks are not insulated in their ontological, a priori coherence. They refer to that which exceeds them and depend on that relationship for their development. Sustaining that possibility, however, requires a subject for whom the blow of experience awakens an existential self-reference, a cutting back into oneself as the only adequate rejoinder to the way in which experience cuts into us. The self-reference of subject is not the attainment of an a priori rationality, a cogito of logical forms whereby one polices experience. It is the act of descending into those conflicts and instabilities that reveal one's inner world as a place of unknown depths.

Most internal "agons" are unworthy of the name because experience in the sense articulated above only happens when trauma and crisis finds the beliefs and ideas on which one's ego-identity depends lacking, inadequate, groundless. In fact, claiming that "the self has been called into question" is a singularly inadequate description of how, for the ego, questioning serves as but prelude and rhetorical ploy preceding the predictable reassertion, via the answer, of pre-existing guarantees. Experience sustained as ontological risk moves in a radically different medium and direction, toward what Kafka called the point that must be reached, "the point where there is no turning back," the realization that one must open oneself up utterly from within. The self-reference of the subject then finds "self" and "identity" given over to a self-mediation that is existential and in which one existentializes oneself from within. A true agon only commences when that register of inwardness is engaged and sustained. The inner world is no longer hedged with substantialistic guarantees. One is here one with oneself in an abjection that seems impassible. The primacy of affect in the psyche's constitution announces itself. But that primacy opens up a self-reference in which affect is so overwhelming that it threatens to dissolve the very possibility of any coherence of "self." Engaging that condition leads to the following definition of internalization.

3. Internalization is the rush of a sudden blow down into the deepest register of the psyche and the attempt by a subject so addressed to sustain the revelatory power of that blow. The blow is the recognition, one with shattering and primitive affects, of a radical otherness within the "self" as one's founding condition. Becoming a subject depends on surmounting the force of a prior determination. The popular saying, "I am an Other," here receives the concretization that makes it imperative to track down the ways in which the voice and command of the Other controls one's psyche. Everything one has profoundly resisted knowing about one's life must be confronted on an inner stage where the "I" lacks all identity and control.

If this experience is welcomed in Keatsian "wakeful anguish," it produces an attunement to oneself at that register of inwardness that most people spend their lives fleeing. Recovery of the wound one is addresses what was crypted in the original repression of traumatic experiences. Contact is thereby restored with the subject as a *who* asking of traumatic experiences the question *why*, that is, subjectivity as a self-reference that is existential. Trauma hollows out in us an inwardness that is defined by two things: (1) a subject at issue, experiencing itself as a who rather than a what, due to (2) the power of certain experiences to activate and reveal the question why in its true ontological situatedness. "Is there any cause in nature that makes these hard hearts?" As the genesis of subject as who/why catastrophic anxiety is the experience that both creates inwardness and grounds it in the necessity of reversal. The force of every subsequent experience is its potential to reactivate that dynamic of subjectivity by prying open those places in the heart that, without trauma, remain closed. Internalization thus hollows out within oneself the space of the tragic, that space in which suffering is willed and becomes the act through which one makes one's original traumatic experiences the conscience that informs perception whenever the world cuts deeply into us and we dare to know the dark motives at work in most human relations.

The experience described above is the basis of what I term the existential a priori, which is an epistemological principle radically different in its operation and results from the conceptual a priori of the Kantian tradition. Its development is given over to experience and depends on those agons in which the who/why mediates itself. Such a possibility is present, for example, in the experience of cruelty and humiliation. When we are humiliated two things happen. We experience ourselves as a who, as a subject who can be wounded in one's being. We also learn that such is the purpose of cruelty. Cruelty is a special act: the attempt to hurt people in their souls, to get at a person's self-worth and do permanent damage there. Why? That question, too, is given to us in its primacy by humiliation. Humiliation puts us in a position to discover the psyche and the true intentions of the Other. Wilfrid Bion asserts that inquiry, the search for knowledge, begins when "love is doubted."[9] We here suggest a darker origin. The knowledge we seek and flee when we experience humiliation is a knowledge of the darkest motives from which others act when their actions strive to drive a stake into our hearts. The two questions that found philosophy thus find in the existential a priori the dynamic that gives them the power to overturn all stable theories of ego identity by exposing the psychological conflicts and avidities that inform human relations.

4. When subject as who/why sustains itself as the living of this question, internalization becomes the act through which psyche puts itself at issue by giving the answers attained through agon the power to change the way one relates to oneself. Internalizing has become the act whereby a subject's *self-reference* becomes an *existentializing process.* Subject has attained a situatedness in which, qua psyche, one is engaged and at odds with oneself at the core. Reflection, as Hamlet practices it, has replaced the way Kant and others use it to establish the rational limits in which thinking must acquiesce so that experience will retain an a priori order. A radically different possibility arises whenever experience is given the power to unleash a process in which defenses in all three of their primary forms—as motives, as reasons, and as affects—are submitted to the process of deracination. The structures on which one depends for the maintenance of one's identity—and the adaptation of experience to those structures—are now seen as the barriers to experience, not as the a priori principles that make it possible. Experience in turn is now felt and willed as something that must be sustained over against them, even at the risk of confusion and unintelligiblity. The hermeneutic circle has become an existential process where repetition is no longer possible. The possibility of *taking action within oneself,* at that register of one's inwardness where such action will affect a complete transformation of one's psyche, has become the dynamic that structures one's subjective self-reference.

5. To put the foregoing in concrete terms that cut to the essentials,

internalization is the act in which one's extant psychic structure is shattered in a way that proves irreversible. The only authentic response is to undertake a complete transformation of oneself. That possibility, however, requires an agon based on principles that are prior to the terms of rational deliberation and mediation, and radically different in their operation. Internalization is the situating of oneself within that register prior to rationality where living resides in the power of the world to bite into the structures and defenses upon which subject as psyche—and not simply as mind—depends for its maintenance. Engagement from its inception transcends the limits of the ratio. The internalization of experience grounds a radically different logic, based on a dynamic of inwardness and self-mediation that is independent of the structures whereby the ratio organizes the world. In sustaining the affective discordance between experience and the concept, inwardness is born, one with its task: to make this contradiction the basis of a self-mediation that will be dramatic rather than rational and that will preserve the reality of drama against all efforts to subsume it under structures of intelligibility based on the hegemony of the concept.

As such, internalization founds a process that has the power to produce a complete change in the subject's relationship to itself. That is why internalization continually exceeds the concepts we form of it and the explanations we set down in an effort to arrest it. Whenever reflection quickens existence, both realities exceed their previous form. The evidence that this process has commenced is also felt and suffered long before it is cognized. Internalization begins when we are arrested by an event or experience that destroys some fundamental belief on which we depend for our "identity." This is the sense in which experience is inaugural. Which is why we strive so hard to assure ourselves a priori that such an experience will never—and cannot—occur. For once it does, being-at-risk outstrips all previous identities as it assaults us from within.

6. We can now formulate, as a final definition, what properly belongs at the beginning but couldn't be said until now. Internalization is the circle of engagement that founds and defines our being as existential subjects. It is the act whereby psychic structure was first constituted and is reconstituted whenever experience impinges upon the register of the who/why. Until, that is, self-reification conquers all. Contra ego psychology (and object-relations theory as currently practiced) internalization is not the act that slowly yet inexorably builds up those structures that plug us into the ratio, the socius, and the forces of normalization so that once the basic ideology and subject-positions are firmly in place we live assured of our ability to adapt and accommodate everything that happens in life to the system of guarantees. Internalization is precisely the contrary: the continual pressure of those possibilities of self-reference and self-mediation that break with the

hypnotic power that normative and normalizing structures have over us by submitting them to a scrutiny that reveals their hollowness and with it the need to develop a radically different way of knowing and living in the world.

IV. Internalization and History

In evoking two ways to view internalization, sections two and three introduce concepts and oppositions that will be developed at length in what follows. Even in their present form, however, one point is clear: it would be hard to imagine a greater contrast than that between the two concepts of internalization. The differences are fundamental and establish an opposition that is not open to mediation. Tracing the implications of this opposition for the study of history will enable us to highlight the main issues that confront the discipline.

The problem of internalization identifies both those events that concern the historian and what must be done in order to comprehend them. History has the power to bring our concepts and beliefs—and our understanding of what it means to be a human subject—to a crisis because in it traumatic events confront the system of guarantees with the reality of radical, unendurable contingency. Insofar as history is, following Nietzsche, an affair of value for "spirit," the traumatic event is the object of historical inquiry.[10] The following sequence outlines this idea through a series of definitions. As internalization, the task of writing history is to preserve the traumatic meaning of events by comprehending the place in the psyche from which the event derives and the acts of self-mediation that are required to comprehend it at that register. The historian seeking such a subject faces a twofold task: (1) to find situations with the power to make such a claim upon us and (2) to preserve their revelatory power, however disruptive, in the process of explanation and narration.

An Event is an occurrence that throws the entire system of guarantees into question. It does so through the power of violent, shattering Images (Auschwitz "liberated," Hiroshima photographed from ground-zero, "the smell of napalm in the morning") to confront us with an experience that challenges our beliefs and frameworks. The image has that power because images (1) eradicate defenses, (2) tear open the buried conflicts of the psyche, and (3) thereby bring us before a knowledge of realities that exceed the ratio. Such is the revelatory power of the Image in its immediacy before discourse turns it into a concept. If one resists that transformation, however, and strives to move in the medium of the image, everything changes. The old principles of explanation ring hollow, while hypotheses of another order find in their image their empirical bases. Deracination is the term I have chosen to identify the principle that shapes the process that ensues. *Deraci-*

nation entails the following steps, which derive from a single necessity: that of constituting the "meaning" of an event in a way that preserves and maximizes its impact on the historian's psyche at that register which the image opens up in us. Conceptually, that act requires no less than a transformation of the conceptual order itself. For that order forms a seamless unity of guarantees and principles of explanation with each plank playing an important function in sustaining the total edifice. Its interrogation requires an examination of the following sequence of interdependent issues.

1. For most historians, the ratio provides the order of concepts whereby facts and explanations are determined so that what happened and why is constituted in a way that exorcizes everything threatening to that order. Traumatic events are thereby deprived of their power to become the imperative of a countermemory. To preserve the image, the first task, accordingly, is to reverse that condition by undertaking a critique of the ratio itself and the ways in which it limits the nature of thinking. The Heideggerian question *"was heisst denken?"* here takes on this determination: what is required to make conceptualization "adequate" to what exceeds and resists it?

2. That effort, in turn, involves a crisis for the two practices that grease the engine of the guarantees: the narrative forms and the rhetorical operations whereby history is written so that the author-audience relationship will move *from* and *to* the reaffirmation of a shared ego identity tied to the essential beliefs and values of the humanistic tradition, which thereby once again proves itself through its power to provide a narrative explanation of historical events.

3. From the interrogation of numbers one and two comes a deeper crisis. The sum total of cognitive and narrative practices that make the discourse of history flow now reveal their grounding in the need to protect and affirm certain psychological motives (desires, fears, and defenses) that are essential to the identity of those who need the system of guarantees in order to maintain themselves. For the critical historian the exercise of suspicion has led to a new hypothesis, which also provides the primary canon of a method *in statu nascendi:* history, as usually practiced, involves complicity in a cover up; it is the system of acts we take so that we will *not* know what happened. Or, to put it in terms that carry the proper sting: it is a practice we create so that an essentialistic and humanistic view of human nature (and the psychological needs that underlie this view) will control the way events are understood and narrated so that their disruptive implications are contained and certain needs reaffirmed, even if a fairly long detour through horror is required before "morning dawns, excellent and fair"[11]—that is, before resolution through narrative produces the cathartic assurance that cleanses heart and mind of all we refuse to know.

To reformulate Walter Benjamin, the primary danger to the dead is their sacrifice to the needs of history's humanistic audience. Constituting that recognition implies the need to write history in new ways, ways that put the audience on trial, exposing defenses and rationalizations so that the existential claims of the subject will become the dynamic that shapes the historian's relationship as writer to the reader, in a rhetoric now based on the recognition that internalization and the ego are incompatible forces, with the defense of the latter the motive behind the explanatory and rhetorical operations that derive from the system of guarantees. A new kind of narration with a radically different "rhetoric" of address is required. History as internalization of the Event is the systematic discovery of the guarantees as acts of refusal that we must eradicate in order to know our subject. Doing so, however, requires a radical act of self-overcoming in which one does not simply question beliefs and desires but tears them out of one's heart and mind in an endeavor to attain, through that act, a new order of self-reference and with it the following definition of history: history as internalization is the suffering of Events at the psychic register of the who/why, the register where, over against the ego and its ways, an existential subjectivity awaits the deracination required to reclaim it.

History as *hermeneutic of engagement* unlocks this possibility in three dialectically interconnected stages: (1) engaging the Event unlocks the power of the traumatic "unknown" to shatter the known; (2) engaging oneself as subject requires risking one's self-reference in the act of knowing; (3) the result is a critical engagement in writing the Event dedicated to a deracination of traditional discursive and rhetorical protocols in an effort to evolve a language where new narrative and dramatic forms shatter or replace the entire economy on which the ego-ratio depends. Thereby the circle of knowing is no longer arrested by the act of writing but breaks from within, ruptured by the pressure of the Event to weigh as nightmare on the very being of language. History, so understood, is a process through which one strives to take action within oneself in order to achieve a knowledge and a way of being that is fully situated in the world. To activate that process one must engage the risk that an Event has the power to deracinate one's identity and the entire system of ideas and guarantees grounding that self-reference.

One upshoot of that act is a recovery of the dialectic of Eros and Thanatos as a way of thinking about history. In anticipation of later developments (chapter 4, part 2), I only present the basic lines of this idea here. The depth-charge sounded by an Event is its ability to reveal that the relationship of Eros and Thanatos is not eternal but historical to the core with the end of that dialectic entailing the possible extinction of one of the terms. This is the spectre Freud exorcized by establishing a dualistic way of conceptualizing the two categories. The alternative is an immanent dialectic, one where history as contingency subjects everything to irreversible change with Thanatos a force in culture dedicated to the extinction of Eros and with the power to bring about that closure to the "eternal" dialectic. Traumatic events constitute an abrupt and painful reversal of the "eternal" dialectic because in them we fund Eros deprived of all assurances. Contra Freud, there is nothing universal, biological, or ahistorical about "the eternal battle." Both terms are fully implicated in history, caught up in processes capable of producing irreversible transformations. Forces in the psyche opposed to life, which we have persistently marginalized in proclaiming our humanism, rise up in the Event to challenge all we believe about "human nature" and history. Rather than a world grounded in love, the primacy of goodness in "human nature," the achievement of rationality and the ameliorative virtues of the social process, the Event reveals a world in which envy and hate stalk life, seeking a final solution that can only come with the extinction of the antagonist. After such knowledge we can never begin again, cleansed of history, restored, through its narration, to some essential humanistic identity, with all our fundamental beliefs in essential goodness reaffirmed, Eros again pristine and empowered. Feeling the pressure of death as it weighs upon and works within us becomes the gauge that measures the depth of our participation in history. The Event rends all the masks that enable us to conceive evil as an aberrance. Existential contingency unseats all essentializing views of human nature, revealing historicity as a process in which Thanatos may be the drive informing "the reality principle." There is nothing in "human nature" that protects us from this eventuality. Positing an essential, and always recoverable, nature outside history is not the solution but part of the problem, the way we blind ourselves a priori to our situation.

Internalizing this idea requires confronting the primacy of Thanatos in the psyche and in history. Time then cuts back into the very life of "spirit." The proper use of history is to disabuse us of anything that protects us from recognizing that the significance of an Event resides in this: in it a culture's desires and discontents are bound to one another in such a way that the through-line that has been organizing the life of the quotidian expresses itself in a quantum leap toward the future condition required for its full realization. In the traumatic event, a long labor gives birth to an epiphany of sorts. The quotidian is stripped bare, the masks torn away, however briefly. Processes that have been developing, under the veil of their denial, assert an underlying truth. What history has been moving toward for a long time finds in the Event the form adequate to it. Something that has been in process at the deepest place in a collective psyche explodes—and nothing is ever the same. An Event shatters the continuum with the annunciation of a new world order—then blasts that news to the deepest recesses of the psyche.[12] For in the event, two realities reveal their simultaneity: the core disorder of the human subject and its irreversible determination in history.

That is why the study of history requires a deeper order of "psychoana-lytic" exploration than has yet been attained. One knows an Event and sustains that knowledge only insofar as one gets to that dark theatre in the psyche from which Events derive. Conceptually, this implies an even more radical change. For these reflections on "the eternal battle of Eros and Thanatos" give us a genuine experience of what immanence means and why it deprives us of all essentialistic guarantees regarding human nature. In the Event, history takes place and is made at the very core of the psyche. The conflict that grounds the dialectic of Eros and Thanatos stands forth clearly in the leap to a new determination. The disorder at the core of the psyche reveals itself with a *blinding clarity* as it seeks to resolve its discontents by giving history the direction required to bring things to their proper end.

In the Event the collective psyche makes a thrust toward a "final solu-tion." In it the true imperatives of what is called the Symbolic Order[13] stand forth in an interpellation that holds all audiences under the gaze of a "smug certainty," an absolute power beyond any appeal. Dialectically and histor-ically the deepest meaning of any Event is this: it brings us before an irrevers-ible determination of what we call the human. Internalization therefore becomes the act in which one constitutes and sustains the inner meaning of an event by unleashing its power to challenge every value, including the ability to "go on being," to remain alive as a psyche. History as "an affair of value to life" becomes the act in which the historian allows the event, in its disruptiveness, to impinge at the deepest register of the psyche—with the risk of inner death the only proof of engagement. Methodology now begins not in the Kantian affirmation of the necessary, a priori limits of rational inquiry but in the evolving of *concepts* that are *agons* and that challenge habitual modes of explanation in order to point toward what has not yet been thought or suffered. That effort, however, entails a prior problem that derives from perhaps the primary way in which the guarantees block the way to other inquires. I refer to the problem of language and the magna carta proclaiming the truth of what is finally a very agreeable idea: that about which one cannot speak clearly one must consign to silence.

V. Language, Discourse (-Communities), the Problem of Style

You spoke and a line snapped shut like fate.
—Rilke, "To Holderlin"

In attaining an existentialized concept of internalization we have created a new and perhaps insoluble problem. What we wish to render into words runs counter to the dominant way in which language—and its a priori status in determining what we can know—is deployed to eliminate precisely the problems we want to engage. Especially that thing called "inwardness," which linguistic analysis (and here deconstruction and Anglo-American analytic philosophy concur) has now rendered non-existent, innocuous, evanescent, lacking any significance. Like Faulkner's Benjy we may forever find ourselves "trying to say" what language has already consigned to the flames. This may, in fact, be the ego's final revenge on internalization and the subtlest way in which the ratio undoes all efforts to constitute an inwardness opposed to its rule.

Two roads diverge here. Our effort will be to take the one less traveled; except, that is, by poets and those like Heidegger open to the need for "a poetizing of philosophy." To concretely reverse the limits currently imposed on language, however, requires a style, a way of writing with this end: to make passion become a discipline of the concept—a style in which thought is the cutting edge of passion and preserves that ground as a psychological energy that is compressed into words in an effort to activate an agon.

That quest defines the problem of language: the wrestling with words in the search for formulations that have the power to leave a permanent record in the psyche they address and to activate that agon in which subject in its self-reference finds itself at issue and at risk. Such an agon demands a language in which drama is logos and not just rhetoric. When other modes of writing—demonstration via the ratio, the essentializing rhetoric of humanism, the consensual agreements that unify discourse communities—rule the inevitable result blunts this process, for drama activates principles of mediation that are of a fundamentally different order than those that structure the ratio. The only language adequate to the dramatic process is one where words *synthesize* an *energeia,* a dynamic in which knowledge is the very act of thinking striving to condense awareness in articulations that can't be forgotten or discharged because words are found that arrest the "soul" and blaze a conscience into the memory. Language as drama is *concept as act,* words speaking directly from the register that "cuts back into life." Style has become an existential project: to make the discipline of the concept and the life of passion one in formulations and definitions that take away all hiding places, that strip us down to nothing save those conflicts and contexts in which, through agon, we determine our innermost being. Language as impassioned perception is only as good as the passion it quickens and sustains by planting discord in beliefs and confidences, a process that applies to author as to reader since to say certain things is to bind oneself ethically to them.

I term the primary unit of such a style the dialectical sentence: the attempt to find for the concept the conciseness and intensity of an expressive form that arrests the subject and activates the possibility of inner change because articulations have been created that are "pure" and leave no exit, no escape from the claim they make on us. Allusion is an essential part of that style because, as Eliot taught us, allusion creates a language whereby the texts central to our cultural memory become present as painful echoes inhabiting a voice that is striving to write the history of the present by returning the reader from the world of rhetoric and "the generalized other" to the space of that essential isolation in which all the real decisions are made. Such a language is passion-driven-inward, striving to implode at the quick of the subject in order to activate an existential process that necessarily begins by depriving us of all the ways we construct a "world in the head" in order to bring experience within the confines of the reasonable.

We thus attain a new idea of the concept, or what may be more appropriately termed the *concept-image,* since the conceptual order here strives to take on the kind of force that artists frequently ascribe to the power of the image. Rather than cleanse itself of imagistic residues, concepts here embrace the metaphoric properties and affective connotations of language. Against an analytic language that situates thought in a purely mental space, language here strives to become a force-field inserted directly into that register in the psyche where subject first engages the process of taking action within oneself.

To affect that movement discourse must create a *dialectical sequence* of concepts that have the structure of a necessary *drama.* Each sentence thus strives to create an agon, epiphanized and driven with a certain force into the reader's psyche. From which the next sentence proceeds in a progression that strives to be irreversible. The sequence is thus analogous to Spinoza's method, but with a radically different "idea" determining the order. For here the dialectical order is one where the condition for the comprehension of each *concept-agon* is its internalization. The discourse thereby seeks an ideal density that retards the reading process while giving it the structure of an inexorable march, an agon injected directly into the innermost hiding places of the psyche and made determinate as a process that is simultaneously conceptual and affective. For that to happen, each structural unit (each section within each chapter and each chapter as a whole) in the discourse must take the *arrested* heart a step further into its own darkness. Only thereby is the reader's subjectivity as self-reference sustained at a register where change is affected through the engaging of its true conditions—the radical uprooting of oneself from within. The structure of the discourse thus strives to be the series of acts one must perform within oneself in order to sustain the movement of one's engagement. To unseat the guarantees one must deracinate the inner basis of one's need for them. That process is what language as drama of self-mediation here strives to realize, by creating a discourse in which the reader is forced not simply to change one's mind but to change who one is, to submit the choice on which one lives to a new decision. Structure therefore strives to be, with the utmost rigor, the agon through which the need for a complete change in the psyche is made inescapable.

In a sense everything said here is an attempt to draw out what is implicit in the concept of risk once that concept is existentialized and given power to assert its *immanence* as the condition that inhabits one's relation to language and one's recognition of the inherent limitations of the conceptual-discursive medium. Integral to this method is the need to return to certain central formulations throughout the discourse and progressively deepen their meaning. In this sense the movement of the discourse can be seen as the opening of a flower—or, by analogy, an attempt within the order of conceptualization to create a structure similar to the one Proust required to comprehend the experience implicit in the taste of a cake dipped in tea. In an immanent dialectic everything is present in the beginning—on August 6, 1945—its unfolding the work of expanding and deepening one's understanding of what is there.

VI. Horror, as Exemplar

> Horror has a human face . . . and you must make a friend of horror. For if horror is not your friend, then truly it is an enemy to be feared . . . horror and moral terror.[14]
>
> —Kurtz in Coppola's *Apocalypse Now*

Horror for us will be an attunement we try to produce, not a concept we employ. Its possibility arises when internalization rubs the guarantees up against a fundamental groundlessness. We then discover that horror has always been comprehended from the perspective of the ratio and the emotional needs of its audience: horror is that aberrance we suffer for a time only to reclaim the essential humanity that delivers us from it. It thus serves as an occasion for catharsis, resolution and recovery, for deliverance from neurotic responses to experience.

When we deal with horror in these ways, it has been contained, but it has not been seen "from itself."[14] To do that one must sustain it as an experience—in its immediacy. Thus: when horror grips us an abyss opens; something has been hollowed out inside us in an anxiety that announces itself, even as we flee, as a fundamental determination of our being as subjects. When horror seizes us, it is in the hollow that we have our being. We have it, that is, in the knowledge that we don't know what it would mean to make a "friend" of horror or constitute its significance because horror is an experience that finds us all in the bad faith of systematic avoidance. Because there is something else we know: horror is the primary fact; we live in its midst and are assaulted daily by its overwhelming claim on our attention—its claim, contra the ratio, to be neither exception nor aberrance, but the rule of things in a savage alphabet we have scarcely begun to decipher. Horror is the eloquent rejoinder to humanistic reassurances about the fundamental goodness of "human nature." It also brings with it a call that has the status of an imperative. For there is only one human reply to horror: a recovery of one's being as who/why.

Such is the space of the authentic historian. It is not the space of objectivity or the concept and no social-rhetorical practice is adequate to its writing. It is the space of a reflection in which anxiety must be sustained, in sufferance, as the basis for the "labor and patience of the negative,"[15] one in which we existentialize ourselves from within by making traumatic experience the basis for a deracination of guarantees. To understand a world defined by horror, we must sup full with it and comprehend it from within by tracking down its origins in the psyche. When horror is so experienced, the condition of the world and the innermost anxiety of the subject meet, issuing in the definition we have been moving toward: horror is implosion into the hollow from which the who/why—one with the howl—emerges as subject's founding self-mediation. Unsatisfactory as definition, but as attunement[16] a beginning, a break with conceptualization as practiced within the ratio and an attempt to give thinking a direction, one where the *image* intrudes on the concept, and where the experience of horror brings with it the recognition that one must write in a radically new way. Writing must become the effort to build structures that will sustain Rilke's imperative: "to wait for that which is concept to again become image" so that Events will return their power to address us with the call: "You must change your life."[18] Unlike Rilke, my task is to attempt this within the medium of a discourse that works *within* concepts, but *from* and *toward* what is beyond them. Conceptualization, so transformed, is the sustaining of primary moods in their revelatory power: the violent arresting of the heart by events, the bite of a contingency that shatters desire, the power of history to put what Francis Bacon terms "a new pressure on the nerves." Such experiences only come to articulation if the violence of events intrudes on the designs of the concept, revealing the limitations of the latter as precisely what must be overcome.

In terms of dialectical method the primary implication is the need to complete the overturning of Hegelian philosophy: a thought dedicated to "the concrete" must become a process in which every concept refers in its inner structure to the primacy of existence and experience. Dialectic accordingly becomes the effort to break systematically with the movement of the rationalist *Aufhebung* by establishing the distinct power of dramatic self-mediation to preserve a world in which historical contingency engages psyche-as-knower in the articulation of an awareness that continuously refers the concept to that which exceeds it. Terence's humanistic motto, "I am human and therefore nothing human is alien to me," finds in horror the only beginning that is adequate to the facts.

VII. A Modest Proposal

We can, in closing, contrast the two views of internalization in terms of what we might regard as the ground experience from which ethics derives. Some events deserve to be internalized at whatever cost; and others don't, even on holiday. A person who refuses to internalize the Holocaust or Hiroshima refuses the duty that makes us human. Those who only internalize what makes them happy and those who always find a way to accommodate experience to "humanistic" preconceptions are subjects whose hermeneutic circle becomes progressively smaller the more it contains. The clearest proof of this is their ability to eternally return to the reassertion of the identical set of universal, ahistorical values; to read everything that happens in life the way Wayne Booth argues we read (or should read) literature—*from* and *to* a stable, humanistic identity. In dialectical opposition to such practices, authentic culture is *Bildung* as an inner ripening to tragic burdens in a hermeneutic circle that expands, but only insofar as engagement descends inward and down, from rational confidences to repressed conflicts. Which is another way of saying that there is more than language: that the Event is inaugural refers to the one constant of experience because the world dives into us with the force of the Furies. Authentic internalization is the attempt to be worthy of our experience, to be equal to the world.

As we will learn, that responsibility reveals "the nuclear unconscious" as not simply another "regional field" within the postmodern sensibility, but the ground phenomenon from which the various ideologies that make up the "postmodern condition" derive, as so many spasms of denial concerned at whatever cost to suppress the reality of the nuclear referent.[18] Hiroshima will enable us to constitute that nuclear Unconscious. The point of that labor will be the possibility of confronting "the postmodern condition" at the correct register; the possibility of writing a "history of the present" in which "the route to the concrete" will also establish the necessity of an existential reversal that we can only undertake once we fully know the hold that "the nuclear unconscious" has in our inner world, and its intimate connection with the dream of reason in the internal constitution of the subject. That narrative does not begin in the desert of Alamogordo, however, but as the next chapter will show, in the titanic wrestlings of the greatest representative of the ratio, Immanuel Kant, with the aesthetics of the sublime.

Three

The Sublime and the Kantian Ratio, or, How the White Man Thinks

Beauty is the beginning of terror.
—Rilke

Stay, thou art so fair.
—Goethe, *Faust*

The true opposition is aesthetics and ethics.
—Mann, *Dr. Faustus*

THE CRITICAL PHILOSOPHY AT ISSUE

Marx spoke about inverting Hegel "in order to extract the rational kernel from the mystical shell." We here attempt an analogous operation on Kant, an inversion that will reveal the irrational kernel that drives the dream of reason. The text making this discovery possible: Kant's discussion of the sublime in *The Critique of Judgement,* sections 23–29.[1]

We will develop three large and controversial theses about the Kantian sublime:

1. That sections 23–29 of *CJ* constitutes Kant's inadvertent and major contribution to psychoanalytic thinking, his understanding of psyche as that which exceeds mind and the ratio. The real subject of sections 23–29 is our *inner world,* in the contradictions that define it at its deepest register.
2. Kant's inquiry thereby establishes the legitimacy and the primacy of aesthetic categories for the interpretation of history. Those categories are the ones needed because they articulate the desires and disorders that determine human historical agency.
3. Uncovering this dimension of Kant's text will bring us to the secret the Kantian sublime harbors as its deepest meaning: the a priori necessity of the atomic bomb for the resolution of the conflict that defines the rationalist psyche.

These are controversial claims and to orient the discussion I begin with a summary of sections 23–29:

Section 23: The sublime as a distinctive form of aesthetic experience is distinguished from the beautiful: the beautiful rests on a harmonious relationship between Imagination and Understanding (*Verstand*); the sublime concerns Imagination and Reason (*Vernunft*) and the order we can discern when both faculties operate at their fullest power.

Section 24: The mathematical and dynamic sublime distinguished.

Section 25: The basic argument set forth. The sublime is not about the object, which is merely a trigger, but about the subject's internal "powers" and specifically what the affects activated by the sublime attune us to in ourselves. In the sublime the Imagination, expanding to its maximum, experiences its inadequacy. The result: an attunement of the subject to a supersensible power within.

Section 26: That attunement defined: the imagination in its failure finds itself referred to reason.

Section 27: The "proper" relationship of imagination and reason is thereby established.

Section 28: An experience of the dynamic sublime thereby produces a conviction of our superiority over Nature, which in turn gives us confidence in our superiority over the "nature (or otherness) within us." The ethical significance of experiencing the sublime emerges as its deepest meaning and value.

Section 29: In a concluding summary Kant capitalizes on the last argument by asserting its contribution to transcendental philosophy. The discourse has established the a priori status of the aesthetic judgment of the sublime for moral and transcendental philosophy.

The discrepancy between our three theses and this summary is evident, and brings the first caveat. Kant knew little or nothing of the meaning we find in his text, which emerges only from a study of the contradictions that shape it. Those contradictions form a system. Kant's text thereby becomes a concrete illustration of Derrida's idea that "coherence in contradiction expresses the force of a desire."[2] Staging that desire, making it explicit, is our purpose. What follows then is *interrogation* rather than commentary.[3] If we succeed, we will show that Kant's text constitutes a massive contribution to psychoanalytic thinking; for what Kant uncovers in this text, at a depth he attains nowhere else, is the *desire/disorder constituting the self-reference of the psyche that underlies and shapes the ratio.* Sublime experience reveals in its innermost dynamic what Kant calls "the subjectivity of the subject."

The summary we've provided above gives a fairly accurate idea of Kant's intentions in sections 23–29. But there's much more going on in the text—and in sublime experience—than Kant's conceptual framework can contain. A subtext consistently disrupts the discourse from within. Our goal is to apprehend that subtext and systematically articulate its most radical implications. Because Kant circles around the problem, producing explanations that often obscure rather than clarify the excess that defines the sublime, we won't follow his discourse sequentially but will group our remarks under a series of topics, each of which brings out a central contradiction in the text, the series itself constituting as a whole the theory of psyche that can be reconstructed as the deepest meaning of Kant's text, a meaning that, I repeat, remained securely locked in Immanuel Kant's Unconscious.

To bring out that meaning, our discussion will move through the following sequence of topics:

1. Kant's view of nature and the sublime object: its irrelevance; the contempt it arouses; and the need to overcome its apparent "independence."

2. The sublime register as attunement to the self-reference that constitutes "the subjectivity of the subject." In the sublime that "within" which exceeds mind and the ratio is given in depth and in a uniquely revelatory way.

3. The affective significance of sublime experience. Sublime affects and the agon they engage reveal the existential imperatives that ground the actual self-reference of the rational subject.

4. In their dialectical connection, numbers two and three define the Kantian quest for inner mastery over the discords that sublime experience reveals in the subject. Nature as an otherness within the psyche is the real subject of aesthetic judgment. Aesthetic education (*Bildung*) is the story of our triumph over that otherness.

5. This connection reveals Kant's true purpose. The sublime is a study of our inner world in terms of its founding trauma. This is the circumstance that mandates the contempt for external nature and the repeated assertion of our need for attaining independence over it. Kant's discussion of the sublime enacts a complex psychodrama, the effort to overcome a terrifying otherness within.

6. Intimations of Immortality. The Bomb is the sublime object that is required to reverse that otherness by fulfilling the desire that Kant calls Reason. Only in the Bomb can the supersensible power within us prove its absolute status by bringing about a total transformation of our dependence on nature.

7. Intellectualization as the Defense that produces Kantian Discourse. Kant's repeated shift from affect and attunement to the conceptual

order is an attempt to comprehend and contain aesthetic phenomena along the lines required by the ratio. The entire discourse thereby exemplifies the system of defenses whereby a rationalistic hyperconsciousness superimposes itself on the aesthetic in order to contain what immanent immersion in its internal dynamics would reveal about subject-as-psyche as opposed to subject-as-mind. Inadvertently, Kant thereby brings to the fore the motives behind the rationalistic flight into abstraction and the insistence on converting experience into terms acceptable to the ratio.

To bring out the dynamic connections between these topics we will structure our discourse polyphonically. Polyphony is the method best suited to bringing out its contradictions because, as we'll see, Kant's text consistently and obsessively circles back upon itself. It is also the method required to engage the seven topics in a hermeneutic that will make the reading of Kant the basis for an act of *deracination* aimed at what that examination will reveal to be the founding disorder of our culture.

But before entering Kant's fertile labyrinth a few more words of introduction are needed. My main thesis is that Kant's discourse on the sublime is really about our inner world—and the presence in it of a "nature," an otherness that terrifies us and threatens us with annihilation.[4] Sublime experience thereby reveals the psyche in its originary trauma and the desire that stems therefrom. Kant, of course, does not and cannot know this. What he knows is that external nature triggers anxiety and an inner "drama" that he wants to master as testimony to the power of the ratio. That drama, however, is one of extreme states and oppositions, one in which we move from feelings of powerlessness to feelings of enormous power. It is defined by an experience in which we initially feel impotent, inhibited, and threatened with extinction by a might that sets us at nought. It is not, in short, the kind of thing conducive to the rationalist in us. Kant's job accordingly is to bring about a transference of energy. The power assaulting us from outside becomes the sign of an identity that in triumphing over nature constitutes the inwardness of the subject. The discourse thereby becomes a testimony to our supersensible destiny, to our duty and our ability to master the "nature" that really matters—those chaotic conflicts and affects within us that must bow before reason and its imperatives.

In its completion Kant's hermeneutic "circle" reveals that the inner world has been his subject all along. When toward the end of section 28 Kant makes the crucial "transition" and says that "nature within" is the true otherness we must master, all he really does is make explicit what the entire discourse has been about. The themes of dependence and independence, of abjection, power, and purposiveness concern a relationship Kant wants to establish within the subject by exorcizing that which disrupts subjectivity from within. As we will see, this has enormous consequences for under-standing the ambivalence with which external nature is treated throughout the discourse, and why this ambivalence points to the Bomb.

Kant's text opens itself to this reading through its utter and blind consistency to its underlying purpose. That purpose defines the true mean-ing of Kant's terms:

1. Nature throughout the text refers to a force in our inner world that overwhelms us.
2. That force defines the initial condition of the psyche and mandates the attempt that shapes Kant's discourse, to reverse that condition.
3. That effort requires making external nature an object of contempt, absolute power over it being the only response that can give us the assurance we need.

And with these three clarifications, we attain the first true intimation of the Bomb—and the deep desire it will fulfill. Kant's text adumbrates a dark telos: the desire to create an object external to us which will bring about a complete reversal of the condition created by that inner object which first traumatized us. There is, as we'll learn, only one object able to fulfill that desire—the Bomb. It alone provides a condition in which the rational subject is sublimely present to itself as a force that is total in its power over Nature, a condition attained by unlocking her secrets and turn-ing them into an expression of our will. Or, to rephrase it briefly here in terms of the subtext driving the discourse: What all traumatized subjects seek is an Event in which they can master and externalize everything trou-bling in their psyche and reduce it to rubble, to an indifferent mass, beneath contempt and concern, annihilated by a titanic act of will. That is why Alamogordo is not enough. It must be dropped—on a city, a place replete with an otherness of the right kind.

I. Affect and Attunement[5]

Kant's initial descriptions of sublime affect derives from a theory of percep-tion that considers such affects as limit cases in an epistemology dedicated to investigating the powers and relations of distinct faculties in the cogni-tion of sensible experience, with the adequation of those faculties to one another the primary concern.[6] With the sublime, however, that system be-gins to totter. Imagination—the power of estimating phenomena so as to present schemata to understanding—is overwhelmed by the magnitude of the data. Affect here strikes chords on a dissonant key. As later examples show, subject as knower is not the actual agent engaged by the sublime, nor do the affects it "arouses" relate primarily to experience as a knowledge affair. In sublime experience the subject is affected by itself at a register of its own inwardness that is extreme and deeply troubling, one in which subject oscillates from abjection to omnipotence, from feelings of elevation bordering on manic diffusion and self-abandonment to affects defined by an abyss in which one loses oneself in engulfment, self-fragmentation, and self-dissolution. If imagination is the power that registers such experiences, it is imagination as we find it first articulated in Coleridge and Schelling rather than imagination as it is defined and functions within Kantian epistemology. In fact, imagination here is no longer a faculty, strictly speaking. It is a psychological register connected to a prior self-reference—of subject, as existence, given over to itself in intense affects. The order of affect that rises up in sublime experience is deeply disruptive, especially of what Kant, following the assumptions of the *Aufklarung,* holds about the derivative nature of emotion, its cognitive "insignificance," and the direction in which the life of affect must move in order to serve the designs of reason. Rationality is precisely what here begins to totter. In sublime affect inwardness is rubbed raw by an agon of extreme emotions that whisper to us fundamental truths about ourselves—about psyche in depth as opposed to mind as ratio, about a "subjectivity of the subject" forged in the crucible of the heart's bitter desires.

In sublime affects, "the subjectivity of the subject," which Ricoeur sees as the question par excellence of transcendental reflection, takes on a radically new determination. Affect here is not something we must get beyond in order to attain objective or cognitive knowledge. It is something we must preserve and deepen as we probe the inner world of its reference. Affect is that self-reference in which the subject finds itself in and through passion. It is that experience in which knowing oneself requires an inner probing of desire that transcends the ratio and the control it tries to impose by defining the nature and proper use of desire. Desire as it rises up in sublime experience attunes us to an inner world that must remain unintelligible to Kant since it entails, as we'll see, a return of the repressed, of what the ratio denies, especially about itself.

This issue is joined in the discussion of what Kant calls *attunement.* Kant thinks of this concept as the principle that will mediate affect in the direction of reason. But what emerges in it is the beginning of a break with reason and the shift toward another psychic register. That shift has enormous consequences. Attunement is significant because it alerts the subject to the possibility of attaining, via the sublime, a unique and privileged insight into its self-reference. Its characteristics suggest moreover that attunement attunes us to something quite different from the kind of rational mediation Kant has in mind. If we stick with the phenomena, before Kant displaces it into concepts, the following picture emerges. Attunement is an awakening to an affective register within the subject that puts one in touch with an inner depth defined by desires and conflicts that are known only in sufferance, in an anxiety demanding an agon that exceeds any discourse of reason and that cannot be comprehended by the ways of conceptualizing and structuring experience that inform the ratio.

Drawing on descriptions Kant scatters at different points in the discourse, we can establish the following as the features that define sublime affect:

1. An inhibition of vital forces followed by an outpouring all the stronger.
2. An elevated judgment of ourselves that comes when we abandon ourselves to an unbound expansion of both imagination and reason.
3. A "mental agitation" rapidly alternating between repulsion and attraction, an experience excessive for imagination, opening an abyss that threatens a total loss of self.
4. The *energeia* of an unleashed might that is annihilating, overpowering, carrying with it the sense of our insignificance when under its sway. What Hegel will later speak of as absolute fear[7] is here experienced as an attraction that exerts a vertiginous pull.
5. Finally, in the sublime a plethora of affective contradictions are experienced in dynamic union: amazement bordering on terror; horror accompanied by a sacred thrill; engulfment in a destructive otherness that exerts the power of a "strange attractor," an *unheimlich* mood that feels like homecoming.

There is something in this more than natural if philosophy could find it out, something central to subject's self-reference that is beyond all reason. Attunement opens this spectre up in us and does so in a mood that binds anxiety to dread. A rift, a fundamental contradiction opens up within subject between its experience and knowledge—with the latter now revealed as the way we exorcize what we do not want to know.

The form this experience assumes in Kant is, of course, intensely subtle: the attempt, in talking about affect, to smooth over the rift so that the right movement—the ascent to conceptualization—will exert its appeal. Our effort, in contrast, will be to solidify the break with reason, to maintain the rift in order to see what emerges when one moves within the "medium of affect."

As always, the phenomena point the way. Before it becomes conceptual, attunement for Kant is a mood, a *Stimmung* and a *Befindlichkeit* that opens up within the subject an inwardness that does not take the form of Kantian rationalism.[8] On the contrary, an entirely different way of being-in-the-world emerges. Which Kant quickly forecloses it. Sublimity is a complex and in many ways contradictory experience—a state of what we might term *dynamic self-opposition*. In it affect turns inward and rushes down to the deepest register of the psyche there to shatter extant habits and structures, awakening (however momentarily) an existential sense of what subject's true condition is and what would be required to assume it. To use a later language, what presents itself here in the order of affect is existence as something one is given over to in a deeply conflicted *passion* that must be sustained since in it one experiences one's being as at issue. In such an experience *subjective self-identity and rational self-identity diverge in a way that is fundamental and that cannot be bridged*. The dream of attaining a substantial identity by adequating oneself to the order of the ratio recedes before a discipline of another kind, grounded in an inwardness of a radically different order.

Kant has to work overtime to give affect and attunement the "proper" direction because every characteristic of sublime experience potentially subverts the concept of rational self-mediation Kant wants to derive from it. All the grand hypotheses that Kant has labored so long to establish about the inner harmony of the faculties in the self-identity of the rational subject and the moral implications that flow therefrom are here thrown into doubt and disarray. Accordingly, Kant develops an explanation of the sublime that amounts to a double transformation and displacement of the experience: first, by shifting from affect to attunement with the "mental" nature of the latter enabling a smooth transition to reason and the "feeling" that we have "a supersensible power within," second, by arguing that identifying ourselves with this self-image is our immanent telos. The power and appeal of the conceptual is thereby assured. At the cost, however, of suppressing everything in sublime affect suggesting the possibility that the deep psychological bases of identity have little to do with "mental powers" and "moral feelings"—except insofar as these ideas provide masks that protect mind, in its narcissism, from that sublime mirror in which nature reflects back to us our true visage.

The sublime puts the critical philosophy in crisis. The experience that Kant claims is needed to complete his project—by establishing mind's unity and the proper relationship of the faculties—may actually subvert his project totally and from within. Contra his best intentions, what Kant perhaps offers us here is this: a systematic picture of how a mentalistic hyperconsciousness superimposes itself on an experience that shatters every assumption which that hyperconsciousness needs in order to sustain itself. Since that hyperconsciousness is also the finest articulation of the western ratio, Kant's text offers us an experience well worth having.

To constitute it we begin with the founding ambiguity within attunement, the discrepancy between a deeply disruptive experience and the interpretation Kant imposes upon it. Developing the latter is for Kant, and he never tires of reiterating the point, the purpose and value of studying the sublime. The sublime provides for Kant a mental attunement—to a mental order. It attunes us to the awareness that we have a "supersensible power" within us, Reason, which offers us (1) an order of concepts that (2) establish the proper way to feel about the sublime so that (3) the primary result of its experience will be respect for the moral law and the rational order within. We thus traverse the greatest distance, moving from the experience of wrenching discordances to the one thing that can satisfy the ratio—a confirmation of our rational identity and its power to provide the guarantees adequate to the mastery of any experience. In its full yield Kant's hermeneutic circle traces this path: a deeply troubling experience of inner turbulence, excessive desire, and raw, contradictory affect is transformed into that feeling of inner contemplative calm that is required to keep the critical philosophy firmly in place as the only inner ordering of the mind that is coherent and moral.

In reply sublime phenomena suggest a different reading. One that reveals deep within not a supersensible power but a *crypt;* a psychic register defined by desires, disorders, and conflicts that cannot be subsumed in a triumphant march toward reason and morality. In attuning us to ourselves, sublime affect directs attention to an inwardness within the subject that is prior to reason and in which we must immerse, without that shield, if we are to learn from within what the sublime reveals about "the subjectivity of the subject," about subject as a who suffered in depth, *in an inwardness where reflection, as existential situatedness, has become a questioning of ontological foundations,* a why that is one with the recognition that impassioned affect is that "cognition" that reveals the world as world and not as object for knowledge.[9] Reflection of this order is, as we'll learn, radically different from the concept of reflection Kant develops in order to impose rationalistic limitations on thought and experience.

II. Deracination as Concrete Deconstruction

Methodologically our task is to develop a way of reading that subverts Kant's discourse from within in order to recapture the drama on which it is based. We do so by returning to the experience in an attempt to preserve and constitute the phenomena over against the framework imposed on it. Abstraction and the lure of the conceptual are thereby reversed concretely and the experience they hoped to contain regained as a theme for another, existializing, mode of thought.

Kant thereby provides the bases for his own destruction, consistently and from the beginning. In moving toward an inwardness that is beyond the beautiful, section 23 introduces an affective order that opens up an unexplored register in the psyche. In the beautiful we have a direct feeling of life being furthered through play. In the sublime, feeling is indirect and comes after inhibition: vital forces, blocked and frustrated, generate an outpouring of increased strength. Seriousness replaces play in what Kant terms "a negative pleasure," a concept to which we will return. Suffice for now the suggestion that desire not pleasure is the appropriate term, since the agonistic experience described here is one in which the subject moves from inhibition to power, impotence to might, abjection to exaltation, from a terrifying abyss to an overweening confidence. Pleasure has little to do with such a dialectic. The dynamics of inwardness revealed here exceed the pleasure principle.

Sticking with the phenomena is the primary source of our counterdiscourse. It is also precisely what Kant cannot do, because the sublime points in a direction sharply opposed to the conceptual. Consider these key characteristics: (1) in "form" the sublime is contrapurposive to our power of judgment; (2) it is incommensurate with our power of exhibition; and (3) it is "violent to our imagination." When Kant then tells us that we judge the experience significant precisely for these reasons, we sense a special pleading. "For what is sublime . . . cannot be contained in any sensible form but concerns only ideas of reason," says Kant. To which one replies, if so what idea does it give reason? And what ideas does it perhaps find wanting? If the sublime tickles us with the grandest possibility—the charge to realize our "supersensible" powers—it also throws into question precisely what they are and what they desire. Unless, that is, we already know—a priori. But then philosophic explanation here amounts to a leap of faith, which then gives itself the status of what I will term a "pragmatic imperative." Kant argues that once we establish that purposiveness is not in nature, nature in its sublime manifestation becomes valuable because we can use it to establish purposiveness on a purely conceptual order. What was affectively overpowering has become useful in leading us to that concept perfectly suited as a defense against any residual anxiety created by the original experience. It does so by displacing the entire thing into a safely intellectualized space, from which Kant can then assure us the sublime "indicates nothing purposive whatever in nature itself but only in what *use* we can make of our *intuitions of nature* so that we can feel a purposiveness within ourselves entirely independent of nature."[10]

We must pause over this passage because in it the need to assert our independence over nature—without and later within—makes its first appearance as the desire that drives the discourse. Why does the sublime in nature engage the issue of independence and then the vehemence with which Kant assures us that nature's independence is only apparent? Does Kant tip his hand here, creating the suspicion that "nature" is a stand-in, a metaphor for everything within the subject that threatens our ethico-rational identity? With these questions the text takes on a new density. The sublime confronts the Kanitan subject with a crisis, an opportunity, and an overweening need. How better establish one's independence than by totally transforming that upon which one "depends"? By bending it to one's will? By forcing matter itself to yield its secrets so that we might unleash what has thereby become a pure and ultimate expression of our power and the confirmation of what we need most—an absolute intuition of our independence? The Bomb is that dream which finds an origin in sublime experience long before science awakens to its possibility. Dependency on nature—and the search for ways to overcome that "condition"—is its unquiet womb.

READING AS INTERROGATION—
KANT'S CRITIQUE OF JUDGMENT, SECTIONS 23–29

We are now ready to undertake a close reading of sections 23–29 in a polyphony of concepts that will make what is sequential in presentation dialectical in apprehension.

I. Beyond the Beautiful: From Pleasure to Desire

Summary of sections 23–24:

1. The purpose of the sublime: imagination harmonizes with the order of concepts—with understanding then with reason—furthering their aims.
2. The sublime is a special order of feeling. The keynote is an inhibition of vital forces followed by their outpouring. In such an affective experience life is furthered indirectly via a *seriousness* constituted through what is termed a *negative pleasure*.
3. The purposiveness found in the sublime is not in nature but in us. Its use once conceptualized is to establish the harmony of faculties and powers. Crude Nature is the trigger; magnitude and might the qualities that shape this experience.

Methodology

Interrogation is the discovery of contradictions; *reflection* the production of new concepts and a new awareness. These two moments constitute the act of critique in a hermeneutics of engagement. *Deracination* is the subsequent effort to enter the psychic condition thereby revealed and attempt its active reversal. We here initiate that dialectic by carrying out its first moment.

In approaching the sublime Kant needs a new term to describe a new pleasure. The beautiful gives us "a feeling of life's being furthered" through a pleasure that is direct for an imagination at play. In the sublime "pleasure" is complex and arises indirectly, in emotions that are of a distinct order, arising out of a complex process in which a "momentary" "inhibition of the vital forces" is "followed immediately by an outpouring of them that is all the stronger." Seriousness, rather than play, now defines the imagination's activity and since repulsion and attraction shape the mind's reaction to the sublime "object," Kant requires a new and richly ambiguous term to mark off this experience—the concept of a negative pleasure. The beautiful charms us; while the sublime moves us: a nice, tidy distinction, but one involving a fundamental shift in the register of the psyche that is engaged by aesthetic experience.

The shift from pleasure to negative pleasure is not (contra Kant) a simple transition within a continuity of experience, but the discovery of a fundamental rift, a basic discontinuity and with it a shift from pleasure to an inquiry into *the dynamics of desire* and what desire (or "negative pleasure") reveals about the "subjectivity of the subject." Unlike pleasure, desire feeds on opposition and struggle. Vital energies are engaged in a traumatic collapse followed by a triumphant self-overcoming. Painful inhibition leads to discovery of an inner force equal to the occasion. Abjection is followed by exaltation, impotence by power. Desire, so understood, is not drive-discharge nor does appetite for the object define its operation. Desire is a psychic complex, at odds with itself, defined by conflict and the necessity of an agon that develops through affects that are "extreme," fraught with anxiety, and that bring all the powers that compose the rational mind to their furthest reach. In activating the register of desire, the sublime also points the way to a radically new understanding of desire.[11] In doing so it announces what will become evident subsequently: subject itself in the depth of its self-reference is what the sublime engages and does so by showing that the struggle to establish subjective identity depends on altering the basic conditions of one's being.

These connections emerge from the cardinal point Kant is at pains to establish. Nature is the trigger to the sublime, but not the object of that experience. The object is our own subjectivity, given, through that trigger, the opportunity to know its inner powers. The sublime is about one thing and one thing only: *inwardness* and the *self-reference* whereby we know ourselves most deeply through an experience that enables us to determine the relationship of our faculties and their correct employment in adjudicating our deepest hopes and concerns. The noteworthy thing about this experience is a circumstance Kant is at pains to marginalize. Anguish is the first and primary reaction to the trigger. And in the anguish here experienced subjectivity as who engages itself in an agon where the movement of affect is the movement of a self-reference, one in which anguish tears open an inner world in which we are for the most part strangers to ourselves, yet one in which the possibility that everything we think, believe, and hope is put at issue. The four questions that for Kant constitute the ultimate concerns of philosophy are directly engaged by the sublime with the fourth (Who am I?) impinging upon the other three with complications they cannot contain. In the sublime the questions *who* and *why* are equiprimordial and become existential and psychological without losing their ontological status. The sublime thereby provides the concrete beginning for the philosophic anthropology Kant hoped to write, but with the implication of a radically new turn within his own Copernican revolution: (1) its opening to an otherness it cannot contain through (2) a recognition that the aesthetic exceeds the ratio in a way that points to the "psychoanalytic" as the new frontier for advancing our a priori knowledge of what grounds and informs the frameworks whereby we know.

I will return to this issue shortly. For now I want to underscore the enormity of the problems Kant faces in trying to adapt the sublime to rational designs. With the advent of the sublime, the subject finds the beautiful profoundly inadequate. Farewell to an idea: the possibility of "stay thou art so fair" before it collapses. Life is furthered only through strife, traumatic experience, and the exacting burden of dread. To know "the subjectivity of the subject" there are "things" in ourselves that we must attend to: abjection, inhibition, terror. Catastrophic images attune us to them. Subject, as psyche, taps its vital energies only after it has found itself faced with the possibility of psychic dissolution. The sublime is a world defined by images and phenomena that have this power.

The threat to frameworks of rational intelligibility is but the surface. Beneath, the real drama commences. In sublime experience the defenses intellectualization provides to keep the world from breaking through our conceptual masks begin to crumble, and with it, the true motives behind rationality begin to emerge. We experience Rilke's insight into the power of all images: beauty is the beginning of terror. The truth reason flees is that subjectivity only begins when burdened by the most painful affects. The inwardness awakened by sublime experience is of an order different from that found previously in Kant and beyond that dreamt of in the ratio. Subject finds something deeply attractive about sublime experience and rushes to meet it with energies awakened after long concealment. Like Kafka's sea frozen inside us, however, they are awakened to a process that may require a deracinantion from within of all we hope to affirm.

This is so because desire, in the sublime, is doubled back upon itself in an agon that has no ready, predictable, or guaranteed result. Affects as psychological forces here meet and clash in extremity. Everything within is submitted to an immanent process that has no a priori limits or controls.

Which is why Kant's assertion of certain victory for the party of reason smacks of resistance to drama and its defining condition. In drama reason is not the director nor does it determine the through-line structuring the process. Saying this, however, amounts to what is today called a "scandal" in philosophy: the heretical notion that philosophic conceptualization is an attempt to escape and then superimpose itself on a prior order that has a "logic" of its own. Moreover, if drama reveals the being of the subject and if philosophic logic is defined by resistance to drama, identity as conceived in the ratio must be re-examined. One may dream with Kant of the one rational resolution to all dramas, endlessly repeating itself, but the medium of agonistic affect establishes for experience a dialectical phenomenology of a radically different order. In the sublime, subject suffers a new determination: one in which it is both the term and the result of a self-reference that is affective and that contains the possibility that certain experiences *existentialize us from within.*

As its inadvertent precursor, the truth of Romanticism haunts Immanuel Kant. The sublime delivers us over to an affective engagement that is prior to all others and deeper. Kant will not dare to say it, but the "truth" attested here is that the goal defining the ratio is the deadening of affect. The great refusal Dante speaks of here finds its origin. And, apparently, with good reason given the world to which affect, as here described, delivers us. Before it is anything else, the sublime is a shattering experience. The surface of ordinary life is fractured by the intrusion of excess and extremity. Habits break down. Perception collapses before images it is unable to process. All of our faculties are checked, suspended, blocked, or exerted under strain and in deliberate reductionism. The continuity of life is rent asunder. The world has become *unheimlich.* We move in the landscape of the waking dream—a realm where projection and an implosive return of projections eradicates defenses, bringing the subject before one thing and one thing only—oneself in that anxiety that one is. Affect here is Keats' "wakeful anguish of the soul," that experience in which one is affected by oneself or, better, infected with oneself. One experiences the call of Nietzschean self-contempt: one is "sickened onto death" and simultaneously quickened by the depth-charge of a "self-feeling" that is deeper than all others. As Thomas Weiskel notes, in the sublime a discontinuity opens up between what can be grasped and what is "felt to be meaningful"[12]—and the latter supplants the former, plunging the psyche into a world of inner conflicts. One inhabits that world only insofar as one knows that what beckons in affect is descent into an inferno that is utterly one's own, and that one has created by steadfastly seeking to avoid it. The sublime is overpowering in its assault upon the subject. Every confidence whereby mind asserts its ability to master experience is shattered. Moreover, power is the essential term defining every moment of the experience: sheer power, breaking all bonds; power over others; the power to destroy; the hypnotic appeal of one's own grandiose fantasies, and, finally, a will to power that has its genealogy in the recognition of one's duty to become the equal to this experience—to live from the sublime register of one's being by taking one's disorders upon oneself in the effort to strip away all hiding places and then deracinate from the core.

One should add that if vast and primitive objects are needed to key the sublime—the sudden rising up of that which is terrifying, that which overcomes all boundaries and sets human life at naught—the true reference of these characteristics is to the psyche and the dynamics that structure it at the deepest register. If an imagination of disaster, of worlds and meanings shattered, breathes through the sublime, the primary reference is not to external violence but to the violence in the human spirit. The tragic has asserted its claims with the problem of subjectivity here siezed at a turning point. As Weiskel notes, "a humanistic sublime is an oxymoron."[13] So, one might add, is a rationalistic account of this experience. The sublime is much more than a challenge, a momentary blockage, to the ratio and the ability of our faculties to harmonize with one another in that incipiently cognitive processing of experience that turns everything into a knowledge-affair. Nor is sublimity yet another genre to be offered up to humanistic interpretation or deconstructive aporia. The sublime establishes the centrality to the subject of desires and discontents that exceed the substantialistic guarantees that the various humanisms strive to impose on experience as well as the impasses deconstruction uses to assure the dissolution of drama.

II. Frameworks: Opposed

If for Kant the struggle to grasp the sublime serves as evidence of the mind's relation to a transcendent reality, it will for us serve as testimony to reason's relationship to a more primary order, that of the Unconscious, and the possibility that this register holds the key to reason's ideals as well as the motives and desires reason fulfills. The authority for that opposition will be provided by Kant himself. For Kant the sublime is a crisis turned into an opportunity. In considering it Kant confronts phenomena that challenge the framework of rationality that structures the critical philosophy. From the beginning Kant's Copernican revolution in philosophy has been moving toward this crisis because it is precisely in the sublime that the relationship between concepts and phenomena begins to totter.

We know only what our framework allows us to know: this principle, which Kant was the first to understand, may here confront a limitation in which one cannot acquiesce because sublime experience teaches us something that contemporary neo-Kantians do not want to know about frameworks. When phenomena exceed a framework they do so in a way that points to another framework, which we can construct only by reading against the grain. In imposing themselves on phenomena, frameworks generate contradictions. In identifying those contradictions we overturn frameworks from within while establishing the credentials of an emergent framework to do the one thing that counts—preserving the phenomena. Moreover, immanence is preserved because the new framework emerges precisely from a discovery of the hidden problems and motives in the framework critiqued. The popular pluralism of epistemological frameworks, each responsible only to their own internal coherence, is thereby supplanted by an epistemology that is dialectical, grounded in an interpretive method that is truly hermeneutic because phenomena are here given the power to shatter frameworks, even to show that some frameworks are better than others precisely by virtue of their openness to complex, disruptive affects and experiences.

The framework that Kant constructs to explain the sublime falsifies the experience. Collecting the contradictions thereby generated will enable us to see the guarantees in their working at precisely those spots where the labor to keep everything moving in the direction required by the ratio is urgent. The through-line of Kantian thought will then stand forth in high relief. The best term for that through-line is intellectualization—the need to transform aesthetic experience into mental concepts so that its unique characteristics will be explained in a way that assures the march of certain ideas and ideals so that the developmental process will confirm an ego-identity in which feeling necessarily becomes "moral feeling," aesthetic attunement "mental" attunement, and with the entire *Bildung* capped by transcendence into a contemplative realm of harmonious rationality. It is, in effect, yet another Platonism, another act of moralism in the face of art, another attempt through intellectualization to conquer for reason everything that haunts and threatens it from within.

III. Purposiveness: And the Contrapurposive

The opposition within the sublime of purposiveness and the contrapurposive brings these problems to a head. Sublime nature is devoid of purposiveness, but the concept is saved through its location, at one remove, in the subject. That argument requires a series of complex transformations. It also dramatizes the difference between Kant's framework of explanation and the one we are evolving. For Kant the new order emerging here must adequate itself to rationality by revealing a purposiveness that has remained unexamined in the earlier critiques, whereas for us the contrapurposiveness of the sublime enables us to comprehend agonistic principles of mediation that exceed any discourse of reason. The question is one of intelligibility; of whether aesthetic experience can be grasped by the ratio or whether it reveals the intelligibility of a dramatistic logic that is independent of the ratio, and that it cannot comprehend or rule.

Faced with this possibility, Reason reveals itself as doubled in a fractured mirror, a demand that cannot know itself as such—nor the motives and conflicts that inform it—because it insists on transforming everything into concepts, into moral and quasitheological ideas, in order to assert a rational identity that is supposedly freed of desire and inner conflict. Held up to nature, however, that mirror necessarily reveals its underlying conflicts in their most distressing form. For in denying and displacing conflicts, reason produces, as in the processing of uranium ore, their "enrichment." Inner disorder isn't conquered, it is transported to another realm where it can claim freedom from the very desires it is thereby positioned to project in a more extreme form. This displacement is the source of the resentment Nietzsche sees in morality, especially Kantian. It is also the motive behind the hatred of Nature that, as a veritable "will to power" (and intimation of the Bomb), drives the necessity for reason to achieve a situation where Nature no longer opposes its desires but realizes them fully, all otherness gone.

In shifting from the "contrapurposiveness" of sublime experience to the purposiveness that rationality can find in "intellectualizing" the phenomena, Kant does not escape the psyche's disorders. He repeats and extends them. The defenses thereby developed do not escape desire, they reinvest it in a narcissistic grandiosity. This is the itch that underlies contempt for the beauty, power, and independence of Nature and the trauma that rises up within whenever nature in its magnificence stirs the embers of the buried life. Reason does not overcome inner disorder, it projects then denies it. Through rationality inner conflict is not extinguished; it is extended across the entire visible world. The struggle to master the resulting projections demands concepts that are of necessity progressively more analytic, mathematical, and denuded. The move toward Nietzsche's "X" has begun. The hidden truth of every conceptual *Aufhebung* is this: nothing is canceled. Instead, what is preserved is rendered avid. And the only thing "uplifted" is the projection of the initial trauma made more regressive through its disguise as idea. We see here the connection in Kant between a superego and an id, between the highest ideals and their sublime genealogy, with both psychic registers defined by the need to assert might, self-aggrandizement, and the need to dominate and destroy otherness. Kant here reveals the inner contradiction that is the primary truth of the rational subject. For us that demonstration is invaluable because it establishes the possibility of reversal. By immersing ourselves in the true medium of our disorders we may attain a psychic integrity that is not based on reason, nor deaf to the actual appeal that is sounded at the depths whenever we speak and act in its name. To do so, however, the "counterpurposive" of the sublime must be comprehended in a framework where conceptualization is not in charge and where reason can no longer split itself off from its founding disorder or deny the results of its projections: "aesthetic education" through the sublime is a process in which imagination is made monstrous, idea grandiose, desire imbricated, the whole thing lurching toward frightful expression, in a blind rush toward a shuddering dawn.

IV. Affect and Attunement in Depth: Inwardness versus the Ratio

Our goal: to comprehend reason as psyche and thereby reverse the hold the disorder called the ratio has over us. The means: an articulation of Kant's subtext as his true text.

In the sublime we re-experience our "origins" and the true conditions thereof. The psyche from its depths projects itself on nature, and "as if a magic lantern threw the nerves in patterns on a screen,"[14] it finds embodied there everything that is dark yet urgent within. In the sublime the psyche presents itself to itself without knowing that fact or the secrets thereby revealed. The repeated shift from abjection to empowerment, from inhibition to omnipotence, from the threat of psychic dissolution to assurance of one's absolute status is the keynote. Of equal significance is the recognition that in both experiences there is something deeply attractive, even thrilling. These characteristics signal conflicts that exceed and deny within the subject all principles of rational mediation. An inner agon of a radically different order is triggered by the sublime, one where we aren't simply given over to the negative pole of the experience, but are deeply drawn by its pull. Vertigo, the specter of engulfment and annihilation, of being overwhelmed by forces beyond our control finds a receptive chord in the psyche. So too does excess, turbulence, and a contemptuous shattering of all restraints. Bottoming out and suicidally plunging into an abyss has a place prepared within us as does destructive energy and an overweening power contemptuously imposing itself on all it regards as small, weak, and beneath it. In its inner constitution the psyche is attracted to terror and already finds "a friend in horror," because the affects triggered by the sublime speak to something crypted deep in our experience.

In sublime affect psyche reveals itself as a reality that exceeds the principles of intelligibility of the ratio. Its mediation, moreover, proceeds through an agon in which sharply opposed forces meet in conflict, without the possibility of a reconciling mediation. What makes the sublime significant is not simply the movement from one extreme state to its opposite, but the revelation of the necessary connection between the two as the expression of the force of a desire and the rootedness of that desire in conflicts that reveal an inwardness where the ratio is still a stranger to itself.

Moreover, when this experience seizes us, there is no escape, no way to shift to ego defenses or rationalistic mediations. Here affect infects. It puts us at odds with ourselves and in touch with an inner disorder that is not open to deliberative reasoning but presents itself in the affective terms appropriate to it. In dread and anxiety we are assaulted by ourselves from within. Being affected by oneself is thereby revealed as the first step in taking action within oneself. Moreover, the ground for that possibility is not mentalist but traumatic. Affect is painful and exacting, not something we can play with or discharge. Nor does its agon proceed from affect to objectivity, rationality, or calm of mind. We must find some way to mediate ourselves solely with the medium of affect. As Spinoza knew, an affect can only be replaced by an affect. Here, however, rationalist and conceptual mediation won't do the job. To move within the medium of sublime affect we must discover a different logos. If sublime affect attunes us to ourselves in depth it does so not by appealing to the harmony of things, as does the beautiful, but by a seizure that abolishes any inner distance between ourselves and affect. We experience the affect we are: affect prior to defenses, prior to the conceptual and emotional mediations we employ to distance ourselves from anxiety and dread. There is no safe distance here—no distance at all. *Inwardness* is what happens when all protections have been eradicated. "For here there is no place that does not see you. / You must change your life." There is no longer any hiding place from inner discord. But to change one's life one must take action within the agon of affect. No wonder we strive to locate the sublime in the external world.

Affect attunes us to the agonistics of a subjectivity that is independent of the ego and its defenses. It is the self-reference that arises when one experiences within oneself the controlling power of an otherness that threatens to engulf and to extinguish the subject. That is what anxiety is. Subjectivity is born in the chilling possibility that one may never be able to oppose that otherness with the force of a mediating desire. That is why the rapid shift in sublime experience from impotence to a feeling of overweening power is both remarkable and utterly ambiguous in its reference. Is it we who move from weakness to mastery or is that shift a fantasy grounded in identification with the aggressor?

Affect as attunement is first and foremost a naked experience of one's inwardness *in extremis,* burdened by the opposition of inner forces that are not yet and may never become agencies. They seize us in the one true immediacy: that of a judgment that is beyond appeal. Affect here is subject in its existence delivered over to the terror of an otherness that attacks it within. Subject does not put itself at issue; it finds itself at issue. One is at issue only when traumatic affect assaults the very possibility of ever attaining agency. We first find ourselves as subjects when we know, in a chilling immediacy, that such is *not* the case. I am the other: that, the most terrible suspicion, is here engaged in the only way it can be—as affect. One here lives in anguish the recognition of a power within that is intent on destroy-ing the possibility of autonomous subjectivity and may already have done so. Beckett's founding recognition—the feeling that one has "never been born properly"—here touches its deepest chord. An inner death is experienced as that action of the other which presides over and defeats every effort to be.

The existential is the effort to give this dimension of experience its full ontological value by beginning with the recognition, contra all cogitos, that in affect one is delivered over to oneself in a way that is primary. Other stances toward the world derive from contemplative and pragmatic ex-ercises of mind. Existence is the prior order they displace. Anguish is the ground-affect that re-activates its claims because anxiety strikes inward with the force of gravity, eradicating all means of escape and discharge. As such it is the call for a certain kind of attention rather than the signal for the automatic and necessary activation of defenses.[15] As Keats' "wakeful anguish of the soul" anxiety is the light that enables us to probe the inner world. For when we refer to ourselves at the register of affect, we are what we feel. Subjectivity then becomes the most rigorous and exacting discipline: to act within oneself by acting on oneself and to do so at and within the register of primary affects.

A reminder. Kant knows nothing of this. Nor could he sustain it since his purpose is not to develop a psychological investigation of affect but to leave affect far behind once he has established a "mental" attunement as the only important thing affect yields. The dominant attitude of the *Auklarung* toward emotion controls the discourse. That is why the foregoing discussion would be unintelligible—and psychologically aberrant—to Kant. The regis-ter of inwardness that opens up here is quite different from the impersonal register of mind as knower and the quasirational ethic of duty that can be deduced from that self-conception. Analogies and explanatory principles based on the framework of Kant's first two critiques thus are of only limited value to the investigation. This point applies with special force to the notion that mind is composed of faculties with fixed a priori powers and functions, which enable us to constitute "experience" as a knowledge-affair. The inner world lived at the register of affect operates by a radically different logic.

The first lesson it teaches: the presence within us of an overwhelming power that threatens psychic dissolution and that mocks all the petty ap-peals and pieties we bring forth in hopes of softening its contempt and cruelty. To no avail. The only way is a harsher process. *Terror begets desire* and the possibility of the only true deliverance: *reversal within,* self-empowerment through *deracination.* In its founding self-reference, inwardness is the strug-gle to survive the threat of psychic dissolution; to confront horror not as an impersonal thing but as the force of an agent within the psyche that de-mands total control over our being. Far more than developmental barriers stand in the way of our becoming autonomous, egosyntonic, morally mature, and socially responsible agents. The inner structure of affect reveals a force of Thanatos within the psyche. As such, affect is a true and concrete beginning for a theory of subject because it gives us over to this: at the origin and center of our relationship to ourselves we find something that opposes the very possibility of subjective cohesion and autonomous identity. Prior to other developmental processes, action must be taken within this realm. Affective inwardness is defined by this seemingly impossible task: to reverse oneself totally from the ground up and to do so, of necessity, as *act* and not as idea. The need is for an affective transformation that is falsified the moment it becomes a rational process. Kant's irrelevance is never more apparent. Everything he celebrates comes only later, to deliver us from the experience that sublime affect engages.

To be or not to be one must act upon a stage where taking action within oneself requires an agon fired in the crucible of affects that are of an extreme and "primitive" order. To find the principles of mediation proper to that realm, one must immerse in that which is labeled aberrant, extreme, even incipiently psychotic. In sublime affect subject is at issue to itself because a crypt has been torn open. The sublime, as psychological drama, is the effort to project that inner world upon nature. When we do so we move in the medium of the waking dream—of the Unconscious as it simultaneously wells up within us and comes back at us from outside. This is what the epistemological ambiguities about whether the sublime is in the object or in us reveals. The sublime puts us uniquely in touch with ourselves because, like Kurtz's jungle, it whispers truths about ourselves we are not prepared to hear, truths about our inner world in its origin and its abiding distress. Repulsion and attraction oscillate in response because capitulation before a destructive force that threatens inner annihilation appears to be the only solution. In tearing open the crypt the sublime plunges us into an inner world that is defined by power and cruelty, one where identification with the aggressor is the dominant response that we project first on ourselves and then by finding someone or something else—nature, a child, the beloved— one can subject to unlimited aggression. The power of the other within thereby becomes one's identity, the a priori door of all perceptions. One flees the terror of self-dissolution by imposing it whenever one finds oneself in a position to make the other—nature, other people, an entire city—the object one annihilates in order to deny that the resulting abjectness is the mirror that reflects one's true image, the spectre one must exorcize again whenever it rises up. Kurtz's "Exterminate them all . . . . Drop the bomb" is an imperative rooted at the heart of the psyche.

Perhaps this is the deepest lesson of the sublime: that there is only terror *in illo tempore,* with catastrophic anxiety the core condition from which the "human" derives. The possibility of authentic reversal depends upon a full assumption of this condition. Transforming oneself radically from within is the act through which one achieves a humanity that one does not have prior to that act. To exist is to be thrown into a condition that requires self-overcoming through a radical deracination. Affective attunement to oneself at that register produces a self-reference in which subjectivity has become a matter of "infinite concern," sustained in a brooding that descends inward toward an "undiscovered country" where one moves in an affective medium that leaves all the old guarantees behind, even when, in deepest despair one longs for the concepts and resolutions they impose upon experience.[16] Sustained as a principle of reflection, this way of being leads to a *thinking*, freed of the ratio: to be or not to be as question lived in an existential process that preserves inwardness as a problem to itself. If this emerges as the truth of the sublime, Kant's discourse will produce as its unintended irony a discovery of the drama of existence.

The countervailing appeal of the Bomb is its ability to put an end to that possibility. Existentializing affect attunes us to the tragic register of inner experience. Rationalizing frameworks explain that experience away by imposing concepts upon it. Inner trauma thereby becomes rational certitude. And with it the fatal transition from subjectivity to substantialism, from inwardness to mind, and the imposition of mind on all that resists its demands. That process proceeds inexorably toward its own sublime spectacle, one capable of bringing the disorder of mind to a "resolution." In the Bomb reason finds the identical "subject-object" to which it can and must say "stay thou art so fair" at the very moment it also says "Now I am become death, shatterer of worlds." What rose up in the desert, in the *jordano del muerto*, at Trinity, on the feast of the Transfiguration in 1945 was an "objective correlative" announcing the glad tidings: that pure mind had finally released itself from its confinement in matter and was now present to itself and absolute in the image of its power over all otherness. One thing alone was needed: annunciation through the perfect genocide.

To comprehend such connections we must, as Freud teaches, "pay attention to the details of our illness" since "there is much of value for our future life" that can only be derived from such investigation.[17] With respect to Kant's discourse, such attention offers perhaps the greatest prize: a discovery of the "reasons" why a psyche would find in the ratio the perfect way to prosecute its desires.

V. From Ambivalence toward the Object to Intimations of the Bomb

Summary of Section 25

1. Nothing that can be an object of the senses is to be called sublime. In sublime experience, imagination expands toward infinity; rea-

son demands absolute totality. The inadequacy of the former *arouses* in us the feeling that we have a supersensible power within us. What is "absolutely large" is not, accordingly, in the object, but in the use judgment makes of certain objects to arouse our mental powers.

2. Indifference to the existence of the object confers subjective purposiveness in the use of our cognitive powers.

3. Thus, "the sublime is that, the mere ability to think which, shows a faculty of the mind surpassing every standard of Sense."[18]

Interrogation

Two fundamental theses are developed here.

1. Nature is an object of great ambivalence. It is necessary as a trigger but must then be treated with contempt and subjected to dismissal.

2. Sublime experience attunes the subject to a special register within its inwardness, which is the source of a privileged insight into mind's unity and the relationship of its faculties, interests, and powers. Thus, indifference to the object's existence enables us to use it to define subjective purposiveness. That purposiveness resides in turn in the pleasure we take in the expansion of our powers, a pleasure that has as its telos a confirmation of the absolute status of that power.[19]

The sublime attunes us to ourselves. But for Kant that attunement can move in only one direction: toward the feeling that we have a "supersensible power" within that takes us beyond the limits of sensation and the trauma it signifies, contingency. For Kant, the most important thing intensely aesthetic sensations give us is the intimation that there is a power within us that can free us from those sensations. The hermeneutic circle of the sublime, which began with sensation as trigger, thus moves toward a dismissal of the object of sense. Such is the logically necessary sequence whereby the "object" reveals its value to the subject. Its magnitude, for example, serves to establish our grandeur. We then return the favor not in a gesture of thanksgiving to nature, but in a dismissal bordering on contempt.

But repeatedly the object sinks to irrelevance and disappears only to return in a more dynamic expression. Kant holds that the senses can only serve as a trigger. *Judgment* uses certain objects to get an inner process going, dispensing with them once they have served that purpose. But this view cannot be sustained. As it expands the imagination actually dispenses with nothing. Nor is anything *Aufgehoben*. What really happens is an "epic" competition among objects. Some phenomena do a better job of stimulating the imagination. When we then seek that which is "absolutely large beyond all comparison," imagination gravitates toward the kind of constructs we find in Einstein and Hawking as witness to the intimate connection between science and the sublime. When Kant says "that is sublime in comparison with which everything else is small," he quickens desire for an object of a certain magnitude, and not for a supersensible abstraction. That is why he keeps returning to Nature with the requirement that each return provide, through the phenomena, a new and greater presentation of mind's power. That search implicates Kant in a question, big with the future: is there a sublime object that would constitute an immediate presentation of the mind in its purest form?

In answering that question section 25 offers a striking intimation of the Bomb in the first of the many necessities it will fulfill. For strictly speaking the Bomb both is and is not an object of the senses. As a release of the energy trapped in matter, it is a transformation of sensation itself. It is also, qua object, a presentation of the power of mind, as ratio, to unlock the energy stored in matter and shape that energy to its will. As such the Bomb confirms, as nothing else can, the power of mind to triumph over nature and to attest that fact purely, with no residual otherness. Everything else is small in comparison because in the Bomb nature, as manifold of sensation, has become energy unleashed in and as an "object" which *is* no more and no less than the force of mind to bend everything to its desire. The a priori desire for the Bomb achieves its first adumbration here. Because the Bomb alone resolves the contradiction that for Kant defines sublime experience: our dependency on nature for a trigger and the need to cancel this dependency by consigning nature to an irrelevancy that is only assured once nature provides, as spectacle, the proof of our superiority.

The repetition of this process shapes the progression of the text. To know our interiority we call repeatedly on Nature, in an encounter that serves that purpose in the degree to which it becomes progressively more extreme. Magnitude has made hot in us the search for extreme sensations. The quest for certitude, tweaked by the dawning sense of a supersensible power within, assures us that the object will always prove unsatisfactory. In seeing nature's unfettered power we unlock our own greater power, which will always cast a contemptuous glance back upon the object which provided the experience required for its development. The name of that glance is science as pure mathematics. Its telos comes to fruition in the Bomb. Was it nature's might or ours that awed the creator-spectators present at Alamogordo? Theological witnesses invoked theophany to describe it. Fermi tried to contain the Event within the terms of the calculus. Only Oppenheimer grasped the *alethia* then concealed/revealed[20]: it is not the power of nature, but our power that was raised to absolute status that dawn. In its sublimity the Bomb as object is the *identical subject-object* before which all other magnitudes shrink because it alone attests the power to destroy as the act whereby mind confirms its identity: splitting the atom; im/ exploding that force; finally, incinerating an entire city. All considerations shrink to indifference before this, the apotheosis of mind: "I am become death, shatterer of worlds."

VI. *The Psyche in/and History*

We are now in a position to see why this achievement marks the *end* of history for the rational subject, the only outcome capable of resolving for it the contradictions within the psyche. Kant, of course, did not bring that psyche into being. He is the *"beginning"* of the History we are here writing, however, because as a philosopher of genius he is far ahead of himself, richer in his contradictions than in his official program, and articulates with blinding clarity what he only dimly senses because he has taken pains to know his psyche only indirectly. In Kant something new comes forth. A rough beast stirring in the boredom of the eighteenth century—and its fascination with something it finds unintelligible, the sublime—here takes a "quantum" leap.[21]

In so doing it gives us an insight into how history is made at the deepest register of the psyche. Certain forces and tendencies build slowly over time and then something comes forth (a critique of judgment, a revolution, a new weapon/technology) that gives them definition, priming a future for what has been blindly struggling to be born. The collective psyche, utterly in history, dreaming transformation and deliverance from the conditions that assault it daily, attaches and fixates its buried life, and its corrosive desires to certain obsessive phenomena, such as the sublime. In doing so, it creates a *force-field* with a *through-line* that matures until it finds epiphany in the Event appropriate to it. (See Appendix A.)

This is the inestimable value of a text like Kant's. It fulfills the past and announces the birth of an idea that is big with the future.[22] Kant believes that he has brought things to a successful conclusion by adequating the supersensible power within to a purely mental and contemplative order. What he does not grasp, and cannot, is that he has actually brought into being what Hegel would call a new *form of spirit*. Kant's achievement is no less than this: irreversibly, in his text, the human psyche in depth—and from the core of its disorder—takes a fundamentally new step, undergoing a complete transformation.[23] The idea that humanity has a history—that the human is utterly determined by the historical, *sans* guarantees—derives from this proposition. Kant's text, as such, is "the beginning of terror" because it shows us how utterly we give ourselves over to history when we feel we can sieze the day and bring "requital to desire," when, that is, the grandest reach of speculation coincides with an ultimate narcissistic theophany.

For us the great value of section 25 is the clarity with which it foregrounds the contradictions that drive Kant's subtext as it moves with quasi-Hegelian rigor from the first twitch of an unintelligible but arresting dream to its installment as the idea and ideal that comes to regulate western consciousness as its *dynamic historical unconscious* and following from it the march toward the one representation that will be adequate: in Hiroshima, in a skull turned inside out, dripping liquid brain, we find the image in which we discern, in inverted form, the truth of all idealisms. Nature in Kant feeds a dream that proceeds apace to the true equation. Pure mind :: absolute death.

VII. *The Scientific Imagination: Kant as Romantic Poet*

Summary of Section 26

Kant again turns to Nature in order to learn what will take him beyond her.

1. To be pure the sublime can't be tied to natural things with a determinate purpose. We must turn instead to "crude nature" fraught with might.
2. Nature is sublime in those appearances whose intuition carry with it the idea of infinity. This experience requires, however, the inadequacy of even the greatest effort of our imagination to estimate an object's magnitude.
3. Through that failure the imagination is referred to reason and the duty to "harmonize subjectively with reason's ideas." To ability to think the infinite as a whole indicates a mental power that surpasses any standard of sense.
4. The mind feels elevated in its judgment of itself when it contemplates spectacles of crude nature without concern for their form. By abandoning itself to the imagination and, once it proves inadequate, by shifting to Reason mind is empowered through this experience, with its inner direction now assured.

Interrogation

1. There is a dialectic within the sublime register. Tracing it constitutes an aesthetic education or *Bildung*.
2. Through this process imagination discovers reference to reason as its telos.

3. This process is best illustrated through what we will shortly describe as the *Aufhebung* of the mathematical imagination: the demonstration, with Fermi's help, of its contradictions, its defining desire, and the hole it puts in the center of its world.

In section 26 the need to return to the object and then overcome it takes on a new emotional valence because a new danger has arisen. The affective register of sublime experience is now defined by the following sequence: feelings of elevation then abandonment, defeat then expansion. The inner dynamic of these shifts holds the key to what this section will reveal in deepening our insight into the psyche.

Kant's concern in section 26 is with a situation where the imagination, faced with the sublime, expands to its maximum and then sinks back into itself. This is an experience of great danger to his project, one the greater Romantic poets confront repeatedly. Though usually described in terms of blockage, what here happens amounts to a depressive crisis, marked by feelings of defeat and a collapse so profound that an abyss opens before the subject. With good reason Kant says he will not talk about this affect directly. For he can't, until he has transformed it into something else and specifically something that will yield a "liking" where "one would least expect it." Thereby depression turns into manic celebration. Blockage, which turns the subject back against itself in melancholic brooding, is transformed into that release from inner conflict that vanquishes all doubts about one's powers. But for this to happen, "crude nature" must be unleashed and embraced, all the better to triumph over it. The indirect and inestimable gain for Kant will be this: the threat that affect plunges us into a "slough of despond" will be exorcized in the joyful assurance of one's power to master internal discord through one's identification with Reason.

Attunement is again significant for Kant only insofar as it motivates a shift to the conceptual order and, specifically, to the ability to think "the infinite as a whole." Crude nature elevates us. We abandon ourselves to the thrills of that experience. But we are then defeated when imagination reaches the limits of its expansive powers and sinks back into itself, in bitter paralyzing defeat. A concept then delivers us—that of the infinite. Once that shift happens the experience we began with is conveniently consigned to the flames, for it has done its work. Nothing else of value can come from it. Magnitude is all and its addressee the mathematical imagination. There is no point in returning to the phenomena with a more Romantic or Husserlian concern for what might be uncovered through patient immersion in its disruptiveness. Kant's phenomenology of the aesthetic is, as always, abridged. Pragmatic considerations are what matters. "Beauty" for Kant can never be "the beginning of terror" because he refuses to let the aesthetic challenge conceptual controls.

We get, accordingly, the stark assertion of what we might term a transition of necessity.[24] Attunement is and must be this: the disciplining of the imagination so that it will not expand blindly, collapse into the abyss, nor implode in despair whenever its expansive efforts collapse. It must instead use the occasion to refer itself to "reason's Ideas" and the "subjective harmony" that is promised when imagination takes that direction. Such is for Kant true education through the sublime: the adequation of our faculties to one another under the dominance of reason.

What section 26 thereby produces is a great act of exorcism—through indirection. The danger vanquished is that imagination will remain immersed in sublime affects in a "wakeful anguish of soul" made ripe by melancholy. And, as Kant fears, at the expense of "ethics," since sublimity here moves in a realm where self-abandonment is elevating; where exceeding limits is a powerful attraction even when the abyss threatens; where traumatic collapse attunes us to the true terms of our inwardness. Depression here presents its credentials as the primary agent of cognition. Rationality in turn reveals itself as mania disguised as mathematics in the displacement required to assure its triumph over inner doubts and fears. For Kant all depressive dangers must be exorcized before they gain a hold over the subject. Otherwise a radically different *Bildung* will commence: a movement of self-reference in which sublime affects burst inward, inaugurating a drama that does not bend itself to reason's operations or ideals. To sever that possibility Kant requires that the imagination educate itself by finding in its inadequacy the call to harmonize itself through reference to a greater power. That connection enables Kant to close the hermeneutic circle that "crude nature" opened by making the return to Nature produce a recognition of its "smallness." The circle ends by canceling what inaugurated it. The motive dominating the fascination with nature thereby reveals itself: nature is prized in its magnificence only so that its smallness when compared to reason can be established. A world that might otherwise distract us from the designs of reason bows before it.

But there is more to the grandeur of reason than meets a purely contemplative eye. The desire that is reason—such is Kant's abiding concern. But his discourse is littered with all he cannot let himself know about reason, especially as regards the two moments that shape the dynamic enacted in mind's relationship to nature: (1) the excessiveness required of the experiences needed to attune us to reason's ideals and (2) the manic nature of the acts required to gain from such experiences the rationalizing results required. Those two moments reveal that reason's relationship to the object is far from a cognitive affair. A better analogue is Melanie Klein's *manic triad,* that is, the feelings of triumph, contempt, and dismissal that ensue when depressive anxiety over a threat in our inner world is overcome.[25] Rage acted out as manic feast then cleanses the psyche of everything that troubles it. I will return to this connection shortly. What I want to do here is suggest the applicability of such categories to the ratio by concluding the interrogation of section 26 with another preview of coming attractions. In its closing lines Kant offers us a new and deeper intimation of the Bomb. The final result of sublime experience is this. Nature shrinks to insignificance and becomes the vanishing term in what is now established as the proper relationship. The boundless reaches of the imagination, finding in the ideas of reason their proper object, "crave" a way to "provide an exhibition adequate to them." What better way than by making that which is already "vanishingly small" become nothing but a pure expression of reason? Such a presentation would assure mind of its absolute status, in and through an absolute triumph over otherness.

VIII. Reason and the Bomb

A. The Collective Subject of History and the Scientific Imagination

Every transformation of affect into something else is a sacrifice and re-education of the imagination; an instruction in imagination's internal limitations and of the frustrations, even the abyss, to which it is doomed if, persisting in reliance on its own powers, it resists reference to reason. Reason, however, also needs imagination and is affected by it. Without imagination's aid certain images would never have the power to move us as they do. Such is the office of the imagination. The imagination is the faculty through which affects are bound to images, thereby giving phenomena a libidinal charge. (Chapter 6 takes up this idea in a context freed of the ratio.) Reason requires imagination to bind desires to imaged condensations of energy that compel allegiance. It must enlist imagination in its service by offering it "ideas" so that imagination will fashion these ideas into images that will arrest, bind, and quicken reason's energies. Imagination thereby offers the necessary reassurance that binds us to the supersensible through a craving for the seemingly "impossible"—a presentation to the senses of reason's ideals. Reason and imagination serve one another because for Kant they are opposite and complementary sides of the same desire.

In offering the only representation adequate to that desire the Bomb completes the education sought by both "faculties." In it imagination finds the visceral and ocular proof of what reason promised when it first offered itself as the solution to the imagination's inadequacies. Images that have fired imagination since it began its re-education through reason are here realized in an "object" imagination cannot go beyond: a spectacle to which it must say "stay thou art so fair" because the image here realizes every desire for expansion and aggrandizement while simultaneously exorcizing any memory of an inner abyss. The abyss becomes instead all that we confidently place forever beneath us, at ground-zero, in testimony to an imagination that has now found something truly "commensurate with our capacity for wonder."[26] Simultaneously, Reason here knows itself in a *coincidence* that gives it certitude and confirms its absolute status in an "object" beyond which it too cannot go and to which it must say "stay thou art so fair" in endless contemplation, delight, and unending awe. Or, to put it in concrete terms, since every desire finds its proper pleasure in the image that triggers its orgasm, the Bomb is that object in the presence of which reason necessarily cums.

The purpose of sublime education for Kant is to assure the subjective harmony of imagination and reason. That goal requires for its attainment a direct presentation of reason's ideas. Only thereby does imagination gain the assurance it has made the right move in re-educating itself by referring itself to Reason. And only thereby is Reason assured that everything constituting the "subjectivity of the subject" attains fulfillment in a condition that knows itself both as pure mind and as the force of a desire. Contra Kant, the harmony achieved here is not one of contrast, but of identity. Reason and imagination have one desire which finds in the Bomb that realization in which its two forms become one: pure mind as pure power unbound and as imagination awed by itself in a spectacle that is, in principle, unsurpassable. In the Bomb all the psychological conflicts and energies invested in our sublime education are *Aufgehoben:* canceled, preserved, and uplifted.

As such the Bomb fulfilled a collective fantasy in a way that bound the many "dispersed" subjectivities gathered at Almagorado into a unity, a single psyche welded by the object to a *project* capable of forging a single will.[27] If, later, some of those participants would describe the Manhattan Project as "the devil's work," that fine afterthought was only possible after science here gave forth another secret: that the purity of mathematics has an intimate connection with the persistence of certain infantile fixations. One witness, in fact, brought that knowledge to the terms of immediate experience. Such is the *Da-sein* of Enrico Fermi and his place in the story.[28]

B. The Triumph of Mathematics

Though Kant is deliberately ambiguous about it, the mathematical and dynamic sublime are not simply different but stand in a necessary dialectical relationship. The best way to underscore this is by articulating the contradictions in the mathematical sublime as they come out in the moment of their greatest celebration. Such is the curious position of Enrico Fermi in the *joranda del muerto.* If the mathematical imagination was defeated (as Kant argues) in its earlier "experience" of the sublime, it makes a stunning recovery at Alamogordo. There its priest, Fermi, turns a speculative bet and a mordant joke into a sublime act of sorts as he calculates, from its wind velocity measured by scraps of paper, the force of the Bomb in order to "judge" the remote possibility that its detonation will incinerate the atmosphere, destroying life on the planet.[29] The answer my friends is blowing in the wind: and Fermi is too fascinated with calculating that fact to look up at gaudier spectacles. Mathematical calculation here triumphs as a way both of seeing and not seeing the truth of the sublime spectacle; as a way of preserving scientific objectivity in the face of an object that has every other witness trembling in religious awe.

But calculus is here also caught in a paradox. Fermi knows that the joke has but one punch line, that the bets he takes are all graveyard humor, and that his "nuclear fear" is itself simulated. Fermi can play-act nuclear catastrophe in detachment because he knows that the planet is not about to be destroyed. He is deadly intent, however, on one thing: the effort to sustain a way of knowing and living that is here challenged by that which in fulfilling it also annihilates it. For calculating the chances for mass death, one brings to conclusion (without *Aufhebung*) the mystique that was invested in mathematics from the moment it became the center of our culture. In the Bomb, calculation receives a new object and a new historical task. The Bomb is significant insofar as it produces data that enable us to calculate the possibilities of our destruction. Blanchot's imagination of disaster here finds its mathematical realization. Though he can't know it, because he remains the purblind positivist forever hiding his psyche behind his slide rule, Fermi's joke participates in Oppenheimer's "mystical" consciousness of Death's dominion and weds Fermi to his eloquent precursor in historiography, Henry Adams, who said this: "No honest historian can take part with—or against—the forces he has to study. To him, even the extinction of the human race should merely be a fact to be grouped with other vital statistics."[30] Desperately clinging to objectivity and detachment, the scientist finds in the Bomb his true vocation: to imagine disaster unmoved and to find in that condition the self-reification of the scientific psyche. The magnitudes measured by an imagination that expands with the Bomb are the calculation of mind as death-work. Mind's innermost power is here presented in the ability that defines it—the ability to annihilate. In Fermi mind as measure of all things measures itself as the freedom to calculate the extent to which pure mind, realizing itself purely, breeds global death. Calculation here experiences its bad faith, which it incorrectly considers its superior irony. Fermi does not realize it, but the joke is on him. The secret is here given out. Calculation finds in "the end of the world" the only sublime object adequate to it. Dr. Strangelove is born. In fact, Fermi has a double, a brother, who has already leapt beyond Incarnation to Parousia. Edward Teller, back at the base, a sulking Achilleus, is busy this dawn with new calculations and a new necessity. With a mind of winter he foresees a really big bang in a vision that leaps beyond the still unravaged landscapes of Hiroshima and Nagasaki to something truly remarkable—the H-bomb, stars wars, nuclear winter[31]. Such are the "objects" upon which the sublime imagination—in its pure mathematical employment—now plays in calculations that expand across the entire visible world, with consequences extending in "half-life" beyond the bounds of recorded time. Death will not stay put. It says NO to every attempt to limit it. It has already cast, as its reciprocative rejoinder, a contemptuous laugh at Faust's dream of an agrarian community. Just try growing something in fields seeded by Edward Teller's imagination.

C. Toward the Dynamic Sublime: The Defeat of Mathematics

But Fermi's victory is also his defeat. The calculation of magnitude ends by shifting everything over to the dynamic register of the sublime. The Bomb is the *Aufhebung*—by reason—of the affective structure that is the throughline of section 26. What is elevated in the Bomb is our own rising up, free of earth, in an ascent of power lacking all restrictions. That is why the Bomb provides an "object" irresistible to the imagination. We needs must *abandon* ourselves to this phenomenon. The defeat of the mathematical employment of the imagination produces an irresistible rush toward the object. The power to calculate now moves wholly within the dynamic register of our inwardness, toward a self-knowledge that expands indefinitely because it is ourselves expanding as pure mind unbound. In a speculative leap, Oppenheimer provides Fermi with the words he too seeks for the new mathematics: "Now I am become Death, shatterer of Worlds." The only *Heimat* now is expressionistic, a mass of energy expanding in tongues of fire before what can only momentarily block a staggered imagination—in the deferral/delay of ethical nostalgia—before it too leaps to be one with its creation: "Death, shatterer of worlds."

Thanks to this development, we can now see why aesthetic education is so dangerous. It is *Bildung* and the self-determination of desire through that agon wherein the psyche gives determination to its being. That is why the determination of a priori necessity, however fantasmatic, is also the binding of a will, a process in which the "logic" and teleology of the one fulfills all that is Unconscious—avid and atavisic—in the other.[32] When we find ourselves truly bound in our feelings by our reasons, attuned by affects to ideas and ideals that are apodictic, we find ourselves at the other end of the convenient belief that emotion is irrelevant, no more than a discharge phenomenon. Feeling here is binding because *desire* is a force that proceeds, in rigorous dialectical movement, toward creations that satisfy the innermost demands of Reason. Feeling is the essence of what we are. Affective agons as aesthetic education produce the deepest determinations.

Which is why a reply to Kant and the Bomb must be forged not in the "cleansing power" of humanistic reflections, but in the crucible of those turbulent affects that for Kant harmonize imagination with a rationality that leads ineluctably to the Bomb. To reverse that telos we must dive back into the fire that refines. This is the task of a cultural criticism that would bind philosophic reflection to the necessity of deracination.[33]

In wrestling with the sublime, Kant formulates a priori necessities that click only when the Bomb exists. Agents who witness that moment provide, in turn, the commentary that enables us to know Kant in the light of the desire that informs the dynamic unconscious that directs Western history. The dialectic of that history reveals the a priori in a new light. The a priori is not pure mind knowing itself purely but the purest manifestation of desire in its effort to invest experience with *guarantees* that assure the coming to pass in history of everything reason refuses to know about itself. The a priori is psyche become pure mind so that it won't know the desires that shape the substantializing self-image it seeks. At base the a priori is this: the effort to assure that certain things must happen and that others cannot, the effort to give history a "goal" and to exorcize or limit contingency.

IX. The Imagination's Re-education: Reason as Sublime Self-Reference

Summary of Section 27

Section 27 enacts the self-transformation that brings the aesthetic education of the ratio to completion.

1. The concept of respect (*Achtung*) introduced. Its function: to provide the key transition. In reaching its limits the imagination finds its vocation: to make itself adequate to reason's ideas.
2. An object of nature is given "respect" because it enables us to intuit the superiority of our cognitive abilities and our rational vocation over the power and appeal of sensibility.
3. We are thereby positioned to consider a new affective complex: that sublime experience in which the mind, in agitation, undergoes a rapid alteration of repulsion and attraction toward one and the same object.
4. This experience carries two distinct affective charges.
   (a) Phenomena excessive to the imagination leave it anguished before "an abyss in which the imagination is afraid to lose itself."
   (b) As attunement to the supersensible, however, that experience is not excessive. On the contrary, it "conforms to reason's law by

giving rise to such striving by the imagination." Imagination's defeat thus establishes its new and proper direction.

5. In an ensuing dialectic of contradictory affects, imagination and reason as mental powers become "harmonious by virtue of their contrast."

6. The sublime is thereby redefined as a feeling of displeasure "about our aesthetic power of judging," which becomes "purposive," once that inability uncovers a greater power within us.

Interrogation

1. Respect (*Achtung*) is the principle that structures aesthetic education. That education is for Kant the movement of the "soul" toward its proper end—that self-reference which establishes the harmonious relationship of its powers.

2. Such education is an inward process: (a) of being affected by oneself, at the deepest inner register, and (b) then reworking that experience so that inner discord becomes inner harmony in an identity that adequates the subject to its supersensible powers.

3. For Kant, the "subjectivity of the subject" is the movement from affective discord to harmony, unity, and the overcoming of inner turmoil. Such is the virtue of sublime judgment: through it we attain an inner condition in which our mental powers become "harmonious by virtue of their contrast."

A. Achtung/Respect

With respect (*Achtung*) Kant introduces the concept necessary to his purpose, which is no less than the transformation of imagination itself. We are at the final turning point in the discourse. It is a moment as dense with suspicion of art as anything in Plato—and with similar results. Aesthetic education for Kant turns on respect. But respect is not itself an aesthetic principle, but one determined by a principle outside the aesthetic. Rather than attempt an immanent understanding of aesthetic affect, Kant seeks a principle capable of arresting and re-shaping aesthetic dynamisms.

It is a watershed moment for Kant's effort to wrest inwardness from the aesthetic and give it over to reason. One direction of experience is exorcized and another assured. Respect is this process: of giving a law to oneself and thereby becoming a law for oneself. The argument turns on the central issue that structures the entire inquiry. To preserve the unity of experience and the harmony of the faculties the shift from the aesthetic imagination to reason must be grounded within the very terms of subject's self-reference. If aesthetic education is the inward process of being *affected by and within oneself,* that process must for Kant produce the *feeling* that one has a supersensible power within. Moreover, that identification must be so total and binding that it harmonizes everything within the subject. The resultant inner harmony constitutes both the fullest realization of aesthetic education and the step beyond it, the development whereby the "faculty" of imagination fulfills itself by making reason and its ideals our supreme objects. All affects and affective energies must be poured into this act. Affect must become reason, leaving no residue. That is the structure which for Kant constitutes what we may term the sublime act: that is, the inner transformation whereby subject attains a rational self-identity that orders everything in the mind to its proper end. Kantian *Bildung* is a re-education and transformation of the imagination. The end result constitutes another chapter in a long Platonic through-line—that of *moralism* in the face of art. The difference, however, is that in Kant's subtler, solider Platonism, art is co-opted rather than banished.

B. Agitation

But in moving to his goal Kant sets loose much that he cannot contain. And that is the text most worth having, if we are to bend reason back against that which it cannot contain. Respect is indeed *Achtung* because it attunes the imagination to a new dream, an abiding fantasy. If imagination is to attain respect—and thereby become a law for itself—it must refer itself to reason's ideas. But how can it do so immanently except by hollowing out a space within itself for a sublime presentation that would confirm that supersensible end? That is, a sublime sensation that would teach us that there is a power above and beyond nature, which we can love (Wordsworth notwithstanding) in a way greater than we ever loved nature, by focusing all of our energies toward providing whatever that principle needs in order to confirm its absolute status.

To get at what's stirring in the subtext of this remarkable development we must carefully immerse ourselves in the agitation that drives it. If movement toward imagination's proper employment is one strand of the discourse, of equal importance is another direction that must be exorcized. *Agitation* in an affective movement of attraction and repulsion toward phenomena excessive to imagination that opens up an abyss within the subject. Affect here engages no less than the threat of psychic dissolution. Kant tries to cast the experience in quasiperceptual terms but what agitation introduces is the possibility of madness—of sublime phenomena attuning us to places in our inwardness that we dare not enter, places where we brood on meaninglessness and consider the absence of grounds. In that realm the psyche is not anchored in ideas and mental concepts but is tied to affects that Sartre will later describe in terms of nihilation, a negativity that feeds on the power of doubt, anxiety, and dread to put us in touch with our inner-most concerns. Terror is attractive and repulsive because it tells us that our inner world is one where terror already has a local habitation and a name. When the abyss yawns, the *crypt* is what beckons and with it the imperative that self-knowledge descend to the most hidden places of an inner world that has nothing to do with rationality. Faced with that prospect, Kant must turn affects into concepts all the better to displace the psychic conflicts they activate. Such is for him our true debt to nature. Thanks to external nature we make contact with the violence of a "nature" within us that we must master.

Kant's way of doing so, however, reveals reason's rootedness in repression. Faced with primary affects, reason rises up offering the imagination harmony through an intellectualization that provides the defenses needed to create an ego-identity and ego ideal powerful enough to make those existentializing, nihilating affects that create the possibility of knowing ourselves and taking action within become matters of repulsion motivating nothing but anxious flight. The achievement of section 27 for Kant lies in this transformation, whereby reason cleanses the psyche of disruption, offering it a way to master phenomena terrifying in their otherness. Reason reads the "abyss" in horror. Imagination then bows before that reading. But what if imagination spoke back presenting reason with a different picture of itself?

C. Reason as Narcissistic Mania

Agitation directs us inward. Mania as defense arises as the only way to reverse that movement through a grandiose expansion outward in search of mirrors to sustain a narcissism made secure through the voiding of inner doubts and fears. In so doing mania brings in its train one of the richest intimations of the Bomb and the problems it will solve. Reason is "intuitable" through imagination's collapse, but the resulting situation is unsatisfactory to both. Reason lacks a presentation that would confirm the supersensible power that has been attributed to it. Yet until that is achieved, imagination harbors doubts and seeds of regression that will keep cropping up until reason presents its credentials in a way the imagination finds compelling. Moreover, since each faculty supplies what the other lacks, what is needed is a presentation that replaces Kant's false infinite, or what Hegel calls a merely additive synthesis, with one that speaks, of necessity, in thunder. $E=MC^2$. Such a formula is sublime because it unlocks nature's secrets as goad to our power, thereby establishing the possibility of attaining precisely that absolute coincidence of the two forces that will satisfy the demands of Kantian reason: nature as force and the force of mind joined in an object-spectacle, which constitutes the purest and deepest auto-affection. The Bomb alone fulfills this demand because in it reason is intuitable directly and absolutely since it is itself the "object" of the sensation here intuited. In the Bomb the self-identity reason offers is confirmed in a narcissism with only itself for mirror. The joy, indeed the *jouissance,* in that attainment is of necessity one with the mania unleashed as desire for its expression: the obliteration of any opposition to that supreme power. In its ordinary employment the imagination is a subjectivity blocked and defeated by otherness. In the Bomb, however, there is no otherness—only boundless self-expression. The only thing exceeding imagination here is reason, but reason present as the highest and purest manifestation of imagination's desires. For what reason offers here is *auto-affection become the identical subject-object of History.*

Irreversible self-determination: such is the lure—and the danger—of aesthetic education. In the Bomb one through-line of that process is finalized, the one defining a subjectivity wedded to the ratio. In the Bomb the fetishized fixation on which narcissism depends finds the objective correlative of its mania mirrored in a triumphant banishment of all otherness. After 1945 it is possible to ask Immanuel Kant a question that can no longer be answered by invoking the old humanistic pieties: what is our supersensible education now that the Bomb has become the sublime object?

One often hears the call for a historicization of aesthetic categories. Bestowing that honor on Kant enables us to re-read Oppenheimer's allusion to the *Bhagavad Gita* as neither humanistic warning nor mystical obfuscation, but as an uncanny revelation of the actual psychic register Oppenheimer speaks from in appropriating the lesson Arunja learns from Vishnu—the irrelevance of the dead, the impertinence of the body count. What Oppenheimer whispers to us in this his Heideggerian "Letter on Humanism" is this: at the deepest register man is a being who wills death and who finds in death the power that regulates the psyche from within.[34] Death is that sublime power that resolves the inner disorders we refuse to confront as well as the strange attractor that draws us to the one object that proves irresistible. "Now I am become Death, shatterer of Worlds." Harry Truman, eschewing Eastern thought, troped Oppenheimer when, hearing the glad tidings from Alamogordo, he proclaimed "this is the greatest day since the creation."[35] He too did not know the extent to which he was right. After Day One, there are only two directions for humanity: toward completion of history's new telos or its reversal through a new "labor of the negative." The latter possiblity, however, would require an imagination led back, contra Kant, to that inner agitation that is banished in the rush of ascent to the Bomb. Aesthetic education would then begin with images of another order, one's found at ground-zero, by an Orphic imagination.

X. *The Dynamic Sublime and the Inner World*

A. *From Unspeakable Horror to Absolute Mastery*

For Kant, section 27 is but a dress rehearsal for the titanic battle with the dynamic sublime that is waged in section 28.

Summary of Section 28

1. The dynamic sublime is nature seen "as a might that" "has no dominance over us."
2. But that is so only if a necessary condition is attained. Confronted with the dynamic sublime "our ability to resist becomes an insignificant trifle." If we view it from "a safe place," however, we discover a sublimity within ourselves: our ability to triumph over any force outside us that threatens our dissolution. This is the key transition in Kant's inquiry.
3. For the immensity of natural forces is nothing to the power of the mind. The experience that threatens our humanity thus yields its greatest confirmation. The sublime is valuable to our education because it saves us from being degraded by forces beyond our control. We thereby discover our true identity: the sublimity of a moral vocation that elevates us above "nature" in all its forms.
4. We thus attain what has been the goal of the entire investigation. We become conscious of our superiority to "nature within us." External nature recedes to the background. The discourse can now shift to the problem of mastering "nature within." The ethical purpose that has shaped the discourse from the beginning comes to the fore.

Interrogation

1. The dynamic sublime activates for Kant a quest that ends with the attainment of a sublime moral character. Such is the process and end of aesthetic education.
2. Three key moments structure this argument.
   (a) The dynamic sublime, like the force of "nature" within us, annihilates the subject. Unless one views it from a safe place.
   (b) The sublime in nature provides us with the opportunity to attain that distance; to practice the operations whereby we may master inner discords.
   (c) Sublime experience thus produces a transference of energy: nature's destructive might becomes our inner might to subdue

the "nature" within us. Subjectivity thereby attains the self-reference that will enable it to bend everything within to the force of a rational, moral will.

In its development section 28 splits in half and that circumstance reveals what actually happens within it: the dynamic sublime experienced in its inherent turbulence motivates, as countermovement, the grand flight of reason required to transform it. After many detours, the dynamic sublime has finally taken center stage. In doing so, it produces a crisis that takes us deeper into the Kantian psyche than heretofore. Kant reverts to the most primitive defense mechanism, splitting, as the only way to get a handle on the psychodynamics unleashed by the dynamic sublime. The section moves in a circle, however, and with its completion psychoanalytic conflicts that have structured Kant's discourse from the beginning become apparent. Structure is never innocent; here it becomes revelation. By the end of the section, the desires and conflicts underlying Kant's thought emerge with a clarity that mandates a psychoanalytic reinterpretation of every term and referent used in sections 23–27. We've reached the secret that drives the entire discourse. The actual referent of the term "nature" is the condition of our inner world. That is Kant's true subject. "Nature" from the beginning has been significant merely as a sign of something within that Kant is finally ready to confront because he thinks he now has a way to master it.

The key dialectical connection is stated in the last paragraph of the section. Now that he is ready to address its deeper meaning, Kant reminds us of something he was at pains to establish earlier. "Hence sublimity is contained not in any thing of nature, but only in our mind, insofar as we can become conscious of our superiority to nature within us, and thereby also to nature outside us (as far as it influences us)."[36] The wheel has come full circle. Psychologically, nature has always meant two things in Kant's text. (1) As "externality" it is significant insofar as it stimulates our awareness of an inner condition. (2) That condition is the reality we keep running up against, brooding upon, and striving to master in our experience of the "sublime." *The sublime in nature attunes us to the conflicts that define our inner world.* "Nature" is that otherness within the psyche that we have not yet, and perhaps cannot master.

From the beginning there has been a strong anthropomorphic dimension to Kant's descriptions of the sublime. Here that dimension becomes explicit in the depiction of what amounts to two agents, one an overpowering and malevolent figure (a truly "moralistic" superego), the other a frightened creature, cowering in submission (an abjectly dependent child). Dominance is the stake of the agon that the dynamic sublime engages and as in Hegel's dialectic of master-slave with surprising results. Kant's effort (like Hegel's) is to invert the initial relationship and prove that nature, however powerful, has no dominance over us. That drama begins, however, with a founding trauma: a situation of total dependence on a dominant power that threatens the subject with extinction. That condition carries as its innermost meaning the suspicion that soul-murder is the desire that animates the other's relationship to us. We find at last what in sublime nature frightens and fascinates us: our own psychic annihilation should a rage that has us as its object be unleashed.

Abjection is the defining condition of the inner world that is activated by the dynamic sublime. Nature in the sublime provides the image that triggers in us a memory that we project back onto nature in a desperate effort to assure ourselves that we have mastered an inner world that is ruled by a force that sets us at nought. In the sublime we face again the deepest horror: our inner world is ruled by a power that demands our destruction and not by development to an autonomous ego-identity. In the dynamic sublime nature at white heat, red in tooth and claw, shatters defenses and bites directly into the buried psyche, reawakening its founding terror. The violent images that arrest us in the dynamic sublime indicate a truth beyond Artaud's wildest dreams. For when all that the psyche has crypted is revived, the force that presides at that register rages in primitive affects unleashed in an aggression that has the psyche as its object.

No wonder resistance becomes the key term in the first stage of the unfolding drama. This time, however, Kant can't shift everything onto a plane of conceptual defenses and controls. Affect weighs too heavily. Intermediate moves immanent within that register are required. Opposing affects must be created and marshalled as a first line of defense. For the first time in Kant, rationalistic mediation gives way to dramatic self-mediation. Kant will finally attempt an agon that moves solely within the medium of affect. To resist psychic unraveling he must establish a countervailing force within the order of affect itself. For Kant, however, affective self-mediation is equivalent to bending everything in a moral direction. In doing so the author of the ethic of pure duty gives us the true genealogy of morals. That dubious ascent begins once the force threatening destruction is characterized as "evil." Anxiety is thereby transformed into a moralizing fear: that we lack the power to resist "evil." Moralizing then structures the subsequent discourse, but without exorcizing the psychological subtext that will undercut it. This contradiction is, in fact, what ethics will here reveal about itself.[37]

In making ourselves "good" subjects we make ourselves beings unworthy of destruction. That transformation also requires the resources of rhetoric, since we must "persuade" a tough audience. The true goal in remaking ourselves is to tame the power that threatens us by tapping its conscience. To do so we create, within ourselves, a new agency, one that, recognizing our virtue, promises protection. We thereby create the illusion that the threatening force has been softened and then transformed into a voice that warmly supports the good intentions of the nascent ego. The superego as ego-ideal has been created. So ends the founding self-mediation in the genealogy of an ethical ratio.

By staging this internal drama, the psyche has taken the action within required to create the space needed to assert control over affect. The necessary act follows—the attempt to affect a complete reversal of the psyche's initial condition. Kant asserts repeatedly that we can only judge the sublime, and experience its proper "pleasure," if we view things from "a safe place." But in psyche, as opposed to mind, the safe place doesn't exist a priori. It has to be invented, and with it the most revealing picture of the genesis of what we now call the "ego." It is a difficult birth to a dubious and troubled function. The problem of the ego is one of generating a transformation from impotence to power within affect itself, through an agon immanent to that register. But Kant is unable to sustain such an agon. We get instead a displacement toward concepts through a use of the defense mechanism known as splitting. Ego and inner world divide in an unbridgeable rift, thus establishing this condition as the true "identity" of the ego. The ego is the effort to repress the conflicts in the psyche from which it derives. But while displacement and intellectualization offer a handle, the ego's work is far from done. The continuing pressure of inner conflicts requires a further battle. In that struggle moralizing interpretations do yeoman service by splitting the psyche's original trauma into a longed-for reification—the opposition of the ego to the drives. We have become creatures full of that nagging otherness we term instincts. This is the repressed truth about ego and "ego development" that emerges from Kant's immanent account of its origin.

The first great arc of the inner experience that structures Kant's text here attains completion. To summarize: Nature's destructive power reawakens in us those primitive affects that return us to a condition of nameless dread and catastrophic anxiety. To flee this state we create, through splitting, new affects and new experiences—evil, sin, and guilt. Intellectualizing activity then provides the ethical safe haven from which we "view" that situation. Thus empowered we proceed to the underlying necessity: a complete reversal of our condition through the submission of inner destructiveness to intellectual domination. The educational purpose of our studying the dynamic sublime is the opportunity it offers to affect this process; to empower ourselves by giving us, at one remove, an experience of power over the internal condition that renders us powerless.

An exorcism is in progress, but it has only begun for we remain largely strangers to our inner world. That is why Kant's "response" to the dynamic sublime in nature necessarily generates double talk. Kant claims to consider "might" directly; at the same time he insists on the need for operating from a "safe place." The result is a twofold distancing from the psychological reality: (1) In sublime nature we project and externalize inner trauma. (2) Viewing the psyche thus "embodied" from a safe place offers the further protection needed to confront that reality. It is as if the Medusa can only be slain after two shields are in place. The ensuing battle takes this form: the destructive might of a "nature" within versus the power of mind to constitute an identity of an entirely different order.

In terms of affect, however, a description of the structure of this experience yields a different and far more complex picture. Fear before "might" triggers the re-awakening of our earliest and deepest anxieties. Need for protection from that realm requires the flight into ideas. Distance then transforms "fascination" with the sublime into the "dream" of attaining dominance over it. The ego has attained its mission. Impotence has generated a *Wille-zur-Macht* avid for transcendance. Which is why the true issue abides. For whenever the dynamic sublime rises up, it rips through all the defenses, returning the psyche to its original, founding condition. Such is the actual condition of the ego: it moves in a circle, defined by conflicts it has not and cannot overcome. Whenever in experience the sublime intrudes, defenses collapse. Humpty Dumpty is then put back together again, but only to await, in eternal vigilance and denial, the next occasion when traumatic reality will again shatter its certitudes. The operations that shape Kant's discourse from within generate a transformation of affects into concepts, psyche into mind, experience into a knowledge-affair. With the moralizing interpretation of sublime experience, the great insaturation has been accomplished. The "safe place" of displacement has become the fortress of the soul's fortitude.

There are two noteworthy things about this achievement. First, the change does not occur within affect but by a shift to its moral re-interpretation. Second, that move conceals an act of despair and resentment: the inability to engage an agon of affect begets a world rank with moral judgment. That condition derives from a single cause. What Kant fears is feeling. He is comfortable with affects only after he has converted them into ethical opportunities. Prior to that, affect is disruptive, a source of anxiety and a threat to psychic stability. It is, for Kant, a passivity of the subject lacking the possibility of an immanent dialectic, mere sufferance void of any possibility of self-overcoming. Only with the development of the ego-ratio can Kant view feelings from the necessary distance. That move defines the ego's essence. The ego is that defensive structure that deadens affect in order to shift all of our energies to the moral interpretation of experience. In their vigorous opposition to psychological reality, the ego and morality are simultaneous developments that reinforce one another. Quite properly the "safe place" Kant has hollowed out for us is identified with "the soul's fortitude." Moral character replaces psychic integrity in a dualism whereby every affect beyond control is labeled evil.

That is why when ego comes incipient superego cannot be far behind and with it an increased hostility to those inner conflicts that one must dominate since one is unable to relate to them in any other way. Sublime education turns on such ironies. Inner fortitude, the "ability to resist" is defined by the need to be a match for "nature's" power. But no dialectic of experience is possible. Instead, Kant asserts the necessity for a *total reversal* of any dependence. We crave a situation in which "nature" will submit totally to our power; a situation in which the natural has no existence except as an occasion for the manifestation of our omnipotent needs. Kant identifies this development with our moral genesis, but its real source is our narcissism, ripened by its founding motive. Inner powerlessness is always rotten with one perfection—grandosity as the blank check that sucks everything in the world into mirroring relations that shatter whenever a hint of otherness appears. The reversal whereby Kant confers stability on the ego derives from narcissism's founding condition: that of absolute fear before the omnipotent other. The ego turns the tables by seeking omnipotence through the imposition of a moralizing will on everything emotionally disruptive. And true to the infantile omnipotence from which it derives, nothing compares in feeding frenzy to the moral interpretation of the world. Nor to the festival of cruelty it will require to complete its formation. Opposition to the "natural" is the essence of that need. Competition and hostility necessarily structure the relationship to nature even in those moments when Kant calmly assures us that "nature" is the unessential term, the weaker force. Mastery is then capped by a gesture of contempt toward the defeated term. "Superiority over nature . . . keeps the humanity in our person from being degraded." The manic triad, accordingly, structures what actually goes on in section 28. Splitting followed by flight into a hyperconsciousness releases one from the burden of inner anxieties, an act followed by the need to proclaim one's superiority through a contemptuous dismissal of the opponent. Ego defenses always require such reinforcing superfluities. Kantian mania presents itself in fairly abstract terms, but the abstractions drip with moralistic and affective connotations in order to solidify a dualism that drives opposed terms to a point of maximum distance. Thereby the most primitive defense mechanisms achieve fruition by reifying a moralizing framework of interpretation that deprives experience of affective complexity in order to reinforce an internal paralysis.

The best evidence of how this framework structures experience is in fact provided by the split structure of the section. Section 28 divides in half: the first half offering a description of the dynamic sublime; the second a series of progressively more abstract statements about those virtues (including those of the warrior and the worshipper) that assure us of our humanity through our triumph over "nature." The first half of the section is full of tension, of charged affects; the second a rhetoric of pieties, postures, and moralistic commonplaces. It would be nice if we could say there was no connection between the two halves. But the truth of the matter is that form here is idea and perfectly mirrors the split psyche Kant constructs in order to escape the claims of the inner world.

B. Agonistic Subjectivity

We pause over what for Kant could be no more than an irrelevant aside. There is another way to react to the inner world pictured here, one that finds in an agon of affect the possibility of a dialectic that will recover within the realm of unbound and "chaotic" forces the creative dynamics of what I will term the *élan conatus*. I use this term to signify a "libidinous" energy that is bound to those affects that define and situate the subject as who/why. When one shifts from the ratio to this register, a dramatic way of relating to psyche's founding condition emerges: for whenever cruelty attempts soul-murder, it generates, in its wake, the affective turbulence of a defiance bound to sufferance. In this agon no dualism avails. "Spirit" here is *at issue to itself dialectically in an inwardness that is defined agonistically*. The domineering presence of a malevolent power bent on soul-murder and the affirmation in the teeth of that cruelty of subject as who/why makes turbulent affect the alembic whereby subject engages a relationship to its deepest inner conflicts. Subject as who/why is the refusal of the other's judgment—and the repression of that refusal. Sublime experience reopens this realm to the possibility of agonistic reversal. The ego is defined by its opposition to this process. It does so by installing itself, like Pandora, atop the crypt in which primary affects are buried. Moralization is the act that solidifies its reign by substituting for existentializing dialectics a dualism in which suspicion of feeling, distrust of passion, and contempt for the body begin their long march toward the ego's true goal—the deadening of affect. Thanatos is the force that reigns in those interpretive frameworks that progressively alienate us from affect so that experience can be turned into a knowledge-affair; all things submitted to the ratio, deprived of any being but the knowledge it sucks from them.

Nature thereby becomes the thing that is hated, an object of use and contemptuous disposal that must be submitted to our will. In dominating nature, subjects attain the illusion of inner dominance; in imposing our will on nature we assure ourselves we have triumphed within. Nature becomes that other we must treat with contempt—especially when she shows herself in power, sheer magnificence, radical independence, unravished splendor. Such qualities stimulate a need for competition, requiring a clear victor. And so we go forth subduing nature in order to extinguish something in ourselves we are intent on denying. Which is why co-existence is untenable. We must eradicate the spectre by squeezing every energy out of the ecosystem, leaving as testimony to our will the scorched earth at our backs as we rush to greener fields. Thanks to Kant we now know the psychological structure that must be deracinated if we are to address the ecological crisis. The death of nature derives from an inner necessity, present everywhere today in images appropriate to it. Nature for the ratio is a gigantic refuse dump—the landscape we litter with our waste products. The only thing we can give back to nature is what leaves her properly defaced, battered, fecalized. Everything that creates terror and loathing in our inner world thereby finds in nature its objective correlative—the whole earth Hiroshimaed as the final solution. Reversal of this telos is impossible within the terms of the ego-ratio, for what it cannot see in each ravished landscape is the human face mirroring back to it its true inner condition in grimace and skull-chuckle, that of a self-reference that finds Hosannah only in the advancement of destructive energies.

Nature is a historical category, submitted not only to production, as Marx shows, but to our innermost necessities. This is the great lesson Kant teaches us: nature must be overcome, annihilated, for every time it rises in beauty, terror, or simple independence the fit returns. The control we seek eludes us. When nature triumphs, the ratio shudders with the return of the repressed. That is why our rainbow must become a million golden arches streaming across the rain forest, pointing to the pot of chopped meat at the end as a fitting imaginary for the technological imperative that has now wired the globe for the only kind of communication that any longer makes "sense," one in which nothing can be said.[38]

In subsequent chapters we will take up directly the agon of affect we have here pried loose from Kant's efforts to intellectualize it. For now what is important is to see that Kant has no room for such an agon because for him everything in the realm of powerful affects must be submitted to a single judgment through the use of a single defense mechanism. *Evacuation* is the name for this defense: the attempt to deny inner conflicts by projecting them upon external representatives and objects, with full permission thereby given to vent our frustrations upon them. That is why we incessantly search for the perfect landscape, the one annealing act that will sanctify our rage. Such an act would have to be a marriage in which soul-murder as destructive *m/other* and ego as *phallic son* would find *a dream object* capable of condensing and expressing the true terms of their relationship. Or, to put it in popular terms, consider this hypothesis: if the reason boys build penises for themselves is to impress their mothers, eventually the need to evacuate the rage accumulating in the failure of that effort will require projection upon an other who in defeat will be unable to cast a Sartrean glance back at the aggressor. The m/other's destructive power would then be fully invested in the son's freedom to unleash the energy compressed in her dominance over his psyche in an act in which the son's founding paralysis would make the two one and inseparable through a total liberation of the destructiveness defining the relationship. Such is the lure of evacuation: to do unto the other, in a finalizing way, what was done unto us. It is also "the perfect incest,"[39] the act that brings everything to interpretive closure in an event where *jouissance,* evacuation, and self-reification become one.

Such was the collective, historical unconscious of a "typical" American boy at a moment of genius: the moment when, a new Adam, he named the plane that would carry a bomb named "little boy," after his mother, Enola Gay. The common man is also a poet and has his sublime moments. The only irony is this: if the *facts* did not exist, we would have to invent them, so appropriate is Paul Tibbets' action to the psychic register speeding in his obedient hands to incarnation at Hiroshima. When the time is ripe, history finds in the commonest of men the proper words. (I return to this example in the next chapter.)

But then language is a matter where not even Kant is innocent. Throughout section 28 his language reveals the affective register of his struggle with the sublime and how objective philosophic language often reveals with the greatest clarity the motives that inform it precisely when it claims to purge itself of affect. For in section 28 rhetoric takes over—and drips subtext. We are told that aesthetic education confirms our "superiority over nature" and is invaluable because it "keeps the humanity in our person from being degraded." A moralized fear thereby begets the need for a contempt that is then solidified by reminders of all the ways in which the object does not even deserve the status of an object. We, not nature, are the object of the sublime experience; our supersensible power its tenor. We therefore conclude by enacting the proper revenge on what previously seemed to have such frightening power over and within us.

What Kant thereby attains is truly miraculous: an affective transformation without a direct affective confrontation. This is also the circumstance whereby he is hoist by his own petard. What is glossed over in the march of arguments that even Kant describes as "subtle reasoning," "high-flown" and "far-fetched," is the need to suck up the affective energies that can be derived from a host of activities (ranging from the warrior to the saint) and re-invest them as rhetorical commonplaces in a hyperconsciousness that is thereby fitted with the emotions it needs to act as the censor who provides the *ego* with the auto-affection required to confirm its ability to master and regulate the psyche. Sublime education here becomes a voice that teaches and preaches. And its native eloquence is pietistic, moralistic, and (of special note) military. The intention is to fit the ego-ratio with the virtues needed for it to secure its function—that of keeping the psyche in line. Thus the praise of military virtues right next to moralistic and religious reflections on the need to prize humility above all qualities. Most revealing of all perhaps is the use of arguments suggesting, in language close to de

Sade's, the necessity of war, lest indolence toward affect corrupt the psyche's structure from within. War is indeed the appropriate metaphor for what has gone on here: the aim of the entire discussion being to fashion a warrior's will to do battle, whenever necessary, in our unending duty to dominate the nature within.

XI. Sublimity and Theology: The Superego . . . and the Bomb

War also provides the basis for the transition to theology, and through it, to the final act needed to complete the psyche that Kant fashions in sections 23–29. As capstone to our sublime education the deity now rises up, sublime in his wrath, present so that we can complete our education by attempting the sublimest act of judgment, with God that before which we are rendered "utterly impotent." Supersensible power here is no longer within us, but infinitely above us. The only transformation possible is an internalization that installs that Deity as the supreme inner voice regulating the psyche's internal structure, thereby giving final determination to the entire set of relations that have been developed in our dealings with the sublime in nature. The ego, as a defense structure vigorously opposed to the reality of everything it cannot master, here achieves as necessary reinforcement the command that keeps that identity fixed in its self-reification. Sublime experience here results, accordingly, not in the manic triad (as before) but in the construction within of a new regulatory agency.

Storms, tempests, earthquakes no longer suggest the terrifying m/other. They now represent the Deity in his might. So fathomed His wrath generates a new "mental attunement"—submission and worship in "contrite and timorous gestures and voice." No rivalry and no sense that the "supersensible power" is within intrudes on this experience. Judgment here requires "quiet contemplation," free of affect. Conforming to god's will is the only possible response: any other feeling is "reprehensible." Humility is the sole attunement, producing the right "mental" direction and activity: a "self-reprimand" that knows that only endless discipline will eradicate the defects of human nature in us. In a parody that inverts the true process of taking action within, abjection here becomes the only inner action that is any longer possible. "In his will is our peace."[40]

With this attitude in place Kant draws a striking conclusion. In realizing that our true vocation is "sublimely above nature," we internalize two regulative ideas: (1) an insight into the sublimity of that Being who arouses the deepest respect in us and (2) a recognition that our attitude toward nature—without and within—witnesses to the ability that this Power has "endowed" us with to align the structure of our psyche with His Being. In dealing with nature correctly, we participate in the Deity. The supersensible power within is now aligned to the Deity in an identification that provides the basis for all future dealings with "the sublime." As superego the Deity commands and confirms the acts we perform whenever we are confronted with the sublime. The ego now has the armor required to master anything that "nature" can throw at us as well as anything that may rise up from an inner world one has now crypted beneath an impregnable repression barrier. It is a sublime moment and thus full of the seeds of future conflict: of the future itself perhaps in a subtext pregnant with the Bomb.

What follows attempts to describe the actual relationship among the forces and agencies that make up the psyche Kant has constructed. The goal is to reveal the conflicts that persist in that psyche's finished form as they beckon toward the future that will be required to bring the underlying configuration of desire that persists as its unconscious to closure in an ultimate object. In section 28 two sublime experiences are inextricably bound to one another and then split violently apart. One is tied to the maternal object; the other to the absent Father. The first is defined by terror, engulfment, nameless dread, catastrophic anxiety. It requires triumph and annihilation. The only way to be sure of our identity is by opposing this power in a struggle to the death. The second is defined by respect, humility, obedience. We fulfill ourselves by bowing before it. The way to true and lasting identity is by making this power the internal regulator and judge of everything we do.

The maternal sublime is associated with destructive and libidinal excess, with wild desires, with energies that resist any confinement or limitation. Seen in terms of it, the ego is the structure that has its being in an effort to defend against the pressures and anxieties that maternal destructiveness creates in a psyche overwhelmed by its demands. Its effort is to develop defenses and, from them, an adapted life of conflict-free operations. Defenses function as signals alerting the ego to the need for flight; the conflict-free realm of social and ideological conventions provides the means of self-regulation whereby experience is transformed into concepts and the kind of emotions that conform to these concepts. The end result is that we become strangers to ourselves in our inner world, seeing it as a realm of impersonal forces we must repress because the ego's identity depends on establishing such a relationship to the unconscious.

The ego thereby created then finds in the paternal superego that other sublime in which it must invest itself through fealty to the power of "sublime" abstractions and ideals to provide the imperatives that compel obedience and worship. Intellectualization, the operation whereby the ego earlier attained an identity opposed to instincts and the "Id," thereby achieves the libidinal charge required for the ratio's self-reification: the father of absolute law as internal regulator and as object of a "masculine," warrior's love.

When we compare the two sublime experiences, the picture that emerges is that of a split psyche with enormous energy invested in both sides of the split—and the necessity of its maintenance. That condition is the essence and identity of the ego. Ego is the eternal battleground between the energies locked in the maternal id and the energies lodged in the paternal superego. Unbeknownst to the ego is the defining fact that those energies mirror one another in a relationship that exposes the desperation of the favored term. The "Law of the Father" is the mirror-double of the destructive m/other—bound to the same inner necessity. Superego is the murderous id regained, fulfilled in Duty as the act whereby one attains a total evacuation of psychic conflict and with it the possibility of self-mediation. "In his will is our peace." All we have to find out is what He wants? Aggressivity is the key to the answer. And the lesson it teaches is that a psyche bound to the superego is not an *Aufhebung* of inner conflict into the realm of pure ideas but a recovery in resentment of violent energies. What was sundered and repressed in the construction of the ego is now regained, with war the proper image for the attitude that such a psyche takes toward itself. The true law of the superego is this: an aggressive war to extinguish everything destructive within the self by evacuating it onto objects. Through that process an identity is forged in which mother and father join hands wedded to an inner rage that can have only two issues—implosion within or massive evacuation without. Such is the true state of the "oedipalized" child—the destructiveness of two parties, in the hatred that binds them, become the aggression that their offspring projects upon the world.

The above completes one strand of a speculation. The other involves "the death of god." It can be schematized as follows. God is the sublime object. And in Kant's official text the subject finds in God a supersensible power outside itself greater than the one within. However, that discovery violates the inner logic of the sublime, which is the overcoming of whatever appears independent. Thus, the esoteric text: God is dead :: God is risen. For God is the sublime projection of our supersensible power become the object of our own absolute reverence. God is our narcissism fulfilled, mirrored in omnipotence. Which is why identification with the superego is always followed by a liberation of aggression.

It is never enough however. Inner discord remains. A final transference is necessary to "heal" the split psyche. The ego must find a way to marry itself to the maternal, so that all the psychic energy condensed there will be invested in the "son" as the agent-who-acts. Sublime action bears this burden: to give the inner world of psychic turbulence the stamp of one's independent agency by finding a way to blow the forces that "rage" within out into the world. The destructiveness of the m/other must become the aggressivity of the son, seeking identity and *jouissance* in a deed. All other erotic possibilities must be sacrificed to destructive rage. The phallic ego can only save itself from implosion by "identifying with the aggressor." The destructive m/other thereby becomes one's own destructiveness. The result: an irresistible pleasure is now found in every opportunity to destroy. For the superego that such a psyche creates for itself is and can be nothing but the refraction of self-hatred. And since the object of hatred is one's own inner "nature," the only way an implosive turning of the subject back upon itself can be avoided is by investing one's hatred in objects. Only by inflicting pain and suffering, by breathing the spirit of punishment into all occasions, does one banish the spectre of otherness within. The innermost demand of such a psyche is to void itself of Eros. The only thing that can bind it to itself and to the world is the insatiable "pleasure" it finds in cruelty and the search for a way to give that principle sublime expression.

This is what the vaporized people of Hiroshima represent. They are everything small, contemptible, sneaky, "japanese" in the psyche. And as such they must be regarded as an indifferent mass—men, women, children, the old, young, base, excellent, and fair—merged indifferently as one. This is sublime genocide. The other is everything the psyche must treat with manic contempt in order to satisfy the imperatives of the superego. For until such an object is found and subjected to "justice" through the necessary deed, the ego remains haunted by the possibility that what it hates still remains within. Genocide is a psychological necessity for one kind of psyche. As "nuclear unconscious" that motive finds its first ghostly articulation in Kant's struggle with the sublime.

XII. Coda: Crypt

Kant ends with a final bath and a mopping up operation, providing a series of conceptual summaries on the meaning of the sublime for those who need further assurance regarding art's contribution to enlightened morality.

Summary of Section 29

1. For mind to comprehend the feeling of the sublime it must be receptive to ideas.
2. Though culture reinforces these ideas, they aren't simply conventions. They are a priori and provide the grounds in us of morality. The name for that wondrous inner presence is moral feeling.
3. Through its working, aesthetic judgment raises moral feeling from empirical psychology to the status of the a priori. Thereby aesthetic education becomes the handmaid of ethics and theology.
4. As such it plays a pivotal role in completing the critical philosophy, both morally and theologically. We now know that correct aesthetic

judgments are based on a priori principles and thus form an integral part of transcendental philosophy.

5. Aesthetic experience is thereby deprived of its dangers. The poets, wings clipped, have been let back into the republic of the enlightened.

Interrogation

A different conclusion, however, derives from the subtext. For none of the above assertions preserve aesthetic experience from within. They constitute, instead, a system of displacements that are valuable precisely because they reveal conceptualization as the pale afterthought of an overpowering experience. Rather than attend to the truly sovereign duty and immerse in the immanent logic of art, Kant transforms the aesthetic into yet another occasion for insisting on the need to give primacy to the moral interpretation of experience. His deepest need—like Plato's—is to bring the aesthetic in line with the moral by purging its deeper and darker complexities. These realities remain foreign to him because he is blind to the power of the sublime to give us a world that exceeds "reason." As a result he is even more blind to reason's crypt and the motives that drive its search to forge in history a form adequate to it. Thanks to Kant, we now know that psyche with the mask of rationality in which it conceals itself stripped away. Which brings us to our deeper task: to understand it from within. This will be the effort of chapter 4.

Four

The Psyche That Dropped the Bomb

> Then everything includes itself in power
> Power into will; will appetite
> And appetite, that universal wolf
> So seconded by will and power
> Must make perforce a universal prey
> And last eat up itself.
> > —Shakespeare, *Troilus and Cressida*

> Experience happens when the tedium of habit is ruptured by the sufferance of being.
> > —Samuel Beckett, *Proust*

> I had entered that dream-state in which you run without moving from a terror in which you cannot believe toward a safety in which you have no faith.
> > —Rosa in Faulkner's *Absalom, Absalom!*

> In order to save your life you must lose it.

OVERTURE: THE EGO AND ITS PLEASURE

A Note on Structure

The dialectical relationship of chapters 3 and 4 is the identity of perfect mirrors. Chapter 3 shows that rational, logical mediation is a lie. Chapter 4 shows what dramatistic mediation is and how its malign form is the underlying principle structuring the ego-ratio. The two chapters thus stand in a necessary connection, with the latter the dark double and ground of the former. We thereby see the superstructure and the basement in their identity. To which chapter 5 will reply by developing an agon where dramatistic self-mediation creates, from the ground up, a radically different structure of self-reference issuing in a radically different psyche.

On Method

In history collective agents find in action a way to pour the pressures of their culture into a project. Thereby a collectivity moves to the act that will give fitting expression to the desires that drive it. This is the register at which we will here present, from within, the psyche that found its "objective correlative" in the Bomb. Our goal is to articulate this Unconscious in a systematic way by beginning with the founding disorder and tracing the sequence of self-mediations that structure that psyche from within as it proceeds to the form required to resolve its conflicts.[1]

Thanks to Kant such a description of the ratio is now in order. For in Kant on the sublime the superstructure reveals its rootedness in desires and conflicts it can neither resolve nor comprehend. Another kind of analytic is required to bring it to self-knowledge, one that enters mind's inner world and attempts to know it without imposing defenses and guarantees. Such an analytic must try to get at everything the ego-ratio does not want to know about itself in order to hold up to the ego the mirror before which it shatters. The theory of **the crypt**, which I will articulate in this chapter, is an attempt to construct that analysis through a systematic reconstruction of the inner world of the ego. Since this inquiry breaks with the relationship most audiences have to the ego-ratio, a few clarifications about the argument that follows are in order. The purpose of the inquiry is to make possible a radical act. Once we see the inner world of the ego for what it is we will have no choice but to abandon the ego and begin again with another principle of self-mediation.

To motivate that effort what follows offers the ego-ratio a tragic experience of its own internal structure. Critique here aims at the very foundations of the structure that issues in the ego. The hermeneutic circle here is one in which the concepts and guarantees that the defense-ego uses to contain threats to its identity are precisely what the examination strives to expose and deracinate. The reader's "good faith" is accordingly called on in a new way. As a negative capability: the exercise of a systematic suspicion toward one's habitual principles of explanation and response sustained through the pursuit of underlying conflicts and motives that can be known and become an active part of one's self-knowledge only if one refuses to return to the guarantees. The shock of recognition here strives to activate in the reader that Nietzschean self-contempt we discussed earlier. While this is the "rhetorical" relationship that shows the deepest respect for the reader's existential possibilities, it is also the one sure to activate defenses in ways that make their operation mandatory for many audiences; even as "that which goes without saying," since the best defense is to repel a threat without letting oneself know one has done so.

Concretely, the stakes of the inquiry can be thought of along the following lines. Once we enter the crypt, the developments that are required to extinguish its founding anxieties stand forth in their true visage. We then learn all the ways in which ego development is a cover-up whereby the archaic avidities prosecute their claims in an unbroken chain. That chain reveals the actual sequence of mediations that generate and structure the ego. Seen from within the ego reveals its actual unity. It is not the movement toward mastery of internal conflicts through the achievement of a rational, conflict-free ego sphere that issues in mature social agency in a progressive community. It is, rather, the structure needed so that the culture it serves can project its disorders with the greatest assurance that the underlying anxieties will be vanquished and the darkest desires fulfilled. Description from the crypt reveals that rationality and ego development are quite different from what we assert when we celebrate reason and its ideals: that is, the bonds of love, moral development, the social process, generativity, maturation, stable object-relations, and the rhetorical universals of humanistic conversation.[2] In bringing that culture before the Bomb as the Event that fulfills the contradictions and desires that shape its inner logic, the ratio is offered a new knowledge of itself and the conditions of its pleasure. Moreover, cathartic exposure here offers neither resolution nor renewal; for, as we will see, after such knowledge there is no forgiveness and no way of going back to the world of the guarantees.[3] Deracination offers the only meaningful response.

Kant and Freud supplement one another in providing the starting point for the inquiry that follows. Kant by teaching us, against his official intentions, that defenses become concepts exist to protect avid desires so that they can be projected as ideals and imperatives charged, through their restraint, with an accumulated aggression that is either dissembled (religion, the ethic of duty) or openly announced for the world to see (the Bomb). Freud by showing that the ego is indeed a pleasure-ego with a double relationship to the detour called reality: an agency constrained to defer pleasure until a way is found, at a later time, to get pleasure in a form magnified and enriched by that delay. Time may have a wallet on its back in which it keeps alms for oblivion; it also has a monkey, a signifying ape, for whom all losses are restored when one is finally able to seize the day and fulfill the resentments bred by the self-lacerations of festering desire.

Historical time sucks energies from a psychic register that wombs itself, in sublimation, until the day when desires can finally reveal themselves in a demystified form. As in the Bomb: where the purest ego the culture has devised—objective science—attains a pleasure in which it is given to itself as the identical subject-object of a pure auto-affection; objectivity triumphant as omnipotent narcissism in unending masturbation before the one mirror that guarantees that "mirror on mirror mirrored is all the show" since here pure mind has freed itself of every restriction. Pleasure for the ego-ratio is here attained in what is truly paradise regained, since with the evacuation of aggression and of every internal restraint, the founding condition of the psyche is abrogated. As we will see, everything that the ego, as a defensive structure, exists in order to contain and deny is here released and set completely outside it. The ego's identity is here assured because everything that haunts it from within is now projected and fully externalized. *Jouissance* of necessity defines its relationship to the object, which is why subsequent statements of remorse reek of bad faith. Like all tragic agents the ego-ratio brings about the thing it fears and denies, and then recoils in utter estrangement from the recognition it thereby creates for itself. Our goal is to give it back the tragic knowledge of itself it denies. This is the drama we will now set forth. To tell that story we must remain at the sublime register, but now work totally from within its crypt, since this is the register from which the sequence of mediations that extend the founding disorder derive.[4]

Here too Kant offers us an inadvertent insight, which we may use by way of transition to the investigation proper. It comes in another reversal that turns the circle in which Kant's thought moves back against itself. Kant's aesthetic is founded in the idea that in the Beautiful we apprehend the "subject being born," the first paring off of incomparable powers.[5] What he learns only later is that in the sublime subject is *reborn* through the recognition of a deeper truth about itself. If beauty dreams harmony, the sublime returns the ego to the actual conditions of its inner world. This is the necessary dialectical connection between the two—a connection in which the sublime performs the *Aufhebung* of what beauty projects by embracing the disorder that it displaces and denies. In the sublime, beauty finds what was suppressed in its birth—the true conditions of its origin. Retroactively, Beauty thereby becomes in Kant what it was for Rilke: "the beginning of terror."[6] What the psyche flees through pursuit of the Beautiful returns in the Sublime to announce itself as the origin and the immanent telos structuring the ego. That telos thus traverses and transfixes the Beautiful, driving the psyche to seek out phenomena and expressions that will mirror its inner condition in sublime objects and acts that are beyond its "imagining" yet utterly appropriate to its desire.

THE EGO'S CRYPT—
THE INNER STRUCTURE OF AN ANTIDIALECTIC

My purpose in this chapter is to describe Hell—from within. To trace, at the level of primary affect, the sequence of self-mediations whereby human beings murder their own souls. The eight sections that follow constitute the progression of an antidialectic, the series of malign mediations required to bring the founding disorder of the psyche to the perfection it will find in the ego-ratio. The real function of ego development is thereby revealed. To bring out that underlying truth each section that follows deliberately moves in a circle in order to represent what the psyche does to itself when it resists drama. The result is a vast and vicious circle of repetition—an antidialectic where ego development is but the disguise in which the founding disorder becomes progressively more virulent and less checked by countervailing possibilities. That is the sad consequence of the attainment of a psychic structure that has cleansed itself of anything within that opposes the conditions of its perfect self-reification.

In exposing the truth of that process, the Bomb will once again be our Vergil. As we will see, the Bomb is the objective correlative that reveals what the ego seeks and desires from the beginning. As referent it thereby offers at each stage the deepest insight into what actually transpires in the drama that follows. That drama, in contrast to chapter 3, reveals the founding disorder not in its sublime guise, but from its basement. Each structure of ego development is thereby presented with the masks stripped away. The total structure then faces the possibility of implosion once it becomes evident that the vast circle is one of destructiveness seeking, through repetition disguised as development, the modifications needed to escape what haunts it from within by projecting it without. We thus attain the only proper name for the structure of self-mediations that solidify the ego: the process whereby death-work empowers itself in the psyche. For the perfection of this anti-dialectic gives one *carte blanche* to do the most horrible things in the assurance one is protected from any future knowledge of one's motives and of one's actual, unconscious intentions.

I. The Psyche's Founding Condition

A. Catastrophic Anxiety

We begin with an effort to describe what is the deepest experience—the one most deeply denied. Catastrophic anxiety is that fear that haunts us from within,[7] the fear that one has already been annihilated; that, like Beckett, one has "never been born properly" and never will be because inner paralysis is the psyche's defining condition—a truth attested each time when, striving to cohere as a subject, one collapses before the tidal wave of an aggression against oneself that rises up from within. An unspeakable dread weds the psyche to terror. All other forms of anxiety are pale after-thoughts. There is a threat worse than extinction. The deepest self-knowledge we harbor, the knowledge that haunts us as perhaps our deepest self-reference is the fear that our inner world is ruled by a force opposed to our being. Death is the icy wind that blows through all we do. This is the anxiety from which other anxieties derive as displacements, delays, and vain attempts to deny or attenuate our terror before a dread that is nameless and must remain so lest despair finalize its hold on us. In catastrophic anxiety the destruction of one's power to be and the ceaseless unraveling of all attempts to surmount this condition is experienced as an event that has already happened. That event forms the first self-reference: the negative judgment of an Other on one's being—internalized as self-undoing. Postmodern posturing before the phrase "I am an other" here receives the concretization that shatters "free play." There is a wound at the heart of subjectivity, a self-ulceration that incessantly bleeds itself out into the world. The issue of the wound is a soul caked in ice, in a despair that apparently cannot be mediated: the nightmare state of a consciousness utterly awake, alone and arrested, all exits barred, facing inner paralysis as the truth of one's life. We ceaselessly flee this experience because if it ever comes down full upon us an even more terrifying process begins: an implosion in which one's subjective being is resolved into fragments of pure anxiety that leave one incapable of existing as subject except in the howl to which each suffered state descends in a final, chilling recognition—that everything one has done and suffered is but sound and fury, signifying nothing. One has become a corpse with insomnia. Identity and self-reference thereafter ceaselessly circle about that void.

This is the hour of the wolf, where one is arrested before the primary fact: at the deepest register of the psyche one finds a voice of terror. Fear of psychic dissolution is the ground condition of our being as subjects. Subjectivity is founded in anguish before the dread of becoming no more than bits and pieces of pure horror, fleeing in panic a voice that has already overtaken us, resolving our subjective being into traumatic episodes of pure persecution. At the heart of inwardness a malevolent spirit presides. To put it in nuclear metaphors: catastrophic anxiety is the threat of implosion into the other's unlimited destructiveness. To complete the picture we need only add Winnicott's point: people live in dread of this situation, projecting fear of a breakdown into the future, because the breakdown has already occurred.[8]

B. Exorcism through Evacuation

And so a *crypt* is built to contain this anguish and repress the experience that is its cause. We organize a "life" of identities and stabilities to give ourselves the illusion of escape. Unable to reverse our condition we take up the only alternative. We try to *evacuate* the whole thing: to blow it out into the world and invest it in objects that are fitted to receive the full brunt of one's discontent and powerless to reply. *Projection,* the ego's priest, is founded in identification with an internal aggressor. That is the complex that informs the effort to lodge our disorders and forbidden desires in others so that we can wage an attack on our inner conflicts then watch the ensuing spectacle from a safe distance. Evacuation thus finds in projection a prime agent of human perception and the secure base for the perpetual, mutual defeat that Sartre finds in all "concrete relations with others." We're always on the lookout for a chance to make someone else bear our discontents. But it's never enough. Satisfaction eludes us. We keep erupting, bleeding from within, in a leukemia of soul that rages whenever we see those who have in "their daily lives" "a beauty that makes us ugly." For then the *projections return* with the force of the furies. Envy and resentment erupt as the assault within our inner world of the truth of our "character"—a truth we deny by reinvesting it externally. This grows apace over the years and then we long for a lasting deliverance, a final solution in the dim recognition that when projection proceeds from the register of catastrophe it requires and longs for a grand exorcism. What we seek incessantly is a total evacuation of all inner discord, a complete and lasting externalization in an ideal victim, one in whom all that haunts us will stay outside, lodged in the world in what Hegel calls a "standing negation"[9]. Our need is for a subject who is destroyed and lives on, proof of a sublime aggression sculpted in time.

The Bomb provides such an opportunity. The criteria required to exorcize catastrophic anxiety finds in it the conditions for expelling the most primitive anxieties in the perfect objective correlative. The subject voids itself of its core anxiety—the inability to reverse inner destructiveness—by becoming the power to destroy, unbound, raining judgment down on a mass of subjects who are indifferently bound together as fragments of pure suffering unable, after that action, to ever form any identity except as walking corpses, *hibakusha,* deadened affect delivered over to the condition of death-in-life.[10]

Projection here succeeds because in that shattered mirror one sees oneself reflected as the equal of the power within that originally proclaimed one's utter worthlessness. Malign "reversal" has grown to the event. All inner anxiety about one's power to be resolves itself in the power to act free of restraint. We have become the thing we feared. Its destructiveness is now ours and nothing else has being.

C. The Contradiction: The Sublime—From the Crypt

The mediation traced above is driven by a contradiction about which it circles endlessly. That is what the sublime object of the ego-ratio reveals when read from its crypt. Sublime action seeks an absolute reversal of catastrophic anxiety in the absolute affirmation of unshakable guarantees. Catastrophe must be reversed because it is that experience of contingency that underlies the horror of contingency in all its forms, the force driving the search for the guarantees needed to contain it. In catastrophe contingency is the other's will as unbounded, unlimited destructiveness. The threat of extinction is the "restraint" here placed on subject. This restraint is prior to the dialectic of "desire restrained and checked" on which Hegel grounds his phenomenology. Desire here isn't restrained and checked—it is turned back against itself in torment. The other requires my destruction for their pleasure and assures that end by colonizing the psyche with an aggression that renders impotent every effort to make a beginning, a tentative move toward independence or self-cohesion. There is no exit but one apparently: identification with the aggressor. I become a self by turning someone or something else into an object delivered over to the true golden rule: do onto others what was once done onto you.

This logic maintains because catastrophic anxiety internalized is death-work as the self-mediation whereby we enact the command of the Other. The only way out, the only way to finalize this process, is evacuation through a lasting exorcism. It alone confers on the psyche a certitude beyond all cogitos. It is also the mediation that finds it, in flight forward, already, in its primitive imaginary, one with the Bomb. In its inner world, the catastrophic subject experiences itself as full of death, disease, corruption. The Bomb alone has the power to cast all "nuclear waste" outside and beneath oneself in a way that indefinitely extends the temporality of that act. Radiation disease is a death that works inward—invisibly, yet inexorably. Death thereby breeds itself forth into an indefinite future, omnipresent in a working, a *différance* that begets delayed effects as further insurance against *Nachträglichkeit*. The extension of death's dominion attained in the Bomb serves one grand function: to prevent the return of projections by extending the temporality of the deed into a future that is lived, by its victims, as a judgment that is inevitable, irreversible, the antithesis of Benjamin's messianic time, ticking—a plea to delay death that can only be answered by death.

The Bomb thus serves as *felix culpa* to an inner necessity. To do its job a sublime event must exorcize everything within the subject that makes it an object of its own contempt. What better way than Orwell's boot brought down in an act of splitting that magnifies the distance between the terror on the ground and the view from above. Catastrophe is now fully outside oneself located in an other who has become nothing but matter, body become spectacle of pain frozen forever in charred sculptures strewn across a devastated landscape, Laöcoon Munched; but with the Howl silenced and deferred until it erupts later from within the survivors in a semiosis that can only be read by the scientists who planted it there and have now come (as biopower/knowledge) to study their handiwork as it blooms and bursts from deep within the body of the *hibakusha* as further testimony of one's power/*jouissance*. Evacuation is complete. Death-work has been lodged securely in the Other. In the *hibakusha* one gets to see one's Thanatos as a narrative principle, a force in history. One gets to see, over time, what it is like to live death. Soul-murder as the innermost reality of the crypt, produces and finds in the *hibakusha* its dialectical image. As the expressive figura of death incarnate, a terrifying *verveilledoch* here attains its objective correlative.

To purge oneself of catastrophic anxiety, an utterly dehumanized object is not enough. Neither the Sartrean look nor the Nazi act suffice. The disorder of the psyche is deeper, prior to desire (Sartre) and demand (Nazism). The projection of death-work can never rest by simply investing one's self-contempt in another. For evacuation to work, the object must become something one can study, inspect, perform operations upon. Catastrophic anxiety is the a proiri that gives Auschwitz and Hiroshima their necessity in the genocidal imagination. The Bomb constitutes an Event because the psyche reverses its core condition—its cardiac arrest in inner self-loathing—through a projection that is total and irreversible. If the evacuation of trauma is the abiding motive atop the crypt, there is nothing abstract or Lacanian about the Real that results from its projection. Evacuation is that malevolent reversal that condemns one to endless repetition. One blows one's self-hatred and one's rage over that state fully out into the world but is thereby rendered powerless to do anything but gape in rapt amazement at one's creation. That is perhaps why, for over fifty years now, whenever given the opportunity, Paul Tibbets has proudly repeated the declaration that he has not had a moment's remorse or regret. Death-work externalized leaves one a spent and reified subject, lacking any power other than the endless repetition of one's deed.

The wheel thus comes full circle in the only justice granted such subjects. When catastrophic anxiety is only mediated by death-work, the affects that compose subjectivity are rent assunder and scattered in pockets of pure persecution. With each attempt to compose an inner self-cohesion, death-work, as internal saboteur, rises up in a renewed attack on the effort to be. Using the Bomb to reverse this disorder produces as its result a perfect, attic justice. Guilt and remorse are denied the doers of the deed because to feel such things is to renew a process of self-unraveling. What the Bomb was meant to deliver one from has become the guardian of untroubled sleep. With the call of conscience rendered impossible, the subject becomes overtly psychotic and must cling ever more desperately to an untroubled memory of the sublime event. The subject thereby pronounces, without being able to comprehend or mediate it, the truth about itself: in the ravaged landscape of Hiroshima the founding inner world of the psychotic—a world of utter fragmentation and the obliteration of every term of reference—has finally found a home to which it must say "stay thou art so fair," a home in which nothing inhuman is *unheimlich*.

II. The Manic Defense against Depression

A. Triumph, Contempt, and Dismissal: The Manic Triad

With the expulsion of catastrophe, the psyche leaps to a new determination, ready to harvest a rich reward—the banishment of *depression*. (I discuss depression as wakeful anguish and draw out the countervailing, tragic self-mediation it makes possible in chapter 5.[11]) Depression is the psychic register where soul-murder, as inner voice, sounds its darkest chords. A shadow keeps falling across the ego and its acts, a voice that speaks a message more insidious and more powerful than the threat of extinction, replacing it with words that shatter all "developmental" illusions.[12] There is something worse than non-being. Catastrophic anxiety appeared to be the ultimate beginning, but it was really a stand in. There is a more intimate voice, one that convicts us in our being of failure, worthlessness, a fundamental inadequacy, a voice that strips us of our "achievements" and our phantom identities. The renewed assault of catastrophic anxiety is thereby increased by the recognition that every effort to surmount our condition only returns us to a worthlessness that our failed efforts only serve to deepen. The condition we hoped to surmount through our deeds transcends them. We touch here on the paradox from which mania—the elation that ensues whenever we feel we have triumphed over internal conflicts and banished them for good—draws its energies. Insofar as action is an attempt to overcome depression, a degree of mania always attaches to it. Our ambitions are large, the energies we invest in them great, because there is much they must transform. Mania and depression are doubles forming a single complex in the ordinary working of which depression rules. Projects collapse or end in boredom. Even genuine achievement partakes of Nietzsche's "melancholy of things completed." As Mary did the body of her son, depression receives us back into the place prepared for us, that of a sadness beyond words that eventually turns into a vigorous attack upon oneself. We attain the loneliest recognition: action doesn't deliver us, it only delays. Unless, that is, there are acts where manic elation finds lasting, orgasmic investment in a unending auto-affection.

For that to happen, however, mania must unlock the triad that structures the inner transformation it tries to bring about. In the dance of elation, mania too often disguises the fact that it is an act of aggression on an object, unleashing a process that fears and refuses to end. The underlying truth of elation isn't release or celebration but attack. It is not enough to escape inner torment. As Melanie Klein argues, a *triumphant* assertion of *contempt* and *dismissal* is required in order to proclaim one's victory over the sources of one's depression. Mania is the jubilation that supervenes when one feels that all inner sources of torment have been vanquished. The attack on external objects is the proof of this achievement, the act required to keep the process from turning back inward.

It is also the circumstance that hoists mania by its own petard. The fit always returns until the proper object and the perfect expression is attained. As Hamlet knows, elation is but sabbath on the Ixion of depression. When the dancing stops and the music ends, the object of hatred within rises up, "unbated and envenomed." Mania is a desperate effort to sustain the illusion that one has gained a lasting release from that object and thereby entry into a world where everything flows magically in a stream of realized desire. The underlying truth returns once the stream reveals itself as a tidal wave of aggression that will brook no opposition, that mocks all prohibitions, and that finds the celebration of destructiveness an end in itself. Another apparent reversal of our inner condition has transformed us into the thing we flee.

In mania the most violent deeds are possible because they have already happened in the subject's inner world. That is the key to understanding the triad—and its object. If all joy wants eternity, all mania seeks the finality of death. Triumph must be the absolute overcoming of all inner prohibitions against wreaking violence on anything that raises the spectre of depression. That violence must, in turn, be externalized in a rush of projection on as many targets as one can find, sustaining the process being the only thing that matters. Contempt solidifies the utter indifference, the coldness and cruelty visited upon the objects of one's scorn, the need being to belittle and dehumanize. Dismissal then finalizes success by banishing anything that might arise in the wake of destruction to trouble the mind with afterthought or forethought. The fascist stance is here attained: self-righteousness wedded to brutality. The goal of the manic triad is the elimination of every seed of inner conflict. Mania practices a scorched earth policy. This drive defines each moment of the manic structure. The only limit mania fears is an end to the process. For that is the moment in which the aggression that has been unbound in the manic high turns back inside to attack its true object in a suicidal implosion.

A contradiction stands at the center of the manic-depressive cycle, seeking a solution that only the Bomb provides. To comprehend that contradiction, we must tunnel back into the depressive condition from which mania derives and study its internal structure. When elation ends and reflection returns, the manic-depressive confronts a single truth. One is oneself the object of depression—and that is the truth one cannot admit. Accord-

ingly, an effort is made to split into three what is really a unity. The inner
world of the depressive is the product of that split. This is its structure:

1. The subject as object of inner mourning.
2. The inner other or saboteur[13] whose judgment makes that condition one of endless suffering, incapable of mediation.
3. The objects—within and without—onto which one projects the
   aggression wedding the subject to the saboteur.

The genealogy of human destructiveness springs from this structure.
For in depth destructiveness is what happens when a subjectivity defined by
self-loathing finds in cruelty the only release through the free projection of
all the hatred one feels toward oneself in one's inner world upon a host of
objects (persons, values, institutions, beliefs, etc.). Aggression experiences,
as heightened pleasure, the boundlessness of cruelty. Elation then beckons
with the discovery of new targets, richer occasions, with but one proviso—
the feast of aggression must never end. In mania one finally knows who one
is and what one wants: that the music, *le Sacre,* not cease until one explodes
from within in a rage that has become absolute "in and for itself," beyond all
restraint or law.

This logic rules because elation offers the next step in the anti-agon,
the malign reversal of the psyche's internal condition, that we are tracing. In
mania the aggression that the other has projected into me becomes my
aggression, but now free of the other's chains and increased as a result of
that "reversal." As such it must be projected onto objects that will necessarily
have two characteristics, the second of which must remain disguised: (1) the
object must be beneath us and thus deserving of contempt and (2) it must
be an appropriate stand-in for the true object of our hatred. Unable to
confront the inner world directly, one must locate its characteristics in a
substitute. To cite the most familiar example: the hatred of men toward
women invariably derives from an inner world in which women are feared as
that greater power before which, in weakness, one cowers, the cruel irony
being that in attacking women, one strives to extinguish that which one sees
as feminine in oneself. The perfect mirror is provided by the tendency of
women to trap themselves in violent, masochistic relationships, since that
complex stems from a similar paralysis: the feeling that one deserves the
other who wounds, since no other "bond of love" satisfies the need for self-
undoing.

The virtue of the example is the deepened understanding of aggression it offers. The object of aggression—both within and without—is always
double: something one hates and fears in the other because it resembles
something one hates and fears in oneself. Aggression aims at the frustrating
terms of an internal relationship in an attempt to annihilate the bind that

locks it in endless frustration. It is the fantasmatic effort to take action within through the travesty of that possibility—violent pseudodrama as a substitute for the real thing. Which is why elation, the victor's crow over the defeated opponent, is the most evanescent and deceitful of moods, an invariable prelude to a deeper, often suicidal, return to the lacerating core of the depressive subject. Elation is magical thinking "dancing in the dark," fearing and knowing one thing, that when the music ends we learn that the song has been about death.

B. *From Wakeful Anguish to the Big Sleep*

Depression and mania, as affects, are perfect mirrors. The slough of despond defining the former must be matched by any equally massive outpouring of affects that deliver consciousness from itself. Only by pumping up the "good feelings" and keeping them at a pitch can the inner state of the psyche find relief. From which we can derive the proper definition of elation: elation is hysteria in panic flight from inwardness, acting out its despair over any possibility of taking action within. Which is why when the dance ends, one returns to ground-zero and finds nothing changed, since the innermost belief fueling the manic process is that one can do nothing to alter the sense of fundamental badness that reigns within.

Unless a new object, the right one, can be found and a final solution attained through an act that would leave in its wake an objectification to which the psyche could always return to reassure itself of the triumph over all inner restraints. In such an object elation would find its dream fulfilled: that of perpetual masturbation before an image that forever stiffens one in the hastening of a climactic *jouissance*. For all its energies, elation is a premature ejaculator who has but one goal: the triumphant extinction of inwardness. That is why there must always be something world shattering about this state. In elation one feels messianic, at the center of things, ready to render the ultimate truth of experience and bring everything (oneself, the other, one's entire history) to a final determination.

That dream blossoms with the Bomb. The narcissistic grandiosity that is at the center of elation no longer holds itself apart, in sublime reserve, indifferent and superior. It here acts in a world become pure field for its sovereign will. The observed of all observers, one is now also the object of rapt attention for an audience awed by one's performance. Within the manic subject's inner world a remarkable possibility here beckons: the true audience that has always presided in disdain over one's efforts will be transfixed by one's act. The inner condition that mania tries to reverse finds in the Bomb its deadly *Aufhebung*. Depression presides over all efforts as the internalization of the judgment that is seen in the face of the m/other as that other turns away in indifference and scorn.[14] Elation is the recovery of that gaze become adoration. Thus, naming the plane Enola Gay weds the mother to the son in the news to be broadcast shortly to an awestruck world. One has finally done something that makes the m/other proud in a recognition that can't be revoked. That is the key to elation. Elation dreams the reversal of one's inner world through a triumphant externalization. That is the logic of mediations that weds it to the Bomb. In the Bomb the inner tie binding m/other and son is epiphanized in a world that has become pure theatrical space for a cruelty beyond Artaud's imagination. It is a final, annealing act because in it two depressions have been laid to rest.

The depressive always harbors one hope about the Other's cruelty: that it too is the product of depression, grounded in sadness, dissatisfaction, and a loss that one can reverse through one's achievements. This is the source of the fantasy that one can "humanize" the other's aggression, save the other from themselves, and bring about a genuine change in that hardened heart. To rephrase Nietzsche, one would rather have a sad object than a bad one. For then destructiveness does not form the core of the other's relationship to me. The depressive's deepest fear—that hate will prove stronger than love[15]—is vanquished. "What does a mother want?" It is a question Paul Tibbets pondered, in chaste reserve, until the moment ripe for an answer.

III. The Fractured Mirror and the Psychotic Core

In weaving its illusions, mania affects a transformation in two other inner structures that also decompose whenever depression levels the loud claims on which they rest. Both derive from the psychotic dimension of the personality and both, for reasons that will emerge, have risen to a position of dominance in "postmodern" society. I refer to *narcissism* and its crypt, the schizoid personality: the perfectly self-enclosed subject and its guardian, the deadening of affect.

A. Narcissistic Grandiosity

The split on which narcissism depends and the grandiosity it requires find in the Bomb the mirror required for their finalization. Narcissism is the beautiful, empty face we erect atop a crypt, the aloof countenance of a beatified self that has escaped the judgments it visits on all others. As unlimited power the look attains in the Bomb the gaze that cannot be disrupted—the gaze upon itself, confirmed through the image reflected back to it from a face at ground-zero , the fragmented, Picassoed face of the other, caved in upon itself, broken into shards of weeping without sound. Narcissistic perfection lies in a self hollowed out from within so that it will coincide with the image of detachment and indifference it uses as the lure to fascinate all other subjects by refusing to take any notice of their being, let alone their efforts to gain its recognition. Aggression finds in Hiroshima the perfect Image for the relation it seeks to others. For the narcissist we are all "always already" *hibakusha*. In two ways: as the occasion for the cruelty, rejection, and humiliation on which the aggression underlying narcissism projects itself; and as the object of rage on which narcissism vents itself whenever its self-image is disrupted. In the American gothic, Paul Tibbetts fathers Patrick Bateman, both desperately seeking through narcissism to contain the underlying psychosis that matures in virulence, enriched like uranium ore, by this malign self-mediation. Narcissism provides the coldness required for self-righteous murder.

B. Expelling Psychosis: The Schizoid Condition

Psychotic anxiety derives from two terrors: (1) the fear of being fragmented into bits and pieces of unremitting psychic pain, unable to form a self that doesn't dissolve immediately into the howl; and (2) the even greater fear of being compressed into an "identity" subjected to ceaseless persecution, claustrophobia finalized with no exit tacked up over the door. In crypting these inner worlds, the psychotic register of the ego traps itself in a malign representation of what Melanie Klein called the paranoid-schizoid condition. At the schizoid pole, the deadening of affect forms the abiding desire, since withdrawal from the world is the only way a psyche rent in pieces, each bearing the force of destructive aggression, can flee a contact with what simultaneously assaults it without and within. At the paranoid pole, however, the inner certainty persists with malevolence stalking the psyche in an attack that is inevitable, since it confirms what the psyche knows it deserves. The result is a consciousness disjunct condemned to oscillate between the positions in the paralysis of a psyche incessantly traumatized in its inner world. Until the Bomb delivers it, that is, by reversing and resolving psychotic anxiety in a cleansing act that expels both sides of the split by locating them in an object that stands at a distance infinitely outside and beneath the subject. Through the creation of that object psychosis displaces its condition, assuring ascent to the narcissistic "stage of development."

A perfect circle has been drawn. It is, however, a self-reifying one and teaches us the invaluable lesson that there really is no development in the movement from paranoid-schizoid operations to the self-cohesion of narcissism and the subsequent ego developments that narcissistic cohesion supposedly makes possible.[16] Something of a radically different sort comes to pass through these self-mediations. The psyche has found a way to resolve its conflicts by creating a structure in which death-work regulates the psyche from within. As Beckett argues, death may be slow work: it is not, however, a maze without a plan. There is a *praxis of self-discharge* that becomes habitual through the operations of the anti-agon we have been tracing. It is now time to give that process a name—Thanatos as self-mediation—and to articulate its logic in systematic, metapsychological terms. This will be the task of section IV.

IV. Soul-Murder Perfected: Death-Work as Self-Reference

Soul-murder[17] is the process whereby the condition of abjection deriving from the other's destructiveness becomes death-work as self-reference and self-regulation. A complete reversal of the psyche's condition is thereby effected in a solution that is in its way final. The psyche takes the terror that haunts it from within and masters it by becoming it. Death-work thereby becomes the principle of self-mediation regulating all our significant behaviors. Three acts are needed to carry out this drama and seal the wound that festers at its center. Those moments are (1) abjection reversed, (2) blockage overcome, (3) aggression unbound. Through their ministry death woos the subject by offering the anti-agon required to reverse the horror of its founding condition. Tracing that process will reveal how death, working within the psyche, raises itself to the status of a "metapsychology."

It attains that status because the process we here describe involves a *transfer of energy* that produces a complete restructuring within the very inwardness of the psyche. By the end there is nothing left to "cut back into life." Spirit has been extinguished. Metapsychology, as we will use that term here, is the effort to articulate *in dramatistic terms* the process that takes place in depth whenever the psyche enacts a complete transformation in its self-reference.[18] Here that process reveals the three steps needed for the soul to impact itself in ice.

A. Psyche's Inner Structure as Anti-Agon

1. Abjection reversed. Tunneling inward, we find at the heart of the psyche not *accedie,* but abjection.[19] And for the abject soul, blockage appears total. In a cardiac arrest of soul, striking our heart we hurt only our hand, reopening channels of self-laceration into which we rush imploding into a void. At the core of our self-reference, we are turned to stone by a murderous presence. Impotence is a poor word for such a condition. Psyche at its abject foundation lives in constant torment beneath a force that rages whenever the slightest sign of spontaneity threatens to mitigate its judgment. At the core, abjection is experienced as that primitive affect that permits no mediation. Self-torment as self-unraveling is one's permanent condition. Undoing as the "defense" that brings everything down to a zero-sum game is here experienced as the psyche's innermost necessity. To escape abjection all energy is centered in the unremitting task of severing connections. Such is the way in which death first installs itself in the psyche.

In doing so, however, it gives birth to its antithesis. As Hegel shows, the virtue of blockage, of restraint is that it establishes the possibility of a fundamental change in one's self-reference. That possibility finds its origin in abjection, because abjection is the situation that mandates the necessity of taking action within. Death-work organizes one response to that challenge. Subject as who/why slumbers as the other. And they exhaust the alternatives, since abjection is that affect whereby catastrophic anxiety brings the subject before the primacy of its existential self-reference. The trauma that founds the subject is experienced in abjection as an *energetics* that must be projected upon. The dialectic in which the psyche is grounded—and the two antithetic structures of self-mediation that derive from that condition— are here joined together in their fundamental and unremitting opposition. The goal of death-work in developing its anti-agon is to repress and extinguish an agon that is equiprimordial with it. Tracing that process thus reveals all the ways death installs its sway in the psyche and why the possibility of its reversal depends on a systematic understanding of those structures. If that study creates the desire for a recovery of the who/why, in its abjection, as the basis for the only genuine self-mediation, it will be because giving death scope also reveals how its opposite slumbers within it as a reversal that becomes possible only when one summons the will to act within the inner structures created by death.

2. *Blockage overcome.* Overcoming the force of inner destructiveness requires an equally massive energy. But how reverse death? How transform that energy, except by indirection, imitation, and repetition: by collecting certain shards of pain in order to reverse abjection by centering a fledgling "identity" in them. It is, of necessity, an identity "restrained and checked," deferred and delayed and as such the first inwardness: inwardness as holding oneself in, anticipating revenge. The child beating the stuffed toy has found a way to become, like the ant, "a centaur in his dragon's world,"[20] avenging himself, in blind imitation, on the giants who stalk him in his primitive imagination. Here's real fort/da had we the strength to see it. The encopritic condition. In unbound violence the other's hatred becomes one's violent protest. Bits and pieces of pure rage accumulate and coalesce in the only "identity" one trusts. Thereby blockage grows toward a reversal as fantasy plots narratives that move inexorably to those grand festivals of cruelty in which, after long delay, one can turn the tables and do unto others.

Inside, however, death has not been reversed. It has been empowered, extended in an internalization of soul-murder that has as its true object, of necessity, the extinguishing of one's being as who/why. The autistic child is an uncanny representative of condition general. Like the sleepless Macbeth, the psyche that embraces death has "caught the nearest way": *reversal by repetition*. That principle here provides the first coherent self-reference, one that acts, with a twisted authenticity, within the chamber of horrors that is the register of primary affects. (The term authenticity is appropriate here because what we are about to describe reveals, sadly, why for many subjects the murdering of their own soul is their only fully human act.) The self-mediation affected here has this form: one takes the most terrifying affects and experiences and from them composes an identity, an *affective coalescence*, which empowers one as a force within that primitive realm. An agon with the destructive other thus commences based on a correct "interpretation" of the other's actions and intentions and a suitable response. But reversal just as surely fails here because sustaining a destructiveness mightier than the deadly force that continues to burn like a stake in the heart does not surmount the need for repetition but assures it as an identification with the aggressor that is solidified and then projected, without and within.

3. Aggression unbound. To make death-work, as energetics, form an identity, one's own power must prove stronger than the destructive force that maintains its command by assaulting any threat to its dominion. The only way to silence inner doubts and fears about its return, a revenant descending in flames, is by giving oneself the one proof adequate to the situation. Therefore, one seeks out occasions for an ever-increasing expression of one's own aggression. That demand forms the circle that the psyche here proves powerless to sever. To assure that reversal and self-empowerment has taken place, one must contract an accumulated aggression now refined into pure hatred and inflict it on objects that are appropriate because they reflect one's original condition. One continues to live that trauma, but with fear now become hate and freely projected onto substitute objects. Those who live in horror of the return of their original abjection thus find it "sublime" to cast off all restrictions—to brutalize women, children, blacks, gays, jews, in the delight and rectitude of the fascist moment. And they must sieze that opportunity whenever or wherever it comes, even in the smallest of rooms and occasions: as when Herr Professor, seeing the craving for recognition in a student's eye, stiffens to the pleasure of making the "scene of instruction" one of humiliation. . . .

B. Thanatos Takes a Bow

With the completion of the tripartite structure described above, the psyche achieves self-identity in the first full flush of Thanatos. Death-work has found a way to extend itself by co-opting the possibility of its reversal. It thereby attains the first confirmation of its sublimity. Increase of power, the fundamental dynamic of the sublime, is here established as a "quantum mechanics" within the psyche, one that establishes a theory of Thanatos that is not abstractly "metaphysical" but is firmly rooted in experience.

Here is the tale it tells. In the initial situation that generates psyche, as opposed to behavior, death is primary, its power absolute and unbound. Thanks to the previous description we now know that the power to structure is the secret of death's appeal. Death doesn't extinguish, it organizes. Discharge of energy in the great bliss of release from tension is but its sabbath moment. Thanatos is a bureaucrat, an inveterate capitalist: concentration, growth, extension are its goals. Rather than an instinct seeking discharge, Thanatos is a colonizer intent on building within the psyche a culture appropriate to it. From which we derive the following as its initial definition: death is the work we take up from within in order to make the voice of the destructive other the term of our self-reference.

1. Ego as culture of death-work. This drive informs the culture death creates for itself. Hatred, envy, cruelty, vain condescension, and petty vindictiveness: such are the self-mediations that create an inwardness that nurtures itself on affects that harbor resentment while hollowing out objects and occasions for its expression. Rather than spend itself in abrupt or noisy discharge, death works best when it stores aggression and builds upon it. Holding back and holding within nurture rage, hardening the heart through repetition. In the resulting self-reference, subject attains a substantiality from which everything then flows with a perfect symmetry, derived from a single principle: those murdered in their souls can only repeat that act—within themselves and upon others. In the abjection of victims, one finds the perfect object. The wheel has come full circle. That which attacks us from within has become the basis of our activity.

Death-work has thereby evolved a structure ruled by three principles: (1) increase of aggression is mandatory and finds in that inwardness that nurtures resentment the perfect womb for its development; (2) repetition, however, always requires a greater expression, an expansion of the field over which aggression holds sway; (3) the attempted reversal of one's founding condition thus moves in a vicious circle. That circle binds destructive energies to a growing contempt for any restraint on their expression. Two forces come to synthesis in this self-mediation: the destructive terror at the core of the psyche and the destructive rituals one has organized to counter it are now one in a marriage that constitutes the unity and identity of the psyche. The threat of implosion has become the force of explosion.

To finalize the process, everything within that must be vanquished for death to secure its reign seeks an appropriate expression. This desire points to a new and frightening theory of repression and the repressed. To achieve lasting peace we must turn ourselves inside out. The primitive terrors that freeze the life-blood of the psyche must find an expression that roots them in the world. Acts are required that reduce the fractured beings on whom they are inflicted to the abjective correlative that is incessantly sought: one must devise humiliations that reduce the other to the stark, arrested eyes of the animal caught in the headlight of one's vindictiveness.

Structurally, death-work attains that maturity through three essential transformations:

(1) abjection, the internal regulator attacking the psyche from within, is reversed through repetition;
(2) destructiveness is thereby compressed in an identity where blockage is overcome in an aggression that awaits occasions:
(3) in which, unbound, it can celebrate the overcoming of its initial condition by delivering the other over to it. To rewrite Nietzsche: Thanatos is the death that cuts back into life: with its self-brutalization it increases its power.

It all works because death provides the energetics of a hermeneutic that forecloses the circle of its self-reference. Step one: thanatopic anxiety remains unbound until inner destructiveness is channeled through an attack by the subject on its own being. Step two: that capitulation binds aggression to resentment, the a priori that has as its inherent demand an attack on life itself. With that principle as the door of every perception, the dead proceed, on all occasions, to oppose anything that escapes their condition. The great reversal has occurred. Step three: implosion-explosion, the dark doubles, organize a world that has become the field for projections that must increase hate because the abiding pressure of the trauma within can only be relieved through festivals of cruelty.

Thanatos must find and create objects for itself. That is its logic as a force in the personality and in history. Evacuation is the categorical imperative that drives the dead in an *Aufhebung* where to be aware of limitations is, indeed, to be already beyond them: since every blockage nurtures resentment and the need, at a later date, for that greater cruelty required to satisfy what festers within. This logic gives us a true picture of what happens to one's inwardness in what is called "identification with the aggressor." That act is usually viewed from the perspective of the ego and its defenses. We now see the underlying motive that makes that account as blind to the true conditions of its prison-house as Ugolino and as unaware of the magnitude of the reversal that is required to undo death's inner dominion. For to reverse death, as we will see, no less is required than a self-mediation that deracinates the hold that death has at the center of one's self-reference.

2. *More die of heartbreak: a phenomenological description.* Before that task most subjects shrink in perpetual fear, contracting their being into ego-identities based solely on consensual validation and reflected appraisals. The result is lives that are called normal, ordinary, healthy, but that can only be described, in an rigorous way, by the steps of another logic; that whereby subjects in "quiet desperation" and in despair over their inner world, die of heartbreak and then ulcerate their being forth in activities that can have only one goal—mutual, collective deadening. What follows outlines the deep structure of the process.

1. In the original traumatic experience that creates the psyche, destructiveness is introjected, creating massive anxiety.
2. Self-destructiveness results in suicide or suicidal behaviors.
3. Or it is displaced and delayed through aggression coalesced then discharged on "appropriate" targets, "significant others."
4. This process gives concrete relations with others a dramatic structure that proceeds inexorably to a final venting, an attack in which the weaker party finally takes flight or is destroyed.
5. Either result produces in the victor the moment of crisis. With no object present, projection turns back inward. The repressed drama of the subject collects around its abiding discontents. The loss or absence of the other leaves only three possibilities: (a) A new object is found, but the new cycle of abuse must correct what went wrong and thus perfect the system of cruelty. (b) The old object is regained but the cycle now proceeds from the point previously reached; the object of attack being that in the other's psyche that enabled them to gain a brief, phantom independence. (c) Inner destructiveness, finding no object, completes the inner return and "eats up itself."
6. Kill or be killed thus reveals itself as the logic that shapes the buried history of many a life, the calcifying truth of most human relationships. As such it is also the point at which metapsychological description starts to burn. For once this structure is known, there is no hiding place, no illusion that after "bad experiences" one can return to a cleansed beginning. Choices made at the deep register of the psyche are irreversible, time and experience the slow articulation of their meaning. Once we discover the ways our lives are dedicated to death, we have only one choice: to reenter the crypt and summon the courage to take action within by confronting all the ways that death has in us "a local habitation and a name." But

because that act demands unremitting struggle with the voice that haunts us, in most cases something else comes to pass.

3. Intimation—Revelation I: over Hiroshima—the voice in the clouds. Serial killers repeat their act because they find no release, no lasting evacuation, however grisly. They lack and forever seek the perfect object. The few lucky ones who succeed attain a state of sublimity from which there can perhaps be only one "regret." Such a man is Paul Tibbets, who has maintained for fifty years a remarkable consistency. Unequivocally and on every possible occasion, Tibbets has stated that he has never felt the slightest remorse and has no regrets about having dropped the Bomb. We trust this account and applaud it. What Tibbets cannot tell us, however, is why his conscience remains clear. Or what he envisioned when he "ushered in the nuclear age" with these, his first words to the crew following the bomb's detonation: "Gentlemen, you have just dropped the *first* atomic bomb in history" (italics mine).[21] We cannot know the nuclear future Tibbets foresaw at that moment. Nor his "disappointment" over the past fifty years. What we can know is this. Tibbets found what he was seeking: the act needed for his Thanatos to reify itself. Tibbets can have no remorse because on August 6, 1945 he died. His psyche fully evacuated its condition, achieving the lasting peace of its own reification. The rest is but quotidian time. Thus Tibbets' Nietzschean blink as "the last man" who was among the first to walk through Nagasaki and gape in vacancy becoming, in his own words, a "tourist," purchasing rice bowls, noting the efficiency of the Japanese in cleaning up "the mess," his nose dumb to the smell of death pervading the place.[22] Absence of affect in Tibbetts is not a mask but a permanent condition. Scientific objectivity, distance, and lack of concern is not a pose, or a discipline one exerts under strain, but that door of perception which now determines, in Nagasaki and elsewhere, "all that is the case." As such it is the discipline of heart and mind that proves "determinate in the last instance." As it did much later for Tibbets, who could not resist the call, when it came, and he found a chance in 1976 to re-enact his mission, and drop a "bomb" complete with simulated mushroom cloud to the cheers of an admiring throng, at the annual air show of the Texas Confederate Air Force, an act solidifying his claim as the apostle of the postmodern imagination.[23]

Death is that discipline which takes anything that "hath a daily beauty in it" and turns the situation to advantage. Historically it moves inevitably to what may today be the true dialectical opposition: the grandeur in a blade of grass to a perception cleansed of death-work versus the death of nature as the demand required to bring the "rationality" of the evolving global technoculture to a point where everything external corresponds to what gnaws at it from within.

V. The Law of the Son

A. *The Phallic Ego and the Attainment of (Phallic) Identity*

We have now traced the structure of self-mediations that issues in the ego. What follows presents the truth of the proclamations this structure makes about itself when they are reinterpreted from its crypt. We hear often today that the phallic stage is the achievement of identity through ascent to the Symbolic order and "the Law of the Father," a development that supposedly overcomes pre-oedipal conflicts and the self-dissolution they threaten.[24] It is a tidy myth, concealing through projection-denial, the lower layer that is its life-blood. That lower layer, moreover, reals the truth about social and cultural relationships when identification with the phallic remains an obsessive fixation, a scene of instruction and unending rivalry.

As our culture demonstrates with systematic regularity, aggression is not overcome in the Symbolic and the social orderings it makes possible. It is extended through a malign reversal that assures destructiveness of new objects and a new direction. Socialization establishes ways of relating that displace and forestall inner torment by contracting all feelings into issues of power. The secret of the system derives from the totemic icon on which the whole thing turns. For phallicized subjects, the inner world is intolerable because with the achievement of phallic identity inner destructiveness centers itself in self-persecution and self-loathing. Inwardness itself becomes the thing one fears because it is connected with sinking into an abyss of affects associated with failure, passivity, feminization, worthlessness, and loss of control. Being emotional equals engulfment in the realm of the mother, who speaks in a voice that "unmans." The phallus as weapon is the reversal that frees us from that voice. Through its assertion all acceptable feeling becomes concentrated in an object defined by the power of its imposition. (That the penis is a tongue—this is the forgotten language, forever lost to those trapped in phallicized identifications.) Speaking ill of the phallic order, however, belies the primary fact. For in it two amazing reversals are affected.

Maternal destructiveness is the psyche's founding anguish; weakness, impotence, and uxoriousness its products, which are overcome by identifying all such feelings with the "feminine" and then extinguishing the entire complex by attacking its externalized representatives: women, children, nature, "men" who refuse phallic identification, and so on. Because such acts stem from the traumatic memory of our deepest humiliations, however, the change they affect involves a complex self-mediation. In an effort to concentrate one's destructiveness on those affects that make us weak and susceptible, the phallus provides the reversal that banishes those feelings by providing a principle of self-mediation that identifies strength with the pitiless judgment one now passes on everything that once made one an object of humiliation. A principle has finally been found that makes possible the creation of a crypt in which one packs ones heart in ice by burying every experience that could deliver us over to the anguish of the who/why. This is the story that the phallus, a flaming sword atop that crypt, desperately denies. For to tell it would show that the phallus is not the Law of the Father's Symbolic social order delivering us from the claustrophobic world of the pre-oedipal and incestuous Mother. That picture is valuable as a counterphobic defense of the Law whenever it comes under attack. But thereby a deeper necessity is also served, which is to prevent our seeing the symbolic order for what it is: the censor we establish to crypt the conflicts of the inner world and thereby sustain the repression of those truths about normalcy, the ego, and the social, cultural subject that stand forth whenever the symbolic order emerges in its true light: as the mediation whereby subjects bind themselves to bureaucracies and interpellations that discipline and punish all concerned,[25] since the system has as its informing principle the attack on any and every thing that can be feminized or so labeled whether by men or by women. Socialized in such practices the collective subject wages an unending effort to exorcize the deep terror within by attacking whatever can serve as its representative. And so the penis becomes a battering ram that hammers away at everything that scares us, rape being, from this perspective, literalization of the dominating trope— rigor mortis of soul made present to itself in its objective correlative.

In the phallus father and son come together in one thing—the desire to put an end to inwardness and the affects that define it by making it impossible to regard those feelings as anything but a disorder that deprives one of masculine identity. The result: men can't communicate with one another honestly about their feelings because the phallus functions a priori to castrate that possibility. The threat of exposure as "feminine" is the mutual betrayal that polices all occasions.

In the larger social context that threat also provides the glue that holds the Symbolic system together. Externalization requires organization; it needs a bureaucracy, even as Kenneth Burke shows, "of the imagination;"[26] a system of rituals, rites of passage and of bonding, even sacred games. The world must be made safe for the phallus. The only law capable of assuring that is objectification. Bergson's comic therefore becomes the ruling principle that always takes command over those areas where the "feminine" and other countervailing behaviors could ooze through. Order is *Ordnung*, never more so perhaps than in the academy. After all, there are certain analytic rules that all responsible discourses must follow. Thought is a social, communal, professional activity: the a priori conditions of rational communication are all ye know on earth and all ye are permitted to know.

They determine what counts as a legitimate speech act, which is why eventually, as a host of commentators today assure us, "we" will put an end to all this postmodernist gibberish and restore objectivity, common sense, and the essential truths of humanism to their rightful place on the throne.[27]

Be that as it may, the energy fueling the fortresses we build against unreason derive from the relief those structures offer at a deeper register. The Symbolic order of the phallus is the perfection of a circle. That circle marches to a logic that has this structure:

1. The world of the m/other is seen as an unmediated realm of primary affects and primitive conflicts which, for the nascent subject, breed terror as the founding self-reference.
2. The phallus offers a way to negate the negation, to reverse the reversal: to institute the claims of binary logic as scorched earth policy.
3. Male identity is the ascent to that order; male solidarity the process of torturing all into submission to its rules by extinguishing all feelings save those that are rational.
4. That commitment solidifies itself by projecting aggression on anything "identified" as feminine.
5. Phallic identity thus affects a double reversal: (a) one's inner weakness is projected and denied, (b) on what becomes, through that process, a suitable object of contempt and aggression.

The Symbolic order thereby achieves its deepest purpose by offering constant occasions for a manic release of depressive tensions. Once the institutionalization of rationality is in place, the system is fool-proof for its hermeneutic circle now rests on an "ontological" principle that extends reason and exorcizes otherness in one and the same act. Phallic power is a principle that affirms itself as tautology, whenever it speaks, with no recognition of the irony. Denying otherness is the one way it always goes beyond the principle of contradiction.

In summary, the phallus affects a self-mediation that submits the self-reference grounded in the M/other to a complete reversal. The organizing principle of the process: aggression. The result: the first proof of death's ontological power. In the phallic order destructiveness reveals, in a systematic way, that it needs no principle outside itself to bring about a complete transformation of the psyche. Thanatos thereby establishes its credentials as a first principle, a true beginning. And in so doing it achieves what will become the principle of its development: eroticizing itself is the act that gives Thanatos the power to annex and extinguish its other.

Once destructiveness has been made a specifically male thing death-work—as self-mediation and as hermeneutic circle—achieves a perfection of sorts. If the m/other triumphs in the inner world by making subject doubt itself, the father principle enacts the needed reversal by making the overt violence of those whose only distinguishing quality is greater physical power the omnipresent threat capable of ending every debate. The Phallus has one grand meaning for the psyche, and for both genders as they reconfigure power around it: the power to do hurt of those whose wound is salved daily by those little murders that offer but momentary relief from a project that is self-contradictory and unrelenting—to destroy without in order to eradicate within.

B. *The Little Lower Layer: Phallic Identity as the Perfect Incest*

My effort, throughout, is to formulate a logic, to show that the psyche, in its most violent acts, moves with rigor in the circle of its own self-entanglement, and is always supremely logical in taking the steps need to complete its imprisonment. That logic is, however, the anti-dialectic whereby the true agon of subjectivity is refused; and with it the recognition that the bond binding the energies that coalesce in the phallic ego is grounded not in the Law of the Father but of the abiding presence of the destructive mother. The attempt by men to convince one another that they are powerful because they have escaped what they all fear is a quest that reveals their actual view of the feminine: the mother not as angel in the house but as Spartan presence. The m/other is the one who sets goals in which one always fails, even when one carries out the founding judgment's fundamental fantasy and comes back, like the Spartan soldier, on one's shield.

The prospect that paralyzes Lacan and others is that the "bond of love" with the m/other is such that father and son have no real or independent access to one another. Their alliance is the supreme myth on which the Symbolic rests, but the truth of the relationship is defined by the effort, together or in rivalry, to escape the m/other's dominion. Through rituals of bonding/bondage, the castrata seek ways to deny their shared state or to triumph over one another in battles where the winner always loses, uneasy being the head that wears the crown. For the entire thing is staged by both parties for one audience, the m/other, who passes judgment on the competitors, with the judgment of "impotence" the ever-present threat. In the phallic order, the incestuous is not surmounted: oedipal rivalry solidifies its power to subdue all human relations to its demands. Identification with the aggressor, the defense on which the ego's identity depends, rest on the marriage Hamlet speaks of: one in which the Law of the Father stands in permanent terror of the engulfing Mother.

That recognition amounts to an implosion of the Symbolic, revealing the trauma of the Real as something it can neither contain nor deny. Least of all by magical thinking; as in the curious Lacanian plea/demand that the m/other accede to the Law of the Father and thereby save the son—from herself. And the perfect incest that beckons—*das ewig weiblich*. As owl of morning, it led one dutiful son to an act of "poetic" genius.

C. Intimation—Revelation II: Tibbets' Agonistes

As Tibbets notes, in narrating the naming of the plane, "they gave planes some pretty strange names in those days, and I didn't want any of that."[28] A new Adam must bear Adam's curse. The act of naming must bring to fruition the erotic truth of the Symbolic tie that binds the doer to his deed. Many American planes bore the names and figures of sexualized women pictured dealing death: of Eros celebrated as a destructive force—a bare-breasted woman, not Slim Pickens, riding a hungry phallus down into the earth. True revelation demands that those precursor images return to the source. Back home, a proud gal sits waiting under the apple tree. In dream space and perfect symmetry the son finds union and *jouissance* in her name, Enola Gay. Put it all together it spells M-O-T-H-E-R, the word made flesh and blazed into the body of the other with a sudden blow that shuddering dawn. Abjection reversed. Blockage overcome. Aggression unbound. The mother's judgment of the son has become that bond of love that requires raining an ultimate terror on the earth to substantialize its reign.

Tibbets' "genius" was this: he saw the son's destructiveness as the m/other's objectified, seeking a form adequate to itself. Tibbets, the Spinoza for our time. The Law of the Father, in might military, as the reversal that fulfills the m/other's commandment by externalizing it. The wheel thereby comes full circle, with destructiveness turned back upon itself in a concerted attack on the very things it nurtured in order to secure its power—weakness, fear, humiliation, abjection. Projection now serves as testimony to the m/other's power. In creating the *hibakusha*, totally dehumanized representatives of those inner qualities that are hated and abhorred, Tibbets completes the self-alienation that is the logic of war's development. And if history teaches us one thing, it is that with each step in that ghostly process the chances of reversal recede. Destructiveness follows an unconscious logic of implosion that finds realization and reification in the Bomb. That is why Tibbets can only gape in rapture, his attention forever fixed on the triumphant eradication of his own inwardness in an evacuation that voids the possibility of any subsequent ethical awareness. The point Canetti seeks, the moment when history disappears, was attained August 6, 1945 in the extinction of "conscience." Implosion alone now sustains the psyche's self-reference, with involutional psychosis the only way left for agents to pass judgment on themselves. And thanks to Tibbetts, that possibility too has perhaps been rendered no more than a last "humanistic" nostalgia.

VI. Intersubjectivity: "Concrete Relations with Others" as Mutual Deadening

A. *Group Psychology American Style*

The Bomb establishes the terms of collective behavior in what will come to be called "the postmodern world." It is the act needed to put everything on a firm and lasting foundation. For the phallocrat, "other people" are one of two things: those one abases and those who, as audience, witness that process, arrested by its power, compelled to undertake its internalization and imitation. The big Other,[29] the one who is always looking at us, most intensely perhaps when we are alone, offers one avenue of escape from the threatened judgment. That is why group psychology is always incipient mass psychology and why the psychological disorder from which the Other derives its power is revealed once there is a sublime *object* around which a mass of subjects can libidinally coalesce in order to be freed through collective identification with it of all inner doubts and anxieties. Such an Object, as magnet for a group-in-fusion as collective will, has the power to gather together in obeisance those who stand in sublime awe beneath its power. Power alone then offers the interpellated "we" the only identity that protects "one" from classification under the only other label that exists. The Bomb contracts all human relations into ones of domination or submission. The only subjectivity it allows is collective and blindly submissive. Beneath it one stands arrested in the blink of Nietzsche's "last man." For under its rule, one is either the nameless, disposable victim or the adolescent bully who here begins to strut and fret his hour upon the stage of world history in what is perhaps a true revelation of the American character: brute might celebrated in the violent rupture of all "humanistic" limitations, the bliss of aggression unbound. As Harry Truman said, "This is the greatest thing in history." There is nothing we can't do to other human beings—and, in the Bomb, *we* know it.

Being and Nothingness (1943) was a prophetic book, not of existence recovered but of dialectic dissolved. All that was required to create a world adequate to it was the coming of the Bomb. The Bomb is the identical *en-soi pour-soi*—the Look that turns everyone into a thing. Especially those subjects who coalesce as *Massenmensch* in the rush to embrace it as *das Ding*, the "brute Thing" that eradicates the threat of any Look with the power to reify those who have already reified themselves in its image. "We" need no longer fear the look of the other because the power of an oppositional subjectivity, what Hegel terms a free consciousness, has been banished from the earth. After the Bomb, there is only *en-soi* as pure expression of the truth of the rationalistic *pour-soi*. The Cartesian quest for a certitude that banishes all doubt here finds the only lasting, clear, and distinct foundation: true freedom and autonomy is the power to compel submission by flicking the switch that turns the look of the other en masse to a blank white screen, no trace left of the tortured visage and the howl that the irradiated victims hurl back from ground-zero in a final fury of the question "why." Free at last of any threat from that Other, a new populace comes into existence, a smug one immune to any rhetoric addressing it as "mon semble, mon frére." In the Bomb that audience finds a judgment beyond appeal; it comes in the power of that sublime object which fascinates and fixates all subjects to *center* all desires in a final configuration of Hegel's "society as a community of animals,"[30]—animals who will live condemned to the ceaseless consumption of images of themselves. The point Canetti seeks has been found: postmodern hyper-reality has arrived. Baptized in the logos that will shape the future, held in sublime *fascization,* a crowd gathers to memorialize the blessed Event.

B. Intimation—Revelation III: The Los Angeles Coliseum, Navy Day, October 27, 1945—The First Super Bowl

Sartre, in nostalgia, looked back to the French Revolution to conceptualize the possibility of an authentic group-in-fusion. We, condemned to historicize that idea, turn to the L.A. Coliseum and Navy Day, October 27, 1945.[31] On that day a crowd numbering over 120,000 gathered for a simulated re-enactment of the bombing of Hiroshima, complete with a chemical mushroom cloud, which rose from the fifty year-line to cheers, fireworks, the rippling flags of a rapt throng. The age of simulation had begun.

In the Coliseum, the news broadcast on August 6, 1945 as message to the world rises up again as symbol, a great attractor, for an audience come together to participate in the birth of a new form of theater—that of a performance art dedicated to the satisfaction of a collective mania. That theater draws on two circumstances for its power: first, the isolation under the Bomb of each subject in a dread so omnipresent that it is the only experience left of individuality; second, the gathering of such paranoid subjects[32] in a collective bow before the re-enactment of that subjection, followed by a rush of ascent straight from the sublime register to embrace and consume that object. Einstein's challenge "to change the way we think about everything" is here resolved, not in a Rilkean embracing of the flame but in collective reification. The consumer society is here born in the panic that will fuel its narcissitic fixation on its own emptiness. In its birth "the society of the spectacle" announces its truth: spectacle here is both scene of global instruction and also the theatre where an audience *cums* to the ritual that confers on it a "lasting" identity: the *howl of joy* that rises as a single voice in a hymn of praise to the burgeoning cloud is the collectivity in hosanna before the image of their inhumanity as it blossoms before them, big with the future. Those gathered in awed attendance at that spectacle are sublimed by the unspoken prayer that rises with the object, the plea to be assured of only one thing: that one never find oneself the object of this savage god. The most primitive bases of group psychology here coalesce in the performative act that seals the *fascization* of the American character. For fascism is this: self-brutalization made the basis for self-certainty in the reduction of all human relations to awe-struck obeisance in "Yes" to the blow, the effort to kiss the boot as it descends. Leaving the Coliseum the crowd finds that like Adam and Eve leaving paradise "the future is all before them," for the manic ceremony now finished is but prologue to the swelling act in which the collective psyche celebrated here becomes a society of consumers who feed incessantly on their own death. The postnuclear subject is this: the *void* that cannot be filled and that sucks everything into itself in the endless proliferation and rush to the next new image, the next new need.

C. Nuclear Fear: 1945–   : A Tiger's Leap into the Future

For celebration always begets as aftermath the return of the reality it was meant to exorcize. Therein the *pour-soi* that sought reification in the Bomb reveals its inner condition as the logos that will shape the American character in the fifties as it fashions a mind of winter for itself by referring everything to the one fear that has now become absolute. That self-mediation cancels the principle of subjectivity on which Hegel based the phenomenology. Nuclear fear is the *felix culpa* that completes the work begun in the Coliseum.[33] Psychic numbing thereby becomes the through-line shaping all social structures. The deadening of affect is the act proving that one has internalized the Bomb. Thus the explosion of the mental health industry and the obsessional need behind the plethora of psychologies dedicated to purging everything that troubles the subject within.[34]

That fact is not without its irony. The term *psychic numbing* was first introduced by Robert J. Lifton to describe the psychological effects of the Bomb on its victims, the *hibakusha*. The term may already have contained another signification, however, as projection and uncanny prophecy of the only way that those who used it could "learn to stop worrying and love the bomb." A psychological category constructed to objectify the victims and turn them into discursive subjects for knowledge/power finds its true referent in the processes that structure the ghostly solidarity of the victors. That irony, however, contains no possibility of reversal. Another exigency drives the process of psychic numbing. Nuclear fear is this: the anticipation that somehow, someday the position will be reversed and one will become the victim. Those who find in this fear signs of an American conscience, of guilt gnawing the subject toward recognition and renewal, convict themselves of the worst kind of ahistorical nostalgia. The real pursuit is what D. H. Lawrence, apropos of World War I, termed "the process of intrinsic death." If, as

Doris Lessing argues, "the bomb has already gone off" within us, it is because after it we live in one world, with psychic numbing perhaps the only telos capable of producing Eliot's "unified sensiblity."

The justice of the postnuclear condition is that it falls with special force on the victors, because they know one thing with Cartesian certainty. They used it. The Event in the L.A. Coliseum brought as its glad tidings the cancellation of Emily Dickinson's message to the world. The only space within where a subject can retreat in solitude to take up the burden of one's being is now a space where the Bomb is omnipresent and omnipotent. And it has already gone off, because with its use, a deadening implosion at the deepest register of our inwardness takes place.

One often hears this charge from those who were around in 1945: "Where were you during the war? You don't know anything about how we felt? I'll bet you weren't even alive then." There is in the statement a disingenuous honesty. A shout went up with Ahab/Truman. Americans took joy in the Bomb and that affective experience went straight down to the deepest register of the psyche, in a hosannah that would prove irreversible. To be in history is at times to make a choice that no afterthought can alter. The aporia of "remorse" is this: on August 6, 1945, the collective psyche made a decision that it can neither admit nor renounce. It felt good. It was a sublime moment. Casting all moral considerations aside, a populace embraced the news in thanksgiving and a revenge long delayed. That is why fifty years later that populace and its historians still clutch at virtually any datum that can be unearthed to "justify" the act, or, at least, to sustain that "debate" and the need for further historical research. We must find a way to "save the conversation," to block interpretive closure, to keep both sides of the debate in place, marshaling new "facts" to attenuate the deed and the responsibility it imposes. One thing above all is needed: to delay and defer the time when one has to *internalize* what happened on August 6, 1945. Histories are written so that history will never be experienced in a way that brings the subject before itself in depth. The two sides in the Hiroshima debate have a secret to hide—one they share with most Americans—their complicity in preventing this encounter. And as long as one bathes the issue of closure with humanistic guarantees—such as Lifton and Mitchell's notion that by admitting our errors we are cleansed and renewed—one's psychic position is not really different from those rebarbative ones, such as Professor Fussell, who continue to proclaim their "good feelings" over the use of the Bomb in order to sustain a hysteric defense against what would come with its internalization.[35]

D. The History of the Present

At the end of Don DeLillo's *White Noise*, crowds gather, mysteriously drawn to brilliant sunsets that, they dimly know, stand as signs of the pollution of the planet. They are transfixed by the new light they can just barely discern as it comes to envelope them, because they find in that bright angel of death a ratification of the process that forms the inner history of the United States from 1945 to the present. In their numbness DeLillo's collective subjects, ripe for death, find in those sunsets a last after-image of the founding act celebrated in the Coliseum. Like radiation sickness and ecological catastrophe, cultural death-work comes not in a "screaming across the sky" (Pynchon) but dispersed as an atmosphere, a new *habitus* and Wittgensteinian "form of life" only faintly visible to the ghosts sleepwalking their way across the neon necropolis. As Durkheim's descendant, DeLillo shows us, with the loving attention to detail of the born sociologist, all the ways in which Death organizes a culture for itself: the ways in which it develops as a historical force fatally attracted to the conditions of its own finalization, bound in love to the one binding object of desire.

Our effort in describing the psychological self-mediations that issue in those structures is not a contribution to sociology, but to its foundations. Similar to Heidegger's argument about the "analytic of Dasein," the effort is to establish existential categories that will enable us to chart the quotidian as a desert that grows because it has but one foundation. The power of Thanatos is its ability to annex and change the function of every object in which Eros and erotic longing invests itself. Since 1945 the goal that has driven this process is the panic flight of the collective historical Unconscious seeking a world where it will be safe from the one reality it cannot attend to, the psychotic pressure that has acted upon the nerves since August 6, 1945. It is frequently claimed that the Bomb has given us fifty years of safety from world war. Its historical "force and signification" has been far more basic and primitive. On August 6, 1945, the psyche was turned inside out: everything since has proceeded from the psychotic register.

VII. The Trauma Is the Real: The Postmodern Condition Attained

> No, the sex in my films isn't simulated. That would be dishonest.
> —Marilyn Chambers

Here is a version of things you are not likely to hear when next the good news goes conferenced forth that the postmodern condition has arrived. The Trauma is the Real. All symbolic strategies for displacing that recognition were blasted to bits by the Bomb. That is why culture today moves in the medium of the hyperreal, the simulated, the landscape of the waking dream become collective nightmare in a vertigo of psyche where the mad proliferation of self-canceling texts conceals and reveals the effort to turn horror into the only possible comfort: that of the void, the absence of reference—the endless free play of the signifier, dancing in the dark to *Le Sacre*. In the Bomb the Symbolic order was realized, exposed, and shattered. Reference had finally been attained. Which is why after Hiroshima "language" becomes the culture's overriding obsession as we seek words to deny the Real and render reference impossible or, at least, "fabulously textual."[36] Simulation provides that desire with the perfect symptom: a denial of reality that serves only to confirm the desperate hollowness of that denial. "Deconstructing the subject" then takes the final step. We must unravel our being as subjects in order to gain release from what has become a historical condition of unspeakable horror. If one can dissolve one's being in a language "that speaks us," then there is one thing that can never be spoken. The hermeneutic circle becomes endlessly autoreferential in ludic service to the spasms of non-meaning whereby it hollows out the subjects who embrace it. Undoing, the most primitive defense mechanism, is now the only one left.

This reading is, of course, a far cry from the conscious intentions of those theorists who constructed postmodernism and even further from the eminently "referential" preoccupations of those who career themselves forth by expounding the new dispensation. The inwardness I am describing here is precisely what they cannot let themselves know about themselves because a dialectical beginning would then be attained, with the postmodern seen as the postnuclear and the latter category no longer marginalized, but made the basis for a demystified reinterpretation of aporia, irony, deferral, and delay. Contra his epigones, Derrida did not deconstruct the Cold War; his thought stands, rather, as an essential moment in the change that the nuclear referent effects within the inwardness of the subject.[37] And faced with the historical reality of that change, the various humanisms offer no meaningful counterdiscourse pointing the way to a return to "sanity" and no way out of the historical condition we've described. Their effort, rather, and their unattainable unconscious, is to protect their audience from the one thing that matters, a "pessimism of strength" that would look at history without guarantees, especially those that posit catharsis and renewal as the assured results of every "confrontation" with a traumatic past. Confronted with the Bomb, humanism, like postmodernism, has one goal—containment. "Human kind cannot bear very much reality."[38] And in that fact humanism finds its true definition: it is the system of essentialistic beliefs about the fundamental goodness of human beings that provide the a priori identity *from* and *to* which the humanist moves himself and his audience in dealing with history. Which is another way of saying that humanism after Hiroshima is in the service of death and perforce regards Lethe as "the knowledge most worth having," reinstitution of the guarantees being for it the only way to cleanse oneself of the burden of history.

VIII. Epiphany: The Eroticization of Thanatos

Pleasure under the sign of the Bomb has this essential characteristic: it consists in binding then releasing a destructiveness that voids all inner tension in an aggression that is projected without restraint. Neither the pleasure nor the reality principle can restrain or account for the "expense of spirit" in the resulting feasts of cruelty. For pleasure to work no residual or retrospective consciousness can live on in remorse to trouble the act or turn it back against the self. Thanatos eroticized necessarily finds its pleasure in the perfect psychotic act: one where the evacuation of inner destructivness has become bliss, exorcism made *jouissance*, the subject's giddy self-dissolution into fragments of pure brutality celebrated as a triumphant externalization of all discontents. The sublime drive—the Kantian need for an increase of might in a greater outpouring after every blockage—has a telos that points to one end, which is now fully present in the Bomb as the identical subject-object of history.

As such the Bomb offers a radically new understanding of the "eternal battle" of Eros and Thanatos, one that deprives that "dialectic" of the hidden guarantees Freud established in proclaiming it. The Bomb shows us that the dialectic is historical to the core. That recognition spells the death of dualism and the guarantees that binary logic imposes on history. When Eros and Thanatos are dualistically opposed we are always safe and can always begin again, with hands washed clean of history. Dualism separates its central categories all the better to assure the a priori, essentialistic, and transcendental status of the favored term. As such, dualism is the mother of the guarantees, the permanent ally of humanism whenever contingency threatens its hegemony. With dualism's aid we can always sort things out so that everything we value ends up on the right side of the Platonic "divided line." That is why after every holocaust we rediscover a cleansing, healing power within. In learning about evil one always learns about the other, the aberration, the unthinkable—never about the heart of one's own inwardness. Dualism is the conceptual realization of splitting as that defense which enables the psyche to label as "bad" everything within itself it can't deal with. Thereby dualism protects a set of "good" a priori needs from the possibility of fatal contamination by their opposite. Whenever it turns to history, dualism accordingly becomes transcendance playing a comedy, claiming to find as universal in the world what it imposes ahistorically from above.

When Eros and Thanatos become historical categories, in contrast, they bite into us, disrupting and challenging the very "life of spirit" by delivering us over to a process where everything is at issue. When opposition is dialectical, not dualistic, everything is subjected to the possibility of irreversible change because the opposition is such that one category can and does invade those realms supposedly secured for the other. Annexation, colonization, change of function are the primary facts: and no essential humanity protects us (and Eros) from such processes. Once aggression was eroticized, the possibility was set that eventually nothing but aggression would produce erotic pleasure. There is nothing that escapes this threat, nothing within the subject that guarantees protection or recovery. Today, rather, in devolution far advanced, the question is whether there is anything left to combat the encroachments of Thanatos. Humanism is the refusal to face this condition. Existentializing dialectic is the antidote. It is that way of thinking that situates everything immanently, in a historical understanding voided of guarantees.[39] Eros and Thanatos are the dialectical categories that make that history concrete in a way that maximizes its urgency. As forces in the psyche given over to history, they are not eternal ideas, but fundamental choices directly felt in the pressure they daily exert upon the nerves and the heart leading to choices one lives out in acts that prove determinative. Existentialized and historicized, the dialectic of Eros and Thanatos is the "concrete universal" that simultaneously defines the world and our responsibility in it. Nietzsche's reconquest of one's humanity is more than one's daily task; it defines our historical situatedness. Before retreating to dualism, Freud noted that his thought contained "the basis for a very grave philosophy." As we'll see, that possibility establishes the tragic as the category that concretizes the dialectic of Eros and Thanatos in a way that gives a new determination to Nietzsche's idea that there is a "highest form of affirmation possible for an existing subject."[40] If "the only death is the death of will" (Roethke), the only resistance that counts is the effort to confront the force of death within and engage it in a battle to the death. To do that, however, one must have an intimate knowledge of the opponent. Sections I–VIII have traced death's genealogy. The task now is to articulate a new *metapsychology*, one that will provide a rigorous and systematic articulation of the force and reality of Death in the psyche.

THANATOS AS SPIRIT IN AND FOR ITSELF

Those alone know death who have gone down into the crypt and struggled to take action within by confronting the full force of the primitive images and affects that define death's strangle hold in the psyche. Lacking that we begin here at the other end, with the condition described at the end of section 6. There the anti-agon of malign self-mediation whereby death installs absolute reign within the psyche attained completion: everything thereafter proceeds with purity and rigor from the psyche's psychotic core. Terror and horror have been made absolute, with death-work fully libidinized. Like Faulkner's Rosa Coldfield the psyche so formed has entered that "dream-like state in which you run without moving from a terror in which you cannot believe,"—a crypted inner world centered in two self-references, a heart packed in ice or strewn as howl in bits and pieces of pure catastrophic anxiety—"toward a saftey in which you have no faith"—the sarcophagus the ego erects to contain that Chernobyl through the little murders we commit each day to keep the only anxiety that remains at a tolerable level. Which is why whenever others show signs of a vitality that has not yet been crushed, the Iago in the dead rises up in sacred duty to the principle that centers their being: the lust to remove from the order of being everything that reminds them of the murder they have committed in their own soul. This is the affective structure that forms the core of the other structures that the ego erects in order to build that "world in the head" where objective, detached, conflict-free operations offer the ego a secure fortress, even though it is but a sand castle in which we rupture and bleed from within in that ulcer of soul that "inward breaks and gives no cause without why the man dies." In that process Thanatos, as author, attains the pleasure it requires. But in doing so it also tips its hand, enabling us to move directly into the belly of the beast.

I. *Rethinking Freud: Concrete versus Abstract Dialectics*

What follows attempts to reap the ontological yield of the previous investigations by setting forth, in transparently theoretical terms, the concept and *werkzeug* of death. We offer it here as a systematic alternative to the concepts of Thanatos that have thus far been developed in psychoanalysis. My first thesis: the theory of Thanatos developed in psychoanalysis by Freud and later by Lacan, is a defense against an authentic consideration of the subject. Death is conceptualized as instinct (even as sublime drive) so that we don't have to see it as work, as an utterly human project. That displacement also protects us from seeing the actual way death works as a force in culture and history; that is, through the effort of one kind of human being to eliminate another. Freud's biocultural fatalism is a defense against the actual human tragedy and the only authentic response to it: internal action rather than Freud's Spinozistic resignation before "willed necessity."[41]

In Freud cosmology absolves us of philosophic anthropology. But absolution wasn't enough. Freud's "healthier" followers, the various revisionists, cleansed the psyche of any remaining taint of Thanatos by proclaiming everything connected with that concept the "metaphysical," disposable, non-scientific part of Freud. Thanatos is thereby consigned to silence; except for the brayings of its ape, adaptation to social normalcy as the superordinate reality principle. Fittingly, however, this theory traps its followers in their own self-reification. Since destructiveness can no longer be considered as internal to the psyche, there is no way to see the aggression behind the enforcement of social normalcy as the working of a force opposed to life, with envy the presiding force and internal deadening the end result of the normalizing practices that issue in a strong, healthy ego, well-adapted to reality.

A different and subtler retreat from death comes in the work of Lacan and his circle. Ironically, the means is an abstract retrieval that puts the category of Thanatos at the center of psychoanalytic theory all the better to complete its removal from the human realm. Death in Lacan's hands (and in Derrida's) becomes a linguistic abstraction installed, as such, as the *Abgrund* into which all our efforts to "say" dissolve, as they did for Faulkner's Benjy. For the postmodern sensibility that dissolution is fortunate because death is thereby prevented from troubling our sleep in more personal, intimate ways. As domain of the drive, the traumatic kernel, the obscene *jouissance,* the perverse father of enjoyment, death is acknowledged by Lacan without being recognized.

To see Death's human face we must reconstitute its tragic register and restore death to its rootedness in those human acts that give life the unity of a dramatic process. Cruelty, envy, resentment, a hatred of life and a violent quest to attain that peace which comes only when "spirit" is extinguished are affective forces that structure everyday life. They are so because they are the primary and the necessary issue of the malign self-mediations that are made at the core register of the psyche in an effort to resolve the conflicts that define its condition. Resentment is not an occasional mood; it is the settled attitude toward life whereby certain beings structure their self-reference and their relationship to others. Anxiety for such beings is the *signal* that rises up whenever life assaults them within. For such beings Eros and Thanatos are neither ahistorical mythic abstractions nor biological instincts craving discharge. They are choices lived out in the human dramas through which each of us determines our humanity and the content of our character. As such they are the categories that hold the key to the story each of us would tell from the crypt had we the ability to draw our breath in its proper pain and confront the acts of self-mediation we have taken in our inner world.

II. Humanizing Thanatos: A Phenomenological Description

Humanizing Thanatos along these lines requires a further critique of Freud. Because Freud sees Thanatos as instinct rather than work, he is able to posit quiescence rather than endless destructiveness as its goal. His later concern with aggressivity corrects this view but without producing the required theoretical revision. Human aggression seeks the totalizing of a certain kind of order. A pleasure drives it and that pleasure is not based on discharge but on a frenzy and a glee, a charge of libidinal energy that has the annexing of Eros as its implied goal from the beginning. Regan's "gouge out both his eyes," and not Bernini's Saint Theresa, is the proper image of the *jouissance* it seeks: the saint's intense passivity but pale after-thought to the appetite that drives Regan. Death rises in its cruelty whenever resentment activates the lust to destroy. Thereby death becomes the most preemptory force in the psyche, the a priori of perception constantly at work in all we see and do. The four characteristics that define neurotic behavior— behavior that is insatiable, obligatory, repetitive, and stereotyped[42]—are death's modus operandi. Four better principles of action could not be devised for death to assure its dominion so that one story and one only is obsessively told on all occasions. Death seeks not discharge, absence of tension, quiescence. It is a ravenous hunger, the "pruner with the knife / busy at the tree of life."[43] To understand it we must liberate Thanatos from "instinct" and see it as an active dynamis, a desire constantly at work in the psyche, fitted daily with perceptions and a host of obligatory tasks; an energy seeking rituals not in order to bind and discharge the pressure that weighs on it but in order to celebrate itself and extend its scope. Inverting Coleridge, for the dead and dying, death-work is the primary imagination: the prime agent of human perception and action; a repetition in the waking mind of the eternal act of hatred in the thanatoptic unconscious. Discharge of tension is but a moment, the blush of triumphant closure, in the battle against life. In its wake the *lust-prinzip* driving Thanatos quickens to hemorrhage out into the world. The dead are infinitely busy and only pause to gather themselves within the void of a negativity that demands deeds in a ceaseless effort to destroy that vitality that sets their teeth on edge.

III. Death-Work versus the Death-Drive

Death-work versus the death-drive: this formula provides the key to all that follows. My effort is to conceptualize death as the psychological reality that informs one of the two ways we live the existential condition that we are as beings who have our *origin* as psyche in the activation by traumatic experiences of subject as who/why.

This dialectic commences when the destructive activity of the other strives to annihilate one's power to be as a subject. The result in some human beings is the effort to expel the anguish of this primary encounter by extinguishing the very inwardness it creates. Death thus creates in the psyche the double register that defines our existence as subjects. Once death strikes inward at the soul, which it also creates through that act, we face the one basic choice: to live the anguish of that origin or to quell it by waging an attack on everything in ourselves that makes us the object of cruelty and humiliation. Inwardness makes us subjects who either bind ourselves to *suffering* or prosecute our own *undoing*.

Only the boldest psychoanalyses descend to this level and confront psyche's still-birth in an autism of soul, an anxiety of "never having been born properly," that can only be addressed by descending to the crypt in which primary effects tied to the experiences of cruelty and humiliation are buried and activating an agon that will sustain the drama locked in those affects as the basis of a self-reference that must be recovered and constituted. Not surprisingly, this register of experience is the one that quasibiological accounts of "early" infant life have striven to exorcize by asserting a "secure base" in which the "bonds of love" are established through the mother's miraculous ability to bracket her own psyche while she nurtures her child, one with her maternal and "cultural mission" to establish "basic trust" as the guarantee that creates in the infant the stable ego-identity assuring normalcy, the development of "good" stable object-relations, and the achievement of socially productive egos that reach fruition in lives lived free from those inner conflicts that could lead to neurosis or worse. Thanks to these "developments" death attains a cogito and a constancy principle that make it equal to all occasions. The certainty of that cogito is its ability to split the surface personality off from its disavowed inner world . A constancy principle has been attained, a mode of functioning that regulates stimuli so that passivity (and interpassivity) comes to structure all relations. The truth that surface cannot face about itself is this: an-hedonia has become the basic self-reference. This arrangement holds because the constancy principle has a deeper spring from which it derives— resentment. Constancy, too, is not a biological or physiological principle and has nothing to do with reality save this: it is the way in which a culture of death creates social structures that secure its dominance in all relations. If the pleasure principle is ruled by the constancy principle, we must take pleasure to its roots and see that true pleasure here comes when death discharges the threat from life by bringing another context of human interaction beneath the sway of resentment and its signifying monkey, adaptation.

Constancy and psychic disintegration are not opposed, as Freud thought, but serve one another in a silent partnership in which psychic numbing mirrors, in malevolent reversal, the inner disorders one refuses to face. In projecting that self-mediation, *passive-aggressive behavior* is the act of genius that produces a quantum leap in the development of Thanatos. The passive-aggressive person satisfies two demands simultaneously: inflicting its burdens on the other and transferring them to the other. As, for example, in the hushed voice always just out of hearing that eventually drives the other person to an outburst that leaves that person with the load of Thanatos that has thereby been deftly lodged in them. Such is true death-work as an "efficient cause" bound to this necessity: deadened inner feelings are projected in an effort dedicated to poisoning others' psyches by creating in them a resentment that will become toxic but cannot be discharged. Such is the cunning whereby the dead find a way to breed death-work in the other's psyche. Wedded to death such relationships proceed toward the desired end: as in unions where a couple, happy at last, police one another so that nothing can or will happen between them. An even more deadly process turns the sexual into a field of aggression in which the extinction of one's vulnerability becomes the primary purpose of sex, with narcissistic mirroring the goal. For this to work one's hatred of the erotic must be conveyed to the other—as a defect in them. Those seeking death-in-life know Eros as the threat that troubles their sleep. The only security lies in making it an act advancing a process of mutual reification.

To bring it off, however, death-work must reverse what may be the greatest act in human history—its founding moment, perhaps, and its finest hour, an event more important than language, logic, play and other purported origins of culture. I refer to the act of relating to another person by turning a biological process (of drive-discharge, stimulus-response) into a distinctly interpersonal and humanizing affair where tenderness, mutuality, and sensual intimacy are prolonged before, during, and after the satisfaction of need and independent of its exigencies. Eros as motive and desire derives from those unique experiences wherein the human being strives to be adequate to the demands of an affective order that is founded in the power of physical intimacy to put the psyche in touch with the need to open itself in and through the drama of intersubjectivity to the necessity of self-overcoming. That is why the battle against Eros, the effort to turn sex into a thing, is so intense. Danger forever lurks in the terror of touch.

Eros is dangerous because every time it arises it challenges the internalized voice and judgments that first established the priority and primacy of Thanatos in the constitution of the psyche. Thanatos is first. Eros always comes after the forces of prohibition and persecution that rise up the moment it solidifies itself as a motive. *Nachträglichkeit* is such that, against the halting annunciations of erotic relating, Thanatos comes armed with the full force of familial and cultural formations that are inimical to the ways of being that Eros opens up in us and bent on bringing subject's self-reference back into line. In the sexual, as in so many affairs of the psyche, Thanatos holds pride of place because of the way cruelty has rooted itself in us so that the primary way we mediate our conflicts is by strangling the very energy we must unlock and sustain in order to undertake the reversal required to attain independent psychic agency. That energy is the Eros in us, but it is always defined and situated by the greater force of self-unraveling as our initial condition. That is why whenever we go inside, looking for a begnning, we find death already installed, waiting. Just as no subject escapes the conflicts of psychosexual experience, no subject escapes the primacy and power of Thanatos within the soul. To be human is to be delivered over to the task of self-overcoming through radical reversal and deracination. The possibility of one's own being is what is at stake in the "death-drive." That is why death, like sexuality, is a conflict that must be lived out in concrete choices and not as some abstract, impersonal force.

If Eros and Thanatos are "eternal antagonists" it is because they are the two *antithetical immediacies* that deliver the subject over to the existential burdens of its being. And like all true dialectical opposites they create an antithesis for which there is no synthesis. Nor any way to establish a logical or temporal point where one term is free of the other. As a concession to the limits of discursive language, I have in the preceding paragraphs spoken of each term separately. Experience only begins, however, when they meet, fused—in opposition: at white heat, with the *élan conatus* created and traumatized simultaneously, made dynamic and existential by the injection of Thanatos into its life-blood. That Event is the origin of the psyche and its definition. Psyche is the act of living a relationship to oneself defined by an agon in which Thanatos remains primary in one sense: its blow is what quickens an élan to persist in one's being that remains vital only through the resistance it sets up to that power. Love is the overcoming of hate, based on nothing more secure than the possibility of self-overcoming that is engaged only when a subject opposes itself to the massive power of death-work in its inner world. There is, moreover, no secure foundation in the psyche guaranteeing this act. On the contrary.

IV. Experience and Existence

Two propositions about the order of experience derive from the above:

1. Death is primary and for most subjects overpowering. The sad and basic fact is that most people spend their lives trying to complete the death-work that rules them within. In terms of "concrete relations with others" that fact constitutes what, for lack of a better word, we call the human condition. The dead crave company. That is the abiding desire of those murdered in their soul.

2. In the dialectic of psyche's self-mediation life is secondary: it is what comes only if and when one reverses the prior force of death. And in that battle Thanatos holds this advantage: it brings to that agon the voice of an internal saboteur who is organized and articulate and has the power to annex and extinguish its opponent. Eros is only vital, as opposition, when it begins with that recognition, for then engagement is quickened by the absence of guarantees. How seldom that happens is revealed by the per-

sistence of binary thought, and the hidden guarantees it provides, even among those who claim to take up the cause of Eros. I refer to formulations such as we get in Brown, Marcuse, and Laing where the dialectic is set up in such a way that Eros provides a separate and independent line of development, which is therefore utopian in its social and historical implications. For us, in contrast, Eros is derivative, that reaction to cruelty which depends for its liberation on the transformation of a prior condition into which it is thrown, utterly, and, as we'll see, tragically. For once Eros is existentially situated the dialectic bursts in a radical recognition of contingency, which teaches us that as historical subjects our situation is that of those born into a late, advanced stage of Freud's "eternal battle" with a deadening end in sight. In terms of Eros that recognition constitutes our responsibility as agents in history.

A. Desire and Its Dialectic

Concretizing that recognition generates a radically new understanding of desire.

We must ask but one question of desire: is it in the service of death or the basis for a movement opposed to it? In an immanent dialectic grounded in an agonistic subjectivity the answer is necessarily twofold. "Desire is death" as long as it remains tied to the original lost object that one has failed to mourn. That failure is the subtlest way the destructive other sustains its internal power with "paradise lost" the nostalgia preventing a recognition of the conflicts of the original relationship. And their deepest result. For what one refuses to mourn is oneself: the child buried in the crypt become the desperate, hungry child who will do anything to gain the love of those who created the primary wounds. As long as it incessantly repeats the quest for a love denied, desire is death incarnate, displaced in the endless pursuit of that perfect, magical relationship that will deliver us from the crypt by restoring what we never had. That is perhaps the deepest spring of the Hegelian insight that satisfaction breeds boredom and the endless need for new quests. Unless, that is, self-consciousness breaks the dialectic of repetitive desire and comes to the one question that matters. Is there some way to reverse the psyche's primary self-reference? Is there a desire opposed to death? And if so, how is it constituted? To engage that issue one must establish the possibility of deracination within the very heart of desire.

To do so one must re-enter desire and sound its deeper chord. Desire is initially for and of the destructive other internalized in death-work as the regulator of the psyche. This is the underlying reality of the "mirror-stage" and the key to the aggressivity that defines it. Which is why, dialectically, mirroring generates in narcissism death incarnate. For narcissism is the "development" that doubles, in fixated repetitions, the hollowness at the core, with rage over that underlying condition the inwardness endowing narcissism with the power to inform the dominant group psychology of our time: the collective effort to support one another in groups dedicated to telling one another what each member needs to hear so that as groups we exorcize together the possibility of confronting anything painful about oneself. The secret of the group: the massive hatred that sustains its exercise of pity.

As long as desire remains the search for the lost object, the pristine origin, it is in love with its own death. In order to initiate an existential dialectic of subject a desire of a different order is required—one grounded in the possibility of an agon capable of enacting a complete reversal within the psyche. Desire as death is the drive toward the dissolution of the dialectic. Desire as self-overcoming is the drive toward its maximization. In this second form desire is inherently tragic, in the best sense of that term, because self-overcoming here depends on an immersion in those "primitive" experiences and affects where subject, as who/why, was first given the burden it then crypted, that of its existential being. When desire is the act in which "spirit cuts back into" itself at this register, a new possibility arises—that of an agon in which the crypt is torn open and submitted, in anguish, to the act of deracination. Desire has become, in short, the desire to take action in oneself by engaging a process lacking all guarantees save one: fail here and death seals its hold over the soul. One's being at issue is what has here become the issue.

B. Desire and/as the Ego

Another choice maintains in the normal course of things. The ego as that system of defenses "vigorously opposed to reality" creates the structures that give death-work the solidity that narcissism could not achieve. This is the function of the system of intellectualizing defenses that discharge tension by creating "a world in the head." That order has one goal—to deliver us from existence. Here are the five key planks in the construction of this edifice:

1. The ego as mechanism of defense is the system of discharge operations whereby death assures the psyche against any intrusion of reality. With this system in place, flight and denial become the automatic responses that click in the moment anxiety is felt.

2. As illusion of identity, the ego is the "self-consciousness" whereby this unconscious extends its rule by establishing tranquilizing orders of mind, action, and feeling. Anytime habit breaks down or shatters upon the sufferance of being, ego-identity restores order by imposing these structures on experience. Inner conflicts are contained by explaining away anything

that threatens to activate them. Of anxiety the ego is now able to pronounce the confident judgment: "it was nothing."

3. The ratio is the hyperconsciousness of this consciousness. It is composed of the system of principles of interpretation, reasoning, and explanation that turn the world into a concept and experience into a knowledge-affair so that we can assure ourselves that intellectual operations are the way to master otherness and attain the contemplative serenity that is our proper end.

4. As such the ratio becomes that sovereign superego which prevents our seeing that agency in its true visage, as the primary agent of death in the psyche. Reason is the mantle that covers over both the libidinal ties and the intense aggression that informs the moral imperatives whereby the super-ego prosecutes its reign in our inner world as that voice issuing the commands before which the psyche bows in an unceasing effort to bring everything in itself and in experience into line with a priori ideas. A perfect and vicious circle has been drawn with morality the knot that assures the power of reason to regulate the psyche. That is why a dialectic of Eros as reversal and experience as inaugural only begins when a battle with the superego is joined internally and in depth. That day may never come, however, since the voice of the superego is not only loudly prohibitive but intensely subtle. Its greatest achievement is the creation in us of the co-conspirator wedded to the founding lie, which we may prove powerless to deracinate: the belief that the super-ego loves us and that we may someday gain, or regain, its love. Thereby a connection between the ego and what is called the *ego-ideal* is formed, which synthesizes the energies tied to the repressed conflicts with the m/other and the f/ather in a single agency that makes imperative the one repetitive action we perform under its watchful eye: undoing as self-unraveling. Thereby the most developed internal structure regulating the ego becomes one with the most primitive operation the psyche performs in deadening experience. Ideology, as the system of ideas and commonplaces whereby the ego is interpellated, is but the tip of the iceberg in which the psyche is packed.[44]

At the deepest register the ego is this: the self-knowledge it refuses. The compensatory structure that suppresses this recognition is the illusion of a substantial ego-identity. The guarantees that flow from thinking of oneself and experience along the resulting essentialistic lines derive their power from the self-reification they assure. This is the tie that binds the order of the concept and the dictates of the superego in that dark doubling whereby they reinforce one another: the former providing the ratio needed to maintain ego-identity by transforming every experience into a conceptualized "world in the head"; the latter by internalizing obeisance as the self-reference that gives that order its "power to claw" and to do so most when disguised in the face of an abiding but eluding love. Under the inextinguishable power of that gaze the ego reveals its final definition. The ego is the structure magical thinking builds to compel the lost object to renounce rejection and restore to us a face bursting with love, now that we've proven worthy of that recognition.

V. A New Theory of the Unconscious

A dialectical metapsychology requires a comprehensive understanding of how death-work operates, one capable of resolving the central contradiction in discussions of Thanatos within psychoanalysis. For Thanatos is both (a) a process of unbinding, of discharging tensions through fragmentation and self-dissolution, and also (b) an act binding the psyche to endless repetitions so that the eruption of the new will always degenerate into the repetition of the same. The persistence of these opposed characteristics points to the dialectical ambiguity of activity and passivity—and the ability of Thanatos to exploit that circumstance in order to triumph in any situation.

The question "whether thanatos is an activity or a passivity of the subject" contains a series of subsidiary issues that point to a single dialectical answer:

1. Is Thanatos aggressive, destructive behavior or a condition of apathy?
2. Is it possible that both states derive from a deeper self-destructiveness and function, accordingly, as attempts to stave off a suicidal depression?
3. Which enables us to pose this question to the inwardness of that lonely process: is suicidal desire unleashed violence toward another or the lure of a Schubertian nirvana freed from pain? Or both, in a fatal complicity that leads to an even deeper question.
4. Is Thanatos an excess, an overabundance of energy demanding a devastating explusion; or a vacuum, a fundamental lack that begets a feeling of non-existence that seeks finalization in the absence or rigidification of affect?
5. Is Thantos fascization or zombification? Is the narcissistic coalescence it seeks a state of fascinated self-sufficiency, requiring nothing outside itself, or one of omnipotent rage, requiring the extinction of everything in the external world that disrupts it?

The answer to these questions is dialectical because death-work synthesizes activity and passivity in a connection that binary logic cannot comprehend. In doing so, moreover, it restores to metapsychology its human

face. Freud's effort in *Beyond the Pleasure Principle* to turn Thanatos into an
instinct, an impersonal biological or "cosmological" force, is an attempt to
escape, through hypostatization, the true horror: that Thanatos is an utterly
human thing, immanent and emergent, its genesis one with the central
human drama—that of the cruelty human beings do to one another and
what, as a result, they do to themselves in the inner structure and dynamics
of their self-reference. Thanatos is a psychological drive wedded to a
demand—self-reification: that is, that we do this brutal thing to ourselves,
no matter how long it takes, and that we make this agenda the goal that
structures every relationship:

The characteristics that Freud identifies with Thanatos—unbinding,
the return to an earlier and simpler state of things, an aggressive attack on
complex structures, and, in collective behavior, the fascistic imposition of
force and its glorification are intelligible not as instincts craving discharge
but as the anti-agon, the drama whereby human beings refuse and dissolve
drama. Freud's shift from psychology to biology and then to myth in defining Thanatos constitutes an effort to acquiesce in that process and then
poeticize it in order to escape confronting death directly, in the only place
one can, within the crypt.

As preparation for that encounter I offer a final set of propositions
that picture Death (and with it the face that turned away at the end of the
previous section) in the moment of its greatest pleasure:

1. In economic terms, Thanatos has nothing in common with the
eventual running down of an Energizer battery. It is an aggressive, insatiable
drive, which necessarily becomes a project: to extinguish life in every field
where spontaneity activates envy in the dead.

2. As such, Thanatos is a libidinized activity that derives intense pleasure from its conquests. The moment of discharge is the delight of *reductionism*—of dominating and destroying complex structures by bringing
them down to a single standard, low and mean. (One of death's greatest
pleasures, accordingly, is the chance to confer non-recognition on genuine
achievement. This is the one profession academics are expert in.)

3. The vitality of Thanatos is the lust to replace the human with the
mechanical, the spontaneous with the programmed, the upsurge of the
possible with the security of repetition, the reduction of lived dialectical
connections to the rigid rules of analytic literalization.

4. Despite the noisy discursive communities it thereby gathers around
itself, Thanatos is defined by the refusal of otherness. For safety exists only if
the "solidarity" of the community is one that keeps psychic tensions to a
minimum. As pleasure and reality principle Thanatos is the force behind
social structures dedicated to the abrogation of human, and humanizing,
conflict and the effort, at whatever cost, to accommodate everything to the

logic of capitalism's dream kingdom—of subjects as empty frenzied consumers actively engaged in the one pursuit that is real, voided within of anything that would refuse or delay this process.

5. To secure this line of thought metapsychologically, Thanatos must be comprehended as an internal logic of self-regulation: as a system of principles of self-mediation that govern a psyche that is turned back against itself, one that must extinguish those possibilities of self-reference that preserve internal agon as the price of existence. To sharpen the bite of this idea prior to its development below, consider its concrete corollary. When sex becomes discharge or domination, the relieving of tension or the giving of pain and thus the act through which couples pursue reification through ritualized repetitions that convey a message of hatred—for oneself, the other, and the body—then the aim of sex is the doing of death and the growth, through the "act of love," of death's power to extend its sway over all the things we do to one another when we leave the bedroom and pretend we aren't enacting in other ways what was enacted there. For the sad and just fact of our condition is that when people die sexually they die everywhere, in every mode of their being.

VI. The Dialectic at the Core: The System UCS Redefined

A. Its Tripartite Structure

A "pessimism of strength" yields the solidest affirmations. As metapsychological effort to systematize the ideas formulated above, I offer as its overture an effort to redefine the unconscious as a dynamic system defined by the agonistic interaction of three structuring forces:

1. There is in us a spontaneous vitality, which I term the *élan conatus*. It is assaulted by the power of death. Crypted it becomes the *existential unconscious*. (To avoid confusion let me re-iterate, this sequence of ideas involves no myth of pristine origins. Everything here is retroactive in a circle of determinations that is activated by Thanatos. Death is the force that creates the *élan conatus* at the very moment it also generates the crypt as the only way to save it from extinctions.)

2. Thanatos as soul-murder strives to create an inner world of perfect hatred. The result I term the thanatoptic Unconscious. It becomes the a priori that informs perception so that death will be projected into every experience.

3. This process gives birth to the Unconscious as that system of defenses which structures and maintains the "identity" of the ego by giving it ways to extinguish inner conflicts. This system, as we

have seen, creates that vast architecture of rationality that has its capstone in the superego as the power that holds the atavism of the entire structure in place by establishing an inner voice that commands assent to the one superordinate command: the locking of the psyche in internal paralysis. With that structure in place, we are encouraged to pursue a "humanistic" and "humanizing" knowledge of our inner world, up to a safe point, that is, but then the whole process shuts down, no longer makes sense, stands in violation of reasonable canons of inquiry, evidence, and discursive intelligiblity. The superstructure thereby attains its end, in perfect adequacy to the unconscious system of defenses from which it derives, by once again closing a circle that is fool-proof, and puts an end, a priori, to all disruptions without—or within. Unless, that is, the places where the ratio puts a stop to reflection are precisely where another kind of reflection begins, by re-awakening the deeper, crypted register of the Unconscious and the possibility buried in it—the possibility of acting in a way opposed to death.

B. *The Existential Unconscious*

For whenever this register is activated the psyche experiences a new upsurge of the who/why before the possibility of taking action within. The true dialectic of the subject is thereby joined. That dialectic has the following internal structure:

1. Cruelty in attacking the soul creates the nascent inwardness that, to escape extinction, buries everything vital in itself. The energy condensed and bound to the resulting opposition between Thanatos and the *élan conatus* forms the nuclear core of the existential unconscious. Through the creation of that register, the psyche is existentialized and exists for the first time voided of any guarantees protecting it from the power of death. For now the only way one persists as a subject is through the sustenance of one's being in sufferance. But as Eliot says, "human kind cannot bear very much reality," and so a crypt is built to preserve the who/why from the threat of dissolution, which comes from two sources: (1) the overpowering nature of its own anxiety and (2) the annihilation threatened by the internalized other should one oppose that power.

2. There is one way, however, in which the existential Unconscious as who/why persists: in the questions that erupt in the course of experience whenever cruelty brings us again before the dialectical connection in which the existential unconscious is grounded—the equiprimordality of overwhelming terror and the upsurge of one's passion to be. In rubbing raw the sores of that discontent, traumatic experience reopens our contact with

ourselves in depth. The quotidian thereby becomes a world haunted by the power of suffering to reclaim those subjects who find *reversal* the only adequate response to the continued call of the crypt in them. This is the circumstance that makes the surface of our lives worth living, with the heart's intermittencies and its lacerations ripening us toward the day when the conflicts of one's inner world make necessary the one action that matters: that of taking action within by engaging an agon that demands no less than a complete reversal of the entire structure of the psyche.

3. Experience thereby reveals its deepest meaning: as the process, the possibility, whereby the who/why is recovered in recognition that our duty to ourselves is to return to the original, traumatic contingencies of our being and activate now the agon that was frozen then. "Is there any cause in nature that makes these hard hearts?" The existential Unconscious was born when this question first came down upon us through the power of the other to smite the heart. It is only answered, accordingly, when the register where those experiences are buried re-awakens the who/why as the basis for an ontological understanding and transformation of human experience. To do so, however, one must undertake the only kind of action that is possible when one finds oneself delivered over to that realm, an action in which the "self" is no more nor less than the labor to sustain a tragic self-reference lived from within the crypt.

4. Subjectivity is the tragic burden that this process imposes on us. For we speak here not of a "true self" buried deep within, but of a self-reference demanding that we turn ourselves inside out by deracinating every self-mediation that binds us to Thanatos. To be a subject is to live the recognition that one must reverse oneself—totally—with no guarantee assuring reversal. The minute one looks inside there is only one thing one can be sure of—the discovery of monstrous things about oneself, the possibility of a self-knowledge no agon can surmount. The existential unconscious harbors one recognition as its innermost knowledge—the possibility of a failure that will prove irreversible. Authenticity only begins when one risks oneself within the anxiety of that awareness. When we speak about the necessity for an absolute reversal within the psyche—and with it an overturning of the entire order of living we have constructed in order to avoid that task—we must always remember that in its reawakening the existential unconscious tremors in the recognition that failure is the most likely outcome of tragic struggle. More die of heartbreak here too, but with a pain of another order, since failure here reveals to the subject inescapable truths about oneself.

In phenomenological terms, we can conclude by offering the following picture of life as seen from the register of the existential unconscious. Tentatively, the existential subject buried in the crypt sends forth "feelers" that are repeatedly blocked or crushed. Just as repeatedly existence erupts from with: as that self-laceration in which one either dies and killing oneself lives on; or as that perpetual dissatisfaction that disrupts every complacency without ever knowing the inner fire in which it burns. Until, that is, the process matures to that crisis in which the inner "narrative" of one's life constructs the situation that brings one to a recognition of the soul-murder that presides over one's being.

Annunciation and retreat so often characterize the upsurge of the existential unconscious because the magnitude of agonistic reversal breeds despair over the possibility of actualizing its demands. For each struggle invariably reveals the power and the advantages possessed by the antagonist. While existence broods, the antagonist does not doubt or delay. It attacks. Indeed, the *constancy* of that act is what defines death as the other unconscious, the one that has already begun to work its insidious processes within the psyche long before any attempt is made to reverse its sway by engaging the agon it awaits in smug readiness at the prospect of savoring the delights of a final victory.

C. *The Unconscious as Agon*

The dialectic of the unconscious is activated only when the agon of existence and Thanatos is engaged. Until then, nothing is *possible*. Moreover, engaging this agon requires defining it with precision. That effort entails the following sequence of propositions.

1. The existential unconscious is created at the moment soul-murder enters the psyche. Inwardness is the simultaneity of those two forces in the inescapability of the agon they create. In its deepest resonance, existence is the anxiety of living in the knowledge that one is situated within and without in a world given over to death.

2. The purpose of death-work is to extinguish the existential Unconscious. The existential unconscious, in opposition, is the call from the crypt—the *cri de coeur* that is reawakened in the violated and astonished heart whenever the sight of cruelty re-awakens an original assault and an insurrection at the deepest register within. We remain alive as long as this can still happen to us. But whenever it happens, the question "to be or not to be" is one with the pessimism of strength that will be required to sustain it. In bringing us before this, the true "labor of the negative," saying *no* to death reveals itself as the a priori upon which the existential Unconscious is based. It is an a priori different from all others because it has its being wholly in its existence. And as existential Unconscious it is, contra Freud, the one negativity that knows no No.

3. In the agon that defines it, the Unconscious is the most active, the least reified dimension of our being. No id defines it. No desires or object-

relations remain immortal or unchanging in it. The agon waged by the two forces that constitute it continually disrupts all stabilities, presences, closures. Both forces destroy all peace with the opposed choices they impose on us as we struggle our way through each day. Until we sleep and find no relief from what can now be established as the true author of dreams: the existential Unconscious in its effort to produce the image that will awaken and arrest the psyche by shattering the ego and exposing the crypt. (See chapter 6 for detailed discussion of this concept.) Dream, so understood, is neither wish-fulfillment (Freud) nor a short-take on one's psyche as a whole (Fairbairn). To complicate Kafka, it is the call from deep within the frozen sea for the ice-axe. Dream is the effort by the existential Unconscious to present itself with images that reveal to it the truth of its inner condition—the truth staged when all excuses and all ego structures have been laid to rest. For then primary process ideation is one with the truth of one's deepest self-reference: the presentation of "self" in the primitive, archaic images that represent one's traumatic experiences in their originary force and impact. At the deepest node of every dream we stage again the horror of our psychic birth, with the core conflicts that structure our life epiphanized and envenomed. In dream we are once again present to ourselves at the origin, in the full anguish of experiencing our being as burden.

4. The existential unconscious is thus the call to assume a labor defined by an ideal suffering. A self so grounded has no identity prior to or outside that labor. Its only being, qua psyche, is its effort to engage the conflicts and imperatives of its inner world. As such the existential unconscious is an epistemophilic force. Unlike most philosophic systems, however, the knowledge it seeks is of what Heidegger terms *existentia;* i.e., those structures that define our being only insofar as they maximize our situatedness. Which is why, contra Heidegger, to describe such structures is to engage them, their knowledge implying an impassioned projection of oneself into the terrifying contingencies they reveal.

5. Its mode of being fits the existential unconscious to that task, however, because one thing alone defines its being—drama. The sole demand at this register of inwardness is that the psyche engage itself, totally, with no hidden guarantees controlling that drama or assuring it a cleansing resolution. In the existential unconscious all one finds are conflicts, agons that must move to crisis, arrested dramas that must be engaged in their starkest form. There is nothing *substantialistic* about the existential Unconscious. Dramatic self-mediation is its sole principle of operation, sustaining that process its founding desire.

6. If catastrophic anxiety is the source of death's power, the existential Unconscious is the only authentic rejoinder because it concretely sustains both the impact of that trauma and the possibility of its reversal. Existence is the only meaningful reply to the stake that soul-murder plants in the heart.

And that is why, for some beings, the existential Unconscious is inextinguishable as that principle of immanent critique and interrogation that disrupts all discourses and all situations in order to alert us to the traps set by the ego-ratio and the culture it serves. To distinguish such a hermeneutic of engagement from other interpretive theories, one might put it thus: the existential Unconscious provides the "basic mistrust" that enables one to see the massive avoidance behind the proclamations of "basic trust," "the bonds of love," and all the other assurances on which the ego depends for the solidification of its retreat from life.

VII. The Last Word: Thanatos—In Reply

Death in reply presents the perfect symmetry of its internal structure. For death, as *existentia,* has three primary functions, which are all finally one. Death-work is the drive (1) to destroy the original other who murdered us in our soul (2) by destroying ourselves through (3) the creation of intersubjective relationships and social structures in which everyone and everything is ruled by death, a vast necropolis in which the only company we keep is that in which, tranquilized together, we are relieved of the burden of existence and the itch of any residual anxiety over that loss. Such subjects need no Coliseum in order to embrace history with the proper *enthusiasm;* nor any help finding in history signs of progress toward the desired end. And that is perhaps the most eloquent reply death makes to the argument I have constructed here, adding as grace-note the reminder that I'm the one who keeps saying everything is historical. But to engage the issue raised here we must return again to Kant and his pivotal significance in feeding the dream of reason.

Five

From Enthusiasm to Melancholia
as Sign of History: Or, Reflection
from Kant to Hamlet

I have made a dream poem of humanity. I will cling to it. I will be
good. I will let death have no mastery over my thoughts. For
therein lies goodness and love of humankind, and in nothing
else.
                              —Thomas Mann, *The Magic Mountain*

It is not to be—what we call the human—Beethoven's 'Ode to
Joy.' It must be taken back. I will take it back
                              —Leverkühn in Mann's *Dr. Faustus*

Why finds no answer.
   —Nietzsche

You must turn yourself inside out and see the world with new
eyes.
                              —Marat in Weiss's *Marat/Sade*

THE HISTORICAL VALIDITY OF AESTHETIC CATEGORIES

I. Poetic Thinking as Ontological Regression

Art as ontological regression[1] begins when one sees that the question "why"
finds no answer within the terms for thinking provided by one's culture.
One must begin again by entering the wound at the heart of the system and
seek therein the terms for a new beginning. That act requires a break with
the entire system of guarantees, with all the assumptions that shape the
structural logic whereby the system maintains control over every inquiry,
with pre-determined results. Ontological regression becomes necessary
when one experiences the system as contradictory from the ground up. A
new way of perceiving, thinking, living, and acting must be found and then
preserved against all efforts to restore the reign of rationalist mediation.
   When art is so understood, as an original way of knowing that is
opposed in principle to the ratio, its primary significance is as a psychologi-

cal category. Art, as I will use the term here, thus refers to a way of structuring one's psyche, a means of self-mediation radically different from the three ways of being that constitute the parameters of current psychology—the neurotic, the normal, and the psychotic. As we'll see, artistic mediation gives birth to a psychological integrity that transcends these categories and the understanding of experience that derives from them; for through artistic self-mediation a reality opposed to both the pleasure and reality principles is sustained.

Art thereby establishes the true opposition that grounds the possibility of a concrete dialectic. Art's ontological power derives from its attunement to the conflicts of the inner world and the preservation of that attunement as a way of understanding experience. As Rank argued, artists are those for whom life presents itself as a problem.[2] "Why finds no answer" because for such beings the question "why?" can only be answered by exploring the original contingencies of one's being.[3] Those experiences in which the "who" of subject is bound to the "why" of cruelty. Such experiences create psyche as that memory which is bound as permanent record to those experiences that are in most of us lost and strenuously repressed: the images and affects that preserve in its immediacy and its rawness an awareness—inarticulate and profound—of soul-murder as the desire and intention of the other incarnated in the *act* that gives it away. Image as affect preserves that act as Event—as the truth that can be known only when all the masks are stripped away. (As we will see, the dialectical system of such Events, stored in the crypt, constitutes the Existential Unconscious.) The artist is one whose heart and mind is so arrested by such Events that they illumine every subsequent experience; as that repressed register that persists in the anguish that informs perception, the conscience that gnaws away at every consciousness. The artist is that being whose consciousness is constituted—and haunted—by the search for principles of self-mediation that will enable one to know the crypt and to lay bare its power to illumine what is really going on beneath the masks of normalcy.

To be an artist is to sustain a fundamental difference in the way one perceives and the thoughts to which perception leads. For most human beings, perception is either habit, as a way of discharging phenomena through selective inattention reinforced by normalizing interpretations; or projection, as the opportunity to feed one's psychological disorders and deny that fact in one and the same act. For one who sees the dominance of these practices, perception becomes what it is for the artist: the collision of two orders—the unconscious and the quotidian—in the dialectical connection that reveals their identity. In apprehending the unconscious as the register from which people act, the artist strips away the masks, bringing everyday life to an awareness of the psychological disorders that inform it. Sustaining this dialectical connection is the task of artistic representation.

Art is an effort to go to the roots of the human disorder, know it in its horror, and reverse the hold that death-work has over us by bringing an audience to the recognition of the need for a deracination at the core of the disease. Art is our most violent knowledge because it roots out every guarantee that would compromise this process.

II. *Kant's Theory of History: Enthusiasm, Progress, and the* Sensus Communis

What has any of this got to do with history? Aesthetic categories, especially rarefied ones such as the sublime, may be invaluable for studying the claims of the romantic imagination, but when history is one's subject one's concern is with the actions of pragmatic beings. Moreover, knowing the intentions of such agents and the circumstances that motivated their actions requires a painstaking concern with matters of fact and policy, which should convince anyone that "the agents who make history" have little of the poetic in their nature. History as a discipline seems to depend, in fact, on protocols of inference and explanation that are resolutely "hard-headed," even reductive, especially when one is talking about figures such as Truman, Byrnes, Groves, Stimson, Tibbets. Such are the predictable objections and one would expect a rationalist such as Kant to provide a sound a priori rationale in their support. Turning to him, however, one finds something subtler, something that reveals a new contradiction at the heart of the ratio's relation to history.

For Kant the sublime was never merely an aesthetic phenomenon or category. It was a force in history and, under the right circumstances, a category of historical knowledge and historical explanation. The burden of Kant's thought on history is to show that the ratio has its own sublime category, which is always present in its dealings with history. That category, and not empirical considerations, shapes what goes on in the discipline. It casts its glow on all the facts, bathing them in an aura that awaits those moments when vast tracts of quotidian time coalesce in events that assure historians we have found what we have always sought in studying history. Long before Nietzsche, Adorno, Benjamin, and others, it was Kant who first established the legitimacy of aesthetic categories in historical explanation and charted the basic logic for their use. He did so, moreover, in full recognition that his study of the sublime formed the basis for understanding an event, the French Revolution, which brought every idea and ideal of the *Aufklarung* to the point where a sublime category, *enthusiasm,* alone proved adequate to the task of comprehending history.[4] Long before Nietzsche, Kant knew the use and abuse of history for the life of enlightened spirit.

In taking up the Revolution, Kant's focus is not on fact but on the affective register. It is there he argues that the Event has an irreversible and lasting impact on the entire European community. Moreover, within that audience those who view events from a certain distance are for Kant uniquely privileged. They occupy the space of the historian. It is not, as we'll see, the space of a disinterested objectivity but, rather, one where rendering the sublime judgment produces a transformation at the deepest register of one's self-reference. In the enthusiasm of that audience Kant finds the affect that serves as what he terms the *sign of history;*[5] that is, the evidence, for subjects living in a world that for the most part seems to drift aimlessly, that history has a meaning and a direction; and, fortunately, one that confirms the philosophic beliefs about human nature dear to the *Aufklarung*. For our purposes the most significant thing about this line of thought is that for Kant affect is what confirms rational beliefs and does so because it gives us a knowledge of history from the inside. In enthusiasm, history is known in a way that assures us that a humanizing telos is in charge. This happens because the right affect, triggered by an event, blazes that certitude into us, banishing all doubts.

To contextualize this issue dialectically—and tap its value for histories concerned with events quite different from the uplifting and progressive ones that Kant celebrates—we need add only one complication. In proclaiming enthusiasm as the sublime historical affect, Kant mentions another affect endowed with a similar power. Kant terms this sublime affect "a vigorous melancholy."[6] It is, as we will see, the dialectical opposite of enthusiasm and as such the affect appropriate to the constitution of another, alternative history—one which begins with signs quite different from those that catch Kant's attention.

The significance of melancholy only emerges, however, after one sees what is afoot in Kant's effort to read history in terms of the sublime. For Kant that story begins, interestingly enough, with boredom. As Samuel Holt Monk shows, fascination with the sublime coincides with the sense of boredom that pervaded eighteenth century society. One source of that boredom was the perception of history; and it is here that Kant first finds the necessity for a sublime transformation. For one cannot live long in history, however universal one's essentialistic beliefs about the goodness of human nature, without needing to find some way to mediate those contingencies that suggest that human suffering is the only thing that increases in history. Delivering the *Aufklarung* from the threat of a suicidal depression is for Kant perhaps the most important function of the events in France.

Kant begins with the bad old things, the news. It has not yet become "the morning prayer of modern man." If we stick to immediate political history all we see, Kant says, is "chaos." Moreover, the primary affect this arouses in us is an *unwillen*—a mixture of indignation and depression. Raised by reflection to an idea, that mood begets this concept: history is a desultory spectacle in which blind chance rules. Since that is so, however, one constituent of the sublime experience is now in place. The desire for transformation ripens with the sight of battlefields drenched in blood. Reason is more than scandalized by the facts of history. It is mocked, relegated to the ivory tower, a signifying ape mouthing grand ideals in a world that is rent in two: reason on its throne, one with the human essence; the world utterly outside it, ruled by blind chance, or by even darker forces about which reason wishes to know nothing. In such a situation the negative, as spectacle, serves as a turning point for reason. Nurtured by nausea, boredom, and despair, the ideas of freedom and progress grow big with the longing for some realization that will break the chains that seem to bind humanity to blind necessities. We look to history for a Sign, an Event (a *Begebenheit*) that will banish pessimism and provide evidence that humanity is making progress in history. That hope, raised to the level of an idea, gives the philosophic historian what he seeks and what the Event must provide: an indication that humanity is capable of being both the cause and the author of its progress.[7]

Event thus becomes the magnet around which every humanistic guarantee of the *Aufklarung* gathers seeking succor; even perhaps a way to fashion a grand master-narrative that will enable us to warm ourselves over the bodies of the stacked corpses that grow skyward as Kant's time gives violent birth to ours.[8] Such is the possibility implicit for Kant in an Event. Once found it provides that *ecstasis* of temporality which redeems past and blesses future generations without perishing of the present.[9] At a stroke and in all three of its modes, the Event delivers us from historical temporality as blind chance and enervating contingency into time as messianic deliverance. It does so, Kant argues, because the Event (1) recalls, (2) reveals, and (3) anticipates what we are as human beings at the universal register of our humanity. It thereby guarantees the continuity and the sense of progress we need in order to live in a world we can gladly and fully inhabit. Chaos and chance are but the products of a superficial, empirical reading of history. Bound to that wheel we fail to see and stay the true course. In the Event, however, we recall and recover the abiding values of the cultural past while embracing a present that has already become a new frontier we can celebrate as we go forth, ready to forge in the smithy of a soul become spirit, the uncreated conscience of a humanity that the Event has freed to enter history, certain that every humanistic value it seeks will be realized there as an end. In the Event the ratio finds itself one with the world, the guarantees primed by the sublime affect required for their ratification.

Who would not delight to find oneself in history when such is the case. One hears in the background the strings of "Freude" and because he is playing here for the biggest stakes, Kant extends his arms to enfold the largest audience. History is meaningful not just for the actors, but for us (*fur uns*), the larger audience who assemble in awe, made present to ourselves as subjects in a new and privileged way by the Event. Our rational self-reference is here identical with our historical being. The psyche is thus cleansed of anything that would disrupt the perfect coincidence of inwardness and existence in that self-presence. In the news of the Event, we hear with eager ears a music that rushes down to the deepest register, banishing all doubts, confirming all hopes. In fact, Kant here gives us perhaps the first philosophically incisive explanation of why "news" obsesses us and how the media plays on that psychological register. History exists in the dissemination of events as they are reported in order to produce certain affects in an audience. The actors, Kant says, are too close, too caught up by the brute blood of the deed. The true meaning of events is always constituted at a certain distance, for an audience, through mediation by the proper witness. History as Event, as sublime sign, lies not in the deed but in its reception. Signs deliver their true affects and convey their deepest meanings only when made public to a large and cosmopolitan audience. In Kant's reflections on the revolution that audience is the *Aufklarung* itself as a public group-infusion. As with the sublime in nature, it stands at a certain distance from an Event but in readiness to enter a privileged space, that of a reflection on the meaning of history as revealed in the affect that the Event has awakened in a mass audience. The task of the reporter-interpreter is to provide the mediations needed to bring this audience to the state required for the Event to do its work within them.

We have entered a space fraught with ideological implications. It may, in fact, be the originary space of ideology as a scene of instruction and interpellation. Before it can become so, however, it is for Kant a state of inherent contradictions, which require a series of moralistic qualifications that bribe the superego only to recede as Kant warms to his topic. Events in France have moved Immanuel Kant at the sublime register. He is, however, deeply troubled by the connection of those affects to deeds of a morally ambiguous nature. Like a good liberal humanist he needs to find a way to control the phenomena so that everything will move in the right direction. To do so Kant will employ the conceptual strategies he developed in order to master the sublime, with the appropriate judgment now brought to bear on history. As art of historical memory, the rhetoric of humanism will thereby reveal its true intention and its necessary deceit: the need to construct and position the audience in order to assure essentialistic values as the conditions of historical reception.

The news of the Revolution in France aroused profound feelings throughout Europe, in audiences far removed from direct participation. (To get some idea think of the response throughout the world to the early days of Tienenman Square.) A vast audience, not universal, though close enough Kant argues, cutting across class lines and educational strata, was moved by events in a way that engaged with a certain urgency all of the questions and ideals that shaped the *Aufklarung*. In the gathering of that audience, distinctions of class and nation slip away. Class is here the disappearing term, "the vanishing mediator," for a "universal" audience that comes to the event bearing universal concerns.[10] Those who love humanity and long to see signs of reason and the ethical in the world respond to events in France with "a universal yet disinterested sympathy." That audience, however, harbors two contradictory needs. The desire to sustain an ethic of disinterested imperatives requires that one preserve, rhetorically at least, a certain detachment and rational control. But since reason here gives the warrant, the time is also ripe for the celebration of ideals long repressed. That is what enthusiasm initially amounts to: reason surprised at itself, caught up in events that bring its deepest concerns and ideals to a pitch in a tumult of affects that also threaten reason with loss not only of control but of its very identity. Unless, that is, the proper act of interpretation seizes the sublime occasion. To that end Kant performs a complex rhetorical act in which he is both the general audience sublimed by the Event and the speaker who addresses that audience so that its participation in the Event will move in the right direction.[11]

To do so, the philosopher-rhetorician must perform a complex act within himself. An inwardness must be forged: one that will enable one to enjoy and justify certain extreme affects, but only because they have been centered in values that are solid and that provide directions assuring us that feeling won't go too far. Such is the problem the humanistic interpreter confronts whenever the sublime (Rilke, Kafka, Dostoyevsky, Beckett, Pynchon) knocks at the door, presenting the crisis endemic to humanistic interpretation. Sublime awareness, while acknowledged (even applauded), must be contained, with the disruptiveness inherent to it purged. Such is the condition of pleasure Kant will impose on enthusiasm to give it the proper shape and direction.

The key to that mediation is the idea of "a universal yet distinterested sympathy." Its function is to protect us from the chaotic and demented enthusiasms of crowd psychology while enabling us to participate in an Event in a way that is "wishful" and charged with affect. We thereby attain a new and privileged position: that of the perfect audience, the ideal future historians, spectators who are not directly engaged, but are far from disinterested and can therefore unite with the actors at a register that goes beyond the intentions of those agents and the confusions of the moment to that which is universal and sublime in their deeds. Our participation in events is empathetic, even vicarious. Because we stand at a safe remove from the immediacy of direct engagement, we can pour ourselves into events without reserve, then withdraw whenever necessary to a more disciplined "passion."

Kant has here constructed for history and its audience the space of theater and is thus prepared to repeat and appropriate the lessons of the *Poetics.* (The theater Kant builds for his audience establishes a psychic space analogous to the one offered the audience at the L.A. Coliseum in 1945. I will return to this connection for in it enthusiasm as sign of history finds fulfillment in its ghostly *Aufhebung.*) Like Aristotle, Kant's purpose is to establish an affective structure: one in which emotional participation in a drama structures the process of judgment whereby the psychological meaning of an event is constructed in and for an audience. Enthusiasm as sign of history can only do that job, however, if Kant can purge it of those characteristics that also suggest to Kant that it is at best a borderline condition verging on dementia.

What, then, is enthusiasm? As Kant notes it is "a modality of the feeling of the sublime" possessing those characteristics we identified in our discussion of the dynamic sublime in chapter 3. Specifically, it is "an *extremely painful joy.*"[12] Moreover, its sublime power, qua affect, is indicated by the qualifications Kant introduces in order to tame this affect in the very process of defining it. The joy that wells up in enthusiasm is blind and, as Kant quickly notes, does not "deserve the approval of reason." Sublime affect taps another, deeper register. In enthusiasm only a narrow margin saves the psyche from collapsing into dementia and a *schwarmerei,* an uproar of exaltation that serves not as a sign of history but of a deeply rooted illness. At first glance all that saves enthusiasm from this fate is its transitory nature. But thereby, as Nietzsche would say, the affect, like the will, is saved and freed to do its work in the discourse that follows, unhampered by the ethical and rational considerations that Kant earlier introduced to qualify his own enthusiasm and hedge his bets.

Kant's statement that the connection with dementia deprives enthusiasm of ethical validity cuts two ways. It preserves the transcendental purity of the ethical and the categorical imperative from the Event while cutting the Event lose from that ethical limitation. Kant is explicitly conscious of the former connection, but his discourse moves within the spell of the latter. That spell establishes the power of aesthetic categories to reveal the truth of Events by showing us how deeply, in our enthusiasm, we participate in them, despite misgivings and afterthoughts. Ethics aside, enthusiasm is the "tensor of a *Wunsch*"[13] in which an infinite idea—that of history as a progress toward freedom and humanistic ideals—finds the Event capable of exerting a force that unifies the faculties and capacities of all subjects who witness or merely hear of it. In the Event those subjects are "hailed," interpellated, and bound together in a sublime feeling that is communal and provides the basis for a community in which everyone would be "*perDu*" in their humanity.[14] Enthusiasm is *Yes* from the pores to being-in-history and with one's whole psyche harmonized by that affirmation, regardless of whatever ethical qualifications and safeguards later reflections introduce. The painful joy one experiences here is similar to the joy Heidegger speaks of as the mood in which the analytic of finitude completes itself for those who find Being-in-the-world the source of the grandest sublimity—that of having one's existence fully at issue.[15] Enthusiasm is the painful joy of being delivered over to history in the full acceptance of that engagement. No longer is history boredom, chaos, or the motive for transcendence. It is a field for the realization of one's innermost possibilities. Which is why this Kantian joy pains with the intensity of a commitment: that of staking everything in a historical situation where to be is to act. Joy here pains to the core for it has become engagement. In the revolution, people committed themselves to their history as a world-historical project entered without reserve, unto death. The actors engaged in such action, and those witnesses moved in enthusiasm by it, are subjects who have overcome all essentialisms and all otherworldliness. They have embraced their finitude in its radical contingency.

Little wonder that everything connected with the Revolution should be for Kant the cause of an extremely painful joy since he is forced here to comprehend the "end of philosophy," in both senses of that term. In the Event all of philosophy's ideals are both "fulfilled" and delivered over to history as that contingency with a blood on its hands that can never be washed away by a return to ahistorical imperatives. The "tensor of a *Wunsch*" that Kant here feels is the anguish between (1) embracing the Event and the world struggling to be born in it and (2) preserving, over against it, one's ethical purity and one's substantial identity. The beauty of the situation, as we'll see, is that the contradiction can't be resolved, since the Event brings to pass, qua affect, everything that will keep reason caught up in an enthusiasm it can neither master nor deny.

To regain control, Kant therefore replaces the joy of the tensor (the register of the dynamic sublime) with a spatialization (a mathematical sublime) that brings the dynamism of affects to a halt so that he can sort things out and reassert certain guarantees. But not without the memory and the scars of the prior experience, which force Kant to redefine his favored concepts as he reasserts them. The key move for Kant is from "an extremely painful joy" to what he terms "an agitation in place." The latter state is the movement back and forth, and without the possibility of a resolution, between attraction and repulsion toward one and the same object; in this case the revolution in France. On the positive side this state of oscillation retains sublime affect because it prevents any easy discharge. At the same time, it involves a shift from an engaged agon to the recovery of Kant's particular brand of speculative humanism. The "Kantian turn" here requires an extremely subtle argument, however, in which energetics of necessity precedes hermeneutics. What can one do with an unresolvable agitation in place but spread it out and displace its anxieties by broadcasting it to others? The historian as rhetorician is born—one with the need to deny the psychological anxieties that inform such discourse. The lack of resolution is precisely what makes the good tidings and the bad share time as a source of reflections on the nature of our humanity and its historical dilemmas. Enthusiastic affect is thereby transformed, attaining the status of a judgment that looks at the excesses of the actors caught up in the Event from the proper ethical and humanistic distance. As a sublime act, however, this judgment retains the sublime power of enthusiasm, but now cleansed of all pathological tendencies. We can have it all. We stand, in fact, at the origin of modern politics and its grounding in collective, "mass" psychology. And because this possibility comes when the circle of boredom, historical pessimism, and the aimless "chaos" of political rule is shattered by an affect that has its historical significance in its power to bring a new community into being, the relevance of Kant's discourse to future historical Events (in Los Angeles as well as in Germany) is considerable. Enthusiasm is not private and that is perhaps the deepest lesson it teaches about affect in general.

An audience moved to enthusiasm by an Event finds affect spreading in two directions. Within one finds in it the basis of community. Those moved by enthusiasm join hands with all other subjects in recognition of a shared humanity. What Hegel will shortly announce as the dynamic of history and of interpersonal relations—the demand for recognition implicit in subjectivity—is here felt and given in experience as a bond uniting subjects in a humanistic community apprehended *in statu nascendi*. Such a bond is the antithesis to Hobbes' view of society as a community of animals. Nothing negative, brutal, or tragic grounds Kant's social contract. Its affective ground is that of a communal feeling in which a universal humanity becomes concretely political. The audience addressed by Events at the register of inwardness where universal ideas and ideals reside as personal concerns is moved by the Event to perform a necessary judgment. In that judgement enthusiasm achieves its final form as a universal awareness that gives birth to a new reality. Kant terms this new and marvelous agency the *sensus communis*.[16] It is a consensus in which all subjects unite in the agreements necessary to ground the eventual attainment of a universal human community. Consensus is perhaps too weak a word for what happens here. In enthusiasm one shares with other subjects the experience of belonging to that audience of which one is happy to be a member because it gives one a participatory recognition of what all human beings whom the Event has made present to one another in their essential humanity will one day come to share. One is here *"per Du"* with humanity in its universal, transhistorical being.[17] Moreover, the power of enthusiasm is such that it immediately and necessarily carries over into shared opinions, beliefs, ideological commonplaces, political and social agendas in a grand rhetorical celebration of the shared feelings that root such edifices in the ego-identity affect here confers on all subjects. A consensus is reached and with it a turning point for history. The *sensus communis* provides the basis for producing the fundamental *contents* that will constitute for future generations a rhetoric of assent to a shared world in which humanism will always find a way to harmonize away discord and discontent by preserving the common ground that is here established as the underlying truth of history.[18]

The "rationalistic" qualifications Kant reintroduces at this point therefore serve a new function. Reason is no longer a way of transcending history, but a way of assuring that history will march to the drum of the *sensus communis*. As Kant notes, the consensus is *de jure but undetermined*—a sentimental bond, with the sentiment constituting the appeal to a community that will only come to fruition when *de jure* status is attained. That process requires history. As its servant Kant offers a new understanding of the role of culture and education in furthering that process. The first task, which constitutes the act of "humanistic" hermeneutics, is to preserve the sublime affect from the dangers inherent to it. As Kant notes repeatedly, enthusiasm is an extremity constituted by a radical heterogeneity. It must be rescued from its excesses so that its value can be assured. That process requires teaching in a curriculum organized around an "aesthetic education of mankind." Kant did not recognize it, but a massive change in the relationship of disciplines is implicit in this discovery. Culture and *Bildung* must now turn on the study of literature because the aesthetic provides the categories alone adequate to understanding history and our participation in it. The historical validity of aesthetic categories requires that the study of literature become central to the very act of philosophizing.

Such a revolution is demanded because there is now a certainty that outweighs all other considerations. The French Revolution as Event has assured us that progress is the through-line of history, universal "humanity" its goal. That sign of the times is irreversible and no legitimation crisis can dislodge its power in us. Certain Events cannot, Kant asserts, be forgotten. History as cultural memory has a content. A permanent record is engraved on its tablets. And it is engraved as affect, not as idea. The new way that fact situates the human subject in history is the true fruition of enthusiasm in providing the guarantee that underlies all others, the assurance that history will eventually serve the humanity in us. What Kant first established through his painstaking consideration of the sublime has now come to pass in and for history. A sublime affect (enthusiasm) has produced a complete and irreversible change within the self-reference of the historical subject. That achievement will not be sacrificed to boredom and the return of quotidian time. It abides with us, bringing the comfort of all those memories that culture as aesthetic education provides to nourish us in our historicity. The past is thereby redeemed as ecstasis of the future. We are finally at home in history. Everything is just a matter of time. He may speak to the contrary, but enthusiasm has here triumphed over everything else in Immanuel Kant's conceptual and affective arsenal.

Aesthetic education also sets the task for those of us who live in a far different time. To repeat our debt to Spinoza, a sublime affect can only be replaced by a sublime affect. Enthusiasm triumphant takes root at a place in the psyche that can only be engaged and reversed by an agon that unlocks countervailing affects that operate at the same register. As overture to that agon a final word on enthusiasm is in order. What we seek and find in beauty, according to Kant, are those affects that correspond to the subject "just being born"—that harmonious paring off of incomparable powers that give us joy in a sense of life as limitless possibility. In beauty the human subject is fully and harmoniously present to itself with the world all before it, one with the rush to embrace life as that great adventure where every desire that gives delight in being alive will find fulfillment.[19] Life, of course, inevitably proves disappointing and we pine, until history renews us, offering itself as the substitute for hopes and dreams gone astray. Such is the source of our abiding interest in history. As Kant teaches, the "subject just being born" renews its enthusiasm for life whenever history provides the sign needed to trigger the utopian dimension of a deathless nostalgia. Enthusiasm then banishes long apathy and makes us once again at home in the world because an Event attests that we are progressing toward the realization of an order of desires capable of creating a communal identity where beauty reborn as hope promises the transformation of a re-infantilized world. What never was—paradise regained—persists as the deathless memory that is brought to a new issue by the power of Events to bind the subject irreversibly to belief in the inevitability of historical progress. Enthusiasm guarantees an essentialistic humanism as the inner teleology that will determine the eventual state of the future. This is doubtless why it is so hard, even after hopes are dashed or the true facts accumulate, to demystify an Event, why we long for Camelot and feed on its nostalgia over those long stretches when the guarantees go "underground," awaiting a Gulf War.

Enthusiasm is double vision—and Newton's sleep—the leap from the transcendental guarantee to the Event it baptizes and back in a single bound with no intervening distance. In its embrace we learn that the philosophers don't even interpret the world differently. They only appear to, misrepresenting themselves most when they claim (like Kant) to proceed from pure, disinterested reason. Like everyone else, when they find the time ripe they can't wait to crow. The affect-charged moment, the moment of enthusiasm, is not the philosopher on holiday, having a momentary lapse, but the philosopher in celebration, casting off all restraints to celebrate the moment when those guarantees without which life would be meaningless stand forth in triumph.[20] Those, like Kant, who have reflected most deeply on the ratio know that reason is never enough. Sublime support is needed. Certain emotions must be cultivated, others banished. Sustaining the temple of reason while living in history requires that the guarantees be solidified at the register of those affects that determine the psyche's self-reference. Such is the role of enthusiasm in guiding the ratio through history. And in exorcizing another affect, which as we will now see has the power to produce a historical consciousness of a radically different order.

HISTORY AND "VIGOROUS MELANCHOLY"

I. Aesthetic Reeducation

We, who stand at the other end of Kantian history, know with Benjamin, that there isn't a "document of culture that is not also a monument to barbarism." We suspect, with Broch, that while "Hegel called history the path leading to the self-liberation of spirit, [and] it has become the path leading to the self-destruction of all values."[21] Like Kant, we have signs but they are given in events that cannot be read by interpretive frameworks grounded in enthusiasm and the guarantees that shape humanism and affirmative culture. They teach us, instead, what Kant was really up to when he set out to vanquish his contemporary Scholsser's pessimistic view of history. In doing so Kant's effort is to banish his own depression and that of his age. Enthusiasm is that motive: the guarantee of progress "a priori," of deliverance from all nagging doubts and contradictions about one's world; and with it the assurance that the brutality that is the dominant fact of the "news" will not bring humanism to an integrity crisis. Within the ratio enthusiasm is the sublime affect because it delivers one from the threat of inner deadening, that psychic numbing which for Kant seems to be the inevitable result of depression.

Depression thus haunts the glad tidings as the spectre that must be banished because it cannot be constituted. This circumstance involves Kant in a paradox, which provides for us a major opportunity. For Kant lists "vigorous melancholy" as a sublime historical affect that is equal in power to enthusiasm. He has, however, no reason to develop that affect and no way. Enthusiasm vanquishes depression by voiding from within the subject everything that causes it. For Kant nothing "good" can come from depression. It is for him a passivity of subject, a slough into which one descends in a self-torment that, over time, produces only inner deadening and suicidal despair. Kant cannot constitute the power of "vigorous melancholy" because depressive inwardness for him lacks any means of self-mediation. Kant is devoid of negative capability. What Keats embraces with gladness as "the wakeful anguish of the soul" signifies for Kant a state of paralysis before the

abyss. Banishing melancholy is enthusiasm's true task and that is why supple-
mentation through a cultural-educational program dedicated to transmit-
ting the hopes and ideals that bind all subjects to certain shared values is
required. We call this operation the humanist tradition. The negative, however, keeps intruding to trouble the guarantees. It must be eliminated, or at
least contained, marginalized. That is why behind every humanist one finds
a Grand Inquisitor, who preaches that certain moods and thoughts are too
hard for humanity to bear because they have proven too hard for him to
bear. When one's profession is to cleanse audiences of painful and
dangerous feelings, exorcism structures one's relationship to traumatic
events. One can learn nothing from such Events because one can't internalize depressive signs and engage them in an agon that puts one's values at
issue. They can only serve, instead, as the signal that the operations of
humanistic rhetoric must commence. In that labor depression is no more
than the *felix culpa* that challenges humanistic ideals all the better to serve
their greater proclamation.[22]

Kant is the master of this motive because he renders any other outcome moot. The possibility of a dialectic of enthusiasm and melancholia as
sublime affects in history contracts for Kant into a single, reifying conclusion: enthusiasm is irreversible, while melancholia is *sinnlos*. The possibility
of finding in melancholia the basis for an understanding of history that will
provide a systematic alternative to enthusiasm is severed—bluntly and
finally.

Our purpose is to restore that possibility, through a systematic articulation of how melancholia satisfies Kant's criteria for a sublime affect (1) as a
sign of history that (2) in mediating an Event (3) issues in a judgment (4)
that is binding on a "general" audience, thus (5) creating a community
grounded in a consensus of shared beliefs, values, and hopes about political
and cultural history, which (6) the dialectic of Event and sublime affect, in
their immutable connection, has established as irreversible and beyond
doubt, thereby constituting (7) a permanent memory that serves as (8) an
inner regulator of the psyche and (9) the basis for a culture and *Bildung* that
will preserve and extend the values that melancholic reflection on human
history establishes.[23] As a systematic dialectical alternative to the guarantees
that inform humanism and the ratio, the rest of this chapter is devoted to a
development of the above formulation.

The notion that Depression might have an inner working (*werkzeug*)
signifying a "wakeful anguish of the soul" and thus the basis for a self-
reference capable of affecting a total change in the inwardness of the subject is an idea that does not and cannot occur to Kant. Such an inwardness
remains foreign to him, for like all apostles of the ratio Kant is unable to
mourn. Depression can never be for him an occasion for self-overcoming
through the deracination of guarantees. It is, rather, a passivity that even-

tually passes to find all the guarantees restored. Or, failing that, it is a dangerous state from which we must be protected since nothing good can come from it. Culture, as *Bildung,* has in fact a sacred duty: to banish depression by finding ways to play at giving it a hearing all the better to reaffirm an essentialistic humanism as that standard of judgement which looks on depressive experiences with sympathy and understanding, to be sure, but in the certainty that our humanity lies elsewhere. Humanism thereby attains its deepest purpose: the dialectical possibility defining the inwardness of subject is inverted. The tragic possibility that judges and measures us is brought within the confines of the prison-house. Its relationship to depression brings the primary defect of humanism to the surface. That defect is the need to contain those experiences that maximize our situatedness by activating that wakeful anguish in which we experience our existence as at issue.

Exorcizing that self-reference is the inner necessity that drives the humanistic relationship to history. Perception can't be "learned" because we can only see the world through filters in which we are already reassured. Events trouble us, but we always find a way to restore the guarantees—and with them the dawning of new enthusiasms. Enthusiasm thereby reveals that truth about itself which Kant refuses to confront. Enthusiasm is the affective itch of the pressure to forget anything that would radically situate us in the world. In our dealings with the world we move *from* and *to* a fixed identity, with enthusiasm the medium that oils the movement of thought and feeling to a this fore-ordained conclusion. In doing so, enthusiasm reveals the repressed truth of its inwardness. Sublime affects are that presence to history in which we experience most deeply its workings within us. That conditions is never more true than when affect has as its task the banishing of those feelings that assault us whenever history hemorrhages events that shatter the economy of the guarantees. Explanations must then be sought; troubling possibilities exorcized. Melancholia has broken loose from the chains in which the ratio binds it. An affect of equal power must be called upon to put it in its place. This is the secret of enthusiasm, the truth it cannot know about itself: enthusiasm is a derivative mood defined by the prior condition it strives to contain. The dialectic of enthusiasm and melancholy is thus the true or concrete beginning. And the systematic contrast whereby we will build the case for melancholy:

1. As self-reference and self-mediation, enthusiasm is the sublimity of that *jouissance* that comes with the release from all inner conflicts. Melancholia, in contrast, is the wakeful anguish of that brooding return into oneself that retards discharge in order to sustain *sufferance* as the primary relationship to inner conflicts. Through that act suffering is redefined. It is no longer a passivity of the subject, but a choice and a situating of oneself

within that choice. The loss of anxiety is the only thing such subjects have to fear. For we now know what anxiety signals: the need to learn something about ourselves we don't want to know.

2. Enthusiasm structures experience so that an audience, as *sensus communis,* participates without reserve in expression as celebration through a cathartic discharge of inner doubts and fears.[24] Melancholia is the structure of agonistic exposure whereby one strips the enthusiastic audience of their defenses in order to bar all exits that protect them from their crypt and the dark, suppressed underside of official history. As such its purpose is the creation of an existential group-in-fusion.

3. As sign of history, enthusiasm is the search for Events that solidify the identity of the ego and its ego-ideals, freeing it from inner doubts and fears. Melancholia is the assault of Events that tear open the crypt, revealing its disorders as the force that shapes history. In enthusiasm a sign is found in history that gives humanistic ideas and ideals the appearance of guarantees that have now been realized. The added appeal is that the triumph of "essential human nature" absolves the psyche from having to confront its inner world. In melancholia a sign is found that enables us to gauge the progress of Thanatos. History is known in terms of its psychological rootedness in disorders that transcend the humanistic ratio. Enthusiasm gives the principle of hope the succor it needs to sustain its project against everything it calls pessimism. Melancholia makes grief grieve on universal discontents, deracinating the humanistic pieties that stand in the way of knowing ourselves in depth.

4. This contrast enables us to give the issue of self-reference a further specification. Melancholia is the affect that assures the validity of an agon of existential reflection and self-mediation over against all efforts to limit or dissolve the vital self-contempt in which that agon is grounded. Sustaining melancholia is the act whereby the who/why attains the possibility of a deracination of guarantees. Enthusiasm is the affect that cancels this possibility by making the refusal to mourn the barrier to internalizing any experience that does not reinforce a substantialistic identity in harmony with the guarantees.

5. The aesthetic dimension reveals the deepest pull of each principle within the subject. At the aesthetic register, enthusiasm is the subject born and reborn in a love of those limits through which beauty and the ratio regulate experience in that hidden harmony whereby they reinforce and complete each other. Melancholia, in contrast, offers an aesthetic that works from within the crypt through an active reversal that *deracinates* every motive on which the beautiful depends for its promise to deliver us from existence. At the register to which melancholia descends, beauty is "the beginning of terror," found in images that are incomprehensible to the ratio because they reveal truths that shatter every limit on which it depends.

6. Two fundamentally distinct *projects* result. As project, enthusiasm is joy in the limitless possibilities of a world that will correspond to the hopes and ideals of a subjectivity that coincides with itself in a paradise of harmonious relationships that free the psyche from inner conflict. Melancholia is the howl liberated as the voice of a humanity that finds its non-coincidence with itself realized, as categorical imperative, in the effort to become adequate to the demands of a systematic knowledge of horror. It is the who/why made articulate as the "negative capability" to sustain the sufferance needed to bring deracination to the places in the psyche where it must do its work. Unlike passive mourning, melancholia does not consume itself in a grief that breaks from within, but ripens as a grief deepened through a systematic probing of the darkest psychic registers. In melancholia the howl finds its *Aufhebung*.

7. The difference between the two principles can be formulated as two distinct ways of establishing the relationship of consciousness to the Unconscious. In enthusiasm, consciousness achieves "bliss" and reification through identification with the ratio as a hyperconsciousness. Everything streams upward toward reconciliation in that perfected superego. Conceptual mediation carries every day. In melancholia consciousness achieves the tragic by discovering death-work as the force presiding in the Unconscious. Consciousness thereby becomes a psyche awake to itself as agon in a world now seen in terms of its abiding avidities. In enthusiasm, hyperconsciousness provides subject with a substantialistic identity. In melancholia, uncovering the unconscious activates existence.

8. In terms of history we may summarize the difference thus. Enthusiasm equals the principle of hope as an affective necessity. History is a continuity bent to inevitable progress in an *ecstasis* of temporality that assures *Freude*/joy as the final chorus that unites all subjects in a transcendental hyperconsciousness empowered as collective celebration. Enthusiasm is the *Aufhebung* of all contingencies by a ratio assured that its guarantees are the through-line of all historical situations. The structural continuities thereby established provide the principles of inference and explanation whereby historians know history and become its reliable narrators.

Melancholia is that pessimism of strength that sees history as the progress of Thanatos in annexing whatever threatens its telos. Temporality is the tragic *ecstasis* of an existential self made concrete as a cultural memory that matures only through a descent of Orphic imagination to the nuclear waste left behind and beneath enthusiasm's spectacles. The scorched earth holds the discontinuous story of a contingency that can only be known, in a systematic way, once we fix our consciousness on those eruptions that shatter the masks of ideology. For then continuity grinds to a halt and something else, arresting in its "unintelligibility" leaps forth in violent images that impose themselves on consciousness with a force that "weighs like a nightmare on the brains of the living," since the call, implicit in them, is for a narrative and a narrative voice that will systematically expose the guarantees and establish for history a logic and rhetoric of a radically different order.[25]

Once realized, a sublime affect cannot reverse itself. That is why enthusiasm remains stuck forever in the Coliseum. For a countervailing possibility to exist one must tunnel within the self-reference it reifies and deracinate everything enthusiasm depends upon for its power. That is the task of melancholia: to rewrite history from within by getting at the place in the psyche from which enthusiasm springs and exposing everything that sustains its hold on us. A sublime affect replaces another sublime affect only by enacting a reversal that negates it from within. For that to happen one must seek out the conflicts and contradictions that enthusiasm displaces because it is unable to bear the affective burdens they place upon the subject. The self-mediation enthusiasm flees thereby becomes the space of an agon capable of producing a complete transformation in the subject's self-reference.

To fit itself for that task, depression must be lived not in passivity and the "bitter duration" Rilke describes,[26] in which suffering is endured sans insight until it passes, but as that "wakeful anguish of the soul," which demands and gives birth to a unique order of internal action. That action is the struggle to be equal to one's experience first by unseating all the habits of mind and feeling that would deliver us from what depression engages and then by engaging the battle to know everything that breeds a sovereign disgust with the deferrals and delays one has used to escape from oneself. Depression so lived drives subject inward, to those places in the psyche that enthusiasm crypts. Welcomed in gladness it becomes the basis for a complete reversal in the relationship subject lives to itself. Anxiety is no longer the signal for flight and the employment of defenses, at whatever cost to the possibility of knowledge, but the call to engage the process of taking action within oneself.

Wakeful anguish is the *Aufhebung* of depression; the act that creates the possibility of plumbing the truth of anxiety. Anxiety always brings us before some fundamental paralysis in our psyche. It is always about a concrete, specific situation we have hollowed out for ourselves before doing everything in our power to flee it. Wakeful anguish recovers the possibility of gaining the self-knowledge we fled. It does so by creating within us the space for brooding; that space where we sustain questions about ourselves that gnaw within and that cannot be answered along the lines provided by the ratio. Suffering thereby becomes the regulator of one's self-reference. It is no longer something that happens to us, but something we do in order to become the life that "cuts back into life." Existential experience has found its logos and now moves within what I call the tragic register.

II. The Tragic Register

An event, Kant teaches, is experienced as "sublime" by all subjects, even those who only hear the news. Affect gives out the truth—that there has been a fundamental change and that we live in a new world. Such, Einstein argued, was the significance of August 6, 1945 for human consciousness: with the Bomb "everything changed" utterly "except" the one change that was necessary—a radical change in "the way we think." That task is the moral imperative that the Bomb placed on all subjects and it did so in the immediacy of affect long before ways were found to displace that knowledge in the hiding places of mind. On August 6, 1945 "vigorous melancholy" became the human condition, the sublime affect that alone attunes us to what in fact happened that day. Knowing the meaning of the Bomb depends on constituting the "range of disclosure" implicit in "vigorous melancholy."[27]

What happened on August 6, 1945? Melancholia responds to the question taking up Einstein's challenge from within by making horror "the medium of the notion," the medium in which one must mediate oneself in order to sustain the impact of the Event at the appropriate psychic register. This is not to deny the obvious fact that most of those who were horrified that day found their way back to normalcy. The danger is not that we cannot get beyond horror, but that we can. For in losing horror one loses the possibility of a knowing that sustains the impact of the Event in the immediacy of a perception, a cognition through sufferance, that is sustained in questions one refuses to compromise or renounce. When this happens experience moves in a direction antithetical to the ratio. Resistance to one's own inner death is here the Cartesian proof that one has begun to internalize the Event. Knowing history is to risk the possibility of losing one's ability to continue on in life. Faced with Hiroshima one can, indeed, die of a heartbreak from which there is no recovery. How was it possible for human beings to do this thing? To put it in Kantian terms, what must human beings be like for Hiroshima to be possible? What are the a priori conditions in the psyche that ground this possibility?

The first thing a "vigorous melancholy" knows about itself in its historicity is this: one's ability to resist the force of Thanatos within is at issue and will be determined by what one does in confronting an Event. In taking up that burden, melancholia establishes what is the ultimate dialectical connection: one's humanity and one's historical situatedness coincide in an inwardness that is defined by one's relationship to what Kant calls the sign of history. Since August 6, 1945 that principle means that to be in history is to be a tragic subject doubled back upon oneself, brought to the necessity of self-mediation at the place in the psyche the Event has torn open. The writing of history now moves within the tragic register. That dialectic, which I will formulate below, has become the psyche's inner imperative. Living it out thus constitutes what, contra Nietzsche, has become "the highest formula of affirmation possible for an existing subject."[28] Here are the essential steps:

1. The tragic register is reached when the cruelty of human relations is sustained as the basis for a theory of "human nature" that eradicates the guarantees that have been erected to assure "fundamental goodness" and reduce cruelty to a secondary and derivative status. Cruelty is the origin. Becoming human requires a self-mediation that depends on the reversal of a fundamental disorder.

2. This is the agon through which subject as who/why matures by making King Lear's question "Is there any cause in nature that makes these hard hearts?" the discipline that lays bare the avidities that inform everyday life and that dictate deracination as the only legitimate response.

3. Experience as *Bildung* thereby becomes the basis for a new phenomenology of spirit, one grounded in the process of tragic self-mediation. That *Bildung* begins when ordinary emotions no longer work to contain or discharge the burden of experience. Their continued appeal becomes, instead, the source of an anxiety of a new order, one where living without their protection activates a depth-psychological agon of primary affects that seeks out everything one does not want to know about oneself. *Self-contempt* has become the basis for a self-regulation that is ethical, and that remains so only insofar as one refuses to draw limits to the interrogation of hidden motives and the deracination that such knowledge mandates. (As we will see, we have here attained the ground for an ethics that refuses to compromise our duty to ourselves as subjects.)

5. As a hermeneutic circle made existential, deracination has become the dialectic defining one's humanity. Internalizing that imperative brings one to the tragic task—that of self-mediation from within the crypt. Through that agon "the life that cuts back into life" becomes self-reference and self-mediation. Self-contempt has become authentic suffering. One has attained the point Kafka says must be reached. Anxiety now has no way out, no relief or release. There is no choice but the agon of action within.

III. The Aufhebung of Anxiety

Anxiety is now one with the discipline of psychoanalytic self-interrogation. As mood, as Heideggerian *Befindlichkeit*, anxiety now signals the need to take action within oneself at the deepest register. To the effort to uncover the conflicts and motives that have structured one's life, one now brings a new demand—reversal. Completely transformed, the function of anxiety is now the need to eradicate defenses in order to bring oneself "before the law" of

Freud's central contribution to our humanity. The Unconscious is not dormant. It is what you do—to the other. Confession and good intentions are meaningless. The only way to reverse the condition that informs our actions is by taking action within at the deepest register. Knowing that, one attains authentic melancholia: the ice-axe is finally aimed at the right target.

When this happens a new affect regulates our self-reference. The immanent movement of self-transformation implicit in melancholia has begun. Normal mourning has been brought to the point where one now "grieves on universal bones" and acts in an agon dedicated to bringing about a reversal in the very structure of one's psyche. Melancholia is the power that lights up all the dark places within where one must take that action. The "negative" has finally become an "authentic force in the order of being"[29] because here the being of the subject is that upon and within which it works. Inwardness has become the movement whereby experience matures to tragic agency. That agency may be defined as the effort to attain an ideal suffering. These are its conditions. The tragic agent is one for whom the wound at the heart of subjectivity is both the object of knowledge and of an agon in which one grieves one's way toward a new humanity by attempting to act from within the crypt. The awareness of one's deepest disorders thereby becomes the attunement to one's innermost possibility. Tragic agency begins with this insight: whether we know it or not, we all act from the crypt. What we have to learn is how to act *within* it, how to engage an agon in which we reverse ourselves from the ground up. That process, as we'll see, is one of affective and dramatic, as opposed to rational, self-mediation. It is the ability to act *at and within* the affects that we are submitted to when our disorders assault us with catastrophic force. Melancholia as self-reference is the determination to sustain this register of experience and bring it to issue. Tragic passion is the result. It is that agency that reclaims the who/why as the basis of one's being in the world.

IV. The Aufhebung of Thinking

Heidegger asserts, "the most thought provoking thing about our most thought provoking age is that we are still not thinking." Centering one's being at the tragic register attunes thinking to the necessity for the complete transformation needed to realize that idea. Thinking now becomes what it was for Hamlet, the philosophic agent who still offers the richest articulation of its inherently tragic structure. For Hamlet thinking is not a reduction of mind to the conditions of analytic precision and propositional statement. Thinking is interrogation and anguished meditation. As reflection it breaks with the conceptual limits that have previously controlled thought in order to descend to those places in one's interiority that one only gets at by pursuing an impassioned self-reference. Mood is the way to that knowledge but only if the revelatory power of basic moods to illumine concealed truths is sustained. Thinking is the question "why" lived out as the basis for a cognition that issues in an existentializing knowledge. In that dialectic, reason is the cutting edge of passion, the principle of articulation that has as its purpose the maximization of affective engagement. The result is the outstripping of all guarantees in a *desire become a project:* that existence be laid bare in its contingency so that contingency will become the defining term of one's self-mediation.

Thinking, so understood, is a systematic attempt to overcome the limits of the ratio. One who thinks with Hamlet no longer strives to impose conceptual limitations and logical dualisms upon experience so that the head can be free of the heart, knowledge cleansed of affect, and the "sin of existence" absolved once knower and known have been separated from one another in tidy boxes and objectifying relationships. As Hamlet shows, to know is to plunge oneself into the world, to engage in an act that offers no fixed protocols, protections, or predetermined rational results. Tragic thinking is the outcome of an immanent critique in which experience takes on the power to transform the very nature and process of thinking. (The above paragraphs, as prelude to its detailed definition, attempt to free the tragic from the ways it is understood when defined within the framework of humanism and the ratio, so that we can see it from itself, liberated in its existential and psychological primacy from the limits that those frameworks impose to deny the challenge it poses to the assumptions on which they depend.)

V. Melancholia and the Tragic Historian

These issues take on a special intensity when one tries to bring the tragic to history. To talk about the claims of tragedy as a literary form is one thing. But to suggest a tragic principle at work in history and in the public actions of responsible men and nations activates powerful defenses. Constituting it entails the following sequence of changes in the historical disciplines. To open history to a tragic understanding one must (1) blast the continuum and the guarantees; (2) liberate contingency in a radical way; (3) then track down the connections that emerge among phenomena and situations that are widely dispersed and appear discontinuous, (4) by unearthing the core disorder that informs the development of a collective agency (5) which comes to fruition in the combined efforts of the institutions required to give hegemony to the psychological disorder at the foundation by its solidification through collective action.[30] With such a hermeneutic in place the writing of history becomes the effort to sustain the affective register of

Events, by developing explanations that do not mitigate these primary "facts."

For that to happen, however, the tragic historian must synthesize three contexts of psychological investigation in an evolving, dialectical logic. (1) Psychotic anxiety must be uncovered as the motive shaping the development of the interlocking agencies needed to evolve a collective unconscious that is both historical and decidedly non-Jungian. (2) The connections thereby established must be grounded in an understanding of Thanatos as the totalizing logos that unites widely dispersed agents in the contribution each makes, from their particular station, to a demand that finds epiphany in the Event. (3) Understanding the Event must, accordingly, lay bare the psychic register at which one must act in order to address and reverse what it reveals as the human condition. The labor of the negative thereby attains a determinacy that opposes all transcendence—and all nostalgia. The study of history brings melancholia to a new self-mediation—dread. That category is now the one that quickens perception to a knowledge of death-work as the logic behind the slouching of events, in quantum leaps, toward what is for that telos the only resolution that makes sense.

Tragic knowledge is the effort to get inside that process, in the realization that knowing death-work from within is the condition required for its reversal. To do so the historian's task is to apprehend death-work as the force moving events by locating those (1) *turning points* in that history that persist as (2) *force-fields* giving history a (3) *through-line* binding the past to the present in a temporality that *implodes* toward the future. Comprehending the historicity of death-work as *ecstasis* of temporality requires developing what I term a logic of the anti-*aufhebung*—a logic that apprehends death, *in statu nascendi*, in a past we are finally able to recover because we have eliminated the guarantees that consign to silence everything that would contribute to that knowledge.

Tragic existence is that hermeneutic of engagement that meets the totalizing logic of Thanatos with the only valid rejoinder: a counter-*Bildung* grounded in principles of dramatic self-mediation that cancel the logic of rational self-mediation Hegel used to structure his phenomenology of experience. At first glance, of course, this prospect looks like a vast anti-*Bildung*, a Kantian *unwillen*, redolent of cultural despair. All the places in culture where one hoped, with Goethe, to find oneself nurtured, have become prison-houses where one now finds death-work disguised as the "bonds of love" that unite "objective spirit" (family, church, state, legal and political institutions) in a *Heimat* and *habitus* constructed as a testament to the guarantees. Authentic *Bildung* begins when one systematically suffers the collapse of these foundations and internalizes that breakdown as the overture to reversal rather than despair. One who takes up that process finds counter-*bildung* in this: history is the basis for a knowledge that brings the subject to the necessity for reversal through an agon of deracination that must bring about a complete change at the deepest register of the psyche. The inwardness of subjectivity and the inner meaning of history now meet, establishing the true dialectical opposition. Horror is met with the only appropriate rejoinder: the rooting out from within of everything that makes one complicitous in its production. Change in depth has become the demand that historical investigation now places on the knower. Thinking about History is anguish sustained and lived out as one's primary relationship to the facts. In that mediation Hans Castorp was only partly right: to be stronger than death, love must reverse death concretely by taking up all the ways the world is given over to its operation—and perfection.[31]

The most revealing way to picture history as counter-*Bildung*, however, is in terms of those for whom histories are written. To reformulate Benjamin, the greatest danger to the dead is their sacrifice—to the needs of the audience.[32] To write history from the tragic register one must reverse all the ways in which the demands of the audience control the writing of history in order to guarantee the reassertion of the guarantees. This happens through the functioning of three factors that supplement one another in a process that is simultaneously cognitive and rhetorical: (1) the disciplinary protocols whereby facts are determined and the "soundness" of hypotheses evaluated; (2) the rhetorical contract whereby a language of shared beliefs, desires, and values structures the relationship of author and audience so that certain assurances are guaranteed and the appropriate cleansing operations performed; and (3) the narrative paradigms whereby a sound and reliable authorial voice creates patterns of desire and expectation that shape the narration of events and our involvement in them to assure a resolution that fufills predetermined emotional needs. When we read (and write) history, all three variables work simultaneously *in* and *on* us. Only a systematic break with these practices will produce the alienation-effect required to reverse their reign. The tragic historian's task as writer is to "get the guests" by exposing how the guarantees shape the writing and reception of history so that anything that could shatter their economy is exorcised. To enact that reversal concretely, the writing of history must become an *agon* in which the appeal of the guarantees is engaged then blocked and thereby doubled back against itself by the power of the Event to generate a counter-discourse. The Event is the true *Entfremdungseffekt* and writing must do everything in its power to release its impact.

As we will see shortly, this effort requires perhaps the greatest break of all. For there is a single principle that underlies the three operations described above. It is the principle behind our need to write histories—and the hunger that finds ratification in the product. That principle is *catharsis:* the ritualization of events so that a collectivity will derive from history the succor it needs to sustain the beliefs and guarantees that deliver it from trauma and contingency. History qua catharsis is the process whereby that community is created, reinforced, and reaffirmed. As such, catharsis is the ground principle that maintains the entire system of guarantees, the necessity that underlies all forms of historical narration within the ratio. And ironically, as we'll see, its subtlest and most complex operation is developed in the structures it has evolved to contain the tragic by appearing to realize and embrace it. To engage that issue we need as our Vergil a new guide. For to overcome the pull of catharsis one must find in melancholia a way of thinking and being that does not purge itself of the tragic but sustains its power to activate the only dialectic that is concrete, that of inwardness and existence.

HAMLET, THE CONTEMPORARY OF THE FUTURE

To be aware of limits is to be already beyond them.

—Hegel

The previous section establishes the task for melancholy; to generate from within melancholic experience a radically new understanding of thinking and the dynamics of reflection.[33] If melancholia is that internalization which preserves the hermeneutic of historical engagement in its intrinsic and irreducible complexity, then *thinking* must be reconstituted along the following lines. Reflection is dread, the attempt to open up for conceptualization a disruptiveness similar to that which Artaud ascribes to the valid image. To think existentially, concepts too must preserve the conditions of their origins. They must come upon us as great calamities and address us with a vehemence that refuses to release us from their grip. For that to happen concepts must become *questions,* kept open as such in the claim experience makes on us by eluding our conceptual grasp. A question remains existentially alive only insofar as it forces upon thought the condition Rilke described when he said that in order to keep thought alive we must wait for that which has become concept to again become image. Only thereby can the primary awareness of anguished perception remain the reality directing thought. Reflection, so constituted, offers a systematic contrast to the concept of reflection that informs the ratio and that was articulated with greatest clarity by Kant. The task of reflection, Kant argues, is to establish the conceptual limits in which thinking must acquiesce. Through reflection the ratio thereby confirms and reifies itself. Melancholia replies by seeking for reflection a different dynamic, derived from the unique powers of a neglected discipline. That discipline is soliloquy. *Soliloquy* is that brooding on the question who/why that produces a complete transformation in one's self reference and one's relationship to the world. (As such it is, as we'll see, the *Aufhebung* of melancholia, the act through which it gives itself irreversible self-determinations.)

The five soliloquies that follow attempt to illustrate the distinct powers of soliloquy as a process of dramatic self-mediation that sustains a way of thinking that is radically different from the limits that define thinking within the ratio. In keeping with that logic, each soliloquy is also the *Aufhebung* of the one that precedes it, the total sequence forming the immanent movement of thinking from the ratio to the tragic.

I. First Soliloquy: Toward Subject as Who/Why

There is a register of the psyche where certain questions are lived in passion. The determination so to sustain them is, in fact, the proof that one understands their claim and responds from the appropriate inner register. Subject as who/why is that self-reference. It is also an experience most subjects will do virtually anything to escape. For once relate to oneself as who/why and all is changed, utterly. Disquietude now haunts all presences. Flight only delays a judgment that persistently rises up from within. "I have become a problem to myself" (Augustine) and that condition transforms all situations. I am a *who* defined by the question *why* and it dives, like the furies, into the most hidden places of one's psyche. Subject as who knows why as a existential question that is addressed, first and foremost, not as philosophy traditionally asserts to Being-in-general or to the cosmos but to one's inner world in the anguish of the discovery of buried conflicts that must be engaged in agon and sustained as such against all attempts to dissolve them by substantializing either the question or the questioner. "Why finds no answer" (Nietzsche)—except through agonistic descent into the interior. To be a subject is to reactivate the *élan conatus* of one's being as existentializing passion and engage it utterly in the struggle to know the truth of one's inner world.

If one has the passion for this act there is in fact only one fear: that one will compromise the process by reductively imposing the ways of thinking and living that ruled before the question who/why bit into the psyche at this register. One glimpses here the origin and true function of the ego and the ratio: the dissolution of existence into the formulae of mind. Schopenhauer defined genius as the ability to sustain, for five minutes, an awareness of the arbitrary nature of everything that most people regard as certain. Existence is that act, but sustained in a temporality that can't end, since it reverses time by hollowing out within the subject the space of an inwardness in which the question of existence, brooded, takes on the scope appropriate to it: that of a world submitted to that interrogation for its determination.[34] With the ego gone, the holes in the world become its defining characteristics. The act of questioning becomes a process uniting the ontological and the existential. Why is here ontological because it insists on making an in-depth knowledge of the psyche's disorders the basis for a comprehensive understanding of the ways in which those disorders structure the world. Who is here existential because it finds within itself both the source of the problem and the terms of the only possible solution. As a who I am now at issue as a question to myself that can only be answered by taking action within the crypt, since I now know that it contains the experiences upon which I have never ceased brooding, those experiences that first delivered me over to myself as a subject, as a who existing thrown into a why that must be fathomed. Inwardness is the development of the dynamics of this self-reference. Its first product is a transformation of the nature of reflection.

II. Second Soliloquy: The Life of Questioning—Reflection as Interrogation and Self-Mediation

When it moves within the medium of tragic awareness, reflection becomes an interrogation defined by the asking of existential questions. Contra the Kantian tradition, reflection is not the application of fixed logical and rational principles to practical and "metaphysical" problems so that they can be reduced to manageable terms and thereby solved. Or, lacking that, dismissed as unintelligible given the limits beyond which thought cannot go since the duty of reflection is to show that the solution of existential problems lies in their disappearance (Wittgenstein) or the triumphant demonstration (Aristotle) that where there is no answer, there is no question.[35] Thinking as existentializing reflection arises when a radical discrepancy is felt and sustained between meaning as defined by the ratio and those experiences that are valuable precisely because in them what is confusing, unintelligible, and abnormal asserts its power to assault our concepts and introduce a rupture with normalizing modes of behavior. Reflection then becomes *interrogation*, the effort to sustain questions as questions, not as preludes to answers. Questioning becomes the effort to produce that next, deeper question that overturns the prior order of thought. This is the dialectical structure of questioning. It is short-circuited whenever asking questions is seen as the repetition of an identical act rather than the immanent movement of a radically destabilizing process. Questions generate deeper—and more powerful—questions because of the gaps, complexities, and wounds that each successive question opens up in the given. A question, properly grasped, is a great gap in being. "Is there any cause in nature that makes these hard hearts?" That gap is widened by further questions in a dialectic where questioning as overturning produces as its *content* the new *context* that is submitted to the claws of the new question. The movement of questioning thus generates an understanding of concrete experience as the density of a progressively deepening context of relationships and responsibilities. Questioning thereby finds in self-mediation the only adequate reply to the situation it has created. It has produced its own *Aufhebung*.

Questioning now moves in the medium of a radically new interiority, which is not that of a substance with either an a priori mental essence or the stability of a social, consensual identity. Interiority is subject as an anguish at issue to itself over the one question that questioning has now made concrete—to be or not to be—as a force that simultaneously exposes the world in its mendacities and the "self" in its appalling inauthenticity. Questioning has become the act whereby a subject brings itself before issues of "infinite concern."[36] We have entered the space of reflection according to Hamlet, that room where the bright lights are always on, focused in a self-interrogation that drills a conscience into one who is held awake in that ideal insomnia which annihilates the "sleep of reason." In the ensuing dialectic, thinking finds a new definition. Thinking is now a deliberate, impassioned attempt to turn thought back against itself and all available solutions. Questioning is the radical, impertinent act that breaks with the hidden concepts and guarantees Socrates cleverly imposed to structure the act of questioning so that the ratio (Platonic style) would control the process of questioning in order to guarantee that everything remain in the head, in a clear conceptual space. Hamlet's effort, in contrast, is to turn questioning back upon itself so that it might discover the motives and conflicts informing rationality and reveal them as that which most deserves to be called into question. This act is the watershed moment in the movement from mind to psyche. The logic of the ratio is no longer able to control or comprehend the process of reflection. A discovery of psychological motives casts a skeptical light on all its certainties. As Hamlet realizes, we think as we do so that we won't have to know certain things. And as he discovers, sustaining this insight brings one to the knowledge that virtually everything in the ratio is rhetoric, a vast argument from consequence that has as its overriding motive the Grand Inquisitor's belief that people are too weak to sustain the act of questioning and need answers, however arbitrary or existentially limiting. Socratic questioning is the parody of existential questioning; the operation through which mind gains training in the procedures that eradicate existence.

The "scandal" of thinking finds its dignity in the courage that defines it. Why should thinking be restricted to what makes sense? Why should we stop as soon as we find the solution that discharges what otherwise creates anxiety; the limits in which we happily acquiesce because they give us a way to coincide with ourselves in a world we can readily inhabit? The world in the head is one where thinking is like the longing for "catharsis" and works best when it dissolves itself. Or, to put that operation in its true light, when thinking has nothing to do with dread and is permanently safe from the sense of incredible joy and liberation that wells up in some beings when interrogation "goes too far" and discovers that reflection is not an after-thought but exists as an independent power with a sovereign duty: to over-come all the concepts and arguments that are used to contain it.

Questioning is that gap in being that existentializes the subject *in* and *through* the discovery that why finds no answer and no exit. As subject one has become the questions one asks: and in so being one has outstripped all essentialisms of mind. Experience has taken on a new definition and direc-tion. Experiencing oneself as a question is the ground for a new interroga-tion: that of the ratio as a system of motives, not reasons; which exist to deliver us from the world, not to know it. Thinking becomes, accordingly, the effort to recover everything sacrificed to their design. One who is not awed and overjoyed by this prospect has not felt its power. To know the world in which we suffer, love, and die, without interposing the comfort of self-deceit, is to live in the gladness of being.

A thinking so quickened finds *beginnings* in contradictions—in the embarrassing, discarded fact, the image that is true insofar as it is violent, that which in horrifying us arrests and compels attention. The purpose of thinking is no longer to minimize any of this, to explain it away so that the ratio's handle on the world will be restored, but to maximize it so that contingency becomes the Real in which we situate ourselves. The process of thinking now has a logic that is one with its existential ground. Hegel's "to be aware of limitations is to be already beyond them" is true only if the production of questions that overturn the entire previous framework of thought also produce the subject ready to engage that context. Reflection must existentialize the subject who enacts it. The only way to sustain that possibility is by rooting out every assumption whereby thinking tries to protect itself from within. Reflection as hermeneutic of engagement thereby existentializes both thinking and the thinker. The circle in which it moves is radically different from the "friendly confines" of the humanist tradition.[37]

Reflection now has a double task, the bringing together of two op-posed forces in a single act, which issues, each time "soliloquy" remains true to itself, in a new determination of the subject's inwardness. Reflection as engagement is the attempt to preserve and deepen those experiences that most completely deliver subject over to itself. It is the ability to *mediate* experience by resisting discharge through the creation of an inner tem-porality that is wedded to an endless brooding directed at the most hidden places in the psyche. Reflection as soliloquy is both the way one knows one's psyche in depth and the act that sustains that knowledge in agon. Reflection has attained its innermost dynamic. It is the act in which the identical subject-object engages itself in an impassioned effort at deracination. That process, in turn, has two objects, two moments: (1) it is the overcoming of less exacting ways of thinking and (2) a rooting out of the psychological motives and disorders that underlie them and are sustained by them. Genuine thinking "cuts back into life" in two ways simultaneously. The limits it transcends bring it to the hiding places that must be engaged in an agon that must, of necessity, issue in a new self-reference.

Hamlet again points the way. In him interrogation seeks that beginning which deepens and maximizes the burdens of existence. Through that act the why is no longer worldless or abstract. It is directed at—and into—the who. Existential questioning is self-mediation. The self-reference of subject is the questioning of itself; thinking the attempt to grasp, live out, and articulate the logic of an engagement that moves in a circle that develops only insofar as reflection progresses into the crypt in order to know and overturn a world that now stands starkly illuminated by it. In authentic reflection thought explodes from within then throws itself out into the world. "The name of action" resides in that dialectic: in the power of thinking to expose, in their necessary connection, the disorders of two realms. Thinking thereby attains a true or concrete beginning. The circle of hermeneutic self-engagement has issued in a situation where contingency is now present in its true bite—without and within. It is not a momentary departure from reason, but thought's fundamental condition. And as such a condition that brings about a fundamental transformation of anxiety. Anxiety is now existence and contingency rubbing one another raw in an embrace that has become a ripening.

III. Third Soliloquy: Thinking as the Cutting Edge of Passion

Thinking begins in passion and produces a deepened passion as the act that sustains our engagement in the world. The circle of reflection is not a movement of ideas but of *affect,* from its immediacy to its fullest meditation. *Affect is the reality of our being as act.* It is the way we experience the burden of responsibility for our existence in an anxious awareness that is accepted as a destiny acted upon or fled in panic and the superimposition of defenses to shut down the world it alone puts us in a position to cognize. The purpose of thinking is to maximize the demand that the affective register places on us; to make affect the self-reference in which we judge ourselves so that perception becomes the conscience of consciousness. The daily news is not a morning prayer, it is a *pensum; amor fati* the energy one invests in concretizing a commitment to contingency. Passion, so understood, is the being of a subject whose being is determined by its historicity. It is the *élan conatus* in its existential and historical *Aufhebung;* the category of passion does not refer to ordinary emotions and their ways, but to life itself at that point of inner intensity where existence is either engaged or deadened. It is our self-reference in its existential historicity. Passion so understood is the discipline that distinguishes human beings from one another, the standard that measures our choices and our conduct by maximizing our responsibility to the world. As such passion is the way we live out the original choice that informs the subsequent choices that determine what is called our *character*.[38] For choice determines us existentially only insofar as it is invested in those values whereby we judge ourselves. Passion, as the way one maximizes those affects that existentialize us, is the act that grounds the dialectic of inwardness and existence in immediate experience. As such passion is the basis of engagement and its medium. The deadening of affect, as Beckett shows, is hard work. Even harder is answering the call that passion constantly places upon us. If we live, for the most part, between these extremes, it is also true that in the process an agon is working itself out and moves toward situations in which our choices "present the bill." Reversal and recognition haunt us because they are the way in which the affects we live structure our experience.

Passion, and not the ability to think, is thus the distinctive act that makes us human. That is why any attempt to *change* must work within affect itself to bring about a reversal that only becomes possible when those buried affects where terror abides are met by an equal passion. Depressive brooding is not a worldless mood that consumes itself within, but that self-laceration that mandates self-overcoming. It binds what are called extreme, pessimistic, "neurotic" affects to that which authenticates them. The process of taking action within oneself only begins when dread has articulated and brought us to that agon where one exists fully for the first time through the act of putting oneself totally at issue. This is the "life of questioning" brought to prime. Self-reference as self-mediation within the crypt thereby becomes a passion of the soul, the principle of self-regulation one brings to every experience to assure its deepest engagement.

None of this speaks ill of reason. On the contrary, it gives us a way to reclaim it in the dignity of its true office. Reason is the cutting edge of passion. The clarity of acute thinking is its ability to render inescapable a knowledge of the affects that actually structure our life and the actions we must take not to dissolve passion but to maximize the power of its engagement. What follows schematizes that dialectic in order to define its primary terms.

The world is given to us through the revelatory power of primary moods. Mood is that attunement in which inwardness binds itself to the world in affective cognition. When the fundamental contingencies bite directly into a subject who is made at issue to itself in that experience—a heart made alive to itself as passion—then knowledge is suffered as the delivery of one's being over to a situatedness that is primary and that cannot be transcended. Existence and ontology have become one. Mood sustained thus issues in existentializing affects that bring us to a new understanding of our fundamental condition. For such affects bind our being to the world as that reality which is prior to desire. For the right subject, that fact creates engagement, whereas for most it is the beginning of resentment. This split constitutes the significance of primary moods: in them we are situated at the turning point of our being, where choice proves determinate.

For those who follow the road less taken, thinking becomes the effort to sustain the revelatory power of such moods through the creation of what I term inwardness. This is an interiority radically different from all others, defined by the effort to preserve events in their power to force us to take action within ourselves at the deepest register. Inwardness as self-mediation is the refusal of all essentializing protections. Its first issue is *passion* as a law of self-regulation that is both the origin of thinking and its primary result. Passion is not a passivity of subject and there is nothing private or "subjective" about it. Nor is it a barrier to correct, "objective" perception. It is a *choice* that concretizes itself in an act: the determination to sustain an existentialized relationship to the world by refusing to renounce the power of questions-lived-in-sufferance against all efforts to escape the situatedness they impose. As such, passion is the *élan conatus* of the subject recaptured as existential historicity. In that dialectic passion and thinking are one. Those who lack the former invariably compromise the latter; as in the Western logos, that great inversion whereby mind separates itself off from that which measures it.[39]

To summarize the preceding structure: (1) mood is attunement, (2) thinking method, and (3) passion the end. *The passions of the soul* are those affective determinations that derive from this dialectic. This category refers to a dynamic of self-reference that is radically different from ordinary emotions and their modes of operation. Passion as self-mediation is the process of infecting ourselves with ourselves in order to take action within ourselves. The affects that compose this dialectic (anxiety, dread, melancholy) have their being in the process whereby they rub themselves raw. Affect as self-mediation is an agon immanent in affect that depends on nothing outside affect to generate a fundamental change in our self-reference. Affect affects itself, producing its self-transformation. But "to want the change" is here "to embrace the flame." Its first product is a new definition of reflection.

Reflection is self-mediation as affective self-determination. That dialectic is defined by the search for a new principle of "absolute knowing"; a principle of affective self-reference capable of addressing all the realities left behind in the march of Hegel's rationalistic self-mediations.[40] Melancholia is that determination. It is the world grieved in a perception/cognition that refuses to release us from its demands. Thought as passion is the effort to sustain that energy through a radical transformation of what we think of as "mind." This transformation is the subject of the next soliloquy.

IV. Fourth Soliloquy: Thinking as the Movement from Mind to Psyche

Is the tragic still possible? That is the question at the center of this book. To engage it two preliminary clarifications are needed. (1) Tragedy as conceived by humanism and within the ratio is a repression of the tragic. (2) The poststructuralist dismissal of the tragic as nostalgia is a prime example of the failure of the self-ironizing sensibility to comprehend the tragic dimension of its own "unhappy consciousness" and thereby see itself as a moment in a larger dialectic. These alternatives control discussions of the tragic and need to be transcended. For that to happen, however, despair must be apprehended correctly—as a starting point.

A. Shattering the Ego

When it moves within the medium of affect, reflection is the originary power whereby we exist as subjects and attain a knowledge of ourselves as existence. It is the unmotivated upsurge of that process through which the subject as who/why reverses everything prior to that starting point in the order of being and behavior. Once radical reflection begins "all that is solid melts into air," especially the architectonic structure whereby the ratio limits self-knowledge so that whenever the psyche suffers itself everything proceeds *from* and *to* a fixed identity. That structure is the ego. It grounds the entire system of guarantees so that identity is enhanced and reinforced by reflection, but never existentialized or overturned by it. In the ego I am one with myself in that substantiality from which I reflect and then confidently put an end to reflection whenever it gets out of hand.

Authentic reflection, in contrast, is that self-mediation which brings about a complete transformation in one's self-reference. One is here oneself the object of an interrogation that exposes the ego and everything on which it depends in order to discover in self-contempt the basis for a radically different self-mediation. Melancholia is its *Aufhebung*: the recognition that in the matter of being honest with oneself the ego has nothing to offer. Contra Freud, in melancholy the shadow that falls across the ego is not that of the malign superego but of one's own inwardness announcing the imperative of deracination from within. Taking action within oneself only begins when one tunnels to those experiences where the affects that define one's relationship to oneself are locked. It is sustained only when sufferance preserves that agon against all efforts to return to the ego and its world. With this reversal the true instauration begins. Mind is replaced by psyche as subject's true self-reference; ego identity and defense by agon and affect as the medium of self-mediation.

Thinking is the effort to get us to this agon by showing reason the motives that inform it so that those motives can be interrogated in terms of the desires and disorders that they project and deny. Such a process is radically destabilizing, for with each advance comes the recognition of a deeper disorder, which can only be confronted by finding for thought principles distinct in their operation from those that structure the way of thinking that has been overturned. Reflection so actualized constitutes a dialectical "inversion" of the Hegelian *Aufhebung*. Rather than using the ratio repetitively to explain everything else, we progressively break with it in order to recover the distinct modes of awareness that inhere in orders of being prior to it. The movement from mind to psyche is not simply a shift from the cogito to repressed desires and conflicts; it is a discovery within the life of feeling of distinct principles of self-mediation that both explain the hold the ratio has on us and concretely reverse it.

B. Constituting Affect

Asserting the primacy of affect carries with it the requirement to make its immanent dialectic the process that completes the act of thinking. But how does one think in and with one's affects? First by listening to them as attunements to inner conflicts, not as pressures that must be discharged. Affect gives me the burden of my being in its situatedness by delivering me over to myself as a subject lacking a fixed substantial identity. Everything we learned previously about what it means to keep a question alive as a question must become the way we live our affective life. That method assures one thing: an exacerbation of the affective process so that those affects that put us on trial will be sustained in their power to root out all the hiding places sequestered in those emotions on which the ego depends in order to relieve us of existence. The dialectic of affect is the process whereby we void ourselves of an emotional substantialism. The ego is annihilated by the movement of existential reflection because it is unable to contain or explain the kinds of affects that agonistic self-mediation establish as principles of self-mediation. When one goes deep in the psyche, the ego's ways of feeling are of no avail, except as signs of defense. Such is the just and withering judgment passed on those emotions that have no purpose other than to arrest, smooth over, and resolve the agon that melancholic affects activate in the soul. In the interiority of that theater, self-mediation is not controlled by the ego and does not result in a return to it. Action within is the embrace of a suffering that drives us inward. To know how one "really feels" and then to take up deracination within the order of primary affects brings to fruition the self-contempt on which Nietzsche based the possibility of "living a life that would bear aesthetic scrutiny." It is , for us, the place where all reflection leads. Inwardness is reversal within the agon of melancholia as the affective dialectic whereby the subject, infected by itself, takes action within itself. To do its work nothing must compromise the immanence of this process. That means that the first task is to deracinate the principle that has thus far shaped the understanding of the tragic and that constitutes, as I will show, its counterfeit.

V. Fifth Soliloquy: Melancholia versus Catharsis

A. *Catharsis as Resentment*

Melancholia is the dialectical overcoming of catharsis. Their systematic contrast will dramatize the difference between self-mediation at the tragic register and its abridgment by the guarantees.[41] In the process catharsis will reveal itself as the handmaid of enthusiasm, the principle in our emotional self-reference whereby the ratio controls what exceeds it so that every troubling experience becomes a prop in the program of humanistic education and interpretation.

Let me offer two preliminary definitions to set the terms of the contrast. *Catharsis* is the structure of resolution and discharge whereby painful emotions are prevented from impinging on the ego's defenses. Through that structuring of affect painful experiences are transformed into "pity and fear," and "emotions of a similar order," which share a single defining characteristic: they act upon themselves in order to do away with themselves. *Melancholia* is the structure that sustains anxiety by rubbing raw the sores of those buried affects that must be engaged in agon if we are to take action within ourselves. Affect here does not act upon itself to produce its purgation; it acts within itself to bring about a complete change in the subject's self-reference. While catharsis moves toward Milton's "calm of mind/all passion spent" or something analogous, melancholia is the principled concretization of the recognition that "spirit is the life that cuts back into life." Catharsis produces resolution; melancholia internal revolution.

1. Emotion as defense: displacement, distance, and deliverance. Humanism and the ratio need more than interpretation to control the tragic. What is needed is an a priori way of structuring those affects that tragic experience awakens so that resolution will triumph. The key to that operation is the installation of certain emotions as the *immediacy* that *structures* human response in a way that gives lip-service to the tragic while producing an internal distancing from it. Thereby the moment in which one supposedly embraces the tragic becomes the first step away from it. Such is the function of pity and fear as structures whereby we resist internalization by mimicking it. In feeling pity and fear—whether about a literary representation, a public event, or some personal matter—we step back from anxiety and assert, within feeling itself, a principle that aligns experience, however painful, with the a priori demands of the ratio. Anxiety opens up within us a drama that is exacting and utterly personal. Pity and fear deflect the blow: pity by rendering the internal a matter of sadness over "undeserved misfortune" (as a result of chance or excess); fear by shifting concern to external matters we must control in order to live lives free of unexpected reversals. Together these emotions enable one to manage feelings so that passivity, adaptation, and the maintenance of "identity" control one's dealings with painful experiences. To this end a little tragedy is useful, insofar as it helps habituate us, through the exercise of pity and fear, in exorcizing darker possibilities before they work too deeply upon us.

The philosophic economy that pity and fear serve is the cardinal instance of the attitude toward the emotions that has dominated western philosophy. Emotion is a disruption, a confusion, and a distortion that must be overcome for the subject to preserve the proper relationship to itself and the world. This is not to say that we are devoid of emotion nor that experience is ever lacking an affective valence. Happiness and correct, consensual living lie in nurturing those emotions that harmonize with the ratio. But the negative always rears its head. Something must be done to assure control over those experiences where inner pain begets a dread that threatens the edifice. In this labor pity and fear are far more important than rationality because they have the most important job to do, their task being to bring about from within affect its own cleansing. Catharsis thereby reveals its central function in sustaining the ratio. *Catharsis is the affective wing of the guarantees.* Through its working, disruptive experiences are structured so that they are deprived of their affective power. Pity and fear displace events that threaten to open up the disorders of our inner world in order to short-circuit that reference. They thereby secure, in a concrete way, the primary purpose of all defenses—denial. For in pity and fear denial is not a mental operation, but an emotional act. These emotions give us, in fact, a unique insight into how repression comes into being; and how it is then lived in habits of feeling that persist against all efforts to reverse them. In pity and fear repression drops all the masks and reveals its genesis in the three cardinal operations that define it: displacement, distancing, and deliverance.

1. *Displacement* is the act that deprives anxiety of its ability to refer to the actual conflicts in our inner world. Through it those conflicts are consigned to the "unconscious."[42] Anxiety activates an inner threat that must

be denied by displacing it so that attention shifts to something else that stands at a safe remove. A massive transformation results. Anxiety becomes vague, meaningless, "nothing" whereas fear rules us because it refers to real things in the real world. It may in fact be said to create that world and the importance we invest in it.

2. *Distance* is thus attained in the pseudosituations we construct then fixate on because they give us ways to vent our emotions, to convince ourselves that we feel deeply, to engage ourselves in hot debates and hot pursuits. All of which is valuable because it provides the illusion of subjective interiority[43] and of drama while delivering us from anything that cuts back into the psyche. Through these operations pity and fear come into their own. Applied to ourselves or to others these emotions give us a way to limit our engagement in conflicts in a way that externalizes and, in effect, theatricalizes them. Fear keeps certain issues off the table while pity enables us to constitute one another as objects of protective concern.[44] Sympathetic support thereby becomes the mask for mutual avoidance. Pity and fear are the means whereby we build communities dedicated to the dissolution of drama.

3. *Deliverance* ensues through two finalizing operations: (a) the discharge of painful affects through the blank check pity and fear give to indulging those feelings and sentiments that bind us to the surface of human motivation; (b) the reinforcement of those operations through the "moral" judgments they dictate as the only sensible, sound, mature way to adapt to life's conflicts. Discharge thus finds completion in a set of quasirational commonplaces about "experience," which provide pragmatic directions for future conduct. The wisdom of experience is attained: one now knows how certain situations, which could become "tragic," can be avoided once the proper principles of human response are in place. It is a mistake to underestimate the significance of pity and fear. Through their working— and it alone—the ratio achieves the reification it requires.

2. Catharsis and the guarantees. In the marriage celebrated by pity and fear repression and the ratio become one. To see if that bond is a solid and lasting one we must take up pity and fear once more with a deeper probe into their affective dynamic. Pity and fear are prototypes of those affects that serve the needs of the ratio because they put us in the position to act as the moral judge of our experience while instilling in us the feeling that doing so flows naturally from common and universal principles of human response. The resulting judgments perform the necessary function. They secure the rational order of experience by identifying what happens when one "exceeds," violates, or ignores its norms. Pity and Fear thus reinforce one's identification with—and identity within—the ratio. As the working of the guarantees within the structuring of affect, they are the primary way in which the opposition of philosophy to the tragic receives support from "experience." *Emotion and judgment of necessity unite in the working of pity and fear.* That is the key. There is no way, once they are in place, to respond to tragic beings except as ones who are, by definition, aberrant, confused, and perplexed in the extreme by virtue of their departure from the proudest product of pity and fear—an essentialized human nature. The tragic world becomes, accordingly, a break with the "order of things," deprived of any power to impinge on its ruling assumptions. In looking on the tragic, with deepest sympathy of course, we find, through the exercise of pity and fear, confirmation of an identity that is both substantialistic and pre-eminently moral. The working of tragic justice restores the order of things. This remarkable fact is the function of the destruction of the tragic protagonist. Tragic experience is thereby "deconstructed." The exception that measures us, exposing the psychological bad faith of the theories that have been advanced to contain it, has been given the quietus. The basic line of thought on tragedy since Aristotle thus constitutes a double line of defense against the tragic register of experience. Through pity and fear that which could prove disruptive within is "aroused" all the better to be purged. We entertain and even indulge tragic affects in order to master the methods whereby we discharge them. The ego thereby finds a way to structure experience so that it cannot occur. In learning the habits of feeling that are compressed in the structures of pity and fear we find the praxis sure to result in our self-reification. Resentment has succeeded in constituting itself as a structure, as a principle capable of determining the inwardness of the psyche.[45] In so doing, however, it also tips its hand, offering us a great lesson. There is nothing mysterious about repression. One who understands pity and fear sees how it operates, and why, under its rule, "why" finds no answer.

Understanding the confines of its hermeneutic circle brings us back to the possibility of a true beginning. One critiques a guarantee by exposing its contradictions. But we only overcome an emotion by constituting everything it prevents our being able to feel. This is the route to real change, moreover, since it restores our contact with that within ourselves which defenses displace, but with those conflicts now engaged in affects that strike at the quick of the psyche. In rejecting pity and fear, we attain the possibility of reversal through action within because we now exist at the affective register where one confronts both the fault lines and the turning point of one's being.

B. Melancholia as Self-Overcoming

1. The agonistic structure of experience. In the tragic "human nature" meets its antipode. If pity and fear work upon pity and fear to rid us of "these and similar emotions," melancholia "checks and restrains" everything that contributes to discharge and tranquilization.[46] Fear, as Heidegger shows, creates a world of "concerns" to sustain the displacement of anxiety. Pity, especially toward oneself, completes the process by depriving affects such as dread of their revelatory power. To regain that power we must attune ourselves to everything within us that moves in a direction opposed to catharsis. Rather than working upon itself to bring about its resolution, affect must act upon itself in order to tear open all that is buried and impacted within it. Conflicts sustained must deepen affects by refusing to dissolve contradictory pressures. *Intensification of affect* thereby becomes a process that blocks escape routes in order to bring us before conflicts that are more deeply buried and that find no solution along normal, ordinary channels.

The movement from anxiety to melancholia is, for us, the prime example of how affect transforms itself by deepening its burdens. In melancholia, painful affects act upon themselves in order to maximize their power to disrupt the subject at the inner register. What ensues is a precipitate descent toward affects that are more exacting, violent, and revealing precisely insofar as they bring the subject before itself, stripped of guarantees. Lacking any way to transcend upward, one must work on oneself from within affect by taking up the immanence of its agon. The revelatory power of melancholia as dread is thereby attained: the ability to penetrate to that which is most archaic yet intimate and utterly personal in our inner world and engage it in an agon of reversal. Affects thus issue in a self-knowledge that of necessity engages itself in an agon in which each affect generates the more painful, more primary affect that is needed to advance and deepen the process. Melancholia is affect driven inward and rubbed raw, affect made the crowbar that pries open the crypt.

The dialectic of affective self-mediation has this structure. Beginning in an anxiety that has become existential, each step in inner descent strives to discover and proceed to a more primordial conflict, by unlocking the power of dramatic action contained in a more "primitive," exacting affect. In that dialectic, *reversal* proceeds through the following *progression*.[47] *Melancholia* turns subject away from discharge and back against itself. *Anxiety* as wakeful anguish is thereby reclaimed. It has become that which, turned inward, unlocks what is crypted and frozen within. *Brooding* thereby becomes the act whereby *dread* hollows out a world of painful connections as the setting for a drama that drives inner conflict to the terms of the starkest illumination. In that *Aufhebung, melancholia* becomes that grief-work which refuses to relinquish the burden of self-knowledge to forgetting, catharsis, and the exigencies of normal "mourning." *Memory* has become an agon in which we know the truth of our experience only insofar as we insist, in *Passion,* on exposing that truth, without consolation, and against all appeals from pity, piety, and nostalgia. Such is the "behavior-arc"[48] of authentic depression as the affective process of self-mediation whereby one attains tragic agency. As a result of that process, reflection is now the act that existentializes the subject by rejecting anything that would limit the effort to engage everything pent-up and concealed in the psyche. This is the telos of melancholy. Melancholia is that affect that acts upon and deepens itself in order to reclaim the original trauma and the original contingencies of our being as the context action must sustain "or lose the name of action."[49] If one's life has been the slow living of a despair over never having been born properly, melancholia returns us in anguish to the dread of that condition. And thereby to reversal as the lasting rejoinder to the deadening of affect and its signifying monkey, the ego.

2. Insight as method

> The most valuable insights are arrived at last,
> but the most valuable insights are methods.
>
> —Nietzsche

The previous paragraph outlines the structure whereby within affect one takes action within oneself. Certain affects have the power to bring us before ourselves. They yield their meaning, however, only if they are lived within an agonistic logic of self-mediation and not a conceptual or rational one. Affect is then "the life that cuts back into life." Discharge refused hollows out inwardness as the space of inner action. In the ensuing drama, turning back and turning inward are one in an endeavor to bring about two fundamental changes within the order of our affective life: (1) normal, ordinary emotions are exposed as defenses through a critique that cancels their appeal; (2) that act empowers the *negative* with the force to become a principle of affective self-mediation through an agon in which the only thing that delivers us from affect is *deracination;* that is, tragic action within those places in the psyche that affect reveals as the site of our most traumatic experiences and deepest, lasting concerns.

The road not taken is the true labor of the negative.[50] The dialectic of dramatic self-mediation is a process radically different from rational self-mediation. It is also a principled alternative to Hegel's dialectic because, like his, it is grounded in reflexive principles that provide the basis for a comprehensive understanding of concrete experience.[51] In its *immediacy* affect contains the possibility of an *immanent* dialectic that depends on nothing outside itself to generate an existential phenomenology that sustains a principled resistance to conceptual mediation and the appeal of all the modes of deliverance from experience that it offers. As such, melancholia is "spirit" as "the life that cuts back into life" *comprehensively* and *dialectically.* Those affects that most people regard as vague, indeterminate, and unintelligible because they are beyond the range of disclosure given to a "humanism" of pity and fear are the *moments* constituting the structure of a *logos* that makes melancholia no less than this: the process through which total exposure within brings about a total change from within. Melancholia is the who of anxiety sustained as the why that drives out everything substantialistic in us so that the wound at the heart of the psyche and the cruelty at its lacerated center will be lived, suffered, and passioned forth in existentializing self-mediations.

The trouble with most responses to psychological pain is that people don't know what really troubles them and won't stay for an answer. Anything that halts displacement, defense, and discharge creates panic and an anxiety that can have but one meaning: the need to escape, at whatever cost, self-knowledge be damned. Such is our being as creatures of pity and fear. Which is why authentic drama begins only when we are arrested, turned violently around, and sent back into the cave. Anxiety is then the light in the darkness, the signal to attend, not to flee. What the ego sees as the necessity to enact denial, is for tragic agents the opportunity to engage the possibility of reversal.

To do so, however, a further inquiry is needed. Everything said thus far amounts to an argument for the ontological primacy of the image as the reality that gives the subject the only adequate insight into itself and its situation in history. Traumatic images are for agonistic self-mediation what concepts are for the ratio. Developing this idea is the burden of chapter 6.

Six

Those Images That Yet Fresh Images Beget

A man's [sic] work is nothing but a slow trek to rediscover, through the detours of art, those two or three great and simple images in whose presence his heart first opened.

—Camus

We must return to our childhood because we must discover its poison.

—Rilke

Marat, these cells of the inner self are worse than the deepest stone dungeon. And as long as they remain locked, all your revolution is but a prison mutiny to be put down by corrupted fellow prisoners.

—de Sade in Weiss' *Marat/Sade*

TOWARD A THEORY OF THE DIALECTICAL IMAGE

My project is to establish artistic cognition as a distinct and primary way of knowing. Here that task will take this form: to construct a theory of the Image that will not sacrifice the image to the concept, but will preserve and articulate the unique order of awareness that it inaugurates.[1]

In the course of a fascinating and frustrating discussion, which will take us directly to our central concerns, Silvano Arieti establishes the following as the defining characteristics of those images that reveal a special creative dimension of the psyche:[2]

1. The image does not strive to accurately represent reality nor to initiate a movement from sensation to the concept and abstract ways of thinking.
2. The image preserves an overpowering affect in the expressivistic terms appropriate to it.
3. In doing so it creatively regresses to "primitive" ways of dealing with experience.
4. Those ways constitute the first instance of a refusal to adapt passively to reality.
5. The primary functions of the image, accordingly, are internal: to maintain motivation, transform emotions, and build up inner reality.

6. The result is a particular order of memory—that containing in images permanent records of important experiences.[3]

Something of crucial importance to the reality of the psyche happens in the image. As Arieti notes, however, psychology has ignored the image because, unlike other modes of mentation, it does not point directly to normal, everyday reality and the adaptational functions necessary to assure our accommodation to that domain. Unfortunately, Arieti's work is tied to the ego psychological assumptions that this recognition implicitly calls into question. As a result, he can't constitute the radical implications of his discoveries. Instead, he drives a wedge between the image and perception, art and reality with a resulting split in the psyche and no way to mediate that split.[4] The problem is that Arieti works both sides of the street, without knowing it or facing the implications of that fact. He repeatedly claims that there is a harmony between the world of the image and the adaptational, consensual world of the ego and yet every point he makes about the image reveals a fundamental opposition. He knows he is on to important, neglected psychological realities, but his abiding desire to integrate them into a humanistic ego psychology blinds him to the disruptive implications of the image. Thus while harmony under the sovereign sway of the ego is repeatedly asserted, everything we learn about art and the image reveals a rift in the psyche that the ego-ratio is unable to heal except by asserting the necessity that art's materials be reshaped in correspondence to the ego's demands and thereby integrated into the framework of guarantees that constitute the intelligibility of experience.[5] This relationship holds, however, only if adaptation of the inner world to external reality is the purpose of art and the function of the image in the life of the psyche. The unique power of the image is to prove that this is not the case; to show, in fact, that everything about the image points to a different understanding of the psyche. The best way to develop this claim is by rereading each characteristic Arieti ascribes to the image in terms of its implications for a way of understanding that is sharply opposed to Arieti's. Rather than moving, as Arieti does, from the image to the concept and accommodation to the rule of the ego, we will show how the defining characteristic of the image—"the refusal to passively adapt to reality"—generates a psychological space of a radically different order.[6] Thus, where Arieti points out a discontinuity between the concrete world of imagery and the rules of conceptualization, our concern will be to sustain that break in its ability to challenge the dominance of the latter order. Where Arieti notes that in imagery we regress toward primary process mentation in order to escape the demands of "reality," our effort will be to show that we do so in order to articulate an awareness that again challenges the dominance of the favored term. When he assures us, as he does repeatedly, that all disruptions can be resolved in a harmony in which art finds its proper, and necessarily subordinate, position in a culture dedicated to the ego, our task will be to preserve the rift in order to constitute the full force of art's judgment on that order.

The ground for these reversals is, fortunately, provided by what Arieti identifies as the most striking thing about the image. As he notes, the inner space that is hollowed out in us by the image is "for the most part repressed or suppressed in most adult human beings."[7] That fact is of pivotal significance because it raises this question: why did we ever hollow out this realm if we spend the bulk of our lives trying to forget it? The image puts us in a position to see that the ego's "vigorous opposition to inner reality" involves, of necessity, an equally vigorous opposition to art.[8] This is Arieti's inadvertent message: contra the humanist tradition, it is impossible to constitute the value of art and creativity as long as one is committed to the ego because art's purpose is to expose and deracinate everything on which the ego depends.

Arieti distinguishes many types and levels of imagery. The most significant for his purpose (and ours) he terms the endocept, which he defines as that primitive level of imagery that puts us in touch with the deepest layers of our psychic experience.[9] It is also, as Arieti notes, that order of imagery that is "repressed or suppressed in most adult human beings." But not, he argues, in the artist and in each of us whenever a powerful image tears through the day and awakens us, however momentarily, to deeper conflicts and concerns. From which we quickly recoil, while momentarily glimpsing perhaps the dominant function of the ego: to estrange us from the power of the image to "call us back" to our inner world.[10] In the image *reversal* is present as that *origin* which renews the psyche's relationship to the original contingencies of its being. The surface we call reality is shattered by connections that draw a straight line from the quotidian to Kafka's frozen sea. In the image the "sufferance of being" arrests and assaults us with connections we can only begin to fathom—and assume—by learning to read the image in a way that sustains the violent claims it makes on us. This is the theory of the image we will try to produce by re-reading the characteristics Arieti identifies. Our goal in doing so is to show that a philosophy of concrete experience finds its starting point and its life-blood in the image.

I. Image as Activity

"The image is the first act in which we refuse to adapt passively to reality."[11] This characteristic, which comes fairly late in Arieti's discussion, is first for us because everything follows from it. In the image an awareness struggling to be born opposes the limitations that the ratio imposes to assure that accommodation and adaptation will eliminate from reality all that resists the hegemony of the ego. In so doing the image recovers that original activity in which psyche as *élan conatus* finds in negativity its defining act.

But why does the refusal of passivity require the image? And what, accordingly, must the content and inner structure of the image be? Why is image rather than some other form of mentation required for the psyche to articulate its founding condition? And to draw out the full terms of the problem, if activity requires the image, what is action? If the image grounds both the possibility of action and its terms, it does so by establishing as the conflicts and context one must engage in order to act an existential situation before which most of the things we do "loose the name of action." In their place we see the image of a solitary figure, in melancholic reflection, constituting himself as an agent who, in thinking on action, acts in a way that overturns every belief and convention whereby we secure our handle on the world.

II. Image as Affect

An image solidifies and preserves an overpowering affect by arresting it in an expression or expressive text that finds in sufferance the possibility of agon. In image affect is the antithesis of discharge; the founding of passion as the basis of change and self-mediation. In the image two key issues about affect come before us in a unique way: (1) the question how affects are preserved or dissolved and (2) the connection of that issue to the larger one of how affects constitute experience.

If we want know how "we really feel" (to quote the current jargon) we must gain access to our primary and abiding images. Image is the way mind as psyche apprehends experience at the affective register. Affect is coalesced and congealed in the image, which is why image has the power to reveal how radically primary affects differ from ordinary emotions and the discharge operations to which they lead. *An image is a complex of conflicted affects and motives arrested in a moment of time.* In image experience is epiphanized in an effort not simply to find "the words to say it" but the way to be it, to exist as agent in the concrete situation that the image defines. In image activity and passivity meet in agon. The image apprehends the terms of a conflict where both dimensions of our being are equally and vitally engaged. This happens whenever experience bears down upon us with a force that both strikes us dumb and summons forth the beginnings of action. If image is, as Arieti holds, the first moment in which we refuse passivity, it is no less the case that we only do so by committing ourselves to agon. The image arrests the terms that will define that agon and sets it before us as a complex of connections in which inwardness and existence are dialectically one.

That dialectical connection is the condition that gives the image its affective complexity: the pang of loss bound to unspeakable rage, horror made present to itself in an awareness enacted in the form of primitive immediacies. As Lear says of cruelty: "is it not as if this mouth would tear this hand for lifting food to it?" In breaking with the protective, self-regulating life of emotions, affect in image reveals the psyche acting from the register of its "to be," the register where one is at issue to oneself but only insofar as one engages in agon the existential situation that the image defines. Affect in image reveals the situatedness of the subject as the effort to mediate experiences that are primary because in them the who/why of subject finds its being in act and not in concept or cogito. Affect is overpowering not because a bundle of pent-up frustrations and instincts crave discharge, but because our relationship to the world is intersubjective from the beginning, the proof of that condition being the power of the other to effect the psyche in a way that requires the image as the only adequate response—and adequate idea. The violence of the image is one with its truth: image is coeval with the birth of the psyche as who/why in the conflicts that image hollows out as situations of infinite concern.

Just as our true "emotion" is almost always the one we don't feel or fear to acknowledge, the image is that which calls us back to the affects we must engage because in them conflict is fused in an irreducible complex of feeling. The image puts before us the need to take action in the face of those experiences that continue to assault us because we were arrested by them and have never really gotten beyond them. *To know the repressed one must recover one's primary images.* As such, the image awaits us with the one imperative that is binding: the necessity of taking action within ourselves at that affective register which the image preserves in the density of its immediacy.

III. Image as Perception

The image thereby reveals what perception cannot see and must apprehend if it would cleanse its doors. The fact that the image "refuses to accurately represent reality" does not mean it is opposed to perception, but that it sees everyday life in terms of its psychological truth. The motives, desires, and mendacities that inform what people do are fully present on the surface, evident to an attention that is attuned to the primary fact: that people project and deny their conflicts and then inflict them on others whenever everyday life offers the slightest occasion. Images do not reproduce reality. They shatter the cover-ups in order to reveal what is hidden and yet most active, what "objective" observation absolves us from knowing about what we do to one another all the time. The image perceives the world according to Francis Bacon, in its "pressure on the nerves." It thereby wrests from concealment the subtext that is struggling to emerge—as howl, panic, joy, dread—in the human face and the human deed.

The characteristics that Arieti uses to distinguish the image from perception are actually instructions to perception on how to see the world by entering it. "I came to Hiroshima because I feel that perception must be learned." As Arieti notes, images (a) don't lead to prompt action; (b) cannot be transformed into verbal terms, and (c) qua affect, remain vague and uncertain in their emotional coloring. These qualities maintain because the image arrests the mind with the burden of the world. Prompt action is for the most part discharge, the tedium of habit, or worse, projection followed by denial and that endless getting on with things that estranges us from ourselves. When perception is thus confined to the operations that bind us to the ordinary world and the dictates of consensual meaning, we deprive perception of its innermost possibility. Perception, as shaped by ordinary habits of mind and feeling, is the world had by selective inattention to everything save what reinforces routine. The image, in contrast, is perception arrested before that which must be learned through sufferance. In preventing what is commonly called action, the image creates the possibility of taking action within.

It sustains that possibility by resisting transformation into verbal terms. Images (and any metaphoric use of language for that matter) irritate the literal-minded because they assert connections that violate the rules on which the fact-based mind depends to keep its handle on itself by reifying its relationship to the world. The purpose of the image, however, is not to set puzzles of decipherment for "sense." That way of viewing the matter blinds us to the deeper circumstance. An image is a creative, intuitive leap into a different dimension of awareness—one in which connections that are beneath the surface and beyond the literal have become the medium in which thought moves. The image resists translation into precise verbal terms because it knows, before the fact, the limitations of a theory of language where statement, empirical reference, and literalization serve as the models of meaningful discourse. In knowing this the image directs attention to felt connections that burden us with a density and a contradictory valence that must be endured and not sacrificed to those "clearly felt emotions" which give us the world at the moment we dispose of it so that discharge will reign supreme as the operation defining the real. The effort of the image is to arrest and assault us with realities that cannot be dealt with in empiricizing ways; to lead the mind to afterthought and forethought by providing perceptions that must be lived agonistically because the masks and cover-ups have been stripped away. In assaulting the literal (and the literal-minded) the image brings together the "unintelligible" and the "*unheimlich*" in a way that is uniquely revelatory.

That is why the following characteristic, noted by Arieti, is in image a positive quality. In image "something is felt in an englobing way" yet refuses "to issue in a clearly felt emotion." While most emotions fix attention on specific matters at hand and then vanish once they are resolved, affect in the image is *Befindlichkeit* (mood) in its nascent form, establishing the primacy of an experience that has this form: the co-presence of self and world in those affect-charged perceptions that are beyond the range of disclosure of other modes of cognition. The world given to us in the image is torn free of both displacement and repression. It is *Stimmung* as that attunement which estranges us from normal affairs and modes of behavior in order to bring us before something that can emerge only when they slip away.[12] Heidegger argues that mood is prior to cognition and volition and beyond their range of disclosure. What he fails to see is that the image is the act that sustains and articulates this awareness. In recovering primitive modes of cognition, the image rushes down to the deepest layers of the Unconscious in an effort to find a way to "picture" a situation in an expressive text that preserves and articulates its burdens. In image anxiety is that prime "agent of human perception" which finds in primary process ideation and primitive modes of cognition and functioning the only way to sustain the concrete connections that stream forth to an engaged consciousness that has gotten to the foundations of what Coleridge calls Imagination. For image is here one with the imagination's inherent, defining dialectic. In such perceptions the deepest layers of what is locked and buried in the Unconscious bring themselves to bear upon "the remains of the day." The result is an articulation that reveals what is really going on and what is at stake once one strikes through the masks and sees how the repressed stalks all occasions. Image is the effort to preserve this awareness and make it safe against the return of the literal, the consensual, the habitual, and the tyranny of the concept. The "unintelligibility" of the image is a positive, necessary quality; the way in which the primacy of affect in its dialectical connection with the dynamic Unconscious is established and sustained. The image thereby joins Heidegger and Freud in a synthesis neither anticipated.

IV. Image as Psyche

That synthesis holds because the image preserves the real in its inwardness. The primary function of images, Arieti suggests, is (a) to maintain motivation (for absent objects), (b) to transform emotions, and (c) to build up inner reality. What he fails to draw is the conclusion. It is in and through the image that the psyche creates and structures itself; through image that it first comes into being and finds a way to regulate and refer to itself in a way that preserves the conditions of its origin. What is it about the image that gives it this power? And what must its inner structure and internal dynamic be for it to issue in the complex dramas that characterize the inner world of the psyche? These questions lead to others and a deeper reading of Arieti's three points. What is motivation if it requires the image to sustain itself? What is feeling if it needs the image to express and bind turbulent affects? What is the inner world if agon, not concept, is the "cogito" that represents it to itself? These questions are basic and take on their proper complication with the recognition that the images that bear these offices in the psyche are fraught with ambiguity, ambivalence, and buried secrets that must be unearthed. An image sets down the terms for a drama of conflicting experiences and desires that can only be unlocked and engaged by one who opens the crypt of the psyche.

Consider, for example, this complex of conflicted affect. Wallace Stevens speaks in nostalgia of "the mother's face / the purpose of the poem." It is perhaps the same face that Winnicott discerned in the paintings of Francis Bacon—that gaze we anxiously solicit in the very moment it coldly turns away from us. This is the image that haunted Fichte, that one Picasso incessantly paints, that one that exists before Lacan's tidy mirror. At the deepest register of the psyche, these allusions do not refer to separate "visions" but to images that co-exist in dialectic because they condense and energize the radically opposed affects most of us have (though few admit it) for one and the same object, the mother of infancy. As drama, joined in dialectic, those affects thus issue in that conflicted positionality which makes *subject as psyche a being radically divided against itself in its inner world*. This is the deepest function and resonance of the image. The image gives us our primary world, which is one of subject arrested, paralyzed, frozen by presences that rise up, promising magical deliverance in times of crisis, engulfment in ones of terror. The primary images constituting the depth of psychic life must be mediated, but this can only happen when they are joined in drama by a subject ready to situate itself in their clash, a subject no longer using dualism or splitting to escape the task of mediating itself. In defining the agons we must take up, the image offers us a way to re-assume, in drama, the original contingencies of our being.

V. Image as Memory

That is so because the image is the permanent record of those experiences that matter most to us and that await us however deeply or strenuously repressed. The image retains the past that had to be crypted. In an image we freeze an experience and put it on ice. But we thereby also sustain Kafka's "sea frozen inside us" against the forces that would turn the heart to stone. The image retains the truth of the other's action as a matter of permanent concern. By refusing to forget the visage, the voice, the fixed contempt for life and the glee that invariably attends soul-murder we make in the image a haven against forgetting. But to deal with those actions, they must become present to us again in their original force. That is the possibility and the future drama that the image preserves.

In this sense image is the "emotion" we have not been able to sustain but must constitute in order to prove equal to the situation that image arrests, preserves, and defines. The permanency of the image is a direct result of the *agonistic clarity* with which it epiphanizes an event of overwhelming impact and importance. That is why images of this order are repressed in most of us, and why as dynamic Unconscious their continued force erupts within then bleeds itself out into the world with persistent regularity the more we strive to escape or deny the image's claims on us. Image in fact enables us to redefine the dynamic unconscious thus: that agonistic system which keeps intruding on our lives because the conflicts defining the dynamic unconscious create the subtexts and through-lines that inform our actions and true intentions even when the prize is the assurance of continued unhappiness. In making our conflicts present to us in their fundamental terms and their deepest urgency, the image lays bare the *context* that determines the *content* of our lives and the truth of our character, even though most of us strive to know nothing about ourselves at this register.

The image is the indestructible product of those events that are permanent, sustained in a text that shows why they are so while assuring they remain so. Image thereby establishes psychological memory as something quite different from behavioral and empiricist concepts of memory. Memory in depth is that affect charged complex of feelings which preserves the truth of an event arrested in the violence of its expression and thereby made a matter of permanent concern. As such, the image constitutes our first attempt to take action within ourselves in the face of an experience that has the power to strike compliance and passivity into the soul. (It thus grounds the necessary connection between the two terms that define the dialectic of inwardness.)

VI. Image as Creative Regression

The image preserves the possibility of resistence because it regresses to those ways of "thinking" that are primitive, expressive, and that reveal agonistic struggle within primordial conflicts as the core condition of the psyche. In doing so the image shows that the *primitive* is not the irrational or the simple, but that order of complex mediations that are fundamentally different from those found in the ratio. In image regression is progression because it takes us from the ego to the psyche. Regression here serves neither the ego nor as a sign that one has lost control of mature ego functions. It is a sign, rather, that one has regained another way of functioning; one where regression is ontological because it recaptures and then

abides within the movement of an agon that is true insofar as one sustains
the demands and the violence of the most primitive, foundational experiences of the psyche. When such is the case the ego and its ways of structuring experience can serve as no more than a rank and irrelevant intrusion.
The image refuses that pull concretely by representing complexes of subjective experience that establish agon as the only legitimate self-mediation.
When regression moves in this medium we return to the urgency of experiences in which we are one with the other, indistinguishable at the moment
when the other's action drives a stake in the heart. Here is true immediacy,
contra Hegel, the origins for a phenomenology of spirit in which our survival as subjects depends on the concrete mediation of Thanatos.

That drama only begins, however, when regression becomes ontological.[13] That is, when regression attempts to get back to the origins and core
of the human disorder and begin again by undertaking an active reversal of
death-work and everything in the developmental process that contributes to
its hegemony. When regression so descends, death is again known as the
power that presides over a frozen world, that which the dynamic Unconscious arrests in agons awaiting their actor. The image is the prologue to that
drama. It is the call from the crypt for the recovery of one's innermost
possibilities through the assumption of one's deepest conflicts.

VII. *Image as Reality*

The image does not reproduce reality. It shatters the continuum in order to
reveal the Real—to lay bare the psychological conflicts that shape the quotidian. Every image is a great gap in being, a rupture revealing the void at the
center of the ego and the connection of that void to the venom that primes
the self-lacerating heart whenever life presents some fortunate opportunity
to project one's cruelty. Which, it turns out, is virtually all the time.
Projection and denial are the dominant forces that shape concrete relations
with others. The image brings this perception home to us in a way that
situates us within the world thereby revealed. An image is everyday life
epiphanized as trauma apprehended as it unleashes its impact at the
deepest register of the psyche. And as such it is the immortal no made
present and lived as passion and articulate rage. Being assaulted with the
power of the image is the cleansed perception granted to those who view the
world from the perspective of the crypt. In the image the real is sublated in
that call of conscience which, perhaps, makes cowards of us all.

For one formula pulls together the seven categories discussed above.
The image reveals the dynamic Unconscious as the reality that structures
the world. Moreover, the image teaches us that we will only understand the
Unconscious once we develop a dramatistic theory of its internal principles.

Contra Freud and Lacan, the Unconscious is not the realm of pure drive or demand; it is the site of those conflicts that give our lives the structure of dramas that are tragic in their fundamental terms and exigencies. The power of the image is to situate us, however momentarily, squarely before this fact. Image puts us in touch with an order of being that exposes the entire framework of habits and concepts that constitute what is called "the real world." For in the image everything that is sacrificed to the effort to escape experience returns and renews its claim upon us. The truth of the matter is that we don't live in two worlds, we live in one. The image gives that truth to us—as burden. No wonder we strive so hard to relegate the image to silence or aporia, to confine it within the order of the ratio, or to soften and reformulate its "meaning" so that humanistic-rhetorical interpretations will prevail. An image is true insofar as it "says" one thing with utter clarity and in the "terms" that bring it full before us: *"Du musst dein Leben ändern."* This is what the image whispers to each in the heart of their inner darkness. And because we know it, we rush to discourse seeking deliverance.[14]

TOWARD THE CRYPT: THE IMAGE AND INWARDNESS

Nothing can trouble the dominance of the true image.
—Rilke, *Sonnets to Orpheus*

Someday a real rain will come and wash all this away.
—Travis Bickle in *Taxi Driver*

An image is true insofar as it is violent.
—Artaud

I'll show you the life of the mind.
—John Goodman in *Barton Fink*

I. Affect as Agon

The foregoing indicates why an image has the power, however momentarily, to arrest us in our being. Whenever this happens experience rubs against our deepest conflicts and concerns. The quotidian is rent by the eruption of its subtexts. Dialectical connection, not projection and denial, is now the relationship binding the two together. In this: the power of the image to call us back to ourselves by delivering us over to the hidden narrative that as cumulative pattern has proceeded with perfect symmetry to the traumatic events that bring us finally before ourselves. In the image the doors of perception are cleansed in order to deliver us over to ourselves as agon.

An image is significant insofar as it activates that drama. But that is also the problem. Not only of distinguishing vital images from the endless stream of commodified fetishes that flit across the screen of our inattention. But also of developing a method of interpretation able to probe the vital image in order to activate its depth charge. If the image brings us before the buried life of our psyche, that is precisely why the image is repressed, deadened, denied in most human beings. Like anxiety, it is *unheimlich,* unclear, and comes to us in moods that are vague, fleeting, and "unintelligible." As Rilke notes, for most of us the image comes upon us unaware, like that calamity Kafka associates with reading. One is confused, arrested and then assaulted with the recognition that the only response, as Rilke teaches, is the fight for one's life.[15] When waged with authenticity that fight becomes the discipline of *agonistic interpretation:* of learning to read and then re-read the image in order, following Rilke, "to wait for that which has become concept to become again image," so that one can experience it again, in a deepening that completes itself, at each stage of agonistic interpretation, only when the image bites back into us with a renewed violence, which proceeds in a precipitate and determinate way to the crypt. The image addresses the buried life in a "rhetoric" where existence supercedes all need for persuasion, where the route to the concrete is toward the recovery of being as agon. A method of interpretation suited to that process must preserve and articulate that which exceeds the concept by charting, in a systematic way, a logic that is radically different and opposed to the principles of intelligibility of the ratio.

As a guide to reading the image, we can schematize that logic of interpretation along the following lines. The image is not a way-station on the road to logic, ideas, and the concept. Its movement is in the opposite direction—downward toward everything in the psyche that exceeds rationalistic mediation. To sustain that movement one must preserve two things in a single act of mind: (1) resistance to the logic of rationalistic conceptualization and all the ways its assumptions, explanatory principles, and ways of structuring experience inhabit our thought; (2) an articulation of the psychological dynamics that constitute the inner structure of the image that will be strong enough to assure that no sublation of what it reveals will be possible. The result, as we'll see, is a new understanding of inwardness, a recognition of how far most theories both of subject and its deconstruction depart from the agonistic principles of self-reference and self-mediation that shape the true life of the subject.[16] The image creates inwardness by hollowing out within us a space where those situations and events that permanently matter are preserved in a way that fulfills Henry James' wish that we be among those on whom nothing is lost. If internalization is what creates us as subjects, the image is the register where the psychological conditions of our subjectivity are stored in expressive texts that preserve the possibility of agon over against those reworkings of experience that assure the ego both its identity and its control over everything that threatens it.

The image arrests, solidifies, and encapsulates the deepest modes of our affective self-reference in an expressive text that preserves the contradictions that define the agon implicit in all primary affects. Cruelty, humiliation, envy, corrosive love—everything that is prior to "desire and the struggle for recognition" and greater in intensity and urgency—find in the image the origin and ground for a new and deeper "phenomenology of spirit." Image teaches us that drama is the primary mode of our being. Prior to everything else in the order of being stands the image as the call from the crypt, the unquiet voice recalling our utter presence to the world as the deathless demand to take the actions that will constitute the only appropriate response to the traumatic experiences that have shaped our life. Unlocking the world buried in the image thus calls for a renewal of Sartre's regressive-progressive method, adapted to the world of dramatic self-mediation.

II. The Inner World of the Image: Reconstructing the Regressive-Progressive Method

A. Regression

If the direction of most psychological processes is toward discharge and that comprehension of experience which is clear, consensual, and supremely literal, the direction of the image is inward toward what is tangled, exacting, and primitive. Movement within that medium begins with the ability to tolerate within ourselves a regression in which the psyche gives itself over to images that are violent in their yokings and archaic in their content. Regression thereby attains what Keats called "negative capability"—the ability to be in "doubts and uncertainties" without any "irritable reaching after fact and reason"; without, that is, the assumption that regression only works when it serves the ego. Regression is now, instead, the unbound and unrestricted movement of the psyche back to its most heart-wrenching experiences in the awareness that unless one enters without reserve into that "mental state" there is no way contact with the image can unlock and engage its meaning. It is only when Lear, for example, begins to speak of himself in such images that he gets at an understanding adequate to his life and the actions he has performed, since it is only then that their full weight comes back upon him in a self-knowledge that grasps cruelty as an appetite unbound by anything but the need to turn at last and "eat up itself."

If we find it hard to move in the medium of such imagery it is because the interiority of the image *retraces the fault lines of our being.* It does so by reversing the displacements that have issued in the ego in a way that is rigorously sequential because it systematically recovers the repressed conflicts that the ego exists to project and deny. Thus, the movement toward the primitive and archaic is here not a movement toward the unintelligible, but toward that which is stark and unremitting in its clarity—our conflicts and choices made present to us in and at the affective register that defines them. A regression of this order gives concrete content to what we previously termed the logic of the anti-*Aufhebung.* Each step in regressive *descent* smashes a prior *ascent* in order to recover that which cannot be sublated by any exercise of the ratio but must be lived and mediated agonistically. This is concrete deconstruction because it recovers and liberates a content, not an impasse. As such, the image recovers existential agency as a distinct way of being that can be preserved in its otherness over against abstract principles of conceptual and rationalistic mediation that distort and limit its meaning.

As psychoanalysts have learned, something like the process described above is the regressive course of an authentic analysis. The ego is resolved into the images that reveal its fixations. Shattered by interpretation those images betray the underlying fantasies of omnipotence that rise up in their wake, only to decompose in schizoid terrors that must be endured so that one can descend, through them, back to the catastrophic experiences that must be assumed as one's defining burdens if a concrete agon of active reversal from within the crypt is to be engaged. When we speak of subjectivity this, and not ironic aporia, must be the context of our thought. For it is through this drama alone that the foundations of subjective agency are established. Regression must descend to that which is most deeply repressed and live it again, in agon and primary affect. Only then are the conflicts defining the deepest psychic register present in their primitive terms and not in terms of the subsequent "orders" imposed upon them.[17] Such is the justice of our condition. To become a subject one must take up one's entire history at its catastrophic origins. Only a regression that goes to the roots can make it possible to begin again with active reversal and not with repetition, displacement, and false transcendence.

B. Progression

Progression then commences, defined by the burdens that must be assumed. One must go back through one's narrative, through the history of one's choices, and now tell a story that subjects the very structure of one's psyche to the need for a change that can only come about through an agon in which the principles that created the ego are no longer viable. It and its world are precisely what must be eradicated. To do so one must live out the logic that inheres in the distinct modes of functioning immanent in the primitive world of the psyche. Agonistic self-mediation from the crypt must replace egosyntonic modes of mediation and must generate a psychological structure that preserves this difference by finding in the "development" attained at each stage of the agonistic process the principles of mediation capable of generating the subsequent drama required by the conflicts that emerge as the truth of that development. Drama thus generates drama—and in that process the displacements, projections, and denials that shaped one's earlier ascent to the ego are concretely reversed. This is the immanent logic of dramatic progression. The developed structures of the ego and the social, consensual world are stripped bare. The "conflict-free sphere" reveals the motives and projections that rage within compulsory normalization as a "form of life." Normal living stands exposed in its suppressed neurotic dramas. In recapturing the conflicts that drive each stage of ego development one attains a new agency. The task of that agency, however, is to unlock the drama festering in the adjustments and denials whereby the sickness at the core enforces the normalcy on which the socialized psyche depends. (Heinz Hartman and Ludwig Wittgenstein find their dialectical connection in the above paragraph.)

The regressive-progressive method breathes drama into all occasions. It reveals the unity of experience as a unity of conflicts repressed and denied—and thereby become avid. Regression recovers the real. Progression then refuses sublation by shattering each apparent conceptual mediation in order to recover in agon an agency of another order. The image thus makes possible the movement of our being toward that which most deserves the designation the concrete because the world it establishes cannot be sublated or sublimated in the concept, but must be lived through in an agon bound to the primitive terms that define it. For the primitive is here the primordial; not the dissolution of the human, but its first emergence, the binding of subject to an affective dialectic that existentializes us from within. These are its defining characteristics:

1. The image reveals the dynamic Unconscious as the deep principle structuring our lives in a way that gives urgency to this idea. In the image we store those experiences that both overwhelm us and engage our deepest concerns. Reading an image from within activates the effort to constitute a self-mediation that is determinate and irreversible only insofar as it sustains the agon implicit in the image.

2. Every primordial image makes catastrophic anxiety present in a way that reveals cruelty as the founding human condition. It does so by repre-

senting the events of greatest suffering and violence in our experience *as the moments of our first activity.* Just as all matter is frozen light, every primordial image is a frozen agon: the call to activate drama in the teeth of that which threatens the dissolution of drama. *In image soul-murder is fused dialectically with the possibility and beginnings of resistance.* The archaic and primitive characteristics of the image preserve that connection. If the image is the first movement toward activity, it is so precisely because the need for action arises only when there is an assault on our being so powerful and intimate that it permits no otherness, no escape, no objectifying distance. The only action given to us is the attempt, in the image, to freeze the blow as it descends. If sufferance and dread characterize the image, they do so not to signal the impossibility of action but the need to ground it dialectically in a savage and unremitting context. Psyche is born when the need to act is imposed on a subject afflicted and utterly thrown into existence.

3. In order to unlock and engage that agon one must preserve the *double movement* of the image. Image reveals the primacy of two opposed conditions that are one. (a) The weak and evanescent nature of our first actions and their consignment, at the very moment of their nativity, to repression and the power of the Other to impose fragmentation and self-dissolution on our efforts at self-mediation. (b) But in the face of that terror the simultaneity of defiance, courage, and the will to action that the image preserves as an assertion against forgetting. The crypt is that memory where both truths are stored, in their dialectical fusion, awaiting drama.

4. Interpreting an image must strive to unlock that drama in a way that preserves its most exacting terms against all efforts to sentimentalize or mitigate them. That is why the image is the enemy to nostalgia and those half-hearted dramas that end in teary reconciliations at precisely the place where the true dramas must begin. The image is unintelligible to most ways of thinking because it is the call to regress to the wound at the heart of the psyche. That is the condition which it brings before us in a way that is immediate—and blindingly clear.

C. Engagement

The image is the agon of our being, compressed and made urgent in the three phases that define it. The task of interpretation, accordingly, is to produce this sequence. (1) To apprehend the core crypt-conflicts that are arrested and compressed in expressive form in the image. (2) To unlock that drama and bring it to issue through a regressive-progressive articulation of the image's inner structure. (3) To will and embrace the ensuing struggle as the Ixion whereby we exist as subjects. What follows solidifies the claims of the last step.

Contra Arieti, the image is not the record of loss, but of the fight against loss. In image we make a permanent record of those experiences we can never be done with, and can never fathom until we unlock the drama frozen in them. As unconscious memories the image awaits us with "the return of the repressed" now understood as the return of those experiences in which our being was put at issue and remains at issue. Until we act within the agon the image defines, our "soul" remains on ice. In preserving the possibility of that action, the image is the reply, before the fact, to the "postmodern" assumption that existence and anxiety are no more than empty, evanescent moods, of no significance except as signs of a chemical imbalance, or, worse, of a failure to attain the cool ironies and aporias of the decentered, self-dissolving subject. As such, the image recovers the *reference* of those "pictures" that "hold us captive" with a *reality* that cannot be contained by the terms of a Wittgensteinian grammar of language games, social conventions, and the rhetorical contracts and conversations that ordinary language permits. Image is that "private language" which reveals what public languages teach us to hide. In the image the who/why has a concrete referent grounded in immediate experience. Image stores with utter, primitive precision a primary context of human relations apprehended in the inherent violence of the real as it imposes itself on us. Sustaining that reference is assured by the way image represents experience: as a passivity that demands action by delivering us over to ourselves in the conflicts of a *deferred agency*. The image represents the "unsayable" as that which is inherently dramatic. Arieti says the image is the first shift from passivity to activity. A better designation sees it as the first step toward drama—through that originary mediation in which cruelties and contradictions become efforts to act because they define a context in which action is necessary, with all possibilities wholly immanent, submitted to the situation; a world where one cannot think one's way through to a "sensible" solution or sustain that posture as anything but a massive act of avoidance. In the image passivity and active reversal are equiprimordial and concrete. *That fusion of inwardness and existence is the agon immanent in the image.*

The image is thus that cognition which preserves the truth of what every other discourse rushes to deny. For image says "No" on two fronts simultaneously. It rescues an event from silence and forgetting. It then sustains the event over against its domestication through rationalizing explanations. The image makes no attempt "to accurately represent reality" or to adapt itself to socialized conventions because it knows that objectification is the first step toward losing one's experience. That is why every attempt to see the image as an anticipation of the concept destroys the possibility of engaging it as drama. Image arrests an agonizing complex, not an incipient concept. It does so, moreover, at a register of inwardness where activity and passivity, subject and object are joined not in the effort to "know" what counts as a "state of affairs" but in the effort to maximize the terms of one's existence.

   This recognition gives us a way to constitute a new meaning for Arieti's idea that the primary function of images has to do with motivation and affect in the construction of inner reality and why sustaining a break with adaptation and accurate representation is central to this effort. The motive preserved in the image is the mortal No in its refusal to forget burdening itself with the action remembering will require. It is a recognition that the violence done to us must be suffered as the condition for the act through which we give ourselves being. The image thereby provides reversal with its text. In image motivation is not restricted to a grammar of consensual validations and reflected appraisals. Instead, in the image the awareness of cruelty binds the subject in agon to this task: to sustain the duty we bear to ourselves as subjects against all demands that make renunciation, rationality, and conformity to social norms the primary logic of motivation. In the image *motivation is existence projected upon the initial conditions of one's abjection* then sustained as a "conscience" that matures through the refusal to blind oneself to the true conditions of the world.

   In the image motivation is affect and as such the antithesis of a discharge phenomenon. Affect here is the burden one must bear in order to put one's being at issue in a deathless commitment to those experiences that arrest the heart—and defy explanation. Which is why the first task is the refusal to relinquish that dynamic to social conventions and behaviors. Qua motivation, in the image a primary affect becomes a nascent "passion of the soul," and, as such, a categorical imperative that is concrete and historical: our self-reference as subjects delivered to the world in a responsibility from which there is no exit.[18]

   In giving us our being as agon, the purpose of the image is not simply, as Arieti holds, to construct an inner world, but to assure an inner world that will remain fundamentally opposed to the operations that issue in the ego and its world. The first lesson that the image teaches is the necessity to sustain this opposition, to negate the negation, by exposing the ego's founding motive. The reality to which the ego is "vigorously opposed" is the reality of the image, which is why the "developmental process" makes the image something to which the ego can no longer attend. Dissolving its force is the ego's true office. In that process the sacrifice of our primary images is one with the construction of what Winnicott calls "the false self system." Given his unexampled compassion, what Winnicott refused to see is that the purpose of this system is not (as he holds) to preserve the "true self" from extinction, but to complete its murder, to give us an identity that makes us at home in the world by estranging us from our being. Which is why (as Rilke knows) the image lies in wait for us, with the power to renew the rift, to bite into us and restore our being to its proper pain. For, contra Sartre, the image reveals that the subject (or *pour soi*) is not "senseless passion" but *passion projected in agon.*[19]

D. A New Allegory of the Cave

Here is one way to formulate the basic difference between human beings. We are assaulted daily by images that reveal the appalling violence of the world. Faced with that fact most people become adept as a single operation—discharge, the turning of image into fact, object, concept. The lesson of experience appears to be this: learn how to discharge horror so that eventually nothing makes a deep impression anymore, or become the internalization of the pain you see as it lacerates wounds that remain forever open in a sufferance that is saved from despair only by persisting in a question: Lear's "Is there any cause in nature that makes these hard hearts?" . . . Stamp Paid's "What are these people?"[20] *Perception quickened by the suffering that is the world*—that is what it means to be a subject.

The deeper truth is thus that we live in two worlds that are one, inhabited by beings who seem to be from different planets. For some, deadening affect and reducing all relationships to the positivity of fact is the only way to live that makes sense. For others, keeping the deepest wounds alive in sufferance is the only way "to live deliberately."[21] But to so live is to inhabit perception as the pain of the world. Most subjects, of course, succeed in silencing that register. They live, as a result, in a world without images; or, better, one in which everything contributes to one image in a landscape that is utterly literal because the deadening of affect is the one constant that is realized in every perception. For the few the opposite maintains: which is why when image assaults us, we must gladden in thanksgiving, since its eruption means that one remains alive at the deeper registers of one's being.

E. The Motive for Metaphor

For both kinds of subjects, however, the image teaches the same lesson. Simile, analogy, metaphor, and other modes of figurative language arise when literalization is not enough. That is, when we must violate analytic precision and binary dichotomies in order to assert connections we then quickly sever because they assault and transcend common sense, burdening it with the real. Or, to put it in language that restores the correct relationship: literalization is the death of metaphor, the "I don't get it" that reduces mind to a permanently blank slate, Nietzsche's cow one with its blink. Imagery arises whenever we break down extant, reified relations in order to grasp and represent novel, shocking connections.[22] When Coleridge distinguished fancy, which can only passively combine things along the lines of associationist psychology, from the imagination, which "dissolves, diffuses, and dissipates" such relations in order to create something that cannot be comprehended by the ratio, he made the crucial distinction that every subsequent theoretical advance in understanding the image has followed.[23] Imagery happens when we strive to articulate connections that are dialectical precisely because they go beneath the surface and beyond epistemologies based on the dichotomy of the objective and the subjective. The image is that engagement where subject and object are inseparable because reality imposes itself upon us in overpowering affects that are lost whenever literalization supervenes.

"If you could lick my heart it would poison you"[24] The statement is from the penultimate witness to speak to Claude Lanzmann in *Shoah,* Itzhak Zukerman, survivor of the Warsaw ghetto and of Auschwitz, constrained at last to heave his heart into his throat, compelled into language by Lanzmann's insistent will to knowledge. The documentary filmmaker demands a statement as Zuckerman's duty to history. "If you could lick my heart it would poison you." The image is Zuckermann's thrust toward an awareness that can be known only insofar as it is suffered—by Lanzmann and by us—in an awareness that obliterates the documentary form of historical inquiry and with it any distinction between knowing and suffering.[25] The violence of the image, and its truth, is that it contains a cognition that refuses to relinquish itself to the concept. "You killed my jew now I'm going to kill your jew"; this statement, reporting a "fact," said by one Nazi to another, in David Grossman's remarkable novel *See Under—Love* is a limit-case for metaphor: a statement of fact that is already an image—in spite of itself. And as such, unable to arrest its movement to a larger context of meaning where it finds its function in a "fiction" in which the effort to internalize the Holocaust becomes the effort to create images that will give voice to that reality.[26] The image is the native language of our feelings, even when brutalization is the text. Any statement that tries to arrest horror by asserting fact becomes horror as metaphor. Literalization is Thanatos crowing. That is what the monsters of history have to teach us: they always leave an image as eloquent testimony to what really happened.

F. Our Native Language

And so by way of transition back to our primary subject, we advance the hypothesis that the images left behind by the agents who make history provide the historian with primary data. This idea is a challenge to the empiricizing conventions that rule history as a discipline since it overturns the conception of what counts as fact and the protocols whereby some statements are given a privileged status and others consigned to silence as insignificant metaphorical asides. History is full of data with the properties of the image. The problem is that we discard such data in order to stick to the facts. In the process we miss what is most factual in them. Why, for example, should documents that Stimson, Byrnes, and the Interim Committee carefully crafted, both before and after the fact, to construct for public consumption an explanation of why we dropped the Bomb count as solid, incontrovertible empirical data, with the power to cancel certain hypotheses[27] while the abundant metaphors those same agents left behind, languish, a detritus dismissed as irrelevant, deprived of the chance to stand as evidence of intentions that call into question official intentions and motives.

Such a reversal of priorities would, of course, transform the discipline of history in fundamental ways. The hypothesis that the image reveals the intention that was carefully concealed shifts the study of history onto a new epistemological and ontological axis. Consider the following:

—Truman, at the good news from Alamogordo, dancing on the decks of the Independence, in manic glee: "this is the greatest thing since the creation."

—Brynes, in consultation dark to Harry in the night: "Given the money we've spent on the damn thing, we've got to use it. Otherwise you and I are going to end up in Leavenworth and not on 1600 Pennsylvania."

—Groves, in one last ditch effort to "explain" why the ancient sacred city of Kyoto must be the target "so that the maximum moral and psychological damage is done to the enemy."

—Stimson, absenting himself from the key meeting of the interim committee, but cleansed later through his ghost-writer with this line: "it was the least abhorrent choice."

—Fermi and Oppenheimer in the desert, the jokester and the Eliot of the moment, one literalizing dread, the other deliberately abridging allusion in unreadable koan.

—Tibbets' "Gentlemen, you have just dropped the first atomic bomb in history." And then the words of his co-pilot, "Look at that sonofabitch go" . . . later recast for *The New York Times* as "My god, what have we done"—as if an old-new metaphor can bring closure by absolving us of a deed that has just begun to proliferate new images at ground-zero and deep within the cells of the *hibakusha*.

The image possesses all the credentials required to constitute historical data on a par with other facts. It is also capable of bringing the primary canon of historical research—the method of multiple working hypotheses—to a new complication. Open history to the image and the dialectic of Eros and Thanatos may emerge as the only explanation that preserves the data in its economy, the hypothesis that is hardest to eliminate.[28]

Such suggestions are, of course, preposterous to those who know when to label something irrelevant, a remark by Truman (say) that is ill-advised but nothing more, the kind of thing that is noteworthy only for those who want to project a "vapid subjectivizing" on to history. In doing history we know what counts and what to eliminate. And we labor in the certainty that historical intentionality never reaches down into the Unconscious. Especially when the account is written by the victors. At this point in the inquiry, however, another possibility presents itself. As Sartre shows, image rather than statement is the primary bearer of intentionality, especially in situations where contingency rubs up against desire with an urgency that brings forth poetry in minds as different as Tibbets and Rilke. By the same token, recovering the image requires the patient exposing of official "intentions." History is full of such opportunities. The text is given, however, only to that historian/detective who like a ragman gathers the detritus, the throw-away line, the discarded image, and the great metaphoric eruptions of those who must crow poetic as they seize the day—images that reveal their meaning only when, the ladders to the guarantees all gone, one writes history from the same place where it was originally written, "in the foul rag and bone shop of the heart."

The section that follows attempts to know it at that register by developing a theory of the dialectical image as the object (or identical subject-object) that reveals history to us—in its immediacy and its depth.

"WHAT HURTS": THE DIALECTICAL IMAGE IN HISTORY

> The mechanisms of *pseudological fantastica* require,
> to establish deathlessness it is necessary to eliminate
> those who die; a task attempted, when a white flash
>   sparkled.
> —Galway Kinnell, "The Fundamental Project of Technology"

Here is an image that will serve as our guide in what follows: whenever the Owl of Minerva takes wing, a scorched earth is left behind as the place to which Orpheus must descend to write what's needed to win back the human from Thanatos. Each time we impose guarantees in order to explain the past, we hollow out the seeds of a lament that must give voice to everything that is sacrificed to our needs. Everything that had to be sublated so that the ratio might crow thereby becomes the basis for a new evaluation. For the effort to impose guarantees is at base the need to exorcize through transcendence something that points in the opposite direction. There is something in the "facts" that is "more than natural if philosophy could find it out." Anxiety over that circumstance stirs the ratio into operation. An aphorism for historians: there are always explanations—and they are always after the fact. Whenever there is a reality, a "fact" slumbering in the data that reaches down into our soul, exposing what we don't want to know, we seek explanations in an effort to evade what we dare not know. The dialectical image sets that text before us.

If history is "what hurts," it is the dialectical image that delivers the wound to the quick. For it doesn't simply exceed dominant frameworks of explanation; it positively resists and shatters them. Articulating the revelatory power of the dialectical image thus becomes the historian's primary task. Three moments constitute that process. They form a continuum, which we isolate in distinct steps only for purposes of analysis. The first moment solidifies the contribution that the image makes to the logic of the anti-*aufhebung* by articulating the ways in which the awareness it yields exceeds the concept.[29] In the second moment, internalization probes the image's deeper implications in an effort to lay bare the catastrophic register of the psyche as a primary force in the determination of historical events. In the third moment, Eros and Thanatos, as categories of historical explanation are engaged in a dialectic that produces as historical knowledge a depth-psychological awareness of the current state of what we may term "the human condition." In all three stages, as we'll see, artistic cognition emerges as the way of being that revolutionizes everything psychoanalysis has to offer the historian.

I. Art: Between Psychosis and Neurosis/Normalcy

Freud's great and unacknowledged achievement was to show that there is no way to establish a fixed line between neurosis and normalcy. Sustaining that insight leads to the possibility that the line separating neurosis and psychosis also will not hold. If neurosis/normalcy is at base a structure of displacement and denial, its true function is not to deliver us from psychotic conflicts but to assure their projection. This idea spells a crisis for those who have no other psychological categories. If psychosis and neurosis-normalcy are our only options and they double one another, the truth of the surface correctly seen is the howl extended through time, covered by a veneer of civility. There is, however, a third mode of psyche's self-mediation, a neglected one that we only begin to constitute when we realize that art is not just an activity that results in cultural products but a way of being and of mediating experience that cuts a path between psychosis and neurosis-normalcy. Artistic cognition confronts psychotic conflicts rather than avoiding them and finds a way to work on them directly and from within. In doing so art overcomes two inadequacies : (1) in mediating the psychotic conflicts in which the psyche is grounded, art concretely overcomes the self-fragmentation that befalls the psychotic; (2) in refusing flight and displacement, art reverses the projections whereby the neurotic/normal personality enforces that social conformity whereby psychotic conflicts and desires, denied and envenomed, find the disguises assuring their propagation.

To understand art along these lines requires as first task its liberation from the rhetorical tradition; that is, from the view that art is a process of (1) taking pre-existent, independently intelligible statements, themes, and ideas and (2) cloaking them in an appropriate verbal form in order (3) to make their communication vivid, powerful, pleasing, memorable. In such a view artistic form is no more than the container through which concepts and themes are presented, without being altered or transformed in any fundamental way by that process. As such, this view is the aesthetic wing of the ego-ratio, since it assures that conceptual meaning and the forms of life it serves will establish both the limits and the goals of art. In contrast, the theory developed here holds that the *forms of art* are original ways of knowing, independent principles of perception and cognition, which give us a unique and primary apprehension of the real. For one who lives out this way of responding to the world, experience and identity are constituted by principles of mediation that are immanent in art, providing an immediate access to experience that exceeds the limits of the concept and of socialized, rhetorical determinations of meaning.

With these gains, however, comes a great burden, for when conceived of along these lines art is thrown totally into history, that is, into a scene of change and radical contingency, demanding that art, qua form, be capable of radical, fundamental change, so as to "embrace the flame." The ability to change, to remake itself from within must constitute the defining character of art. Unlike other forms of knowing, which are fixed in the a priori functions that define their essence, artistic form must in effect be *sui generis*. Each work of art must constitute an original experiment that need not and perhaps cannot be repeated. Before it founds a "tradition" and sets the style for countless imitators, this is art's lonely, austere office. The artist's task is to invent the forms required by a historical occasion that is itself unprecedented and may not recur. There is no necessity, or likelihood (save fashion and the cash-career nexus) that a given artistic form will ever be used again because that form's raison d'être may be utterly defined by the situation at hand. That is why repetition deadens and why all genres and generic rules smell of death.

Unlike those ways of thinking that rest on a priori concepts and fixed categories, artistic thinking is inherently and openly experimental. It rests on one convention and one only: the artist has no idea what will be required or where the search for principles of artistic mediation will lead in the development of new artistic forms. Artists intuit and feel their way toward the solution of problems that they are also the first to formulate in that prior flash of "intuition" in which art finds its subject. The implications of this commonplace call for no less than an ontology of artistic form as the primary mode of historical knowing. Shelley's great maxim implies an equally great philosophic burden. Art is a knowledge that is radically different from all others and must be liberated from the preconceptions and limitations that rhetoric, humanism, and the ratio keep imposing on it.

This is the sense in which Dwight McDonald could not know the extent to which he was right in his smug yet incisive comment on the inadequacy of the journalistic methods John Hershey uses in *Hiroshima* to the magnitude of his subject. He could not know because the only way to gain that knowledge is to create the artistic form equal to that subject. The new nightmare that entered history in Hiroshima will be known only when when we evolve the radically new artistic forms it requires.

That possibility is grounded, however, in the self-reference that defines art. Art is that mode of cognition that relates to history through the immanent critique of its own forms. That, and not some pure aesthetic demand to be experimental and "make it new," is the source of change in the arts. The authentic artist seeks forms adequate to the comprehension of historical change; forms that will provide an embodiment that "gives the age and body of the time / it's form and pressure"—as in those portraits where Francis Bacon catches "a new pressure on the nerves" or in deKooning's *Excavation* where the fractured psyche is splayed in imploding patterns across a wall "as if a magic lantern threw the nerves in patterns on a screen."[30] For art to happen nothing can be fixed ahead of time; no content or theme can be established a priori without violating an order in which "content" is generated immanently from form's critique and overcoming of its previous limitations. Art is ontological and remains so only insofar as it evolves its "content" by staying true to its own internal logic. That logic is defined by art's radical inherence in the immediacies of affective experience. And that situatedness, in opposition to more abstract, conceptual, and ideological mediations, is the mode of its inherence in history. The "content" of a work of art is radically experiential and we misunderstand it in a way that is fundamental whenever we translate its "meaning" into abstract themes, quasipropositional statements, and rhetorical relationships. Or, to put it more concretely, when we find it impossible "to wait for that which has become concept to become again image" because we dimly know that we need concept because we cannot endure the agon to which artistic awareness submits us.

A. Sitting Shiva for the Human

If the concrete is, as Ricoeur says, "the final conquest of thought," then thought finds in the dialectical image the "identical subject-object" that provides its deepest contact with history. That is so, however, not because, as

Ricoeur holds, the image or symbol "calls for thought" and a hermeneutics of recovery devoted to retrieving universal meanings of an ahistorical (and quasireligious) nature,[31] but because the image exposes the conceptual and existential limits of such ways of thinking while calling for a thought that is dialectical precisely insofar as it moves in the medium of an awareness that sustains the affective and psychological dynamics of experience against all efforts to refashion the real in line with the assumptions that shape the ratio. There are essentially only three ways we can relate to the image. It can be thematized, as in the hermeneutic theories of Ricoeur and Gadamer. It can be deconstructed, as in the aporias of deMan and the trace-logic of Derrida. Or it can be engaged in an effort to constitute the existential, historical reality of its reference. The effort in what follows will be to bring this third possibility to its fullest complication.

The foregoing serves as but prelude to the crucial act. The dialectical image demands not abstract comprehension but concrete engagement. The image is that cognition which strips the world of its phantom objectivity and situates the knower in an epistemological space where impassioned appropriation constitutes the meaning and "objectivity" of experience. This circumstance is a direct result of the image's defining characteristic. *An image allows no inner distance.* It relates to us by seizing us. Images do not persuade us, they interrogate us. They claw at us with the power of events to smash beliefs, concepts, hopes, and defenses. The image is that text which rushes down to the deepest, buried registers of the psyche there to breed a sovereign discontent as the basis for the act whereby we grieve ourselves toward a new humanity. Images "address" us in a way that goes beyond all other rhetorical contracts. Engagement is the only possible reply, the only way of knowing available to us in this realm of being.

To constitute this possibility we must understand artistic mediation in a way that sustains its radical difference from other modes of knowing. The image is the first form and actualization of artistic awareness. The task of preserving its significance as such can be summarized in a single statement: an image is not a way of picturing or presenting a concept. It is a radically different act of knowing with a radically different "content." For the historian, this idea implies a fundamental transformation of the discipline. If art provides a distinct and privileged access to events, the historian must reconstitute the discipline from the ground up by making artistic mediation the model of thinking, knowing, and writing. This necessity is also determinative in a deeper sense because living it out constitutes what it means to be a historical being and, therefore, what it would mean to make the knowing and writing of history a matter of fundamental value for "spirit" in Nietzsche's sense of the term. Perhaps the most striking implication of this dialectic concerns the ways that the dominant rhetorical conventions of historical writing shape the relationship between author and audience so that the danger of history and contingency will be exorcized—for both parties. To reverse that rhetorical contract, one must write history in a way that deprives the audience of all escape routes. Here is true Brechtian labor, had we the wit to seize it.[32] *Writing must arrest, shatter, and expose dominant ways of understanding and the narrative paradigms on which they depend.* The writing and reading of history must become a drama that systematically forces the concept to bow before the power of the image so that the image can do its work (*werkzeug*) in evolving narratives that bring the audience to the roots of a disorder and the deracination consequent upon such knowledge. Narratives so formed constitute concrete reversals of Plato's allegory of the cave, with reader's delivered over to themselves through the power of the image to lay bare all that we prefer not to know.

B. Reading the Dialectical Image: Conceptualization/Catastrophe

The dialectical image is inexhaustible. The stages of its interpretation, however, have a single direction. Each stage is a further descent into the interior and toward a sharper articulation of the connections that constitute the context and meaning of traumatic events. Descent is the process through which the image performs its critique of the concept. Sustaining the image requires at each step the exposure of one set of concepts and the movement toward another. An Event has a twofold significance: the destruction of a hidden guarantee and the call for an articulation that will constitute an irreversible revolution in thought. The two moments in their connection constitute the process whereby the dialectical image enables us to *historicize the present.* To read a dialectical image is to preserve a complex that arrests and compresses time in an expressive density. Tunneling is the metaphor that best describes the tactics of such interpretation. Unearthing the buried dimensions of the image requires a method of decipherment that does not split or deconstruct the image into opposed, incompatible significations but that sustains the contradictions that are fused in the image by seeing the dialectical connections thereby established as ones that take us to the core of the psyche in its historicity. Or, to put it in image: the task of interpretation is to make the crypt speak, like one summoned by Dante, so that a message denied us by the ratio will be brought to human ears.[33] That message is the necessity to constitute catastrophe as a category for history.

Aragon argues that in order to know oneself each person must find that image that for them annihilates the world.[34] Such is the significance of the dialectical image for the historian. It annihilates the assumptions and protocols that have structured the discipline by setting forth what it cannot contain or comprehend. As we saw in chapter 4, the catastrophic register has the power to throw into question the entire structure of psychological beliefs historians have used (whether consciously or not) to shape their "materials" in order to sustain a humanistic rhetorical-ideological contract with their audience. Before the image, all of this grinds to a halt. Crisis, in Heidegger's sense of the term, comes to the discipline. For in the dialectical image catastrophe takes on the status of an ontological question demanding an ontological regression into ways of knowing that are strange and unintelligible to most historians. The psychotic register of experience becomes the primary object of attention. In attuning the historian to that reality, the dialectical image functions like a war neurosis. The traumatic reliving of an Event is the act of interpretation that shatters the ego-structures that make discharge operations possible. As Rilke says, "Here there is no place that does not see you." The desperate repetition of the old escape routes deepens dread, making it determinate. The image thereby brings the question Why to issue in its true force: why finds no answer within extant orders of discourse and conceptualization precisely because they are grounded in a refusal to "go to the roots" by entering the inner world opened up by the image.

In the image, the contradictions of a historical situation erupt, come to a head, and begin to implode. As a result, contradiction here is not only a logical articulation of opposed historical forces, but a revelation of history's human meaning as that weight bears down upon the subject. A new way to locate crisis-points in history, and with it the recovery of a host of Marxist concepts, emerges.[35] Crisis is the real in its movement toward catastrophe. In the image that supposedly impossible reference is torn loose from symbolic shields and presented in its true gravity: Orwell's gigantic boot, updated and known, as it descends. As "sign of history" the dialectical image shifts everything over to the register of the sublime, teaching us that to read history at that register is to unlock the terms of an irreversible dialectic. When the deepest disorders of the psyche stand forth in deeds that are celebrated in their smug certainty, there is only one appropriate reply. That reply is the attempt in reading the dialectical image to articulate the logic of the anti-*Aufhebung* so that Events will be apprehended "correctly"; as the imperative to make engagement the only adequate response to experience. Concepts then become agons epiphanized in their power to arrest and interrogate a subject whose duty, as thinker-historian, is to live out the burdens thinking imposes by developing an order of thought that will be fully existentialized and that will sustain passion as the primary term of every articulation.

I hasten to add the corollary that concretizes. A word, an utterance is sufficient to constitute a dialectical image. And often the most prosaic agents speak the deepest truths. As in Grossman's *See Under—Love* in the reply of one Nazi to the action of another: "You killed my jew, now I'm going to kill your jew." Or this, straight talk from the man from Missouri, circa 1945: "this is the greatest day in history." There is only one condition that must be fulfilled to create a dialectical image. One must give voice to what was never spoken before and which, once said, changes everything by revealing a new configuration of Thanatos—ineradicable and unsublatable, unbated and envenomed.

Like energy unlocked from its long confinement in matter, in the dialectical image the quotidian explodes in revelation: of how separate institutions and disciplines function together to constitute a collectivity that dances to the imploding psychotic through-line structuring the system as a whole. A new theory of agency and of collective intentionality comes into view. The agents required to constitute an Event need never meet, deliberate, and then act together for an overriding purpose to make its demands (and its pleasures) felt as an imperative shaping the choices made by diverse agents at each necessary step along the way. This is the invaluable lesson for a philosophic historian in studying actions such as those that led inexorably to the "decision" to drop atomic bombs on Japan,[36] and the key to knowing why, at the right moment, the sublime force of that Event tweaked even the least among those agents into "song."[37]

In exploding the continuum, the dialectical image cancels two operations that in their "*différance*" have one thing in common. I refer to the effort of the ego-ratio to restore old, explanatory "humanistic" frameworks and the "postmodern" effort to "deconstruct" the image so as to displace and delay/defer its power. The claim that reference is impossible or undecidable is the glib flip side of an a priori recognition: the fear that no reference any longer exists except the nuclear one, descending, on a socius that has become the space of a collective psychosis—with Thanatos the tie that binds subjects in the "rhetorical" contract that creates and sustains the consensual order of the We. The possibility of "absolute knowledge" and a systematic description of culture as what Hegel called objective spirit depends today on plumbing the depths of the psychotic register.[38] And just as the dessert grows, the totalizing power of the dialectical image is its ability to call for *deracination* within the psychic terrain that it lays bare. The image calls for a new kind of conceptualization. The role and order of the concept is to articulate the agons that must be engaged if the disruptive power of the image is to be preserved against the pull of abstract, reductive, and analytic modes of understanding. Concepts as cutting edge of passion are fists aimed at the frozen sea. And that is why conceptual articulation is only a starting point. Because the image invades us and rushes down, with shattering force, to the most concealed and buried places of our psyche, it is there that one must fathom its meaning by living out the full force of the blow. To restate Artaud, an image is true insofar as its violence allows no inner distance. That is the key to its working (*werkzeug*). It assaults the "knower" with the charge of a knowledge that is one with an imperative: "*Du musst dein Leben ändern.*" You must change your life. Conceptualization is but the first moment in constituting the meaning of the image as a dynamic demanding a process in which engagement is not one hermeneutic stance among others in a happy pluralism of approaches, but that prior condition from which other modes of interpretation derive—and which they displace. The absence of inner distance and the necessity of engagement is the dialectical connection that binds the knower to the object of historical knowledge. Because the image seizes us with the force of an interrogation that puts our being at issue, we can only know it by living out an agonistic relationship to it. Because it shatters all defenses, the image leaves no option other than self-mediation through agon. The guarantees no longer work as principles of explanation and no catharsis supervenes to deliver us from the alembic of primary affect. And that drama has a single direction: the movement inward and downward to the questions about oneself the image reawakens in delivering the subject it addresses to the full force of history. In the dialectical image, "the heart's intermittencies" (Proust) and its deathless passions are retained as agons awaiting the process through which subject as who/ why ripens to the permanent claim that historical Events have on us.

DIALECTIC OF THE CONCRETE—
THE THANATOPTIC IMAGE AND THE CRYPT IMAGE

> The Chaconne [in Bach's D Minor Partita for solo violin] is for me the most wonderful, unfathomable piece of music. On one stave, for a small instrument, the man writes a whole world of deepest thoughts and most powerful feelings. If I imagine that I could have created, even conceived the piece, I am quite certain that the excess of excitement and earth-shattering experience would have driven me out of my mind.
>
> —Johannes Brahms

The greatest gift the dialectical image bestows on the historian is this: it teaches us that affect, not reason, directs history.[39] It does so, moreover, by forcing the historian to comprehend history at the sublime register. In the dialectical image we learn not only that the life of feeling is historical, but what the actual psychological principles are that shape the actions of collective, historical agents.

In what follows I will develop the implications of this theory for history by distinguishing within the dialectical image what I term the thanatoptic image and the crypt image.[40] This distinction is analytic and serves to identify the terms of the agon that constitutes the internal structure of the dialectical image. In image the density of the two forces distinguished above are fused—at white heat—in a synthesis. That synthesis reveals the present state of the opposition that defines history. The task of interpretation is to unlock the condition arrested in the image in order to activate the agon implicit in it. Articulating the inner structure of the dialectical image is the act that makes clear and distinct, stark and unremitting, the choices it imposes on us. That effort will take the form of a series of definitions, grouped under six topics.

I. At the Origin: Death-Work and the Existential Unconscious

The thanatoptic image apprehends death-work in the specific acts through which it shoots ice into the soul. In it, cruelty is arrested, compressed, and made a permanent record. Such images apprehend the heart as it contracts; Thanatos at the moment it empowers itself at the core of the psyche. In such images the Iago-driven intentions of the Other are apprehended in acts that give forth the truth, regardless of what is subsequently said. Such images leave no inner distance, no room for denial or delay, extenuation or the cover-up. Faced with soul-murder, action is demanded—even if repression immediately ensues.

The crypt image is the howl made concrete as reaction and incipient action. In it protest is staged in that coalescence of primary affect that gives birth to one's being as a subject. No matter how deeply buried, such images beckon to the future. That temporality maintains because the crypt image "synthesizes" two forces in an exacting dialectical relationship: (1) the truth of the other's cruelty and (2) the refusal to deny or mitigate that fact. Action thereby finds its origin. In this: suffering internalized transforms passivity by bringing the who/why into existence as that passion which is one with the agon implicit in it. This is the sense in which humiliation, for example, sows the seeds of the greatest reversals. To restate Camus, perhaps the greatest trek is to recover those two or three great images in which the heart first closed—in order to make them the basis for its recovery.

Thereby, the dialectic that founds the subject is joined. The thanatoptic image reveals envy in its malignance, cruelty in its effort to find the vulnerability that must be subjected to humiliation, poisoned, and turned back against itself for soul-murder to attain its end. The crypt image is the inauguration of the existential unconscious as the only possible response to that act, the effort in the depths of the arrested, astonished heart to find the will, against forgetting, to preserve that situation so that one may somehow project oneself upon it. The agon that makes us human derives from the clash of this contradiction: death-work, unleashed in the fury of its rectitude and celebrated as such over against the fragility of that which flickers and flares up momentarily in the hot tears and interstices of our humiliation.

The latter, of course, disappears almost immediately, repressed and perhaps extinguished. Existential subjectivity is that barest of possibilities, crypted in images we flee because they bind us to the humiliated child we once were who haunts us from the past.

II. The Origin as Historicity

As historical Event, the thanatoptic image reveals death-work in its leap to outstrip prior limitations in order to attain an irreversible determination of its agenda. When it is met by an equal or greater reaction the thanatoptic image begets in the crypt image the terms for a *tragic agency* that is concretely pitted against death.

History thus remains a battle of Eros against death. But the desert grows and our world abounds in images of Thanatos set free of internal opposition. To engage that dialectic the difference between our situation and previous ones is precisely what must be constituted. For in constituting that difference we historicize the present. The great image, redolent of Thanatos, which begins one of our greatest poems—"April is the cruelest month" remains fully dialectical because in the world that *The Waste Land* represents life still troubles those who have not completed their dying. No such conflict intrudes on Tibbet's moment or on "You killed my jew, now I'm going to kill your jew." That is why such images require a rejoinder that comes straight from the crypt: "If you could lick my heart it would poison you." Zuckerman's image updates the longing for death that is Eliot's moment by defining the situation that is its historical outcome. Such is the burden of artistic conscience. Itzhak Zuckerman lives because he is alive in a dialectic that proceeds directly from the crypt. There is, for Zuckerman, no going back to an explanation that is not an engagement without reserve in an unprecedented historical condition. That is his gift to Lanzmann and the audience: a poison that goes straight to the heart with no intervening distance.[41] In this regard, it is significant that Zuckerman only speaks reluctantly, after telling Lanzmann that his framework and his questions are inappropriate to the "facts." As Zuckerman knows, the Shoah demands an internalization "costing not less than everything," an image that addresses the who/why with a violence that eradicates every defense and guarantee. Because he lives that burden, Itzhak Zuckerman is one of the "unacknowledged legislators" of our time who gives us, in image, the agon defining what is required to exist today as a historical subject.

In the thanatoptic image, death-work realizes a new "inhumanity" by annihilating a prior order of human relatedness. The record of that fact is preserved in the image: the human condition reduced to bits and pieces of pure persecution, shards of unsublatable pain become the permanent condition of the walking dead. "I came to Hiroshima because I believe perception must be learned." In the thanatopic image the historian finds what Aragon sought, an annihilation of the world become an object of one's infinite concern.[42] In the crypt image the who/why finds through ontological regression a way to constitute itself within that situation. The crypt image has its meaning in this demand: deracination through reversal within the agon of primordial conflicts. In the crypt image, the wound at the heart of subject is assumed as womb for the process of taking action within. The core is exposed as an existentializing burden made present in a knowledge of one's complicity in an inhumanity that rises up as a judgment one must assume. The question one asks of one's own heart—"Is there any cause in nature that makes these hard hearts?"—is now lived in images that strip away all protections from self knowledge: "Is it not as if this mouth would tear this hand for lifting food to it?" Psychotic conflicts are again present in their immediacy, but now as the basis for a new self-mediation. That agon begins when psychotic panic is reconnected to the primitive conflicts from which it derives. Fragments of unspeakable pain become present again—as experiences now remembered in their truth. The attempt to know the force of the destructive other in one's inner world is thereby made one with the only appropriate action—deracination. In the crypt image that possibility finds the harsh and concrete terms of its labor.

III. The Heart of the Image: The Psychotic Register Laid Bare

> Black milk of daybreak we drink it at evening
> —Paul Celan, *Deathfugue*

The thanatoptic image embodies psychotic anxiety in its triumphant externalization—soul-murder become *jouissance,* unleashed and celebrated in a festival of cruelty. The crypt image drives that pleasure back with implosive force to the place of its origin. Here are three ways to concretize the terms of the resulting agon.

The thanatoptic image represents, in an omnipotent fantasy, pure mind as pure madness; the ratio overcoming all restrictions in a violent exploding of itself. In such images the truth of the ratio is revealed: the motives it disguises, projects, and denies are made present in their sublime expression. The horror of abstraction :: the abstraction of horror. The crypt image attempts the absolute reversal of that movement. In it omnipotent fantasy reveals itself as flight from inner reality. Deprived of its phantom independence, it is doubled back upon itself. The buried contents it attempts to escape and deny are now inflicted upon it. There are only two options left: claustrophobic delirium or active reversal.

In the thanatoptic image, catastrophe, in its historicity, finds its objective correlative in a psychic fragmentation and self-dissolution that is binding and that imposes itself, on all subjects; both those subjected to its destructive power and the new *socius* interpellated in reverential awe beneath its smug finality, as in the L.A. Coliseum. In the crypt image, nameless dread, makes the only "humanistic" response by hollowing out an inner space where death-work is confronted by images in which suffering becomes an active agency, "signaling through the flames."[43] This is the space of the Howl as the prime agent of historical perception.

The thanatoptic image reveals a new advance in the pacification and internal deadening of the mass subject. In it the true agenda of the nuclear age is revealed. As in the inaugural act when an entire city became a single psyche stripped of all relations save the corpsed condition to which it was delivered. Then, of necessity, in the rush of the victors to mirror that condition: (1) in Amerika's collective fascination with images of its own extinction and commodification; (2) in the hot pursuit of simulation and hyperreality as ways of canceling the pressure of the real; and (3) in the current drive to annex ourselves to a world of pure affectless information, networking the globe in a velocity that eradicates everything save what conforms to the "rationality" of the evolving technostructure.[44] In programming the machine we reprogram ourselves. The lure of that fixation is this: inwardness thereby becomes information, in endless blind permutation of itself.

The sequence sketched here gives us a key to the relationship the image has to time. Temporality in the thanatoptic image is a present big with the future it raises to the status of a categorical imperative. The command implicit in the thanatopic image is to consign to a residual nostalgia whatever fails to correspond to the "forms of life" required for its hegemony.[45] The crypt image unearths the counterforce of a temporality in which active reversal situates the possibility of resistance and historical change at the register of experience where revolution begins with ontological regression, with the effort to remake the human from the ground up. By beginning with the wound, the basic rupture at the heart of the psyche, one gets to the place where death first planted itself and sits empowered. The rooting out of inner death thereby becomes the basis for a praxis that is concretely projected as a perception of the omnipresent ways in which death advances its agenda in the fabric of culture and of everyday life. The negative is thus lived on all occasions as that cleansed perception which sees the world as death's dream kingdom. Praxis thereby attains its true object and its burden. The wound has become the place from which one acts in combating the force of death without and within. The resulting temporality, in resisting the wave of the future, reopens the past as a repeatable possibility, but one that exists only insofar as it is situated and defined by the pressure of the present.[46]

IV. Affect: Its Primacy and Its Dialectic

In the thanatoptic image the burden of affect is externalized and resolved at the sublime register. The detritus of inner nuclear waste is congealed so that the most primitive defense mechanism, blowing away, can resolve all inner tension by evacuating itself upon a world delivered over to its destructive designs. Thanatos fully eroticized thereby attains a triumphant overcoming of its discontents by providing the mass subject it interpellates with the perfect scapegoat—Nature, the other, the jap, the kike, the cunt, the coon—on which self-disgust can vent itself. The rituals and symbols that invest that act with *jouissance* make irresistible the resulting self-reification.

In the crypt image dread, in reply, becomes the basis of self-reference and self-mediation. In such images the existential unconscious projects the who/why as an impassioned confrontation with death at the level of psychic structure. Our duty as historical beings is to create the affect that our situation demands. In the crypt image that task finds the solidification that fixes attention on the necessary agon. To combat death what is needed, above all, is a fundamental change in the order of feeling—a new order of rank grounded in that affect, tragic melancholia, which becomes an innermost imperative because it "names" our historical situation in a way that imposes it on the subject as a passion of soul. At this register, to feel is to take upon oneself the burden of an articulation of the world that does not resolve or "tone down" affect but that sustains and deepens its claim upon us. Affect so constituted is ontological and the equivalent for a thought that is historical of Spinoza's adequate idea. The "right" affect is the one that issues in the knowledge that delivers us over to history, totally and without reserve. In that affect inwardness and existence become one as act.

The fourth section of David Grossman's remarkable novel *See Under— Love* is a sustained effort to constitute such a dialectic of affect. For Grossman we have not comprehended the Shoah because we have not yet constituted the affects required to give it voice. Doing so requires affective "discriminations" of a new order. The character Aaron Marcus defines that task as the necessity to create images that will embody emotions that have never existed before because the historical situation demanding them had not yet come into being. Marcus acknowledges the limits of language ("the fault lay in language," p. 441), and yet asserts the need to find a way to give "voice" to new complexes of feeling: "to breed anxiety with hope, or melancholy with longing," to find the "six shades of feeling, more or less acute, all of them definitely 'primary,'" that exist between "anxiety" and "terror."[47] The effort at naming and "classification" is not for Marcus, however, part of a redemptive aesthetic. It is undertaken, rather, to provide fodder to feed a machine called THE SCREAM. Marcus supplies it with the material it requires through the following acts. (1) He plots "the voids in man's feeling atmosphere" so as to introduce therein (2) "the purest octave of human anguish," to which is added (3) "a subtle note of defiance and a light ring of protest." The evolving complex is then (4) rehearsed until one attains a "feeling" that is "razor-sharp." It constitutes the pure material of historical awareness. (5) One then implodes that matter by whirling it, with "maddening velocity," like atomic particles in a cyclotron, around a Void in an effort to liberate the sound of a scream that will shatter the entire world. (7) But from which there is "no explosion, no disaster. Nothing at all" (p. 424). Marcus thus learns the secret of Munch's painting. No sound comes from that mouth; except for those who (like Schoenberg) have ears to hear a new sound. For them the fourth section of Grossman novel constitutes the dialectically ordered structure of images that define the agon that a historical subject, as narrator and as reader, must enact in order to internalize the Shoah. Reading here engages its innermost possibility, which Kafka defined at age 24: the reader becomes the book, with existential risk made apodictic by the power of authentic art to explode within us. Such works read us and find wanting everything in us that refuses the demand they place on us to take action within.

Those attuned to the history of dialectical art know that there is nothing "new" about Grossman's project, save the explicitness with which he foregrounds it.[48] Creating new affects is the primary business of great literary works. Unfortunately, criticism and literary theory (with a few noteworthy exceptions) anesthetizes the energy of charged affects. Through interpretation the shield is varnished and the Medusa slain. Habitual patterns of response that are redemptive, cathartic, humanistic, and supremely self-serving triumph over all disruptions so that the reader can rise from the book, "calm of mind, all passion spent;" Kafka's experience vanquished, identity restored; with the world unchanged, the recalcitrance of emotion having again defeated affect in carrying us one step further in the practices conducive to our self-reification.

V. The Nuclear Unconscious: The Temporality of the Dialectical Image

A. "Spots of Time"

In its temporality, the thanatoptic image reveals what the past intended by presenting the Event in which its hidden agenda is fulfilled. In this sense, every thanatoptic image embodies a step toward the final solution; what the past, as precursor, anticipated in providing the images that paved the way to future actions. That connection gives us the through-line of history. In tracing that progression the patient historian (Raul Hillberg for example) binds together in chains of steel traces, empirical markers of what we have every right to call causality. He thereby brings to apprehension what the prophetic witnesses to history (Clara Haber, Franz Kafka) fore-suffered in flames.[49]

In its temporality the crypt image projects that knowledge into the future so that the present, in its telos, can be known Now. As example, a date, 1893. That is the year Munch painted *The Howl*, thereby sublating desire into dread, setting the agenda for twentieth-century art: to record in expressive texts the increasing pressure that time since 1893 has exerted upon the nerves. While death hides its agenda until all is ripe for celebratory ratification after the fact, in the crypt image "looking before and aft" plunges into the future so that conditions foreseen can bite back into the present. Such is ecological time, the antithesis of Hegel's Owl.

B. Time in the Quotidian

If Blake saw the world in a grain of sand and it took Proust seven great volumes to comprehend the temporal relations implicit in a cake dipped in tea, it is because the dialectical image compresses in its density the relations that define the intersubjective meaning of an entire historical order. One dialectical image fully read reveals the true condition of the world it epiphanizes. For us that means that the search for lost time finds its beginnings in images animated with the force of implosion. Those seeking such images need not look far. We live in their midst. They compose what has become of Hegel's morning prayer: images, fitted to advancing the deadening of affect, flit across the screen before subjects who sit in paralyzed fascination, horror the one response no longer available—or the one incessantly sought, as the only pleasure. Everyday life abounds in images that reveal the quotidian as death-in-life, with death-work the "strange" attractor and the "magnet" around which dispersed subjectivities congeal as groups-in-fusion, dedicated to the dissolution of subjectivity.[50] "The disappearance of subject" is a process that is lived, in intense longing, long before it becomes an abstract, formalistic theme in a philosophizing in love with the linguistic prison-house because it renders the bars of the cage a priori, and therefore comforting. Popular culture is the mill where death-work ceaselessly churns out signs and traces of itself. In the latest development, subjects now sit in rapt, anesthetized amazement before a machine that annihilates thought in the great rush to reprogram everything to the conditions of information circling the globe in furious motion on that great technological superhighway. Medium is indeed message, since anything other than analytic facticity has become intrusive, irrelevant noise that "does not program." Those subjects who have not purged themselves of everything opposed to the "language" of the computer are now the curious objects of an incoherent and fleeting nostalgia.

In the crypt image these processes momentarily screech to a halt as the anxiety of another self-reference momentarily erupts. Death-work is felt in its Baconian pressure on the nerves. The flow of information is arrested in a knowledge of what must disappear from our lives for the wave of the future to secure its dominion. In such images that which is passing from our lives makes its presence felt, as it flares up momentarily in images redolent of loss and danger—Larkin's animals seen through the eyes of Franz Marc. Do such images provide the terms of resistance or betray lying nostalgia? That is the innermost question that the crypt image harbors about itself—and embodies in the tensions that constitute its internal structure.

For Blake, "he who catches the joy as it flies / lives in eternity's sunrise." We, born into another condition, find our beginnings only when the pressure of death on the nerves receives its "reciprocative rejoinder" in affects that refuse to mitigate its presence in every avenue of our lives. Forster's "Only connect" resides today in a world where, as Musil already knew in 1912, "Pseudoreality prevails." That watershed recognition informs the effort of our finest contemporary writers (Pynchon, Gaddis, Gass, Morrison, Grossman) to represent an order of things in which death informs all occasions, its appeal virtually irresistible for those whose collective quest is to void themselves of all residual inwardness.[51]

VI. The Motive for Art

In the thanatoptic image the death-drive informing a collectivity epiphanizes itself. This is the abiding significance of those images we wrest from the news—such as the spectacle enacted in Los Angeles in 1945. In reply, the crypt image plants a time-bomb in the brains of the living, unleashing a counterviolence by inflicting on the audience it addresses discontents that can no longer be denied but must be assumed as a sovereign duty—that of an absolute reversal of the psyche from the core. The thanatoptic image celebrates a collective mania; the crypt image "gets the guests" in the marrow.

In the thanatoptic image neurosis/normalcy reveals its psychotic bases, with the two known in their complicity and their covert identity. In the crypt image art establishes itself as the only psychological and ontological alternative to that reality. Into the seamless web uniting psychosis/neurosis/normalcy art drives this wedge: it descends directly into psychotic conflicts and mediates them in a way that sustains a break with the ego-ratio. It thereby evolves structures of affect, ways of experiencing and regulating the psyche, that are radically different from the adaptational and consensual principles that give the ego its self-reifying destiny. The artist is neither psychotic nor neurotic/normal. Neither way of structuring experience is able to account for art's "legislative" activities. Gaddis, who defines normalcy as "a well-compensated neurosis" also said this: "art is a counter-attack against nightmare."[52] In the crypt image, this, the true poetic act, first coalesces in the density appropriate to it. Situating us before that apprehension is "what poets are for in a dark time"[53] because the artistic mediation of experience and of history begins there, in the psychic terrain Heidegger refused to enter, the inner depth of the *Da* of *Dasein*.

In the history we are living, the primacy of Thanatos demands of art a radically new relationship to the audience. Art's task is that of Orpheus: to descend and unearth those images that combat and actively reverse Thanatos. Most of us respond to Thanatos with flight, denial, or with a secret pleasure. That is because our complicity in advancing death's agenda must remain unconscious; otherwise we would have no choice but to take up our lives. Art's duty is to force that choice upon us. Doing so involves six steps:

1. By abiding with Thanatos art finds the true labor of the negative in ontological regression.
2. Thereby it internalizes those images that deliver us over to our condition because they fathom the force of death within the psyche.
3. Deracinating action at that register emerges as the only possible response.
4. Orphic descent makes that act possible because it discovers, within the crypt, images of reversal that respond directly to Thanatos by engaging it concretely in agon.
5. The images buried in the deepest crypt of one's humiliation thereby become the life-blood of the only action that truly opposes death—the act of uprooting death-work from within.
6. In art, death, made present in those images that empower it, is brought up against the action those images also hollowed out in us as the only authentic response.

In the clash of images one attains an immanent dialectic that proceeds directly from that register in which history and psyche are one. If Shelley was right in claiming that "poets are the unacknowledged legislators of the world," the dialectical image is the act through which they engage that office.

The "inexhaustibility" of the dialectical image derives from its revelation of the primary fact: historicity. An image is fathomed only when its agon is fully unlocked and the crypt register engaged in the expanding field of dialectical connections that reveal the quotidian in terms of the avidities that inform it. As the call for action within that field, the image gives us the world stripped of illusions, denials, and guarantees. In so doing it awakens the existential unconscious, that vitality buried in the crypt, which can reclaim itself only through a deracination that practices a scorched-earth policy within as the true and decidedly non-Hegelian "route to the concrete." Creating an affective order that is determined by one's existential situation in history thereby becomes the innermost imperative structuring subject's self-reference. Only then is history lived, suffered, and acted in the pores.[54]

In making the case for melancholia as the affect that fulfills these requirements, no attempt has been made to posit an essence outside time. On the contrary, the effort, to put it in quasi-Hegelian terms, has been to show that melancholia is that affect which is its own notion immediately and which, as identical subject-object, the source of the self-mediation that makes subjectivity one with engagement in one's historical situation. In its dependence on art to provide the formal principles making that self-mediation possible this dialectic lives out what Nietzsche intended when he argued that we should live lives that will "bear aesthetic scrutiny"—

> I have found it—paradise.
> It is the sun upon the sea—

APPENDIX A
TWELVE THESES ON THE PHILOSOPHY OF HISTORY

HISTORY AS FACT

1. The dead remain in danger. Of being sacrificed to the needs of the audience.

2. Determining the fact is the historian's sole task. But the fact is often a vast question and a great gap in Being. Such as this: what happened on August 6, 1945?

3. That question, ineluctably, involves another, which can be formulated in its most radical form by putting the issue in Kantian terms: what must human beings be like for Hiroshima to be possible?

HISTORY AS DIALECTICAL PROCESS

4. Thanatos, in its effort to annex and extinguish Eros, is the driving force of western history. Eros, in dialectical rejoinder, must totalize itself by deracinating every realm of experience where death-work holds sway.

5. An Event, as sign of history, is an act in which the eroticization of death interpellates all subjects at the sublime register of the psyche.

6. A collective historical Unconscious thereby evolves, creating the *through-line* that binds diverse institutions, disciplines, and agents in a movement that proceeds inexorably to the next necessary event.

THE TEMPORALITY OF THE EVENT

7. History, as Event, creates a force-field driven by the logic of the next step: this is the law and lure of progress as a movement to "the final solution."

8. The Event thus lays bare the *ecstases* of historical temporality: the violence of the present unlocks the hidden truth of the past and exposes the demand that will shape the future. Existential time is the suffering of that condition as the cause that informs the act of thinking.

HISTORICITY AS HERMENEUTIC OF ENGAGEMENT

9. A dialectic of the Anti-*Aufhebung* articulates the logic required to comprehend history without guarantees. That logic systematically reverses Hegel by revealing all the ways in which dramatic self-mediation exceeds and exposes rational self-mediation. As dialectical system the result is a systematic understanding of death-work in its totalizing power.

10. Engagement is the resulting labor of the negative: the effort to meet the horror of History with the only appropriate rejoinder—an inwardness dedicated to the agon of deracination within the core of the crypt. Only thereby is it possible to confront and reverse the force of death in the psyche.

HISTORY AS WRITING

11. The dialectical image is the reality that delivers us over to that task. As the identical subject-object of history, the dialectical image reveals the necessary connection of what must be deracinated—without and within. Its comprehension can be compressed to a single point of illumination: "*Du musst dein leben ändern.*"

12. The writing of history begins with a search for the forms of artistic cognition and expression required to preserve and constitute the reality of the Event. Style is idea, narrative is drama. Art, as an independent way of thinking, generates a knowledge of experience that is beyond the modes of understanding developed in and demanded by the ratio. The writing of history is the attempt to compress the energy of the negative to the point of an ideal nuclear density. That density defines our duty to the dead: to write histories in which the needs of the audience are sacrificed to the reality of the Event and the existential imperatives it imposes on us.

APPENDIX B
TOWARD CONCRETE DIALECTICS:
HISTORY, PSYCHOLOGY, AESTHETIC ONTOLOGY

This book forms the first volume of a trilogy. Volume Two, *The Crypt,* will develop the theory of the Psyche implicit in it. A final volume, *Dialectic of Aesthetic Experience,* will take up ontology directly: (1) by contrasting, on purely philosophic and methodological grounds, the theory of subjectivity developed in these works with the leading philosophic theories of the day; and (2) by showing how an ontology of being based on artistic cognition enables us to reclaim existence and experience as starting points. The tendency today is to begin with metatheory—and specifically with the hypostatization of language and discourse with a resulting reduction of reality and meaning to the dilemmas of signification. Making the case for "lived experience" and the "existential subject" requires a radically different starting point and procedure, one rooted in immanent investigations of agonistic processes that exceed the limits of both the conceptual-discursive order and its deconstruction and based on architectonic principles derived from the primacy of literature and its referential claims.[1] The contrast with the current belief that everything can be derived from an analytic and rationalistic understanding of language and discourse is, in fact, systemic. And structural: one purpose of the order of the trilogy being to create an *Entfremdungseffekt* by (1) constructing a position that breaks with the metatheoretical assumptions and paradigms that structure contemporary thought (2) in order to see what might emerge to fresh consideration when a radically different way of thinking constructs a concrete and systematic contrast. (By the same token, this is why metatheoretical issues are here taken up at the end and not, as is so often and distressingly the case today, at the beginning.) To orient the reader to the project as a whole—and to where and why various issues will be taken up—I here offer a brief overview of basic theses in the order in which they will be discussed.

A. DERACINATION: HISTORICITY, HIROSHIMA,
AND THE TRAGIC IMPERATIVE

1. Deracination is the practice I propose as a concrete alternative to both (a) the various forms of poststructuralist thought and (b) to the essentialisms of the humanistic tradition. That concept is developed through the interrogation and reconstruction of a particular discipline, history. A single event—the bombing of Hiroshima—focuses the inquiry.

2. Thereby Benjamin's "duty to the dead" becomes the imperative shaping the inquiry.[2] With this result: *memory* is blazed as *conscience* into the deepest hiding places of the historian's psyche through a systematic exposure of the various guarantees and ideologies of explanation that historians have traditionally used in order to escape the reality of their subject.

3. A new theory of thinking and of how to interrogate historical events is thereby evolved. The primacy of the image—and the ontological claims regarding the reality of its reference—becomes the basis for a Rilkean theory of perception that liberates contingency from all guarantees and that establishes affect as the primary register at which we apprehend the world.

4. The Bomb and the Nuclear Unconscious, Hiroshima to the Present. The nuclear unconscious is described through a systematic analysis of "the psyche that dropped the bomb." That description enables us to comprehend American society as a psychotic theatre driven by an imploding logic that has made hyperreality, simulation, and endless, empty narcissism the only remaining terms of reference. The postmodern is thereby comprehended as the postnuclear, with the latter category providing the context that re-reads and re-interprets the former. This is the dialectical-historical connection: the ironic stance of free play and endless deferral are flights from the referent that inhabits them.

5. The deepest implication of that investigation is a reconstitution of the dialectic of Eros and Thanatos as principles of historical explanation—a rethinking that is dialectical not dualistic; historical not essentialistic; irreversible and voided of guarantees; one in which Thanatos, not Eros, is primary both in the internal constitution of the psyche and in a socius that today aspires to attain coincidence with a deadening logic.

6. The internalization of that knowledge becomes the act whereby the "historian of the present" engages the task of writing history. Nietzsche's idea of the proper use of history for "the life of spirit" is reclaimed as a meditation on the tragic imperatives of our condition; and a recovery of existential reflection as the act of thinking required for its comprehension.

B. THE CRYPT: THE INNER WORLD OF PSYCHE AS TRAGIC AGON

The second volume attempts to internalize this knowledge and bring it to fruition in a new theory of the psyche, one that is psychoanalytic yet sharply opposed to current psychoanalytic schools and orthodoxies.

1. Cruelty and Humiliation are established as the experiences that found the psyche. Such realities are not merely important, neglected experiences. They are the very foundation of experience; the reason why there is psyche (rather than simply behavior), the condition of its origin. In humiliation subject as who/why is born in and as the anguish that attends the struggle to constitute one's being in the teeth of soul-murder, the experience of Thanatos as the intention and the action of the other.[3] Thanatos, so understood, is not a cosmological idea or a biological principle but a human act. It is the way that those powerless to reverse the results of their humiliation inflict humiliation on others. The existential register of experience, the register at which one becomes a subject at issue to oneself, derives from the internalization and repression of the self-reference—a subject as who/why that cruelty creates. The heart of inwardness is the continued pressure of this crypted experience over against the displacements constructed to deliver us from it. Those displacements have one master name, the ego, which is here seen in its essence as that structure, that way of being, which is vigorously opposed to reality. Freedom from its rule, however, requires a new *Bildung*, a new "labor of the negative": a descent into the crypt and the activation at that register of an agon requiring a complete reversal of the entire structure of the psyche.

2. Through that process the basis for a new "phenomenology of spirit" is attained, one that makes the continuing significance of Hegel's thought a *moment* within a systematic knowledge of how dramatic self-mediation differs from and exceeds rational self-mediation. For descent into the interiority of the subject now bears the unmistakable stamp of an analogy to Dante's *Inferno*, but with neither Vergil nor Beatrice to provide the guarantees needed to structure that journey. In contrast to current cute, clever dismissals of humanism, this is what going beyond that tradition requires: one must abide within the crypt and confront the force of Thanatos without any shields.

3. The "dialectic of situated subjectivity" inaugurated in *Inwardness and Existence* is thereby put on a new basis. The "route to the concrete" now begins by showing that what the four great thinkers interrogated there could not let themselves know is precisely this: the crypt as the reality that inhabits and is displaced in the ontological primacy claimed for their starting points. As a result, the phenomenological descriptions they offer now yield to *interrogation* a deeper problematic and deeper experience of what

Kant called "the subjectivity of the subject." For example, the dialectic of desire and master-slave in Hegel is now grounded in the prior force of Thanatos and cruelty in the constitution of intersubjectivity. Thereby the standpoint that Lacan and others regard as foundational—the bedrock of desire, even if that desire is of the Other—is referred to a prior, and darker, dynamic—of cruelty—and, of greater significance, to a new possibility. Compassion is that which is prior to desire and the basis for an understanding that will break with the hypnotic force that desire has had over the understanding of subjectivity since Hegel.[4]

4. Establishing the primacy of passion as the *agon* that drives and informs the subject's *self-reference* also produces a transformation in what Heidegger called "the Analytic of *Da-sein*"; that is, a phenomenological description of the basic structures in which the subject's being is at issue. For now to know where one's being is at issue is to find it at issue and engage it as such in a process that is simultaneously existential and psychoanalytic. The result is a hermeneutic that generates as the end result of each interrogation-agon a *content* that *existentializes* those who comprehend it.[5] Passion is this register, the register of affect in which the soul debates with itself the meaning of its being. It thus stands in stark contrast to the defensive functions of ordinary emotions and feelings. Reflection is authentic when it moves within "the medium of passion," opening up what is frozen within to agonistic self-mediation.[6] That drama is one in which the act of existence pits itself against all the forces contributing to self-reification. This is the agon that constitutes the dialectic of lived-experience, the way (contra Sartre) that the who/why gives itself being.

5. The *tragic* is thus attained and its primacy established. All guarantees have been voided; all other ways of thinking about experience exposed and made "moments" within this dialectic. Pantragicism, if you will, but also perhaps the foundation for a new "humanism," one where no essentialistic guarantees or rhetorical delays (pluralism, the new pragmatism, the operationalism of discourse-communities) any longer intrude on the bite of contingency and the utter situatedness of the subject in history.

C. DIALECTIC OF AESTHETIC EXPERIENCE

Part One

The result of such concrete investigations is a scorched-earth policy toward the philosophic positions that define contemporary thought.

1. A critique of social-rhetorical theories of the subject and of operational, pragmatic, and institutional theories of thought and discourse. And

thereby a critique of one of the great reductions: the currently dominant idea that subject is equivalent to subject-position(s). (Among those to be considered here: Wittgenstein, Kenneth Burke, McKeon, Rorty, Foucault, Stanley Fish, Judith Butler.)

2. An understanding of all variants of essentialistic humanism in their essential complicity: the providing of substantialistic guarantees that are made a priori and that therefore define what counts as meaningful and as normal, healthy, ethical, and intelligible in human experience. Humanism is the series of substitutions—via different founding guarantees (god, human nature, the cogito, enlightenment, liberalism and the social process)—whereby the desire for essentialistic guarantees regulates discourse in the human sciences. It receives its quietus when the anxiety informing it is revealed as the abiding motive behind—and within—the conceptual structures whereby it perfects its flight from experience. (Among those to be considered here: Ricoeur and Gadamer, Booth, the neo-Kantianism of Cassier and Habermas.)

3. The recovery of situated subjectivity as the untranscendable horizon that historicizes and concretizes poststructuralism, making it a *moment*, a necessary stage, in a return to dialectics. This argument will be developed through a demonstration of how figures such as Derrida, Lacan, and Lyotard arrest their thought in an effort to escape its richest implications. Thereby we will attain a concrete *reversal* that restores what Hegel showed to be the proper movement of self-conscious reflection: the movement from stoicism (structuralism), to skepticism (poststructuralism, deconstruction), to "unhappy consciousness" and a fully existentialized reappropriation of its ontological status. (A central plank in this argument will be a critique of Heidegger and Sartre and the ways they arrest and contradict their own existential beginnings.)

Part Two

Part I constitutes a systematic effort to reverse the reign of the conceptual in order to establish literature as that primary access to experience that exceeds its limits—and shatters its guarantees. Thought is concrete insofar as it strives to make this idea the basis for a way of thinking that will take as its task the development of *aesthetic theory as fundamental ontology.*

1. Aesthetic cognition is established as an awareness that is liberated from the "tyranny of the concept" and made the basis of a cleansed perception (Blake) that "must be learned" (Duras) in a sufferance that historicizes artistic form. In its historicity, art qua form is the effort to create that which is *sui generis* and not a priori:[7] the artistic representation "adequate" to the

Event (Auschwitz, Hiroshima, Vietnam, Chernobyl) and the "new pressure" that time "places on the nerves" of those who internalize it. The agonistic relationship that such art takes up toward the audience is integral to that awareness: as is the necessity to expose and break with all the ways in which the guarantees structure and limit the forms and purposes (resolution, catharsis, etc.) of art.

2. The study of literature thereby becomes the foundation for an existential ontology that renews the Analytic of *Da-sein* that Heidegger formulated in *Being and Time* in a way that frees that idea from the formalistic and Kantian limits Heidegger placed on it. Art reveals reality in a way that engages the subject in the agon of its existence. In so doing it also renews and transforms the project of Hegelian phenomenology: art as concrete drama provides the model that enables us to describe and interrogate philosophic positions and attitudes in terms of the actual contradictions, desires, and motives that make them intelligible as necessary stages in the progress of a self-conscious being toward an awareness that will bring it into a correspondence with history and the actual conditions of its world. That logic, contra Hegel, is one of agonistic rather than rationalistic mediation.[8]

3. As such, it is the recovery and concretization of what has been the through-line of all my work: the attempt to reconstitute the *existential* and restore its claims on our thought. The only way to do so—and this too has been a through-line from the start—is by constituting a genuine "answer to Plato," one which shows that artistic awareness generates a Knowledge that cannot be comprehended except by overturning the rationalistic and logocentric assumptions about thinking that achieve their first articulation in Plato.

4. And thus we close the hermeneutic circle with the idea that has informed the entire project: the idea that everything is historical and must be submitted to history for its determination. Or, to end with an image, this is why Hans Castorp becomes Adrian Leverkühn, the "author" of *Gravity's Rainbow*.

I have laid out the entire structure of my project here to give the reader a general map and an indication of why certain metatheoretical issues and preoccupations, which usually come first given the linguistic preoccupations of current discourse, can only be taken up later in a project that attempts to recapture the claims of a radically different starting point and its ability to generate a radically different understanding of the relationship between thought, discourse, and experience.

NOTES

I have tried to keep the endnotes as brief as possible, focusing them on the comparison and contrast of my argument with the central thinkers and texts in the different disciplines involved in the inquiry. I also offer a number of notes on methodology. These notes form a dialectical order that is grounded in the concept of dialectic I established in *Inwardness and Existence: Subjectivity In/And Hegel, Heidegger, Marx, and Freud* (Madison: University of Wisconsin Press, 1989) [hereafter I&E]. The present inquiry extends and develops the concept of situated subjectivity articulated there by engaging history, as reality and as discipline. For the relationship of the present book to the trilogy of which it forms the first volume, see appendix B.

Preface

1. I use this term to signify the system of assumptions that inform the logic of reasoning, inference, evidence, and discursive intelligibility that is dominant in western thought as well as the concept of human nature that underlies and is supported by these assumptions. They provide what I later describe as the system of *guarantees*. See below, especially pp. 183–88

2. In *The Phenomenology of Spirit*, trans. A. V. Miller (Oxford: Clarendon Press, 1977) [hereafter *PhG*] Hegel proceeds from Skepticism to Unhappy Consciousness. Deconstruction reverses this movement. My effort is to restore the proper dialectical relationship and with it a renewal of Hegel's contribution to existential thought, but purged of his devotion to rationalistic mediation. In *Inwardness and Existence* I established the methodological bases for such a reading of Hegel and of the other thinkers listed in the title.

3. For a critique of Lifton and Mitchell, and other works that use the framework of ego psychology to make admission of wrong-doing the act that leads to restored health and a successful resolution of the past, see below, pp. 27–30, 128.

4. See Martin Heidegger, *Being and Time*, trans. John Macquarrie and Edward Robinson (New London: SCM Press, 1962), division 2, section 4 [hereafter *B&T*].

5. For a detailed bibliography of historical writings on Hiroshima, see chapter 1, notes 27–29. A further word is in order regarding Richard B.

Frank's recent book *Downfall* (New York: Random House, 1999). Frank's book is distinguished by its thoroughly unproblematic relationship to the only "facts" it regards as relevant and the condescending confidence with which it proclaims the one "case closed" explanation that can be wrung from them. Of greater note, Frank labors untouched by any of the recent developments in historiography and thus there is no way that the issues discussed here can impinge on the way of doing history that his work exemplifies. The saddest thing, however, is the likelihood that Frank's book will define the terms of discussion of Hiroshima in the coming years. Who knows, it took fifty years to expose the first myth constructed to justify Hiroshima; perhaps another fifty will be spent rooting out the errors that will derive succor from the "archive" Frank constructs. Because the one thing a book like Frank's does is save the old debate, as historians pro and contra set out to challenge or support what is, at base, yet another effort to defer and delay a consideration of the primary issue—and the primary fact. What happened on August 6, 1945—and "again" on August 9, 1945? As good historians, before deciding whether dropping the Bomb was right or wrong, we should establish what actually happened on August 6, 1945—and "again" on August 9. This book is dedicated to that prior inquiry. Its attempt is thus to establish the primary facts. In the course of that inquiry, a further irony about the "debate," which neither party seems to be aware of, will become apparent. Developed at length below, I note it here to orient the audience to my effort, like Mercutio's, to dismantle both houses. As we will see, what joins the two sides is their complicity in serving the needs of the audience—one by justification, the other by cathartic resolution—and the system of ontological and psychological guarantees about history that ground and preserve the identity of that audience. Option one: we did the right thing. Option two: once we admit we did the wrong thing, we are cleansed and renewed. (On the second see note 3 above, note 1 in chapter 4 and the critique of catharsis in chapter 5) It is pretty to be the audience of American history: one either gets justification and celebration or cleansing and renewal. Thus the debate that has defined discussion of Hiroshima for over fifty years serves as a perfect instance of Benjamin's insight that "The dead remain in danger." The danger, as we'll see, derives from the system of guarantees that shape the discipline of history. That system predetermines the ways debates are constructed and resolved so that an overriding purpose will be served: the protection of the audience from the questions, thoughts, affects, and psychological experiences that challenge the system of guarantees. Thus, Lifton, for example, cleanses us of the traumatic past in order to demonstrate the abilities of what he calls "the protean self" to forge a better tomorrow. Frank's labor moves to the same end—and through what is really the same relationship to the past. He concludes, in fact, with explicit affirmation and celebration of what has been his book's structuring purpose:

"Had American leaders in 1945 been assured that Japan and the United States would pass two generations in tranquility and still look forward with no prospect of future conflict, they would have believed their hard choices had been vindicated—and so should we." Those who loudly speak against rewriting the past find in this sentiment an ideology they can't refuse, since to invert Nietzsche, it redeems the past and blesses the future without perishing of the present. It also represents a new and burgeoning development in the writing of American history, as witnessed by a book similar in spirit that appeared about the same time as Frank's. See Michael Lind, *Vietnam: The Necessary War* (New York: Free Press, 1999), where one learns that the great relations we today enjoy with the Asian world are the fruit of our wisdom in staying the course throughout that conflict. Bush was wrong. The pen is mightier than the sword. We remain the undefeated champs. Such is the function of such books in their singlular dedication to inverting not just the *ecstases* of temporality, but time itself. Nietzsche was wrong: we can will backwards. And, apparently, if one is an American military historian, one must.

6. See Walter Benjamin, "Theses on the Philosophy of History," *Illuminations,* trans. Harry Zohn (New York: Schocken, 1969).

7. The differences between Foucault's concept of discourse and the one I am developing will become apparent as we proceed, as will the difference between Derrida's linguistic concept of the trace and my attempt to tie that concept to its traumatic historical referent.

8. Chapter 4 is devoted to a detailed and in-depth discussion of this issue in explicitly psychoanalytic terms.

9. For a very different concept of the nuclear Unconscious, see the special issue of *Diacritics* (Summer 1984), which is noteworthy for a striking article by Derrida on the topic. Not the same can be claimed for the efforts of the editor of this volume, Richard Klein, to stake out the exclusive rights of deconstruction to the academic property termed "nuclear criticism," nor for the grandiose claims by many of Derrida's academic epigones that credit for having ended the Cold War goes to deconstruction, thanks to its unraveling of reference. See note 24 in chapter two and chapter 4 *seriatim* for my effort to show, in contrast, that deconstruction is a defense against and displacement of nuclear anxiety. As such it is, of course, one of the more significant instances of the concept of the nuclear Unconscious that I am developing; that is, the ways in which the Bomb is that force within the psyche that explains the social and cultural developments that we group under the concept of postmodernism. Another contrast to my position is, of course, the more orthodox Marxism of Frederic Jameson's *The Political Unconscious* (Ithaca: Cornell University Press, 1981).

10. See the last two sections of *B&T.*

11. The difference between the way I develop this concept and the

way it is deployed in Lacan and in the striking work of Slavoj Žižek will become apparent as we proceed. See especially chapter 4, pp. 140–50.

12. The reference once again is to the dialectical movement Hegel establishes from Skepticism and its reliance on irony as master trope and master narrative, to the tragic exigencies of the Unhappy Consciousness. The contrast between the two was perhaps best formulated by one who lived in deep attunement to the latter. In 1903, Rilke said this, of irony, to a young poet: "Irony. Don't let yourself be controlled by it, especially during uncreative moments. When you are fully creative, try to use it, as one more way to take hold of life. Used purely, it too is pure, and one needn't be ashamed of it; but if you feel yourself becoming too familiar with it; if you are afraid of this growing familiarity, then turn to great and serious objects, in front of which it becomes small and helpless. Search into the depths of Things: there, irony never descends." *Letters to a Young Poet*, trans. Stephen Mitchell (Boston: Shambhala, 1984). If history repeats itself as farce it does so by inverting the dialectical relationship between irony and the tragic.

13. One of the best representatives of this idea as the basis of humanistic interpretation and ethical evaluation, especially in dealing with disruptive texts, is Wayne Booth. See especially *The Rhetoric of Fiction* (Chicago: University of Chicago Press, 1961) and *The Company We Keep* (Chicago: University of Chicago Press, 1993). As we will see, the untapped significance of Booth's work is this: it applies far more tellingly to the writing of history than it does to fiction (especially twentieth-century fiction). Booth's basic argument is that the humanistic tradition provides an ego-identity that functions in the following way: we read (and write) from and to the set of beliefs and values that an enlightened, rationalistic humanism provides. It is thus the basis of both the rhetorical and the ontological contract between authors and readers. As such, it is the way in which traumatic realities are contained—never more so perhaps than when history presents us with such realities. It is then that the system of guarantees goes into operation and writes what readers then read in order to get the closure they desire. The rhetoric of history is, by and large, a consistent and, indeed, primary example of the rhetoric of Boothian fiction and of how the beliefs in which that system is grounded cleanse us of traumatic realities—and tragic necessities. See below, pp. 37–38, 157–58.

14. See Walter Benjamin "Theses on the Philosophy of History," *Illuminations*.

15. As I will show, catharsis in not the end of tragedy but the guarantee that the humanistic tradition imposes on tragedy in order to contain its disruptive power. Chapter 5 is devoted to an extended development of this idea.

16. The allusion here is to Derrida's quite different concept of "force and signification" and its application to *écriture* and history as developed in

Writing and Difference, trans. Alan Bass (Chicago: University of Chicago Press, 1978).

17. My development of this idea attempts to offer a systematic contrast to Hegel's concepts of the Absolute and of Absolute Knowledge. With respect to those concepts and their function as the end of a dialectical system, my effort in the present book is to take the methodological contrast to Hegel, which is articulated in the last chapter of *I&E,* and apply it to history and the philosophy of history. Concretely, the goal is to show that the traumatic event is the referent that, for an existential and tragic thought, performs the function of the "Absolute" by forcing the thinker to become a historically situated being in a philosophic position defined, finally, by a single proposition: there is nothing but history—nothing in the order of mind and "human nature" that escapes that situatedness. Hegel's dialectic, in contrast, moves "within the medium of the Notion [*Begriff*]" and is structured accordingly as a system in which rationalistic mediation subsumes tragic experience. There are, however, ambiguities in Hegelian closure since one primary name for the state of Absolute Knowledge is history. That is why it is possible to read and interpret Hegel along lines similar to the position on historicity I am developing here. See Slavoj Žižek, especially *For They Know Not What They Do: Enjoyment as a Political Factor* (London: Verso, 1991). On "the call of conscience," see Heidegger, *B&T,* pp. 269–280.

18. On the concept of a hermeneutics of engagement, see *I&E* and below, pp. 25–27.

19. *Hiroshima Mon Amour,* script by Marguerite Duras, directed by Alain Resnais. Released in 1959. On *The Holocaust Memorial* see below, Appendix B, note #1.

Chapter One

1. Elias Canetti, *The Human Province,* trans. Joachim Neugroschel (New York: Seabury Press, 1978), p. 69.

2. Developing a critique of historical reason, which was the main preoccupation of Dilthey and other German post-Kantians, does not simply add another room to the critical philosophy. A philosophy of history as a priori framework for explaining events and thereby providing coherent explanations of both past and present may fulfill the deepest of our a priori needs. A critique of historical reason would thus be on a par with the three questions—What can I know? What should I do? What may I hope?—that gave birth to the three Kantian critiques. It may also be the most concrete way to address the question that Kant himself said contained the other three—the question "Who is man?" That question, which Kant saw as the subject of philosophic anthropology, is, as we'll see, equivalent to the ques-

tion of constructing a philosophy of history. The latter task is complicated, however, by the recognition that narrative is the a priori form in which historical explanations are constituted and thus the principle of cognition we must comprehend in order to know how and why the satisfaction of our deepest needs and intellectual concerns comes in and through the telling of stories.

3. Specific references to thinkers listed here will be given at the appropriate place in the inquiry.

4. The opposite view has recently been articulated at its essentializing extreme by Samuel P. Huntington in *The Clash of Civilizations and the Remaking of World Order* (New York: Simon & Schuster, 1996). Huntington's solution isolates cultures, delivering each culture over to the purification of its "essence"—a solution that includes the continued suppression of other/dissenting voices within it. My position, in contrast, begins with the recognition that dialogue is only possible after those deprived of a voice have constituted one.

5. One of my overarching purposes is to show that dramatic mediation (in contrast to rational mediation) is a distinct way of knowing that forms a uniquely agonistic relationship to the audience that such a discourse engages in a process of painful psychological discoveries. In *Get the Guests* (Madison: University of Wisconsin Press, 1994) [hereafter *GG*] I developed this idea as a way of understanding what a drama does to its audience. My effort here is to extend this method to the reading and writing of history; to create for that discipline and that audience the agon that engages the full dimensions of the historical.

6. See Clifford Geertz, *Local Knowledge* (New York: Basic Books, 1983).

7. See below, notes 27–29, for specifics on this issue, and chapters 3 and 6 for further discussion of particular historical agents.

8. In this regard the present work continues the epistemological concerns—especially with the method of multiple working hypotheses as a canon of inquiry—that I first formulated in *The Act of Interpretation* (Chicago: University of Chicago Press, 1979). The method of multiple working hypotheses is here developed, however, in a way that is explicitly psychoanalytic and existential, thus grounding interpretation in the principle reached at the end of the third chapter of that book: "The relationship of the human subject to himself [sic] and the understanding of what it means to be a human being is the ultimate basis of any act of interpretation." My effort here is to explore what that idea might mean for the study of history.

9. Frederic Jameson's *The Political Unconscious* is one of the best recent attempts to historicize this issue. Frye remains the *locus classicus* of its essentialization. The space between the two is occupied, ironically, by the structuralism of Lévi-Strauss. As we'll see, a dramatistic perceptive compli-

cates all of this because the agonistic logic of drama challenges the hegemony narrative currently enjoys. Because it cuts to the core, drama entails a critique of the limits—and temptations—of narrative. For short-hand purposes I use the term narrative here but my point applies to all the forms artists have developed in order to mediate experience. As the term Agon replaces the term narrative the reader will get a sense of the new direction in which I am proposing that we move in replacing narrative with drama as the primary form of artistic knowing that students of culture in a number of disciplines might now use to open up dimensions of their subjects that the narrative paradigm has prevented our seeing.

10. See Hayden White, *Metahistory* (Baltimore: Johns Hopkins University Press, 1973). A central if essentializing text, which did more than any other to put the issue of narrative form at the center of historiography.

11. Hayden White, *Tropics of Discourse* (Baltimore: Johns Hopkins University Press, 1978), pp. 47–48. For a more recent attempt to develop this and related ideas and, through them, a critical appreciation of other theories of narrative and history, see the essays by White collected in *The Content of the Form: Narrative Discourse and Historical Representation* (Baltimore: Johns Hopkins University Press, 1987).

12. See Wayne Booth, *The Rhetoric of Fiction*. Perhaps the primary significance of Booth's argument bears on the ways in which the relationship of author and reader is constituted in works of history. See below, pp. 157–58.

13. In 1946, John Hersey published a book called *Hiroshima* (New York: Knopf, 1946, 1985), a fairly conventional repotorial piece of interviews with selected survivors. In an early review of that book, Dwight MacDonald offered a critique in *Politics* (October 1946) that in many ways provides the through-line for my effort in this book. As MacDonald put it, somewhat curtly, "Hersey has not found the form adequate to the facts. To deal with Hiroshima, a radically new way of writing is required."

14. Thus the argument developed by Stanley Fish in a series of books makes its appearance in yet another field. Predictably and necessarily, since Fish's position offers the readiest way to resolve epistemological problems—whenever and wherever they arise. But through a drastic, "pragmatic" abridgement of its supposed bases in Wittgenstein. For my critique of Fish's position and a resulting interchange, see *Critical Inquiry* 10 (June 1984), pp. 668–717.

15. Heidegger, *B&T,* pp. 36–63. The entire section ripples with implications. We draw out here those that bear directly on the concept of a hermeneutic of engagement. Doing so moves Heidegger's thought in a direction quite different from where he takes his ideas about crisis and the hermeneutic circularity of understanding. My effort to show that the latter principle necessarily leads thinking in an existential and psychoanalytic

direction also constitutes a clear departure from Heidegger and from the formalist and neo-Kantian limits he puts on the analytic of *Da-sein* throughout *B&T.* I discuss this and related issues in chapters 2 and 5 of *I&E.* The dialectic of situated subjectivity constructed in that book establishes the existential context that informs my attempt here to rethink the issues of history, as discipline, and historicity.

16. Heidegger, *B&T,* pp. 149–63.

17. On this concept, see Paul Ricoeur, *Time and Narrative,* 3 vols., trans. Kathleen McLaughlin and David. Pellauer (Chicago: University of Chicago Press, 1984–90). Their shared humanistic assumptions make Ricoeur and Gadamer the best representatives of a traditional and essentializing appropriation of Heidegger's idea of hermeneutic phenomenology. For a magisterial effort to constitute that concept, see Hans George Gadamer, *Truth and Method,* rev. ed., trans. Joel Weinsheimer and Donald G. Marshall (New York: Crossroad, 1989).

18. This is the "reciprocal rejoinder" whereby existentialism and psychoanalysis inform one another throughout the following inquiry in a dialectical relationship or "synthesis" that radically destabilizes both, overturning the limits in which both are currently mired. See below, pp. 145–49.

19. Such an existentialized concept of reflection was the primary effort of *I&E.* For the effort to complete that existentialization, see below, pp. 177–85. Derrida's contrasting concept of reflection and radical self-criticism—and the interpretive procedures required to sustain it—is brought to its ripest formulation in Derrida's *Spectres of Marx,* trans Peggy Kamuf (New York: Routledge, 1994). Rodolphe Gasché, in *The Tain of the Mirror* (Cambridge: Harvard University Press, 1986), focuses on the problem of reflection in offering the most sophisticated and philosophically rigorous interpretation of Derrida yet developed. That examination concentrates on the aporias to which that concept of reflection necessarily leads when it is conceived within the parameters of logocentrism. My effort below in chapter 5 will be to establish the concept and practice of reflection we can begin to develop once we move outside the limits of logocentric reflection and the pleasures of its endless deconstruction.

20. Heidegger, *B&T,* pp. 182–203.

21. On possibility as a category/*existentia* and its primacy over actuality and necessity, see *B&T,* pp. 262–69. Internalizing this idea is the act that founds an existentializing thought, by exposing all substantializing concepts of mind. A new relationship to interiority is thereby mandated. In engagement, alethia as "wresting from concealment" finds one's own psyche the object of dangerous knowledge. One radical implication is the uncovering of the motives and desires that shape knowledge in general. In pursuing this direction engagement is not a continuation of Heidegger's thought but a radical transformation of it.

22. In this connection it is exquisitely ironic that Alexander Nehamas in *Nietzsche: Life as Literature* (Cambridge: Harvard University Press, 1985), argues on analytic grounds that self-contempt is an impossible act. Nietzsche is thus sacrificed to the one grand commonplace of the mental health industry, Nehamas thereby showing that it doesn't matter whether one is an Anglo-American philosopher or a boa-deconstructor: the common pursuit is to convict the possibility of an immanent critique grounded in the self-reflexivity of the subject of logical contradiction. This is another reason why it is so important to distinguish an existential, experiential circularity from the inherent limitation that foreordains any purely conceptual understanding of reflexivity to a violation of the principle of contradiction.

23. The most noteworthy in this regard is the article by Henry Stimson (ghost-written by McGeorge Bundy), "The Decision to Use the Atomic Bomb" (*Harper,* February 1947) shortly after the war fabricating the explanations needed to justify the use of the Bomb. See Bundy *Danger and Survival: Choices about the Bomb in the First Fifty Years* (New York: Vintage Books, 1990). Also, see below p. 213.

24. To say so is not, however, to commit oneself to a Derridean theory of textuality. Another one, which situates the psyche in language in a far more dialectical way, is being developed in process here. See below, pp. 40–43.

25. This is the definition Robert DeNiro offers of acting: "people don't reveal their intentions, they conceal them; and it is in the process of concealing them that their intentions are revealed." Politicians are, of course, the greatest actors and thus the need for such a dramatistic principle in interpreting their words and acts.

26. Two recent collections of essays, spurred largely by the Smithsonian capitulation to the VFW, provide useful overviews of a number of historical issues and the current state of historical research on them. See Edward T. Linenthal and Tom Engelhardt (eds.), *History Wars* (New York: Metropolitan Books, 1996) and Michael J. Hogan (ed.), *Hiroshima In History and Memory* (Cambridge, England: Cambridge University Press, 1996). Editorially, the latter unfortunately sustains fealty to the logic that "there are two sides to every question" and that the history and parameters of historical debates must be structured accordingly.

27. See John W. Dower, *War without Mercy* (New York: Pantheon, 1986).

28. See Gar Alperovitz's recent and massive *The Decision to Use the Atomic Bomb and the Architecture of an American Myth* (New York: Knopf, 1995). Due recognition should also be given to the "limited hang-out" offered in McGeorge Bundy's *Danger and Survival* since Bundy was the ghost-writer of the article by Henry Stimson, which appeared shortly after the war, formulating the justifications it has taken historians fifty years to refute.

29. As in Robert James Maddox, *Weapons of Victory* (Minneapolis: University of Missouri Press, 1995) and in Richard Frank's more recent effort in *Downfall* to unearth startlingly new information on Japan's hidden military capacities and plans to continue the fight.

30. See Richard McKeon, "Philosophic Semantics and Philosophic Inquiry" (ms.), and in *Thought, Action, and Passion* (Chicago: University of Chicago Press, 1954) for a systematic attempt to offer an exclusive and exhaustive description of the different methods that have been developed in the history of philosophy. McKeon's philosophic pluralism is quite different from the eclectic and rhetorically popular ideologies that currently parade under the banner of pluralism.

31. As McKeon shows, the problematic method has as its founding act the strict separating of disciplines and questions. Aristotle, Kant, and Dewey are three great architects in the history of that effort. For the principles on which the problematic method depends and how those principles contrast sharply with dialectical categories, see McKeon, *Thought, Action, and Passion*, pp. 109–24.

32. McKeon's primary example is Plato. In my view that model severely limits his understanding of dialectical thought and its history. See *Thought, Action, and Passion*, pp. 156–64. A far more radical understanding of the immanence of dialectical categories and the kind of mediation required for their development was the singular achievement of Hegel's logic and his theory of the *Begriff* or notion. Heidegger's recognition of the difference between conceptual categories and what he calls the *existentia*— the structures that constitute the analytic of *Da-sein* and the ways in which its being is at issue—is the watershed moment that constitutes the next movement in the irreversible history of dialectical thought, the movement from logic to existence as the architectonic for the development of principles that will preserve the situatedness of thinking in history.

33. See John Dewey, *Reconstruction in Philosophy* (New York: Holt, 1920). Dewey's most systematic efforts to constitute this idea as a philosophic principle occurs in *Experience and Nature* (Chicago: Open Court, 1925). If existentialism is just "pragmatism with a sense of inwardness," as an early commentator on Heidegger put it, the reverse tells us something revealing about pragmatism: that is, the failure to constitute the existential dimension of experience leaves the pragmatist, even one as great as Dewey, repeating the categories Arisotle used to distinguish the theoretical, practical, and productive arts. The only shift is the primacy and comprehensive status accorded to the practical. Deriving a new theory of logic from that principles is one of Dewey's great achievements. No such complexity remains in the new pragmatists (Rorty, etc.) who concern themselves primarily with grounding everything in rhetorical principles—the consensus of professions and discourse communities and the useful "work" we can get

done if we all agree to confine thought to such agreements. See especially Richard Rorty, *Consequences of Pragmatism* (Minneapolis: University of Minnesota Press, 1982). The primary consequence of this "development" is that what pragmatism needs it pragmatically can no longer attain—that is, a crisis or, lacking that, a simple recognition of the existential dynamic that has been sacrificed to its eminently sensible efforts to purge inwardness of everything but useful directions.

34. Spoken in the penultimate interview to Claude Lanzmann in *Shoah.* For discussion, see below, chapter 6, pp. 224–25.

35. Somewhat ironically, military historians (hardly a leftist group) are among the first to have seen the uniqueness of what happened at Hiroshima and Nagasaki and what those events meant for military strategy given the fact that on August 6, 1945 its "object" changed utterly.

36. The construction of this theory is the burden of chapter 4. I should point out here, however, that Lacan's concepts of *jouissance* and of the traumatic kernel will be but a moment within the theory of the Unconscious developed there. See below, pp. 142–50.

37. Adolf Grunbaum, *The Foundations of Psychoanalysis* (Madison, Conn.: International Universities Press, 1993) and Daniel Dennett, *Consciousness Explained* (Boston: Little, Brown, 1991). A scientific construal and then testing of Freud's ideas requires a single-minded focus on hydraulics to the exclusion of hermeneutics in the reading of Freud. And thus the frequent polemic in such works against Ricoeur, Schafer, George Klein, and others who dare to suggest the necessity of a language of existence and experience when dealing with the psyche. That is, the scandalous, impossible idea that it is precisely the strength of psychoanalysis that it is not a science and should not try to become one.

38. See especially Jacques Lacan, *Écrits,* trans. Alan Sheridan (New York: Norton, 1977). Lacan's genius is to elaborate ever more complex schemata for describing a subjectivity internally estranged from itself, condemned by its situatedness in language to repeat in ever more elaborate schemata the representing of the bars of its prison.

39. I allude primarily to the work of Habermas in this sentence because he articulates, with great formalistic precision, the set of concepts, in different fields, that must be brought into a single alignment for a contemporary reassertion of Humanism and the project of the *Aufklarung.*

40. Recovering the historicity of the tragic, and liberating it from irony, requires a journey that steers between the Scylla of Frye's perfected stoicism of the ahistorical imagination and the Charybdis of deMan's skeptical ironization of all forms, with a consequent consignment of the historical to the "unsayable." Unhappy Consciousness as the awareness that reemerges through the dialectical critique of these two attitudes would then find in the tragic the category capable of concretely reversing the movement

of literary theory over the past forty years in a way that would concretely recover history and the real as the forces that generate, within the tragic, the existentializing of its forms. The continued use of Frye by historians as different as White and Jameson shows, of course, the continued power of an essentialistic framework to provide an a priori handle on history and its writing; which then becomes perfect grist for the poststructuralist mill, since irony constitutes the only relationship that a self-conscious thinker could have toward operating within that system. All one need do then is ironize irony, as does deMan: the system of literary forms and tropes then turns on the necessity to unsay itself. The two moments in this supposed development of literary theory thus recapitulate the Hegelian movement from stoicism to skepticism: we essentialize and then we ironize what we've essentialized, closing the circle we then conveniently term "the prison-house of language." Avoided thereby is that which has not been attempted—a tragic recovery of Unhappy Consciousness through a direct assault, with Zuckerman, on the unsaid.

41. This is the relationship that drives a dialectical and historical wedge into the essentialisms of Aristotle's *Poetics*. For an understanding of how that immanent critique overturns the most sacrosanct principle in that canon, the principle of catharsis, see below, chapter 5, pp. 185–91.

42. Robert Denoon Cumming, *Starting Point: An Introduction to the Dialectic of Existence* (Chicago: University of Chicago Press, 1979). This important and neglected work is one of the finer efforts to liberate the existential from the superficial ways it was described, discussed, and then refuted by academic philosophers during its brief American heyday in the late fifties and early sixties.

43. See Hegel's preface to the *PhG* and Derrida's "No Hors Texte," in *Dissemination,* trans. Barbara Johnson (Chicago: University of Chicago Press, 1981). My attempt, in this chapter, has been to use a less radical strategy to achieve a similar end: every formulation advanced here is provisional and will be submitted in each chapter that follows to a deepening that transforms it. In this way the discourse strives to existentialize itself from within—to achieve at the end of each chapter an understanding that will be put at risk in the engagement that necessarily ensues in the chapter that follows.

44. As McKeon shows, these are the primary assumptions that make it impossible for thinkers working in other modes of thought to understand what is going on in dialectical discourse. As long as any of these assumptions remain in place, dialectic remains unintelligible.

45. Methodologically, this was also the basis of my argument with McKeon about dialectic.. In contrast to his privileging of Plato as the pure model of the mode, my view is that dialectic has an irreversible history that moves from Plato, through Hegel's great equivocations concerning logic

and existence and Heidegger's neo-Kantian analytic of Da-sein to a hermeneutic of engagement focused on the development of an existential historicity. My point, simply put: once dialectic opens itself to existence, mediation becomes agonistic rather than rationalistic. Drama becomes ontological the moment one makes that "Copernican" turn, a turn far more radical than Kant's because it situates knowledge and self-knowledge in a process of psychological self-overcoming that exceeds the ratio. Or, to put it in terms of the ontological claims of its informing principle: drama exceeds the concept in principle and in process, which is why a dialectic based on it evolves a structure of thought quite different from that provided, as in Hegel, by logic and the concept.

46. Such an *Aufhebung* is radically different from the kind one finds in Hegel. Both processes depend, however, on a suspensive structure in which the completion of each circle in the hermeneutic of inquiry transforms the beginning. The *Begriff* or logic of the notion provides Hegel's most systematic account of how determinate negation produces "progressive" results in a rationalistic framework. Determinate negation for us, in contrast, is precisely the process of (1) eradicating such guarantees so that (2) the existentializing process will mediate itself through an ever deeper delving into the subject's inwardness.

47. This would offer us a new way to think about "philosophic idealism" and the ideal of a *Bildung* that moves toward sufferance not toward progress; engagement not resolution; inwardness not affirmative culture. The absolute or state of absolute knowledge would then reside in the search for a condition in which suffering is sustained and made determinate against all efforts to mitigate it. It would be a condition, in short, in which the adequate idea would become the ethical condition of one's innermost being.

48. Continuing, the letter concludes with a comment that I can only "answer" by offering the entire book—and the reader's engaged response to it: "You ask too much of the reader, especially in a culture where happiness, at whatever cost, is the superordinate need—and not only among the masses. The guarantees you critique are so deeply embedded in academe— ego psychology, consensual validation, catharsis and historical recovery— that the only thing your critique can and will do is activate the reader's defenses, with predictable results. Your work will be seen as nihilistic and not as an attempt, like Nietzsche's, to expose the nihilism of your opponents, of their 'values' and the ego-defenses on which they depend."

49. Rilke on irony in *Letters to a Young Poet*. For full quotation, see preface, note 12.

50. Thomas Pynchon, *Gravity's Rainbow* (New York: Vintage, 1973).

51. The allusion is to Joyce's comment, through Stephen Dedalus,

about history in *Ulysses.* "History is a nightmare from which I am trying to awake." In keeping with the pattern of images that structure it, the Marxist corollary is suspended until the end of the paragraph.

52. As in this deathless insight of Marx's into the problem and meaning of history: "The voices of the dead generations weigh like a nightmare on the brains of the living."

53. Percy Bysshe Shelley, "Defence of Poetry"

Chapter Two

1. Other hermeneutic theories resist this, the dialectical connection, as did Heidegger, with unfortunate results: the retreat from the analytic of *Da-sein* and its existential implications and the resulting hypostatization of Being. The political consequences that have been the focus of recent discussions of Heidegger follow of necessity from the prior reductions. My effort in re-appropriating Heidegger's "starting point" is to show all the ways in which "we" have forgotten existence—and the consequences of that loss.

Heidegger is one of the primary points of divergence in contemporary thought: one line leading to Gadamer, Ricoeur, and other hermeneutic theories; another to Derrida and the deconstruction of phallogocentric metaphysics. My effort is to construct a theory of the tragic and of situated subjectivity that replaces both positions because it transcends the binary opposition that controls the parameters of contemporary thought: that is, the belief that the only alternatives open to us are ironic, self-deconstructing, postmodern play or a re-affirmation of an essentialistic humanism.

Among appropriators of Heidegger for hermeneutic theory, Ricoeur offers the most significant contrast to my position because he has developed a systematic theory of history, *Time and Narrative,* and in it he attempts to confront contingency in ways that the other two major contemporary hermeneutic theorists render impossible: Habermas a priori, by confining the "real" to the rationally or discursively intelligible; Gadamer by rendering the contingent relatively unimportant to a thought that is always reaching backward toward "tradition" for the "repeatable." Moreover, Ricoeur regards his theory of history and historical narrative as a tragic one and it has been so lauded by no less a historiographer than Hayden White. See *The Content of the Form,* p. 181. White notes that for Ricoeur "the symbolic content of narrative history, the content of its form, is the tragic vision itself" (p. 181). As we will see, however, Ricoeur's position actually constitutes one of the best contemporary examples of the humanistic resistance to the tragic. Tragedy for Ricoeur is the recovery of a system of meaning that is essentially allegorical and replete with the guarantees that structure humanistic thought. See chapter 5, pp. 183–88.

2. For the application of philosophic pluralism to the question of history and its writing, see McKeon, *Freedom and History* (New York: Noonday Press, 1952).

3. For a systematic example of this rationalist, neo-Kantian relating of disciplines in a single line of rational development, see Jurgen Habermas, *Communication and the Evolution of Society,* trans. Thomas McCarthy (Boston: Beacon Press, 1979). Habermas there deftly shows just what positions in the different disciplines need to be combined for the overall project of communicative rationality to attain an overarching interdisciplinary solidification. For accounts of ego psychology that indicate why it fits psychoanalysis so nicely into such a project, see Heinz Hartmann, *Ego Psychology and the Problem of Adaptation* (New York: International Universities Press, 1958) and Anna Freud, *The Ego and the Mechanisms of Defense.* One looking for a contemporary effort to graft all good things onto the ego and to guarantee our attainment of that substantistic identity as the necessary product of what is finally a stark, biological determinism need look no further than Jessica Benjamin's, *The Bonds of Love* (New York: Pantheon, 1988). The most preposterous premise in this work is the one that grounds it: the strikingly non-psychoanalytic notion that while she is providing the bonds of love the good and normal mother brackets her psyche and her unconscious. Mothering is magic and magical thinking: all good things and no disorders come to us in and through the first relationship. Not the least oddity in this concoction is the attempt to graft onto it the most non-dialectical and non-psychoanalytic reading of Hegel on desire and recognition imaginable.

4. W. R. D. Fairbairn, *An Object Relations Theory of the Personality* (New York: Routledge, 1952). Fairbairn's work is not without its contradictions on this issue, especially when the question turns on social and cultural values. And thus the issue here as always is one of interrogation and appropriation—in this case of a bold beginning. Sustaining it requires, however, a dramatistic theory of the psyche. The opposite direction, toward the dissolution of drama, controls the American reception of object relations theory by ego and "self" psychology. In the process all the internal complexities of Fairbairn, Klein, Winnicott, and Bion are leveled off for the sake of a rapprochement with the adaptational agenda of American society. See Stephen A. Mitchell and Jay R. Greenburg, *Object Relations in American Psychoanalytic Theory* (Cambridge: Harvard University Press, 1983).

5. This is one of Winnicott's central insights, the basis for his examination of the false self system, and for his insight into "never having been born properly" as the central dilemma in neurosis. For a striking example, see his *Holding and Interpretation* (New York: Grove Press, 1986). Lacan's great critique of the ego is carried out in the first two seminars.

6. Frederic Jameson advances this definition in *The Political Uncon-scious*. Unfortunately, the theory of history he develops amounts to a struc-turalist containment and anesthetization of this idea. The "hurt" turns into a "cognitive" matter of what we cannot know given the a priori, and finally ahistorical nature of the frameworks on which knowledge and narrative are based. At times Jameson, following Lukács, tries to ironize that situation, making it quasihistorical: i.e., the "a priori" forms of historical knowing correspond to what knowledge must be within capitalism. Of greater note here, for purposes of contrast, is Jameson's use of Lacan to provide the "psychoanalytic" basis for his position; since what Jameson unwittingly puts his finger on is one of Lacan's primary contradictions: the attempt to give an account of a particular historical situation that ends up reifying that situa-tion and hypostatizing it as an abstraction—the Real. In Jameson once again the blow of history—and the hurt—becomes a conceptual dilemma—a problem of "signification." Knowledge of our specific histor-ical situation becomes, accordingly, an abstract anguish about the necessary limitations of our cognitive "mapping" systems. A richer, and dialectically nuanced, reading of Lacan's category of the Real and the development of a theory of history grounded in Lacan's concept of trauma is worked out by Slavoj Žižek.

7. For a development of the concept of melancholia as the way of thinking implicit in this process, see chapter 5, part 2 below.

8. See C. S. Peirce, *Collected Papers*, vol. 5 (Cambridge: Harvard Uni-versity Press, 1935). My development of this idea is quite different from Peirce's, since my concern is not with the semiology of the social but with that experience which is constituted when one sustains estrangement from adaptation to the social as the primary term of one's self-reference.

9. See Wilfrid Bion, *Seven Servants* (New York: J. Aronson, 1977). This is one of Bion's primary insights and the key to his greatest contribution: the possibility of comprehending knowledge—and especially philosophy—psychoanalytically in terms of the desires and motives from which concep-tualization derives. As with Lacan, Bion's limitation is a function of his strength. In both thinkers logical schematism offers what Bennett Simon (in conversation) termed, "the mathematization of pain." Simon's formula, to my mind, succinctly identifies what enables these two seminal thinkers to explore primary disorders of the psyche while avoiding and "containing" the tragic. Tragic experience is placed within a problematic in which Knowl-edge remains a matter of logical and linguistic systematization. Knowledge, accordingly, does not lead to engagement but rather to either an abstract paralysis (the condition of the patient) or an equally abstract mastery (the position of the analyst).

10. To avoid misunderstandings, Spirit or *Geist,* as used here, implies nothing religious, hypostatized, or "germanic." It refers, rather, to a self-

consciousness that tries to sustain the contradictions of one's situation as the moral imperative whereby one attains "character" or inwardness. As Nietzsche formulated it, "spirit is the life that cuts back into life; with its agony it increases its knowledge."

11. The allusion is to the last lines of William Styron's *Sophie's Choice*. Its "aesthetic" containment of the tragic via resolution, catharsis, and cleansing is a good example of how humanistic guarantees as principles of artistic structure contain, in glaring inadequacy, a historical event such as Auschwitz.

12. The allusion here is to Walter Benjamin's discussion of an absurd, surreal, revelatory act that occurred during the early days of the French Revolution. Spnontaneously and independently, throughout Paris, citizens shot the hands off public clocks.

13. This is the option Lacan follows in developing his psychoanalytic theory of history. That theory is not without its force, especially in exposing other ideologies in terms of their repetition of the contradictions of late capitalism. Žižek's focus on trauma and the relationship between the Symbolic and the Real carries this dimension of Lacan's thought into provocative readings of everything ranging from philosophy to film and popular culture. Joan Copjec in *Read My Desire* (Cambridge: MIT Press, 1994) has used Lacan to mount a revealing attack on Foucault and "historicism." Other contributors to a Lacanian theory of history include Juliet MacCannell, *The Regime of the Brother* (London: Routledge, 1991), and Jacqueline Rose, *Why War?* (Oxford: Blackwell, 1993).

14. Heidegger's recognition of the problem is salutary. One of the far-reaching insights of *B&T* is that there are many moods and languages that are beyond "the range of disclosure" of "cognition and volition" as conceived within the Cartesian (or metaphysical) tradition. Tragic literature is one of these. The attempt of the later Heidegger to develop a theory of the ontological primacy of poetry and to remake the language of philosophy in that image, however, constitutes merely one response (and often a self-mystifying one) to the problem, which is older than Plato, as Socrates notes in *The Republic*. Unlike most subsequent thinkers, however, Plato is aware of the central issue: the quarrel between philosophy and poetry is ontological, not rhetorical. It turns on the issue of art's cognitive claims as a unique and primary way of knowing the world. In reconstituting that claim the argument of *Deracination* as a whole may be taken as a reply to Plato through a demonstration, as chapter 6 will show, of the power of the image to go beyond the order of the concept.

15. This is a good example of how an existentializing dialectic concretely inverts Hegel: (1) as practice/process, through the sustenance of suffering contra any *Aufhebung;* (2) as content, through the tragic knowledge thereby liberated from the guarantees that Hegel and others have

imposed on history and experience to give it a rationalistic direction; that is, to arrest historicity and the dark knowledge it contains.

16. The concept of attunement (*Stimmung*) will play an central role in our examination of Kant in chapter 3.

17. Rilke, "Archaic Torso of Apollo."

18. As noted previously, the academic movement calling itself "Nuclear Criticisms" had an auspicious debut in a special issue of *Diacritics*. Derrida led off with an article of considerable power that I will discuss later. One cannot say the same for what followed nor for the subsequent efforts of the editor of the issue, Richard Klein, to stake out his claim for "nuclear criticism" as the academic property of his own curious brand of "deconstruction," one in which he is proud to assert that ethical questions are irrelevant. Klein's main contribution to the academic effort to aestheticize yet another phenomenon comes in *Cigarettes Are Sublime* (Durham: Duke University Press, 1993). Works on the nuclear are, of course, voluminous. Among them those well worth consulting include Derek Chaloupka, *Atomic Culture* (Minneapolis: University of Minnesota Press, 1992); Peter Schwenger, *Letter Bomb* (Baltimore: Johns Hopkins University Press, 1992); J. Fisher Solomon, *Discourse and Reference in the Nuclear Age* (Norman: University of Oklahoma Press, 1988); Daniel L. Zins has edited an invaluable newsletter *Nuclear Texts and Contexts* (Atlanta), a rich source of writing on the nuclear in a wide range of disciplines.

Chapter Three

1. Method is of the essence here, one primary purpose of this chapter being to establish a new way to read philosophic texts. For the reader's convenience, I have divided the methodological notes to this chapter into seven separate entries. As a whole the set forms a dialectical series and should be so apprehended.

Note on method I: Interpretation as *interrogation* is an attempt to reconstruct the psyche and the desire/disorder at work in a text by probing the implications of the text's contradictions. An attempt is then made to historicize that knowledge by connecting those contradictions to the Event in history that reveals and "fulfills" the text's deepest, innermost meaning. Texts from the past (from the tradition and the canon) thereby reveal their hidden unconscious meaning as that meaning comes to fruition in the present. As the pivotal instance of this idea, the present chapter illustrates this method of reading by taking up the contradictions of the *Aufklarung* as revealed by the struggle of its greatest representative, Immanuel Kant, with the idea and the reality—the sublime—where the contradictions of the ratio come a cropper.

Any method is only as good as its ability to engage in the close reading of texts. Here, in illustrating my method, two contrasts with other concepts of "close reading" are intended. First, to the rules that shape "humanistic" interpretation: the confinement of reading to the recovery of the official authorial intention of a text as revealed by the letter of its argument; a practice backed by the prohibition of any attempt to discover or discuss underlying motives, desires, and conflicts, even when they might be eminently present in the gaps and contradictions in the structure of the text's surface. Second, to Derrida and current theories of textuality that focus exclusively on linguistic contradictions in the signifying process.

The assumptions underlying the first position are, in effect, the subject of this chapter. The similarities and differences between my method and Derrida's require a further word of clarification here; especially since both approaches share certain psychoanalytic concerns and can be seen as attempts to realize a psychoanalytic concept of textuality. If deconstruction is the teasing out of warring significations within the language of a text in order to identify its aporias and thereby produce the text's unraveling, *interrogation* is an attempt to think through the implications of what can be made to "speak" once one uses the contradictions and breaks in a text to read the text against itself in a way that is determinate because it produces the text's actual content. The goal of interrogation is to articulate that content in order to reveal its stark opposition to the official program and intentions of the text and the ideological commonplaces the text superimposes on its subject. The upshot is the discovery of what we may term the text's unconscious, the system of contradictions and "desires"—grounded in a psychological disorder—that give the text its actual "coherence," which as the discussion here of Kant on the sublime shows, is a "meaning" that requires time and history to announce itself. Such is the unconscious prescience and significance of a great text—such as Kant on the sublime. It is far ahead of itself in its leap into the "future," into what will be required to resolve the contradictions it reveals in the very process of trying to cover them up—and in the foresight with which it adumbrates what will be required to bring to a final state the desire driving the way of thinking that it represents.

Three steps constitute the architectonic of the method of interpretation I am developing here. (1) The purpose of *interrogation* is to produce the actual content of a text. As such it is the necessary prelude to (2) *engagement,* which is an effort to reconstruct in a systematic way the psyche that shapes the text in order to lay bare the disorder that drives a discourse that wants to present itself solely as an affair of reason. In reconstructing the psyche that dropped the Bomb chapter 4 will provide this service for what chapter 3 reveals. Both steps are prelude to a third (3) *deracination,* which is an attempt to take up the disorder of the psyche revealed in chapters 3 and 4 from within and actively reverse the hold it has over the psyche. Chapters 5 and 6 carry out this project.

2. Jacques Derrida, "Structure, Sign, and Play in the Discourse of the Human Sciences," *Writing and Difference.* For Derrida on Kant, see especially "Economimesis," *Diacritics* 11.2 (Summer 1981): 3–25; and *The Truth in Painting,* trans. Geoff Bennington and Ian McLeod (Chicago: University of Chicago Press, 1987).

Note on Method II: My overriding effort is to show that deconstruction, dialectically considered, is a moment within deracination; irony a moment within the tragic; skepticism a moment in the development of "unhappy consciousness" with the latter category, restored, providing the basis for a new dialectical methodology that will not repeat Hegel but will recover the problematic he first formulated, freed from the rationalistic limitations he imposed upon it; that is, with agonistic self-mediation now supplanting rationalistic mediation. Somewhat ironically Derrida's significance to that program comes from one of his central formulations: "coherence within contradiction must express the force of a desire." If this idea equals teasing out the ambiguities of language and the play of *différance* within signification a more rigorous model of textual dynamics and of interpretation than Derrida's cannot be had. It is also the case that such a conception of "the textuality of the text" derives from the persistence of strategies of close reading (new criticism ironized) that depend on a hypostatization of language in service to the desire for a state of pure autoreference in which fixation on the permutations of linguistic minutiae mirrors a hysteric effort to abolish the outside world—to delay and defer the Real—in order to hold off the paralysis that would ensue should experience shatter the magic circle and ivory tower of linguistic subtlety and refinement.

3. This is the place to note the wealth of recent books on Kant and the sublime. Not too long ago Paul Guyer, in what was then taken as a definitive work on Kant's aesthetic, *Kant and the Claims of Taste* (Cambridge: Harvard University Press, 1979), dismissed the sublime as an irrelevant aside in Kant's third critique. Among recent reevaluations pride of place goes, of course, to Jean-François Lyotard's *Lessons on the Analytic of the Sublime* (Stanford: Stanford University Press, 1994). But see also: Dieter Henrich, *Aesthetic Judgment and the Moral Image of the World* (Stanford: Standford University Press, 1992); John Sallis, *Spacings: Of Reason and Imagination* (Chicago: University of Chicago Press, 1987); Michael James, *Reflections and Elaborations upon Kantian Aesthetics* (Dissertation, Uppsala Academia Ubsaliensis; Stockholm: Almqvist & Wiksell, l987); Rudolf Makkreel, *Imagination and Interpretation in Kant* (Chicago: University of Chicago Press, 1990). See also Zizek's comments on Kant in *Tarrying with the Negative* (Durham: Duke University Press, 1993) and Neil Hertz, *The End of the Line: Essays on Psychoanalysis and the Sublime* (New York: Columbia University Press, 1985). A lot has also been

done recently on Kant's thought on history. We discuss this topic and its necessary dialectical connection with the sublime in chapter 5.

4. *Note on Method III:* To put it in concrete terms: in this chapter Kant's inner world and that of his age is the object of a psychoanalytic reading that is itself deeply critical of current psychoanalytic theories. As this examination shows, the currently dominant school of American "ego, object-relations, self" psychology shares with Kant the psychological disorder that is the object under study in this chapter. As hermeneutic of engagement a double critique is thus developed here. Epistemologically, Kant's text is not exploited as an occasion for some fixed and dogmatic psychoanalytic theory to prove its mastery by imposing itself on the phenomena being studied, but rather for current psychoanalytic theories to discover their limits and the directions in which they must move to go beyond them. A new theory of the psyche is advanced here and in the next chapter. That new theory is the result of an immanent critique of psychoanalysis, from its beginnings to its present state. What happens in these chapters to psychoanalysis as a discipline applies mutatis mutandis to any theory. For the larger effort here is to establish the hermeneutically correct relationship of concepts to phenomena; which is the ability of the latter to question and overturn the former. This is the condition and the opportunity on which interpretation should turn.

5. *Affekt und Stimmung.* In the course of the chapter I will show how these two principles break loose of the rationalism in which Kant contains them.

6. For the statement of how the critique of aesthetic judgment will complete the project, see Immanuel Kant, *Critique of Judgment,* trans. J. H. Bernard (New York: Hafner, 1951) [hereafter *CJ*], pp. 7–34.

7. See Hegel, *PhG,* pp. 114.

8. On *Befindlichkeit,* see Heidegger, *B&T,* pp. 172–179. For the warrant Kant provides for that development, see Heidegger's *Kant and the Problem of Metaphysics.*

9. *Note on Method IV:* Chapter 5 uses the character of Shakespeare's Hamlet as the basis for developing this theory of reflection. The present chapter prepares the way for understanding the revolutionary implications of reflection as it is constituted by that agent. It does so by showing how reflection is constituted and confined in the ratio and the contradictions this construction entails. In establishing the priority and primacy of existential reflection, chapter 5 will complete this critique by revealing the derivative nature of both the concept and practice of reflection found in the ratio. Chapters 3 and 5 thus stand in a dialectical relationship in which the concrete content of the latter completes the critique of the ratio carried out here by revealing the existential reality and activity from which its formalism derives—as flight and then as violent repression.

10. Kant, *CJ*, pp. 83–84.

11. Through a direct consideration of "the subjectivity of the subject"—the question "Who is man?"—Kant hoped to take up in a fourth critique the issues of philosophic anthropology. The entire Kantian philosophy would thereby find its roots in the deepest interiority. My argument is that Kant's discussion of the sublime, in effect, constitutes that inquiry and with it the recognition of which Kant remained unaware—that desire is "the subjectivity of the subject."

12. Thomas Weiskel, *The Romantic Sublime* (Baltimore: Johns Hopkins University Press, 1976) p. 21.

13. Weiskel, p. 3.

14. T. S. Eliot, "The Love Song of J. Alfred Prufrock."

15. The key contrast here is to Freud's late thought on anxiety as the danger signal that serves to motivate the defenses of the ego. I return to this issue and its necessary connection to the role of Thanatos in the psyche in chapter 4.

16. The two melancholy Danes thus link hands.

17. Freud, *Therapy and Technique,* ed. Philip Reiff (New York: Collier, 1952).

18. Kant, *CJ*, p. 89.

19. Kant, *CJ*, p. 88.

20. Richard Rhodes, *The Making of the Atomic Bomb* (New York: Simon & Schuster, 1986). Rhodes is a primary source for details surrounding the behavior and remarks of scientists and others at Alamogordo. See also the memoirs of Frank Oppenheimer and J. Robert Oppenheimer,

For instances of theological responses to the Bomb both then and subsequently one should consult *A Shuddering Dawn,* ed. Ira Chernus and Edward Tabor Linenthal (Albany: State University of New York Press, 1989). The principle of hope springs eternal and has continued for fifty years now to find ways to make the Bomb the occasion for whatever succor hope, *Das Prinzip Hoffnung,* needs to find in the world. See Stewart Udall, *The Myths of August* (New York: Pantheon, 1994) for an enlightening discussion of the carefully crafted moral ambiguities of J. Robert Oppenheimer.

21. Noting this connection is one of the great achievements of Samuel Holt Monk's enduring study, *The Sublime* (Ann Arbor: University of Michigan Press, 1962).

22. The allusion inverts Nietzsche in order to establish an opposition to his concept of the task of the Overman: to redeem past and bless future by perishing of the present.

23. *Note on Method V:* Kant on the sublime would thus constitute an essential moment in a dialectical phenomenology of "spirit" that would be significantly different from the "rationalistic" phenomenology that Hegel constructs. That new phenomenology involves, of course, an enormous debt

to Hegel, especially to the tactics of interpretation that Hegel developed in creating the first systematic way within philosophy to identify and get inside the motives and desires that inform conceptual structures. My effort in this paragraph is to show how the phenomenology I am developing moves in a radically different direction from Hegel's because it sustains both the principle and the experience that he must surmount in order to give experience a progressive, rational structure. Panlogicism or pantragicism? This remains the question regarding Hegel because of all he uncovers before the superimposition of rational mediation. For us, *für uns,* however, in contrast there is no equivocation or any hedging on the radical difference between rationalistic and agonistic mediation.

24. Ironically, Hegel makes this claim for each step, for each attitude considered in the *PhG,* though many of his transitions are, as has been noted, clearly ones of "sentiment." Ironically, it is in Kant that necessity works in a truly rigorous fashion, but as a movement that occurs in spite of—indeed against—the transcendental designs of the author. Whereas Hegel tries to establish a necessity that embraces and dialectically orders the totality of experience, necessity in Kant's operates against Kant's official intentions yet in keeping with underlying motives and desires.

25. Melanie Klein, *Envy and Gratitude* (New York: Basic Books, 1957). For more on this connection, see below, pp. 000–00 and chapter 4. In the present chapter a number of psychoanalytic concepts from a variety of analysts (including Klein, Lacan, Winnicott, Bion, Kohut, Fairbairn etc.) are employed. I trust their general meaning to emerge in the course of the discussion and reserve citations and detailed comments until chapter 4, where psychoanalytic interpretation will be the primary topic.

26. The allusion is to the final pages of Fitzgerald's *The Great Gatsby.*

27. For the concept behind this possibility, see Sartre on the group-infusion in *Critique of Dialectical Reason,* vol. 2.

28. Richard Rhodes, *The Making of the Atomic Bomb,* pp. 435–42.

29. Fermi first played with this bet in Chicago. Several of his colleagues revived it at Los Alamos. See Rhodes, pp. 656 and 674.

30. I am indebted to Paul Boyer's seminal book for this remarkable statement by Henry Adams. See *The Education of Henry Adams.* The prescience and horror of the statement is even more remarkable when one considers Adams's purpose in that book: to attain modernity and with it a new way of understanding and living in history.

31. The notion of the scientist achieving the "mad exploding of himself," which I here apply to Teller, is adapted from Pynchon's brilliant treatment of the scientific psyche in *Gravity's Rainbow.*

32. For a contrasting development of a theory of fantasy, see Slavoj Žižek, *The Plague of Fantasies* (New York: Verso, 1996).

33. *Note on Method VI:* This is perhaps the most revealing definition I

can offer of my overriding purpose: to "repeat" Romanticism in order to liberate its tragic core and thereby historicize its aesthetic categories as principles of cognition and bring them up to date in a theory of the image that enables us to see that today the telos of Romanticism, the Romantic poet's task, is to bring before consciousness images such as this, from Paul Celan: "Black milk of daybreak we drink it at evening" (*Deathfugue*). Such images today provide the basis for a "poetics of culture" that will historicize Nietzsche's call for a radical "revaluation" of values. The result would be a tragic culture based on an ontology grounded in the primacy of artistic, poetic cognition as the one way of historical knowing adequate to our world. Chapter 6 develops this idea of artists as Shelley's "unacknowledged legislators" by rethinking Romanticism's central concern—the nature of the image.

34. The allusions yoked here are to the *Bhagavad-Gita,* and to Heidegger's "Letter on Humanism." Oppenheimer's secret, which he may very well have kept from himself, is this. Vishnu's message is that death doesn't matter: Arjuna can go forth to war cleansed of humanizing twitches. Heidegger's resistance to psychoanalytic concepts is amply documented: thus the considerable irony of this re-reading of one of his more famous pronouncements.

35. Truman, as quoted in Lifton and Mitchell, *Hiroshima in America: A Half Century of Denial* (New York: Putnam, 1995), p. 23.

36. Kant, *CJ,* p.104.

37. My argument here is similar to the one Nietzsche makes in *On the Genealogy of Morals.*

38. The allusions here deliberately yoke Lacan, Pynchon, Lyotard, and Ellul to construct one fitting definition of the "postmodern condition."

39. Faulkner in *Absalom, Absalom!* saw this as the logic that bound the South fatally to its "past." I here try to show that it is also the logic binding the ratio, in fatal futurity, to its defining act.

40. Thus the true, unacknowledged message of July 16, 1945 to theophanic interpreters of the Bomb. In this regard it is worth noting that the disorder I analyze in Kant did not originate with him. But in another dessert with a truly sublime and terrifying author, full of the need to bend everything to his demands. See Jack Miles, *God: A Biography* (New York: Vintage, 1996).

Chapter Four

1. A brief methodological note on the place this chapter has in the structure of my overarching effort to develop a new theory of the psyche. Chapter 4 of *I&E* offered a dramatistic re-interpretation of Freud as part of

an effort to ground psychoanalysis in an existential theory of subjectivity. *GG* used that framework to develop a critique of current psychoanalytic theories through a demonstration of how art—and specifically dramatic literature— can be the source for new and radically unsettling developments in psycho- analytic theory. That demonstration brings with it the possibility of a crisis in which psychoanalysis will be forced to confront the flight from knowledge that controls its effort to limit and often to undo its insight into the depth of the human disorder. The present chapter attempts to get to the heart of the ulcer by reconstructing the psyche that dropped the Bomb; that is, the collective Unconscious that controls our culture as expressed in the Event that reveals its truth.

The allusions in this chapter to Sartre and Hegel serve to indicate the dialectical intent behind my effort, in analyzing the American psyche, to provide a new theory of what both thinkers term "objective spirit" and to revive Sartre's regressive-progressive method, though with quite different psychoanalytic concepts than those he employs to concretize it in the great volumes on Flaubert.

An additional word is needed with respect to two frameworks with which I would not want my project to be confused: (1) psychohistory as practiced by Mazslich and others and (2) Jung's concept of the "collective unconscious." The first typifies a reductive use of traditional Freudian con- cepts in support of what is finally a solipsistic reading of history. The contrast with Jung can be best illustrated through comments on Michael Perlman's Jungian reading of Hiroshima, *Imaginal Memory and the Place of Hiroshima* (Albany: State University of New York Press, 1988). In turning actual per- sons in Hiroshima into representatives of psychological archetypes, Perl- man's book throws into high relief all the ways in which Jung helps us flee history, impose sentimental quasireligious guarantees upon it, and how stark the resulting incongruity is between archetype as inadvertent carica- ture and actual historical agents when one's subject is Hiroshima. No better example could be found perhaps of Benjamin's idea that the "dead remain in danger": for the danger is precisely that the refusal to know their situa- tion will take the form of a pseudomourning ritual with deliverance guaran- teed a priori and ahistorically. When such is one's need, Jung provides the "categories" of explanation. Finally, my psychoanalytic treatment of Hiroshima contrasts sharply with the recent book by Robert Jay Lifton and Greg Mitchell, *Hiroshima in America: A Half Century of Denial* (New York: Putnam, 1995). Lifton and Mitchell's effort is to "cleanse" the American psyche by persuading us that it is time to admit the truth about the bombing of Hiroshima. The guarantee is the assurance that knowing the truth about the past is necessarily cathartic and curative; and in line with Lifton's alle- giance to ego psychology, a perfect instance of the ability of "the protean [American] self" to remake itself in a way that is always liberal and progressive. The book is, in short, one of the clearest examples of how the guarantees form and interpellate an audience in the necessities that humanistic interpretation imposes on traumatic realities. What Lifton and Mitchell offer, in closing the books on Hiroshima, is a celebration of the ideological commonplaces of American ego psychology as the framework that both enables us to understand the past and that frees us from that specter. The book thus forms a striking contrast to the psychological description of the psyche developed in this chapter and a confirmation that the trauma Lifton purports to heal has not yet been known, internalized, or "mourned" and cannot be within the terms of ego psychology. Recent developments in Lifton's thought do not, however, minimize the profound debt that everyone concerned with Hiroshima has to Lifton's *Death in Life* (New York: Basic Books, 1967), a great and humane work of testimony and, as I will show, a diagnosis not only of the *hibakusha,* but inadvertently of the American psyche and the force of Thanatos since 1945 in its constitution. Psychic numbing is, of course, the specter Lifton needs to deny lest he see in 1995, half a century after the Event, how deep the disorder of the American psyche is and how complicitous the beliefs and desires that structure ego psychology—and the health professions—have been in serving to protect that "identity."

2. In his great satiric and philosophic article "Limited, Inc.," *Glyph* 2: pp.162–254, Derrida shows that a single system of assumptions binds together the thought of the "academic community" known as Anglo-American analytic philosophy. In that context, John Searle is, as Derrida shows, anonymous, and justly so, since his thought is underwritten and produced by the discourse community of which he is a proud member.

The concept of the "Inc" has a much broader application, however, and can be used to reveal the common purpose uniting those who often know nothing of one another. I refer to the common set of assumptions, concepts, and commonplaces that bind together distinct disciplines in their contribution to an overarching unity of purpose that constitutes what I will here term "Humanus, Inc." The term refers to humanism as a single ideology that can be identified as the controlling force in the structuring of thought and research in the variety of fields and disciplines all of which are required to realize humanism as a worldview totalized across a culture. (It is not necessary that a given practitioner be consciously aware of the reinforcing work in other fields or the overarching set of grounding assumptions for those assumptions to exercise structural control over one's work; in fact, the general assumptions work best when they remain unconscious, tacit, habitual, automatic; when they have the status of that which "goes without saying.")

To bring out the ways in which the grounding assumptions operate across a number of different disciplines and topics I therefore focus, at different points in the discussion, on "Humanus, Inc." in its philosophic, psychological, rhetorical, literary, ethical, and historical exemplifications. My purpose is to show that the underlying system is the proper object of articulation and critique. An intellectual biography of "Humanus, Inc." today would include something like the following list of reinforcing texts: Jurgen Habermas, *Communication and the Evolution of Society;* Paul Ricoeur, *Time and Narrative;* Wayne Booth, *The Company We Keep;* Hayden White, *MetaHistory;* Jessica Benjamin, *The Bonds of Love;* Heinz Kohut, *The Analysis of the Self* (New York: International Universities Press, 1971); Charles Altieri, *Subjective Agency* (Oxford: Blackwell, 1994); Gerald Graff, *Literature against Itself* (Chicago: University of Chicago Press, 1979); Richard Rorty, *Contingency, Irony, and Solidarity* (Cambridge, England: Cambridge University Press, 1989); Norman Holland, *The Dynamics of Literary Response* (New York: Columbia University Press, 1989); Erik Erickson, *Identity and the Life Cycle* (New York: Norton, 1980); Alistair MacIntyre, *After Virtue* (Notre Dame: University of Notre Dame Press, 1984).

I leave out of consideration here the internal debates whereby the variants of humanism constitute their Christian, rationalist, romantic, evolutionary, pragmatic, consensual, etc. alternatives since my point is that the primary function of such debates and "conversations" is to assure that the set of shared assumptions will define the parameters and possibilities of thought and discourse.

3. For a critique of catharsis and the ways it functions as the ultimate guarantee in humanistic responses to history, see chapter 5, pp. 185–90.

4. Thereby, dialectical reinterpretation brings together a diverse number of psychoanalytic thinkers and concepts in a theory of psyche that is often profoundly at odds with the different analytic theorists on whom it draws. Accordingly, comments on specific analysts and specific concepts and issues in their thought will be given at appropriate places in the discussion.

5. Kant, *CJ,* section 5, pp. 6–7.

6. Rilke, *Duino Elegies,* no. 1.

7. On catastrophic anxiety, see Wilfrid Bion, *Seven Servants,* and the two seminal essays on psychosis—"Differentiation of the Psychotic from the Non-Psychotic Personalities," *International Journal of Psycho-Analysis* 38 (1957): 266–75 and "Attacks on Linking," *International Journal of Psycho-Analysis* (1959): 308–15. On the connection of that concept with the fear of dissolution or, in the words of Bion's greatest patient, Samuel Beckett, "of never having been born properly," see especially *Endgame.* Adorno termed that play the "first work of nuclear art." It is also, in many ways, the last; thanatoptic unbinding being the principle that shapes its agonistic structure. The anxiety Beckett speaks of was frequently voiced by Winnicott's patients and underlies Winnicott's concept of "the false self system."

My effort in this chapter is to show that Beckett's fear is condition general for the nuclear subject; and thus the reason why in analyst's offices today the schizoid and the narcissist have replaced the Freudian "sexual" subject.

8. Winnicott, "The Manic Defence," *Collected Papers* (New York: Basic Books, 1958), pp. 129–43.

9. On this pivotal concept in the Hegelian dialectic of master-slave and recognition, see *PhG*, pp. 104–38.

10. See Robert Jay Lifton, *Death in Life: Survivors of Hiroshima* (New York: Basic Books, 1967) for the striking development of this concept as a way of describing the psyche of the *hibakusha*. We are all in debt to Lifton for his effort here and in other works to preserve the record of those who have suffered in some of the primary atrocities of our time. My concern here, however, is with the limitations of Lifton's framework of ego psychology and its concept of working-through as a way of containing the reality of traumatic experiences.

11. For depression as "wakeful anguish" and the self-mediation it makes possible, see chapter 5, pp. 172–75, 188–90.

12. The thought of Erik Erickson is the seminal illustration of this way of thinking and the structure of relations the ego requires for its development. See especially *Identity and the Life-Cycle*. Ego psychology quickly adopted Erickson's thought, shorn of its internal complications, because it provided the larger cultural and ideological scheme needed to assure "the solidity of the ego." A similar argument is mounted by Habermas in *Communication and the Evolution of Society*, where all good developmental things become the property of the ego in its ethical and rationalistic march toward a realization of the universals of the Kantian tradition. Ego psychology is the perfect match for such philosophic projects because it gives the illusion that the subject can attain a substantialized identity through a developmental process that is irreversible and that thus frees the subject from the threat of the psyche's deeper disorders.

13. Fairbairn develops the concept of the inner saboteur to account for that "agency" within the structure of the psyche that produces its own undoing. The concept has much in common with Freud's malign superego and with the Lacanian Big Other.

14. Winnicott develops this idea to account for the anxious solicitation of the other's gaze as it is represented in the face in the paintings of Francis Bacon. See *The Maturational Process and the Facilitating Environment* (London: International Universities Press, 1965). A similar point about the gaze of the Other is developed phenomenologically by Sartre and in psychoanalytic terms by Lacan. Depression, as defined here, is an attempt to constitute as a principle of inwardness Bion's notion that "inquiry begins when love is doubted."

15. See also D. W. Winnicott, "Fear of Breakdown," in *Psychoanalytic Explorations* (Cambridge: Harvard University Press, 1989), pp. 87–95, one of Winnicott's finest essays on the value of depression; in effect, an assertion that in depression we experience the reality of the crypt and the primacy of its indestructible claims upon us.

16. This is the central contradiction in Kohut's position. See *The Analysis of the Self.*

17. I derive this term from Martin Shengold, *Soul-Murder* (New Haven: Yale University Press, 1987). My development of the idea, however, has little in common with how Shengold deploys the concept. It is closer in spirit to Alice Miller's seminal work on childhood trauma. See especially, *Thou Shalt Not Be Aware*, trans. Hildegarde and Hunter Hannum (New York: Farrar, Straus, Giroux, 1984).

18. For a very different attempt to constitute Thanatos in metapsychological terms one turns, of course, to Lacan, whose complex thought on Thanatos has recently been developed in a book-length study by Richard Booth, *Death and Desire* (New York: Routledge, 1991), which goes a long way toward making clear what Jean Laplanche in *Life and Death in Psychoanalysis* (Baltimore: Johns Hopkins University Press, 1976) worked overtime to render opaque. See also Ellie Ragland, *Essays on the Pleasures of Death* (New York: Routledge, 1995). A detailed contrast of my thought on Thanatos with Lacan's would take us too far afield. Suffice to note here that I plan to take this issue up at length in a subsequent work. On which see appendix B.

19. On this concept and its connection to melancholia, see the work of Julia Kristeva, especially, *Powers of Horror* (New York: Columbia University Press, 1984) and *Black Sun* (New York: Columbia University Press, 1989).

20. The line is from Ezra Pound's "Pisan Cantos."

21. See *The Paul Tibbets Story*, by Paul Tibbets with Clair Stebbins and Harry Franken (New York: Stein and Day, 1978), p. 227. In 1989, Tibbets reissued the book as *Flight of the Enola Gay*, claiming sole authorship. This is the book he sells, along with other memorabilia at various gatherings of patriotic groups. One can, at such occasions, get Tibbets' autograph, but only for a fee. Coffee mugs, T-shirts—with "first atomic strike force" blazoned across them—and other items are also available. A catalogue is available from Tibbets' Book Company.

22. Ibid, pp. 240–44.

23. Ibid, pp. 303–4. In the three narratives cited in notes 25–27, Tibbets provides a primary historical example of what chapter 6 will theorize in terms of the concept of the dialectical image.

24. We see here both the appeal and the inherent limitation of the Lacanian theory of history as the trauma one flees through the Symbolic. The result is an abstract dialectic in which everything turns on the opposition between two hypostatized terms. My attempt here is to situate trauma in

a context that concretizes it historically. Tibbets is thus used to establish the subtext of Lacan's fixation on the phallus—and the paternal metaphor—as a psychological disorder that the Symbolic order does not and cannot surmount. That which Lacan wants to label pre-oedipal and imaginary so that he can leave it behind in the ascent to the phallic order is shown to have the force of a revenant, a power that disrupts the phallic dream from within, both as the deeper "fantasy" informing it and as the pre-Oedipal anxiety that it wants to consign to oblivion as "the nuclear waste" beneath the feet of the phallic signifier.

25. The allusions used here to bind together Althusser and Foucault are deliberate.

26. The considerable value of Kenneth Burke's insufficiently appreciated work as a social psychologist is the power of his categories to unlock the ritual desires and motives that structure social action.

27. This is, of course, a program that embraces both right and left in a "conversation" that is based on assumptions "shared" by the warring parties, by (say) DeSousa, Bennett, Graff, Searle, Fukuyama, and Fish. Excluded from that "conversation" is everything that will be purged once rationality is restored and all the old alternatives once again establish their rule, as exclusive and exhaustive "choices," in an academy freed of its discontents and purged of the specter of postmodernism.

28. Tibbets, *Paul Tibbets Story,* pp. 197–201.

29. For the richest developments of this pivotal Lacanian concept and its significance for social theory, see Slavoj Žižek, especially *The Sublime Object of Ideology* (New York: Verso, 1989).

30. The thing Hegel constantly fears and repeatedly tries to render impossible: the collapse of the dialectic, an imploding, psychotic regression to its beginning but with that state reified, unsublatable, and thus the true and bitter end of history. Hegel's exorcizing dream is of irreversible advance, but such necessity can and must be purely logical. That is why history gives that guarantee the lie—and in so doing our situatedness one of its primary terms of reference. For Hegel's society as a "community of animals" is but another way of formulating what will become the culture of narcissism grounded in the commodity fetishism that animates the "empty" subject of "late" capitalism. Hegel there describes far more than the Hobbesian state. It is one of the most prescient chapters in the book: not a picture of what is surmounted in the modern world (as Hegel thought) but the condition to which it devolves. In that socius, the true tie that binds us: desire commodified, each against all, nothing but endless consumption to fill the inner emptiness with signs that deny that condition by inflicting it, as envy, on the other.

31. Paul Boyer, *By the Bomb's Early Light* (New York: Pantheon, 1985) p. 181.

32. Pynchon is the thinker who develops the richest contemporary understanding of paranoia as the dialectical category that best describes the "post-"modern condition. Plato defined dialectic as the ability to make connections. *Gravity's Rainbow* constitutes the contemporary, historical realization of that "ideal."

33. Spencer Weart, *Nuclear Fear: A Study of Images* (Cambridge: Harvard University Press, 1988). Lacking a theory of the image and any way to interrogate its psychological meaning, Weart's book ends up simply collecting data.

34. It is not without significance that the concern of the late Foucault is mirrored in the work of popular psychologists such as Thomas Moore, Daniel Peck, and James Hillman. For yet another effort to return to Greece in order to recover an essentialistic ethic, see Martha C. Nussbaum, *The Fragility of Goodness*.

35. Paul Fussell, *Thank God for the Atom Bomb and Other Essays* (New York: Summit,1988). See also the more recent *Wartime* (New York: Oxford University Press, 1989) for a reiteration of Fussell's enduring, rebarbative sentiments.

36. This claim was made by a number of Derrida's followers. Derrida, of course, never said any such thing. His own relationship to the nuclear resulted, rather, in one of his most complex and valuable essays: "No Apocalypse, Not Now, Seven Missiles, Seven Missives," *Diacritics* (Summer 1984). I cannot hope to do full justice to the turns of that essay here. What is worth noting, for our purposes, is that it constitutes one of the clearest examples of Derrida's thought as a historically situated response to the postnuclear world. Derrida's attempt in focusing on that world's most important hypertext—the politics of deterrence—is to develop a theory of textuality as a "drama" within discourse that represents and contains historical contradictions. In his essay on the nuclear the contradictions circle around a center that is, as Derrida sees, simultaneously "real" and "fabulously textual." Deterrence is the language and linguistic practice that became necessary once the Bomb existed. By the same token, deconstruction's constant reference to language finds in the logic of deterrence its actual historical basis, its master trope. Anxiety before the prospect of absolute annihilation, is the abiding motive behind the effort to assure oneself that if one can assert a purely textual universe—which, ironically, is the same thing the two superpowers did in that monstrous proliferation of language called the "logic of deterrence"—then one can contain history, can prevent the end from ever happening. If we still take seriously Lukács idea that movements in thought corespond in some way to historical situations—as the manifestation in thought of historical contradictions—then we might see that the connection between deconstruction and the nuclear "Unconscious" is necessary—and total. As such deconstruction constitutes one of the most

meaningful responses to the anxiety of our historical condition, since it takes that anxiety into the very inwardness of thought and language where it simultaneously explodes and implodes.

37. The basis of this desire in Derrida's own relationship to death is admirably acknowledged by Derrida himself in *Aporias,* trans. Thomas Dutoit (Stanford: Stanford University Press, 1993) and *The Gift of Death,* trans. David Wills (Chicago: University of Chicago Press, 1995). The alternative deferred, which just barely emerges in the margins of these texts, is a recovery of the existential.

38. T. S. Eliot, "Four Quartets."

39. This is the effort of the chapter 5 of *I&E.*

40. Nietzsche, *Thus Spake Zarathustra.*

41. This is the concept featured by Paul Ricoeur in his hermeneutic interpretation of Freud in *Freud and Philosophy,* trans. David Savage (New Haven: Yale University Press, 1970).

42. See Lawrence Kubie, "The Fundamental Nature of the Distinction between Normality and Neurosis," *Symbol and Neurosis* (New York: International Universities Press, 1978). A seminal article.

43. See Lowell's great poem, "Waking Early Sunday Morning."

44. This paragraph indicates why interpellation and introjection are concepts that should be joined since the first represents in ideological terms what the latter effects in terms of psychodynamics. On introjection, see Fairbairn and Joseph Sandler (ed.), *Projection, Identification, Projective Identification* (Madison, Conn.: International Universities Press, 1987). For an attempt within ego psychology to purge introjection and other disruptive Kleinian processes in order to assert an adaptational concept of internalization, see Roy Schafer, *Aspects of Internalization* (New York: International Universities Press, 1968).

Chapter Five

1. On this concept and its function in developing a theory of the psyche, see *GG.* For the historian, ontological regression issues in a recovery of the dialectical image. In showing this chapter 6 will, however, develop a theory of the dialectical image quite different from those found in Adorno and Benjamin.

2. See Otto Rank, *Art and the Artist* (New York: Knopf, 1932).

3. See Sartre, *The Family Idiot,* especially vol. 1, for the development of this concept.

4. Among the most important recent work done to retrieve Kant's thought on history, see Peter Fenves, *A Peculiar Fate: Metaphysics and World-History in Kant* (Ithaca: Cornell University Press, 1991); William Booth, *Inter-*

preting the World: Kant's Philosophy of History and Politics (Toronto: University of Toronto Press, 1986); Willi Goetschel, *Constituting Critique* (Durham: Duke University Press, 1994). Lyotard's *The Differend* (Trans. George Van Den Abbeele) (Minneapolis: University of Minnesota Press, 1988) constitutes a remarkable effort to retrieve Kant's thought for a contemporary philosophy of history.

5. Kant's writings on history have been collected as *On History*, ed. L. W. Beck (Indianapolis: Bobbs-Merrill, 1963) For the development of this concept in Lyotard's long meditation on Kant and history, see *The Differend.*

6. For Kant's brief discussion of this concept, see *On History*, "The Idea of a Universal History."

7. Kant, *On History*, "The Conflict of Faculties," part 2.

8. Mark this as the first step in a redefinition of Benjamin's "angel." See below, pp. 233–34.

9. This constitutes a fundamental redefinition of Nietzsche's concept of the Overman. It also gives a new referent to Heidegger's concept of the *ecstases* of historical temporality.

10 On the concept of the vanishing mediator, see Slavoj Žižek, especially his book on Schelling, *The Indivisible Remainder* (New York: Verso, 1996).

11. This is the context in which Wayne Booth makes his major contribution to the humanist ratio. Booth's theory of rhetoric attempts to extend the regulative ideals of enlightenment humanism to the ways we read and judge all works; especially those written in a later and less credulous historical situation, since judging their humanistic veracity is the way we bring them into the fold or exclude them from that canon. For more on this, see below, notes 22, 25.

12. Kant, *On History*, "The Conflict of Faculties." See also Lyotard's discussion of this in *The Differend.* Lyotard's theory of the differend might be seen as an attempt to begin, as we do, with the reality of the event, but to render an interpretation that assesses its meaning in terms acceptable to the the Anglo-American analytic community. That focus is in keeping with Lyotard's argument in *The Post-Modern Condition* that only those continental ideas that can be restated in analytic language have any chance of surviving in a postmodern intellectual community that is defined, for Lyotard, by the hegemony of analytic rationality and its ready translation into the terms of information programming. A capitulation. Nonetheless Lyotard's concept of the differend goes a long way toward creating a conceptual crisis for the analytic community—and its framework of interpretation. Which suggests that irony is perhaps the trope that informs Lyotard's practice/play with respect to the analytic. My effort, in contrast, is to constitute what we can know about history when we stick with the richest traditions of European thought and try to revolutionize them from within so that contingency,

historicity, and the tragic become the basis for a new theory and practice of dialectical reasoning.

13. Kant, *On History*, "The Conflict of Faculties."

14. Thomas Mann, *Doctor Faustus*. This is the "humanistic" "break-through" for which the narrator of the novel, Serenus Zeitblom, longs. However, that humanism is precisely what its central figure, Adrian Lever-kühn, annihilates by discovering and liberating the true ontology of artistic form. For Mann writing this novel constituted his own effort to perform such an act and thereby both cancel his own humanism and become a tragic contemporary of the future and the postmodern. It is a remarkable work and an insufficiently appreciated effort, one of the great examples of a critique of humanism from within. The dialectical series of musical works that Mann creates for Leverkuhn constitute a great example of the power of artistic cognition to revolutionize its forms in order to become adequate to its historical mission. As Mann notes elsewhere, the work was also a deeply personal confession and a judgment on the bankruptcy of the humanist tradition, of which Mann was the last, great modernist representative.

15. Heidegger, *B&T*, p. 345.

16. Kant, *On History*, "The Conflict of Faculties."

17. Mann, *Doctor Faustus*. That which Leverkühn finds it necessary to revoke is the fourth movement of Beethoven's Ninth Symphony.

18. This is the effort of Booth's *Modern Dogma and the Rhetoric of Assent* (Notre Dame: University of Notre Dame Press, 1974).

19. Dialectically, the significance of the experience is antithetical to the "aesthetic of the beautiful." For here Winnicott's "spontaneous vitality" and what I term the *élan conatus* find their origin in the pang of an unspeakable loss. That loss, as Wallace Stevens shows, is what the presence of the beautiful reawakens.

20. This circumstance also suggests why recent attacks on the "apocalyptic tone" in philosophy and elsewhere conceal/reveal enthusiasm as the primary motive (and bad faith) behind one brand of deconstructionism: when we can't cheer ourselves up with signs of the times, we can at least rule out negativity by perfecting a formalism that makes the "tragic" no more than a genre. A tragic relationship to history is thereby tropped dead, to pun on Joyce, consumed in the flames of non-reference. For an ironic and ironizing spirit (which is one definition of deconstruction, especially its deManian variants) the troping play with how genres shape historical narratives is the perfect way to contain the past. For such a sensibility this is the great value that can be derived from Derrida's rich essay on the nuclear. For Derrida there teaches that attempts to tell "our" story tragically fall within the apocalyptic genre. The possibility of historical reference is thus eaten up by the ouroboros of text. The possibility of a "tragic" comprehension is reduced to no more than an exercise in the conventions of the apocalyptic

genre. This reduction provides a sort of austere comfort I suppose. Also the containment of a truly dangerous idea. Namely, that the tragic is that "genre" which is historical in its "essence," an *existentia* that has no fixed content or a priori form. It exists, rather, as the question whereby it throws and projects itself into history. See below, pp. 187–91, for a demonstration of how this concept of the tragic stands in marked contrast to the essentializing function of other literary genres and to "tragedy" as generally conceived.

21. Hermann Broch, *The Sleepwalkers,* trans. Willa and Edwin Muir (San Francisco: North Point, 1985), p. 559.

22. In fashioning the rhetoric that moves this broader non-philosophic audience thinkers like Booth carry out a task perhaps more important that Kant's. For their interpellations stick and take root in the order of affect; in, as we will see below, pp. 185–88, that which is not secondary but primary in the constitution and regulation of the social subject.

23. The attempt in this formulation is to wed Nietzsche and Marx, the inwardness of the former become the praxis of the latter.

24. The great example in this effort is Aristotle, *Poetics.* The *Poetics* is a systematic work because it describes the structure of a literary form in terms of the affective process it enacts in the audience. All of its concepts derive from this focus. Understanding what Aristotle is up to and the various uses to which the *Poetics* has been put are two quite different things. Aristotle establishes the first systematic psychology of form. Pity and fear, as principles of response, structure an action that arouses and works upon those emotions in order to bring about their purgation. Plot is that movement. Emotion is not a by-product of mimesis; it is its structuring principle. The audience is thus the reality that the action acts upon. My effort here and in *GG* is to historicize this idea and move it beyond Aristotle's emotional economy so that the agon proper to a later historical situation and a later audience can be created.

25. One of the primary ways to do so is by showing that history as written, especially along "traditional" lines, is indeed a "rhetoric" in which the relationship of the author as "narrator" to the "audience" is based on a system of reassurances and guarantees. This and not the "facts," is the primary thing we read and respond to when we read a work of history. And thus the untapped significance of Wayne Booth's work on the implied author as the way whereby the system of "humanistic" values that shape narratives—especially perhaps historical ones, where the need for this is greatest—is transmitted to the reader. This relationship is the bedrock of ideological interpellation: for it forms the structure of feelings and value judgments whereby one reads "to" and "from" the identity experienced, reinforced, and self-reified in and through the reading process. Hayden White's study of the genres of historical writing finds its necessary supple-

ment in Booth's *Rhetoric of Fiction*. In fact, Booth has a lot more to tell us about the ways histories are shaped than he does about fiction, which had already gone well beyond the humanistic limitations Booth tried to place on "modernity" in his first book. As a reaction to modern, and by implication postmodern writers, *The Rhetoric of Fiction* is in many ways deeply reactionary. As an account of the rhetoric of history, however, it remains prescient and invaluable in helping us identify the primary way in which the guarantees structure writing in that discipline. By that very token, purging the guarantees requires a break with the Boothian author-audience system in a writing of history based in an agonistic relationship to the reader. Establishing that necessity is one of the primary burdens of my discourse. That project turns on a problem similar to the one Derrida formulates when he shows how the attempt to deconstruct the western logos keeps falling back into it. An affective agon confronts something further—and deeper: the need to engage and actively reverse the psyche of the audience. The implications of that necessity for how one must write history will only become clear, pp. 185–88, when we confront the grandest servant of the rhetorical guarantees, the principle of catharsis.

This is also the place to indicate the contrast of my position with Stephen Greenblatt's Foucauldian "poetics of culture." See especially *Shakespearean Negotiations* (Berkeley: University of California Press, 1988). Noteworthy about Greenblatt's "poetics of culture" is the function of drama in the mediation—and at times the production—of cultural conflicts and contradictions. What Greenblatt's position lacks and what I try to provide is a theory of the ontology of artistic form required to assure drama's ability to perform actions that have such a relationship to history—one, significantly, not limited actions to Wittgensteinian and Foucauldian terms of the social, discursive, and consensual. In that regard, it's worth noting that a negotiation is not a negation and that the latter term alone apprehends the possibility implicit in drama.

26. Rilke, *Duino Elegy*, no. 10

27. A note on method. The remainder of the book constitutes the dialectical sequence required to realize this possibility: the *Begriff* or notion of "vigorous melancholy" as the mood, *Befindlichkeit*, that discloses the situatedness of the postmodern subject in its historicity. As I here try to show, that process is, in many ways, an attempt to comprehend Hamlet as the representative of a certain way of thinking. I hasten to add that what follows is not intended as a full interpretation of Shakespeare's play. It is but prologue to that act—the effort to articulate what makes the character Hamlet, singular, profound, and representative, a major turning point in the history of thought and the experience of subjectivity. My effort here is to show how Shakespeare's insight in creating this character might be, in Heideggerian

terms, repeated, in a different context, that of philosophy, in order to articulate a concept and way of thinking that stands in marked contrast to most "philosophic" conceptions of what thinking is.

It is worth noting, however, that most interpretations of the play *Hamlet* "work" by short-circuiting everything we show to be distinctive about this character. Perhaps the safest generalization one can make about most interpretations of *Hamlet* is that they constitute ways of avoiding and escaping the play—and its protagonist.

28. See Nietzsche, *Thus Spake Zarathustra*. What I advance here is thus an alternative to the formula that leads Nietzsche to "the eternal recurrence" as the highest formula of affirmation.

29. In this sense it cancels the Hegelian, rationalist *Aufhebung*. The result is a recovery of the pan-tragic force that generates the concrete drama of the *PhG* before—and against—the rationalistic mediations that Hegel repeatedly imposes upon that drama. Which is a way of saying not only that the *PhG* is both pan-tragicism and pan-logicism; but that recovering the former is the best way to preserve what is "living" in Hegel and thereby his massive contribution to a fully existentialized phenomenology based on a concept of the tragic that is freed of the logos.

30. Such a framework would be more than interdisciplinary, requiring categories that transcend the disciplines rather than ones that just add up the contribution of various disciplines. Despite their popularity such "interdisciplinary" projects really amount to no more than a conglomerate in search of a synthesis, an indeterminate lumping lacking a unifying dialectical concept.

31. Mann, *The Magic Mountain*, "Snow."

32. Walter Benjamin, "Theses on the Philosophy of History." As we see below this idea undercuts reception theory. The audience is in control. That is the problem.

33. My effort, in effect, is to reverse Freud's great essay "Mourning and Melancholia," with the same text, *Hamlet*, providing the basis. See below, note 48.

34. This amounts to a new conception of philosophic idealism and perhaps its reconstitution on a new basis.

35. See Aristotle, *Organon*. I am indebted for this point to a conversation with Richard McKeon in which he argued this position. The comment is one of the clearest marks of the difference between a pragmatic, operational philosophy such as McKeon's—and its restriction of thought to discursive intelligibility—and a thinking that sustains the excesses and the anguish of a questioning that is lived in openness to existentializing experiences that refuse the confines of social, discursive rules. Long before the party of irony, many, following Aristotle, tried to reduce this specter to

impossibility, aporia, and infinite regress. What it actually signifies, however, is a far greater threat: the threat of an "answer" so exacting that living the question as existential self-mediation is the only adequate reply.

For a rigorous and inherently pluralistic formulation of methodological difference as the basis for a philosophic semantics that will enable one to know the inherent logic of distinct philosophic methods, see Richard McKeon "Philosophic Semantics and Philosophic Inquiry." Such a logic is a far cry from the easy assumption that constitutes what so many so proudly today advance as the ground of their pluralism: the "I'll grant your question but then apply my canons of evidence and correct reasoning to test it." It is a tidy and (unconsciously) vicious circle. For its deepest function is to set up a procedure that assures the impossibility of questioning the rationalistic assumptions on which the position is grounded and of making sense of anything that operates outside those confines. Dewey in *Reconstruction in Philosophy* cites Kant and the three critiques as one of the examples of what he regards as the true "scandal" in philosophy: the scandal is not that we can't bring the disciplines together, but that we ever let them be separated in the first place.

36. Christian regressions aside, the concept that certain questions engage "infinite concern" constitutes one of Kierkegaard's great contributions to the understanding of inwardness.

37. The two best examples are Ricoeur and Gadamer.

38. This is analogous to Sartre's concept of the original choice and its connection to the project, especially as both are developed in *The Family Idiot.*

39. The Nietzschean possibility of living a life that will bear aesthetic scrutiny has its ground in this principle. In many ways the argument of the remainder of this chapter is for a tragic recovery of the concept of "aesthetic scrutiny" against the playful and "aestheticizing' ways in which Nietzsche's idea is currently deployed.

40. For Hegel subject's seeking a coincidence with itself is the condition that drives the *PhG.*

41. See Kenneth Telford, *Aristotle's Poetics: Translation and Analysis.* (Lanham, Md.: University Press of America, 1985). This remains one of the best discussions of how emotions work as principles of dramatic structure. What follows can be seen as a critique of the emotions that inform the *Poetics* and an attempt to replace them with a more exacting dialectic of primary, existentializing affects. Aristotle's great insight is that emotional response is structured by plot. Contra Aristotle, however, poetry and history do not differ in this regard but find in it an underlying formal identity. The theory of affect and of what I term the passions of the soul being developed here is thus the key step in our attempt to construct a dialectic that will preserve internalization against the effort of the party of the ego to undo it at the

register where the psyche must be pacified—the register of feeling. Emotion is the process through which the ratio and "Humanus Inc." has its triumph, and exacts its revenge against existence: structuring emotion is the process whereby "reason" dissolves the force of everything it can't explain through its other operations. For examples of how this assumption controls recent theories of the emotions, see Ronald de Sousa, *The Rationality of Emotions* (Cambridge: MIT Press, 1987), Amelia Rorty (ed.), *Explaining Emotions* (Berkeley: University of California Press, 1980), Robert C. Solomon, *The Passions* (Garden City, N.Y.: Anchor/Doubleday, 1976).

42. This is the "softest" definition of the Unconscious, but it also establishes its naturalistic bases, its origin in processes that are eminently behavioral.

43. As in the easy assumption so many make that we are in touch with how we "really feel" whenever we feel intensely or when, overwrought, we "let ourselves go." Subjective proof of this kind is, of course, a travesty of the subjective and also the reason why "objectivity" takes on a fetishistic character for so many. Both terms in the "subjective-objective" opposition as commonly deployed serve a common end—to prevent our seeing that authentic subjectivity is the most rigorous process imaginable and that objectivity in the realm of human affairs is a flight from its demands.

44. The great and singular achievement of O'Neill's *Long Day's Journey into Night* is to have traced this process from its simplest beginnings to its fullest, fractured issue. Naturalism and tragedy are thereby wedded in a drama that proceeds with precision from the claws in the simplest words and gestures to their cumulative, irreversible, outcome. See *GG*, chapter 4.

45. Nietzsche's great insight into resentment as the cornerstone of pity and of Christianity is one of his finest achievements. My effort here is to ground it in affect—and thereby rethink it.

46. Hegel on desire is the parent text I allude to and also reverse here by establishing an affective process that works outside the principles of rational mediation Hegel uses to explain experience—and especially to explain what happens when desires are "restrained and checked."

47. As such it is analogous to what Spinoza does, as dialectician of affect, in books 4 and 5 of the *Ethics*. My position is, of course, radically different from Spinoza in the affect it champions and the dialectic of affect it constructs to bring that affect to fruition.

48. It is here, accordingly, that we ground our opposition to Freud's account of the relationship between (normal) mourning and (neurotic) melancholy. Freud's allegiance to a reflex arc psychology persists from the Fleiss years and underlies the way in which economic accounts often violate dialectical possibilities.

49. "Or lose the name of action," Hamlet adds. Although this discussion is only a fragment of what would be required to give an analysis of

Shakespeare's play, this paragraph does try to formulate something close to the understanding Hamlet finally comes to in his protracted reflection on the nature of action.

50. We can take that step because we now have a principle of negativity that is radically different from Hegel's and that opens to engagement everything his *PhG* must abridge and sacrifice in order to secure its rational progress.

51. See *I&E*, chapter 5 for a methodological account of the principles that shape a dialectical system. The argument of this chapter is that the criteria there formulated are fulfilled by the theory of affect we have here established. In terms of the history of dialectical thought, however, existentializing affect is decidedly the road less taken. It is, however, the only dialectical principle that earns the "charge" of pantragicism and the only one that is rooted psychologically in the immediacy of experience.

Chapter Six

1. On method, two crucial caveats:

(1) We live in a world in which we are assaulted constantly by images. Most are public, social, shared, ideological; suited to mass consumption; images that tranquilize the mind, creating that oneric bliss that ends only with the purchase of the next utterly needed irresistible object of commodified desire. Such images form the primary interpellations whereby advertising, the media, and the dominant social institutions create and hold us in thrall as (capitalist) subjects. Barthes, Eco, Sebeok, and others have contributed major studies to the semiosis of such images as social texts and "signs" that reveal the *ubiquity of social, historical, cultural mediations* in determining what many people wish to think of as natural, immediate, spontaneous, ahistorical, essentialistic, free. My effort to develop a theory of the traumatic image and what a hermeneutic of engagement can find within it is not without its irony given the way such images are the daily fare of the media. One of the great lessons of contemporary history is that the traumatic image can be exploited, commodified, and its potential thereby deadened. For a striking discussion of this process, see Susan D. Moeller, *Compassion Fatigue: How the Media Sell Disease, Famine, War, and Death* (New York: Routledge, 1999).

I note all this here by way of indicating what this chapter is not about. My concern is with an order of imagery that is both rare and uniquely revelatory and that breaks with the dominant processes that shape collective consciousness. The images that concern me announce the reality of something else. It is, as we will see, the reality of art and its claim as an original and primary way of knowing.

(2) I once considered using the work of a single writer (Rilke, Eliot, Shakespeare) or a single work (a novel rich in compelling imagery such as *Beloved* or *Under the Volcano*, or a historical-reportorial work such as *Dispatches*) as an illustration through the chapter. This would, however, have doubled the chapter's length and would have shifted attention from the image that has already been with us throughout the book—the Bombing of Hiroshima. This chapter is a reading of that image and brings to completion our attempt to probe and constitute its interiority. As such this chapter re-reads chapter 4, giving us a further way to deepen our theory of the Event and the "intentions" of the "agents" who constituted it.

Here is another way to formulate what this chapter is not about. As social subjects we are bathed in a sea of images that ideologically constitute the inwardness of most subjects because the commodified image "delivers the goods" in a text that is immediate in the pleasure and power it promises, the boredom and anxiety it vanquishes, the "identity" it confers on those who rush in narcissistic mania to embrace it and the contempt it visits on those it excludes from the magic circle it draws around the fantasies it creates. When most drop off to sleep the day's residues that form their dreams are a public, social, commodified residue—the Hobbesian detritus of decaying sense derived from the endless stream of images that flit across the screen of a collective consciousness that is emptied of all else save their reception and fetishization. Rather than an "otherness" to dominant ideologies, the image is by and large the realm of ideologies' triumphant circulation and consumption. Proximally and for the most part one finds in most images the conventional, the commodified, that which reinforces and reifies the dominant culture, not that which alienates or estranges us from it. This is especially true today of most of those images that claim to do the opposite: the primitive, the vital, the liberatory, the erotic—these are now thoroughly colonized matters, tokens of the extent to which possibilities once liberatory, and as such existentially exacting, have become what Pynchon calls "mindless pleasures."

This is the place to note the "absent presence" that is at the center of my awareness in this chapter. The most eloquent witnesses to a history defined by the Bomb—the dead and the *hibakusha*—are not directly considered in *Deracination*. This was not my original intention. But I found as I worked on this project that the *hibakusha* required a writing of a different order than that attempted here. The result is this book's companion, *The Holocaust Memorial* (Bloomington, IN: First Books, 2000.) (An earlier version was produced by the Department of Theatre of the Ohio State University in 1998.) This work, originally planned as the final chapter of the present book, attempts to realize the concept of image and of artistic cognition that the present chapter conceptualizes. Dialectically, the play thus completes *Deracination* by embodying its argument.

2. Silvano Arieti, *Creativity: The Magic Synthesis* (New York: Basic Books, 1976), pp. 53–65. This is also the place to note the invaluable contribution of the work of Eva T. H. Brann, *The World of the Imagination* (Savage, Md.: Rowman & Littlefield, 1991) to the study of the image. Brann provides an exhaustive survey of philosophic theories of the image from the ancients to the present.

3. It is worth noting that this idea has been the primary target in the latest effort of "cognitive psychologists" to refute Freud. It would be hard to imagine a better example of basing a critique on a prior misunderstanding. In this regard Ernest G. Schachtel's "On Memory and Childhood Amnesia," in *Metamorphosis* (New York: Basic Books, 1959), pp. 279–322, is a salutary reminder of what Freud actually said.

4. Except, that is, by art's eventual capitulation to the ego. And in this Arieti follows the standard argument of one of the founders of ego psychology Ernst Kris, whose seminal statement of the position is "Regression in the Service of the Ego." *Psychoanalytic Explorations in Art* (New York: International Universities Press, 1952).

5. In this framework this is the function of "form." The cardinal example (as we saw in chapter 5) is the principle of catharsis.

6. Arieti, *Creativity*, p. 54. For Hegel representation/image (*Vorstellung*) was necessarily superceded by concept, with concept (or notion) the medium in which thought must move in order to attain self-consciousness. For a summary of Hegel's argument, see especially the prefaces collected in *On Art, Religion, and Philosophy*, ed. J. Glenn Gray (New York: Harper & Row, 1970). My effort here is to show that moving in the medium of the image follows a "logic" that provides a clear contrast to the "logic of the notion" and that cannot be sublated by it. This argument caps the contrast I've been developing throughout between Hegelian rationalistic mediation and my concept of agonistic, existential self-mediation.

7. Arieti, *Creativity*, pp. 60–62.

8. The latter must, however, be dissimulated. Therefore, literary theory, rather than banishing the poets, must attempt to co-opt them, to pay lip-service to their activity all the better to impose upon it the concepts and "humanistic" ways of living art goes beyond. To restate my favorite aphorism: we don't need censorship, we have interpretation.

9. Arieti, *Creativity*, p. 53.

10. This is the effort of Heidegger's later thought and the reason why poetry is of pivotal significance in it. Heidegger has a deep understanding of the ontological significance of art. Developing a theory of the image, however, is not one of Heidegger's concerns. Nor do the violent energies of modern art, which I champion, strike him as anything more than another reason to retreat into the nostalgia of his *Seinsmystik*.

11. Arieti, *Creativity*, pp. 55. After recognizing that we employ the

image so that we will not "be forced to accept the limitations of reality," Arieti undoes this insight by establishing a relationship that inverts its significance. The resulting dichotomy, between the image and the ego, alienates the psyche from itself.

I focus on the image in infant and early experience here, but what I am saying applies to the status of the image at all points in our life and to both its individual and collective powers. That is, to what we experience whenever an image arrests us and strikes though the defenses we use to shield ourselves from reality. Which happens daily; for example, when, watching the news, our heart ulcers at the face and walk of a six-year-old child, JonBenét Ramsey ravaged to her parent's pleasure.

It is worth noting that recent "attacks" in academic psychology on the importance of the image in constituting and in recovering early experience coincide with the effort to cast doubt on recovered memories of infant and early sexual abuse. Now that the enormity of that phenomenon is becoming apparent, a "scientific" way must be found to destroy—or at least impugn— the data. As long as academic psychology (which Frederick Crews constantly reminds us has rejected Freud) posits adaptation, habit, and socialized behavior as the determining factors in what counts as "real" and what constitutes a scientific explanation, it will have nothing to offer a theory of the image because it inverts, ontologically and methodologically, the relationships that the image establishes. It is significant in this regard that the cardinal functions Arieti finds in the image are precisely matters that have been ignored or persistently marginalized in academic, empirical psychology in keeping with its desire to keep adaptational, behavioral, and quantifiable matters uppermost in its study of the human being.

12. They are thus aligned to the comprehensive force of *Befindlichkeit* and primary moods in Heidegger, the experience of the *Stimmung* as discussed by a number of modern artists, and the *Unheimlich* as analyzed by Freud. All of which provide contrasts with "the oceanic experience." While it delivers us from experience, affect delivers us over to it.

13. For the classical account of regression from the perspective of ego psychology, see Ernst Kris, "Regression in the Service of the Ego." In ego psychology the concern is always to manage and control regression so that the return to the ego directs the "therapeutic" process. Our concern is to move the other way—to constitute, sustain, and deepen the break. When one does so regression is already, in principle, ontological because its movement is against the structure on which the ego depends—and toward the crypt and the necessity of beginning again, from there.

14. For a deconstruction of Rilke's "Archaic Torso of Apollo" and an argument against a "referential" reading of this its final line see Paul De-Man's essay on Rilke in *Allegories of Reading* (New Haven: Yale University Press, 1979). As intertext, DeMan's theory of the image is a primary term of

contrast throughout this chapter. See also his *The Rhetoric of Romanticism* (New York: Columbia University Press, 1984).

15. Rilke, *Fragment of an Elegy.*

16. Subject, self, and identity are here interchangeable terms; and deconstruction is the flip side of the ego-ratio. Subject, as we conceive it, transcends the dichotomy from which both positions derive.

17. This may be the deepest function of the Lacanian Real as a *ding-an-sich* that, qua unknowable, functions to protect the status of the Symbolic order.

18. It is in this context that we would retrieve Adorno's notion that Hitler gave the world a new categorical imperative. See *Negative Dialectic* (New York: Continuum, 1966).

19. There is a dissonance between the ontology of *Being and Nothingness* and Sartre's two books on the image. For all its brilliance, the first work freezes the subject in a Cartesian dualism. The richer phenomenology of choice and character developed in the books on Flaubert depend on a recovery of the image and its significance for Sartre's effort to show how the "original contingencies of our being" structure the psyche and inform its project.

20. The first quotation is from *King Lear.* The second from Stamp Paid in Morrison's *Beloved.* The yoking is deliberate.

21. The allusion, of course, is to Thoreau and the reason why he went to live at Walden Pond.

22. This is the basis for Aristotle's recognition in the *Poetics* of metaphor as the act of genius.

23. Coleridge, *Biographia Literaria.*

24. Itzhak Zuckerman, to Claude Landzman in *Shoah.* At his own choice and on a different occasion Zuckerman spoke at length (though not to Landzman), leaving on tape an invaluable record that has now been published, titled *A Surplus of Memory* (Berkeley: University of California Press, 1993). (Originally published in Hebrew, Tel Aviv, 1990.)

A literal translation would read close to this: "Were there one would lick my heart, would be poisoned."

25. Of course this is why *Shoah* constitutes an immanent critique of the documentary form and the immanent search for an artistry that will be ontologically adequate to its subject. Unlike Hersey's book, it is thus a work that takes up Dwight McDonald's question as the imperative that informs its simultaneous inquiry into history and into the artistic form required for its cognition.

26. This effort makes the fourth section of Grossman's novel one of the most fascinating contemporary efforts to constitute a structure of dialectical images required to constitute a knowledge of the "meaning" of the Holocaust.

27. See McGeorge Bundy, *Danger and Survival* (New York: Random House, 1988). It is interesting to note that the voice and the narrator-audience relationship Bundy crafts for his history is a perfect example of Boothian rhetoric, as is the emotional discharge that the telling of that tale offers author and audience, in retrospective death-bound "conscience." The full magic show of humanistic rhetoric is here on display, doing the work of cleansing for which it was fashioned. In that effort the insistence on facts and the confinement of intentions to the literal meaning of documents still plays its crucial function here by banishing the scandalous idea that we dropped the Bomb to impress the Russians. That work done, the pathos of "mature regret" (shades of Dr. Johnson) then produces a catharsis with respect to those facts that Bundy now confesses can no longer be denied.

28. For a classic statement of the method of multiple working hypotheses, see R. S. Crane, *The Idea of the Humanities*, 2 vols. (Chicago: University of Chicago Press, 1967). Crane offers a rigorous formulation of this concept, yet ironically fact as the sole basis of decision remains for him a matter that is empirical and unproblematic. As a result, certain hypotheses are not and cannot be given the hearing Crane claims to offer them. Like most Aristotelian pluralists, especially those of a Humean hue, the only way to choose among hypotheses is on the basis of "empirical" data. A tidy circle. However, one where some hypotheses are not and cannot be given a hearing since the kind of "evidence" that would substantiate them has been disallowed a priori. Crane thus plays the "pluralist" game in dogmatist fashion, granting a hearing to any "reasonable" hypothesis as long as it submits itself to the test of incorrigible fact. Nietzsche's notion—there are no facts, only interpretations—never gains a hearing. Moreover, the determination of fact is itself a function of metaphysical assumptions that are not examined and can't be because they exist as axioms of common sense: certainties such as the notion that the real is the factual and that conscious, stated intentions are the basis for finding out why historical agents acted as they did; and thus, de facto, the basis for marginalizing or excluding psychoanalysis and the Marxist understanding of ideology, claims of pluralistic openness notwithstanding.

29. This is analogous to the Hegelian *Begriff*. The image contains the necessity of a dialectical movement and this forms its internal structure. The three steps described here outline that dynamic. The first moment (as formulated here) has similarities to Derrida's attempts to formulate a logic of *différance* and the trace. The difference, however, is that while Derrida's categories establish antinomies of signification, ours establish existential situations.

30. The allusion here is to Eliot's "The Love Song of J. Alfred Prufrock."

31. See especially *The Symbolism of Evil*, trans. Emerson Buchanan

(Boston: Beacon Press, 1969), where the religious and christocentric bases of Ricoeur's project become strikingly evident.

32. Since estrangement-effect would become the very process of writing and would exert its force everywhere in that process—from language and style through all the conventions and protocols of discourse to the dominant paradigms and a priori concepts that structure the discipline as a whole.

33. The reference is, of course, to the character in the Inferno who agrees to speak to Dante only if assured that his words will not get back to human ears.

34. Aragon as quoted in Louis A. Sass, *Madness and Modernism* (New York: Basic Books, 1992), p. 135.

35. Since this is a "Marxist moment," I would make it good by suggesting that we can renew Marxism not by schematizing the "present" and the postmodern in terms of its departure from the possibilities characterizing the past (which is the method of Lukacs and Jameson), but by identifying ruptures that situate thought in historical contexts that exceed and shatter prior theoretical guarantees and the concepts derived from them (the proletariat, class consciousness), thereby creating and demanding new forms of collective action. Solidarity would then arise from all that one must deracinate from one's conceptual and affective struggle in order to enter the present.

36. Robert Openheimer, a Hamlet after the fact, said this: "the bomb's use was implicit in its invention." As all accounts of Alamogordo show, that knowledge was also repressed by the creators during the time period of the creation.

37. The reference is, of course, to Tibbets. See above pp. 92, 119–20, 124–25.

38. On the category of "objective spirit," see Hegel, *PhG*, 294–363 and the massive development of this category in volume 5 of Sartre's *The Family Idiot*. What Sartre there offered for the nineteenth century, I attempt here for the one that dropped the Bomb.

39. It is thus the concrete basis for a dialectic capable of inverting Hegel. But unless one begins and abides with the image and finds in its agon principles of development radically different from the ratio, the Hegelian way of thinking will creep back in.

40. I here substitute the term crypt for Eros deliberately. Eros reeks of guarantees, especially in the way it was used by thinkers such as Brown and Marcuse. In contrast, we here establish a context in which it can be posited as a possibility, a project that is defined and historicized by a prior—and tragic—reality.

41. On the *pharmakon,* see Derrida, *Dissemination.* One way to read this chapter is as a presentation of images that Derrida and deMan cannot

deconstruct because they contain *différance* as one of their essential moments. Zuckerman brings us the "gift" of an image that can't be deconstructed because it derives from a principle of reflection that provides an alternative to Derrida's concept of reflection. It has that status because it does not flee history in yet another dream of reason, but takes up history as it enters us at a tragic register that cancels the possibilities—and the appeal—of deferral and delay. In an inadvertent division of labor, deMan carries out the task of anesthetizing for Europe by focusing on the deconstruction of Romanticism and the Romantic image; Derrida on America and the history of the present by deconstructing the nuclear referent. Both attain the desired end—for one absolution from Europe's past, for the other freedom from the fear that haunts the future.

42. See Kierkegaard, *Concluding Unscientific Postscript.* In many ways my argument is an attempt to wrest the idea of "infinite concern" from theology and appropriate it for the study of history.

43. This is, for Artaud, the actor's task.

44. Ellul and Heidegger thus join hands in defining this as one of the primary modes of our situatedness and the negativity we must of necessity adopt toward it. Contra Lyotard, we might put it thus: that which refuses to make sense in terms of the logic of technological meaning is the only knowledge that constitutes the postmodern condition as a condition.

45. See Wittgenstein, *Philosophic Investigations.* Learning "grammar" is ideological instruction. Perhaps the failure to acknowledge that circumstance, and its implications, is the picture that holds us captive.

46. But in a way that fundamentally reinterprets Heidegger's statement of this concept. See below, note

47. Grossman, *See Under—Love,* trans. Betsy Rosenberg (New York: Farrar, Straus, Giroux, 1989), pp. 440–45.

48. Toni Morrison's *Beloved* is an even more compelling contemporary example. A similar effort informs the musical compositions invented by Mann in *Doctor Faustus;* those great expressionistic and surrealistic texts that enable Leverkühn to constitute the "history" of his time by overcoming the artistic forms of his day and the ethical-aesthetic limits that a humanistic interpreter such as Zeitblom wants to place on artistic experimentation and expression.

49. Clara Immerwahr Haber was the first woman to receive a doctorate in science at a German university (Breslau). Her husband, Fritz Haber, developed chemicals used in the Great War. In 1918, after a last effort to persuade her husband to stop, Clara Haber committed suicide. In my long labor on this book she has, above all, remained for me the one who is "still signaling through the flames."

50. The point is thus fundamentally different from Benjamin's theory of the image—and the messianic hope that Benjamin finds in all images

connected with the dream of the commodity. This chapter constitutes, structurally, an attempt to record my debt to Benjamin and the fundamental difference of our positions. (For a briefer and more systematic formulation of the contrast and its function as intertext, see appendix A.) The other primary intertext in the chapter is Heidegger on the *ecstases* of temporality. Certain similarities between Heidegger and Benjamin—probably unconscious to both—are thereby suggested. Namely, the notion of repeatable possibilities as the key to Heidegger's hermeneutic as a theory of history that has similarities to Benjamin's concept of "messianic" time and its ability to recover in the past meanings and possibilities that blast the continuum, thereby becoming for the present its concerns and its conscience. Benjamin's fascination with the image and his way of reading it, even its most commodified form, turns on this issue, which offers me the quickest way to formulate the difference in our positions: there is nothing even remotely messianic about my theory of history. My concern with the past is with the recovery of death-work and its power; not with repeatable possibilities we can recover in a salvationist project, but with a horror we cannot combat because we have refused to know it and to see its history: its power, its appeal, and, above all, its presence in a past that is thereby shot—like time's arrow—into a present we can engage only once we "recapture" that past which even the greatest Marxists have been careful not to know because it blasts every guarantee and every messianic hope.

51. Robert Musil, *The Man Without Qualities,* trans. Sophie Wilkins (London: Picador, 1995).

52. This is William Gaddis' definition of art.

53. See Heidegger, *Poetry, Language, Thought,* trans. Albert Hofstadter (New York: Harper & Row, 1971). In Heidegger's hands the idea leads poets further away from history, however, rather than more deeply into it.

54. The possibility of becoming the only kind of socialist that matters, one who has, as Doris Lessing puts it, become "a socialist in one's instincts," derives from this idea.

Appendix A

1. There is nothing even remotely messianic about my theory of history. My concern with the past is the recovery of death-work and its power; not with repeatable possibilities we can recover in a salvationist project but with a horror we cannot combat because we have refused to know it and its history. But this is also precisely where reversal begins. For that past once known becomes time's arrow shot into a present that is now known and lived with its actual past recaptured, a past that even the greatest Marxists have been careful not to know because it blasts every guarantee and

every messianic hope. That is why it is the past most worth knowing—the one that truly situates our Marxism in an explicit negation of the master-narrative that has so often blinded Marxism. On which see Tucker, *Philosophy and Myth in Karl Marx* (Cambridge: Cambridge University Press, 1961). On Benjamin's theory of history, see Max Pensky, *Melancholy Dialectics* (Amherst: University of Massachusetts Press, 1993).

Appendix B

1. In the position developed here, there is never a moment of presence or self-presence. The current deconstruction of "lived-experience" thus misses the point of what is attempted here. Existence and its imperatives is a force that traverses lived-experience, making its agon one that weds the subject fully to its situatedness.

2. Walter Benjamin, "Theses on the Philosophy of History," *Illuminations.* The concept of melancholy thought developed in chapter 5 has many points of similarity and difference to Benjamin. As will become apparent, the differences with respect to history derive from my elimination of any belief in "Messianic time."

3. Although I discuss the psychoanalytic progeny of this concept in chapter 4, my primary source for it is the indelible impression left on me by the art of Ingmar Bergman, who stated the goal of his work as "getting to the bottom of this matter of humiliation."

4. The importance of the Hegelian parent text is systemic in Lacan: it structures his understanding of the mirror stage, of desire, and of the defiles of the signifier. The "depth" of Lacan's starting point is put in question, however, once one sees desire as a displacement of and a flight from the crypt and the concrete agons it requires the subject to undertake. Hegel's text has, of course, been the primary parent text for the past half century of French thought; grounding it in a deeper dialectic of subjectivity would thus entail dislocations of some consequence.

5. The fusion of the existential and the psychoanalytic is the concrete circumstance that smashes the Kantian limitations of Heidegger's analytic. It does so, however, only insofar as it generates at each step in its dialectic an existential self-mediation to which the subject commits itself utterly.

6. In contrast to the Hegelian "medium of the notion"; that is, of logic and rationalistic mediation. Agonistic mediation is radically different and thus leads to a radically different methodology. Developing the contrast between the two has been one of the dominant through-lines of the book

7. See pp. 151–53. The line of thought leading to this concept is developed in *I&E*. One of Heidegger's primary efforts in *B&T* is to

distinguish concepts and categories that are fixed and essentialistic, and that dissolve phenomena in an ahistorical understanding, in contrast to *existentia* as categories that overcome that practice in principle. Such, I would add, are precisely the kind of categories we must develop for the understanding of history and of artistic phenomena. That effort, of course, leads me far from Heidegger and into sharp opposition to the formalistic, neo-Kantian nature of his analytic of *Da-sein*. To put it succinctly, the problem of thinking historically converges on the problem of seeing art as the model for a cognition that is historical because form for the artist is always *sui generis,* the *existentia* from which other *existentia* derive.

8. Methodologically, this is a central concern. Hegel is a primary source of both possibilities, however, and employed both in the *PhG*. But always with the rationalistic in control—at the expense of the agonistic phenomena that are sacrificed to its development. Regaining their significance requires reading Hegel against the grain, as did Kojeve, Sartre, and Bataille, who said, "He [Hegel] did not realize the extent to which he was right." He didn't because his rationalism prevented him from constituting what a fully liberated endorsement of an agonistic logic of mediation would produce. To take up that task, however, one can't simply extract certain concepts such as desire, master-slave, and the struggle for recognition from Hegel. Rather than just appropriating these ideas, as do Sartre and Lacan, one must rethink them from within an agonistic framework that entails a fundamental reinterpretation of Hegel's founding experiences.

INDEX

A

abjection, 114–5

Act of Interpretation, The, 248

affect

and constitution of psyche, 33, 60, 64–
68, 236, 238, 277, 280

deadening of, 60, 63, 67, 90, 112–3, 128,
142, 143, 181, 190, 210–1, 222–3, 227–
9

existentializing affect, 68, 114–5, 163–6,
180–3, 184–5, 188–90, 205–7, 282

and image and art, 6, 152, 193, 196–201

and Kant

enthusiasm, 154, 156–63, 168, 169

Kantian affective self-mediation, 73,
80–1, 86–8

the sublime affect and attunement,
51–5, 67–8

agon

of affect, 65, 88, 90, 91, 116, 162, 166–8,
171, 278

and image and art, 196–7, 200–11,
222–5, 240, 288

agonistic relationship with audience, 17,
248, 278

agonistic subjectivity, 90–2, 136, 139–41,
238

agonistic self-mediation, 184, 254, 262,
265, 284, 290, 291

the anti-agon, 110, 113–5, 133, 144

of deracination of history and guarantees, 174, 220–1, 225, 230–1, 234, 248

and desire, 58–9

and dramatistic language, 41–3

as existential, 8, 17–19, 148, 291

and melancholic reflection, 179–84,
189, 231–2

and trauma and the tragic, 31–35, 170,
277

anxiety

as existential, 8, 17, 19, 20, 31, 43–4, 65,
168, 170, 180, 185–6

catastrophic anxiety, 33, 67, 87, 94, 103–
8, 147–150, 207–9, 269

and the ego-ratio in history, *xviii,* 214,
238, 264, 273–4

and the image, 199, 204

and Kant, 50, 86, 166

melancholic anxiety, 66, 74, 188–91

nuclear anxiety, 128, 245

psychotic anxiety, 113, 173, 225, 269

thanatoptic anxiety, 118

tragic anxiety, *xvi*

Aragon, 219, 225

Arieti, Silvano, 193–5, 198–9, 209–10, 284–
5

Aristotle, 4, 13, 18, 30, 158, 177, 188, 252,
277, 279, 280, 286

Artaud, Antonin, 175, 221, 289

attunement, 33, 171, 43–4, 64–8, 181–2,
152, 199

Kantian, 51–5, 69, 73–4

Aufhebung, 21, 44, 63, 102, 111, 118, 158,
167–8, 176, 180, 183–4, 255, 279,

the anti-*aufhebung,* 173, 206, 215, 220,
234

aufklarung, 18, 52, 153–157, 253, 260

B

Bacon, Francis, 44, 197, 217, 270

beautiful, the, 166, 276

and Kant, 56, 58, 102, 112, 162

and Plato, 13

and Rilke, 59, 73

Beckett, Samuel, 103, 113, 181, 269–70

begriff, 18, 252, 255, 278, 287

Beloved. See Morrison, Toni

Benjamin, Jessica, 257

Benjamin, Walter, 23, 37, 163, 174, 244, 259,
267, 275, 279, 289–90, 291

bildung, 45, 62, 74, 81, 161, 164–5, 170, 237,
255

counter-*bildung,* 173–4

293

and the systems of guarantees, 18, 37–9, 122, 129, 131, 194, 220–1, 238–9, 246, 268
and the tragic, 183, 185, 228, 256
and the dialectical crypt image, 226, 237
and image and art, 195, 203, 217, 258, 276
and interpretation, 260, 267, 289
see also catharsis; ego psychology
humiliation, 117, 121, 223, 231, 237
see also cruelty

I
image
and affect, 6–7, 152
crypt image, the, 148–9, 222–7, 229–31
as dialectic (dialectical image, the), 23, 107, 179, 199, 201, 206, 207, 222, 271, 274, 286, 287
as agon, 204–5, 208–9, 210–2, 288
and history, 213, 215, 217–22, 234
and the Event, 36–7, 112, 283
opposed to the ego-ratio and guarantees, 23, 166, 168, 194–7, 208
over and against concept, 42, 175, 193–4, 259, 284–5
and Romanticism, 266, 289
thanatoptic image, the, 222–8, 230
theory of the image, 193–203
and History, 13–5, 191, 290–1
traumatic image, the, 282
see also ontological regression
interiority, 27, 70, 171, 178, 182, 184, 187, 206, 237, 250, 283
internalization
authentic internalization, 25, 30–6, 38, 43, 175, 205, 211, 215
and ego psychology, 22, 27–30, 40–2, 75–6, 115, 185, 224, 274
and existential engagement, 21, 237
inwardness
and the Bomb in History, 23, 160, 169, 174–7, 181–5
creation of through the image, 199, 205
and the existential, *xv*, 9, 28, 50, 148–9, 243, 255, 280
inwardness and existence, 196, 201, 209, 227, 234, 237, 252, 283
melancholic inwardness, 163–5, 171, 270

and the subject as who/why, 31, 90, 104, 137, 179, 204
of affect, 64–9, 190
and trauma, 33–5
flight from and extinction of, 111, 117–8, 121–2, 125, 128, 131, 136, 156–7, 226, 230,
and the sublime, 52–6, 58–9
see also inwardness; self-reference; subjectivity
Inwardness and Existence, 237, 243, 247, 249, 250, 266, 282, 274, 291
irony
as historical narration, 5, 18, 206, 236, post-modern irony, *xv, xviii*, 131, 256, 262, 275
and the tragic, 183, 246, 253–4
see also deconstruction; tragic, the
Ixion, 109, 208

J
Jameson, Fredric, (*The Political Unconscious*), 4, 245, 248, 253, 256, 257–8, 260, 288
jouissance, 83, 92, 95, 133, 134–136, 165, 227, 253
Joyce, James, 255, 276

K
Kant, Immanuel
and enthusiasm, 156–165
and history, 4–5, 151, 153–5, 169, 247, 274–5
and reflection, 27, 34, 175, 177
and knowledge, 19, 26, 254, 265, 270
and method, 260–1
and super-ego, 93–5
see also attunement; the beautiful; enthusiasm; ratio, the; sublime, the; subjectivity
Klein, Melanie, 16, 109, 113, 265, 274

L
Lacan, *xvi*, 18, 203, 238, 239, 246, 253, 257–8, 259, 266, 270,
see also jouissance; Real, the; phallus, the; Symbolic Order, the; phallus
Lanzmann, Claude, (*Shoah* and Zuckerman, Itzhak), 14, 212, 224, 253–4, 286, 288